THE POLITICS

of

SAME-SEX MARRIAGE

THE POLITICS

of

SAME-SEX MARRIAGE

edited by

CRAIG A. RIMMERMAN

and

CLYDE WILCOX

THE UNIVERSITY OF CHICAGO PRESS

CHICAGO & LONDON

CRAIG RIMMERMAN IS PROFESSOR OF PUBLIC POLICY STUDIES AND POLITICAL SCIENCE AND CURRENTLY HOLDS THE JOSEPH P. DIGANGI ENDOWED CHAIR IN THE SOCIAL SCIENCES AT HOBART AND WILLIAM SMITH COLLEGES. CLYDE WILCOX IS PROFESSOR OF GOVERNMENT AT GEORGETOWN UNIVERSITY. THEY ARE CO-EDITORS (ALONG WITH KENNETH WALD) OF *THE POLITICS OF GAY RIGHTS* (UNIVERSITY OF CHICAGO PRESS, 2000).

THE UNIVERSITY OF CHICAGO PRESS, LTD., LONDON
© 2007 BY THE UNIVERSITY OF CHICAGO
ALL RIGHTS RESERVED. PUBLISHED 2007

PRINTED IN THE UNITED STATES OF AMERICA

16 15 14 13 12 11 10 09 08 07   1 2 3 4 5

OCLC:76967328
ISBN-13: 978-0-226-72000-5 (CLOTH)
ISBN-13: 978-0-226-72001-2 (PAPER)
ISBN-10: 0-226-72000-4 (CLOTH)
ISBN-10: 0-226-72001-2 (PAPER)

LIBRARY OF CONGRESS CATALOGING-IN-PUBLICATION DATA

THE POLITICS OF SAME-SEX MARRIAGE : EDITED BY CRAIG A. RIMMERMAN AND CLYDE WILCOX.
P. CM.
INCLUDES BIBLIOGRAPHICAL REFERENCES AND INDEX.
ISBN-13: 978-0-226-72000-5 (CLOTH: ALK. PAPER)
ISBN-10: 0-226-72000-4 (CLOTH: ALK. PAPER)
ISBN-13: 978-0-226-72001-2 (PBK.: ALK. PAPER)
ISBN-10: 0-226-72001-2 (PBK.: ALK. PAPER) 1. SAME-SEX MARRIAGE—UNITED STATES. 2. SAME-SEX MARRIAGE—POLITICAL ASPECTS—UNITED STATES. I. RIMMERMAN, CRAIG A. II. WILCOX, CLYDE, 1953-
HQ1034.U5P65 2007
306.84'80973—DC22
2006101402

⊗ THE PAPER USED IN THIS PUBLICATION MEETS THE MINIMUM REQUIREMENTS OF THE AMERICAN NATIONAL STANDARD FOR INFORMATION SCIENCES—PERMANENCE OF PAPER FOR PRINTED LIBRARY MATERIALS, ANSI Z39.48–1992.

CONTENTS

PREFACE

In 2006 same-sex marriage replaced abortion as the focal issue of cultural conflict. Conservative activists have marched in Washington and barraged the U.S. Senate with letters in support of a constitutional amendment limiting marriage to heterosexual couples. Gay and lesbian rights activists have also marched and lobbied and have gone to court to challenge state and local laws that bar them from marrying. The battle over marriage has involved all branches and levels of government and has been the subject of statewide referenda.

Students at Hobart and William Smith Colleges and at Georgetown University are very interested in the issue and frequently have strong normative views. But they frequently find the politics of same-sex marriage confusing. This is not surprising, for the issue is quite complex.

First, same-sex marriage is both a new issue on the national and state political agendas and an extension of a much longer set of policy debates that stretches back for several decades. In many ways, the quest for the right to marry is the logical extension of other efforts by the gay and lesbian rights movement to decriminalize same-sex behavior, to prohibit discrimination in employment and housing, to serve openly in the military, and to more generally enjoy the rights and privileges extended to heterosexual citizens. To the extent that same-sex marriage is similar to these other issues, we would expect public attitudes and policies to grow more accommodating over time, as detailed in separate chapters by Mark Carl Rom and by Clyde Wilcox, Paul R. Brewer, Shauna Shames, and Celinda Lake with regard to matters such as employment discrimination and gays and lesbians in the military.

Yet marriage is, for many Americans, a substantively different issue than employment discrimination. Many see marriage as an institution created by God and consecrated in a church, and most have mental images of countless heterosexual marriages in their minds as they approach this new issue. To the extent that marriage is a unique issue that taps into different cognitive images and emotional responses, the politics of the issue may remain more constant over time.

Second, same-sex marriage is what is often called an "easy" issue for the public to understand, since it does not require complex background information or technical knowledge for one to comprehend it. Sorting out competing plans to lower the cost of prescription drugs requires considerable background information and knowledge of economics, but deciding whether same-sex marriage should be allowed requires a citizen to merely inventory her values.

Yet this does not mean that all Americans find the issue an easy one to resolve. In the heated first reactions to the Massachusetts Supreme Judicial Court decision that legalized same-sex marriage in that state, many conservative groups urged Americans to "protect" marriage from the long lines of gay and lesbian couples that lined up in San Francisco to marry in the summer of 2004. But there is some evidence that this frame is beginning to lose some of its potency as citizens ponder why allowing those couples to marry would destroy the institution.

Surveys show that Americans value traditional marriage and that a majority still believe that homosexuality is sinful. Yet they also value equality, and many have gay and lesbian friends whom they value. Small wonder that polls show such conflicting results, with a majority opposing same-sex marriage when asked a simple yes-no question but majorities also favoring some kind of legal recognition for same-sex couples when asked questions that include the options of marriage, civil union, or no recognition.

Third, in many ways same-sex marriage activates the same coalitions of groups that fight about legal abortion, stem cell research, and other cultural issues. But the coalitions are subtly different in important ways. African American churches have been an important source of opposition to same-sex marriage, for example. And many business groups have opposed referenda that would not only ban same-sex marriage but also forbid companies from providing benefits to same-sex couples. Young people are far more supportive of same-sex marriage than older Americans, adding complexity to the group cleavages.

Fourth, same-sex marriage creates complicated issues of federalism. Cities and counties have performed marriages in violation of state law, and states have struggled in some cases over whether to recognize same-sex marriages performed in other states. Some conservatives have pushed to amend the U.S. Constitution to define marriage for all states, but others object to this national incursion into a policy area that historically has been the province of the states.

In the background of this debate, the constitutionality of the Defense of Marriage Act has yet to be decided. If a more conservative Supreme Court permits the act to stand, then married same-sex couples may well have different rights on vacation in some states than others, and the patchwork quilt of state policies may pose serious complications for gay and lesbian couples. If it overturns the act, however, many conservatives who now oppose a federal amendment may favor one to protect the rights of states to define marriage.

Finally, there is the tension between issues decided by courts and those decided by legislatures. Conservatives frequently argue that they merely object to activist judges, but it seems likely that some states will adopt same-sex marriage by legislative action in the next decade, and conservatives are unlikely to object less strenuously. Yet liberals are also cautious about resolving the issue in the courts, and some gay and lesbian rights activists reacted with some relief when New York's state supreme court did not find a right to same-sex marriage in the state's constitution. Some prochoice activists argue that *Roe v. Wade* actually shifted the momentum from abortion rights groups that were gradually winning in state legislatures to prolife groups that mobilized in the aftermath of the decision. John D'Emilio suggests that attempts to win marriage in the courts have had disastrous consequences. Yet without a national court decision, it seems unlikely that many states will allow same-sex marriage in any of our lifetimes.

PLAN OF THE BOOK

We have put together this collection to help students and faculty better understand the complexities of the politics of the issue. Some of our contributors are gay or lesbian, some are straight, most are political scientists, and some are activists. Not all of our contributors agree on the substance of the issue. We asked them to elucidate various aspects of the politics of same-sex marriage. We did not ask them to be neutral on the issue, for we are not neutral ourselves. But we did ask them to write objective essays that investigate the topic from a variety of perspectives. We did not impose a single theoretical framework on the chapters, for we think that students will profit from chapters that offer policy analysis, social movement theory, interest group perspectives, various theories of public opinion and issue framing, and examination of the behavior of political institutions. Finally, although we sought to reduce overlap between chapters, we understand that individual instructors may not wish to assign all chapters, and so we have encouraged authors to write essays that can stand on their own.

The first three chapters provide an overview of the issue of same-sex marriage from different perspectives. In the introduction, Mark Carl Rom provides a public policy analysis of the issue, exploring changes in the social environment, the interest group environment, and official actions that have created a window of opportunity for the emergence of the issue. His essay also provides a thorough overview of the emergence and development of the issue on the policy agenda. Rom's analysis provides an early look of many of the topics that appear in the rest of the book and is the logical starting point for students wishing to understand the politics of same-sex marriage.

John D'Emilio offers a more personal overview of the issue from the viewpoint of a gay man who has been very active in the gay and lesbian rights movement but also is a distinguished historian of social movements. D'Emilio argues that attempting to win the right to marry in the courts has had calamitous results.

Ellen D. B. Riggle and Sharon S. Rostosky provide an academic analysis of the personal consequences of marriage policy for the well-being of same-sex couples. The authors provide a perspective that many students have not encountered by showing the difficulties that same-sex couples encounter as a result of being forbidden to marry.

The next four chapters deal with interest group politics and with coalitions of groups. Ronald G. Shaiko argues that gay, lesbian, bisexual, and transgender interest groups in the United States have displayed a lack of strategic vision and now find themselves fighting a defensive battle on an issue that was not the top priority for most groups. Shaiko suggests that these groups have suffered from growing pains, a lack of national leadership, an all-or-nothing strategy, a we-they mentality, and a secular liberal identity. He offers suggestions for ways in which the community can be more effective, including a call for the religious Left to be active regarding the issue.

Kenneth D. Wald and Graham B. Glover explore the theological underpinnings of same-sex marriage. In a thoughtfully nuanced essay, the authors suggest that religious teachings concerning the practice are more complex than commonly portrayed. There are disagreements among theologians in a number of religious traditions. Moreover, the actual process by which religious teachings take on political meaning is complex and frequently involves political elites who seek to mobilize the religious.

David C. Campbell and Carin Robinson explore the religious coalitions for and against same-sex marriage. They describe the large, ecumenical, and interracial coalition that formed to oppose it and mobilized after the Massachusetts Supreme Judicial Court decision of 2004. They then describe the activities by such groups, which were very important in referenda to amend state constitutions to bar same-sex unions, and the struggles within the coalition to craft a federal amendment that was acceptable to all groups.

Sean Cahill describes more broadly the coalition of groups that oppose same-sex marriage. Cahill, who writes with the language and passion of an activist, shows how this coalition appears to those who work in the trenches to advance marriage rights for same-sex couples.

The next three chapters explore same-sex marriage as it relates to the mass public. Barry L. Tadlock, C. Ann Gordon, and Elizabeth Popp discuss the framing of the issue. We noted above that many Americans value traditional marriage and morality as well as equality for all citizens. This leads contending coalitions of groups and elites to struggle to define the issue as involving primarily one or the other value. The authors draw on content analysis of interest group Web sites and of newspaper coverage of the issue to argue that opponents of same-sex marriage have been somewhat better in winning the framing battle than have supporters.

Clyde Wilcox, Paul R. Brewer, Shauna Shames, and Celinda Lake provide a comprehensive analysis of public attitudes toward same-sex marriage. The authors argue that this was a relatively new issue to most Americans in 2004, despite having been on the policy agenda at least a decade earlier. Drawing on public and private national and local surveys and on private focus groups, they conclude that there is considerable long-term momentum on behalf of gay and lesbian rights, but they also explore a sizable block of Americans who favor gay and lesbian rights generally but who oppose marriage.

DeWayne L. Lucas focuses on the same-sex marriage issue in the 2004 elections. Lucas shows how partisan elites tried to frame the issue and how it served to mobilize the Republican base and to unify many elements of the party. He traces the use of the marriage debate in the presidential race and the ways it echoed in congressional elections as well.

The next three chapters examine the politics of same-sex marriage in national and state political institutions. Craig A. Rimmerman provides a detailed historical analysis of the two elected branches of national government. He provides details that will surprise scholars as well as students, such as the ad that the Clinton campaign ran on Christian radio touting his signing of the Defense of Marriage Act. He traces reactions by the Bush administration and the Congress to the Massachusetts court case, showing the picture to be far more complex than commonly understood.

Karen O'Connor and Alixandra B. Yanus focus on the important role of the courts in same-sex marriage. After a broader discussion of the way other disadvantaged groups such as African Americans and women have won key rights in the courts, they provide an analysis of the gay rights groups and socially conservative groups that have worked in the courts to affect the legal status of marriage. They then explore the constitutional issues surrounding the Defense of Marriage Act.

Katie Lofton and Donald P. Haider-Markel compare attitudes and statewide voting on same-sex marriage with other gay rights issues. Drawing on national surveys and statewide exit polls, the authors conclude that referenda banning same-sex marriage have majority support in all states. Moreover, voters respond to this issue differently than to other gay-rights issues by prioritizing their value of traditional families and morality over equality.

Finally, David Rayside provides a comparison between the complex politics of the U.S. case with actions in other nations such as Canada and Spain. Rayside offers insights into the unique aspects of the U.S. case—the strong, religiously conservative opposition, the popular fear of social disintegration, and the broader opposition to recognition of de facto couples—but also the strong and organized push for equality for gays and lesbians. His chapter provides students with an opportunity to consider how the politics of same-sex marriage might be different if some of these unique elements of the United States were different.

ACKNOWLEDGMENTS

We thank our editor at the University of Chicago Press, Doug Mitchell, for his support. His assistant, Tim McGovern, was instrumental in moving the book forward in key stages. Elaine Wilcox-Cook helped prepare the manuscript for the press, and Katie Szymanski provided critical volunteer assistance early in the process. Mary Gehl shepherded the manuscript through the production process, and Jane Zanichkowsky was an outstanding copyeditor. The Hobart and William Smith Faculty Research and Awards Committee provided ongoing support for Craig A. Rimmerman on this and related projects.

Of course, this book would not have been possible without our contributors, who provided us with thoughtful essays and agreed to revisions and updating. It is always a joy on a project like this one to choose the best possible contributors and then have them all agree to contribute.

We would also like to thank our students—gay, lesbian, and straight—who have showed interest in our research, encouraged us, and sometimes thanked us for our endeavors.

When this project began, Clyde Wilcox was working with two young women graduate students who have both contributed to this book—one an evangelical Christian who has now married, and another a lesbian who was in a long-term relationship but could not legally marry.

We dedicate this book to couples in love everywhere.

INTRODUCTION

THE POLITICS OF SAME-SEX MARRIAGE

Mark Carl Rom

Same-sex marriage was one of the hottest issues of the 2004 electoral season—perhaps *the* hottest. In May the Supreme Judicial Court of Massachusetts ruled that the state could not prohibit same-sex marriages under its constitution (Arce 2004). This ruling produced enormous backlash, and the voters of thirteen states quickly amended their constitutions to codify the definition of marriage as an exclusively heterosexual institution (Peterson 2004).[1] President George W. Bush came out in support of a federal constitutional amendment to ban same-sex marriage. It is possible—although the issue is hotly debated—that these amendments helped Bush clinch the election by raising turnout among conservative voters, especially in Ohio, the state that provided his margin of victory (for example, Lewis 2005; Hillygus and Shields 2005; Lochhead 2004).

How did same-sex marriage come to play such a prominent role in the agenda of American politics in 2004? How can we understand the politics of this issue? In this chapter I offer some tentative answers. In doing so, I focus on three critical topics (largely following Kingdon 1997): the social environment, advocacy groups, and the work of public officials.[2]

Life happens. That is, the world we inhabit is constantly changing in terms of social norms, demographic characteristics, religious beliefs, economic activities, and many other features. Sometimes the changes gradually unfold. At other times, striking events such as a terrorist attack or a hurricane occur. Slowly changing conditions or rapidly occurring shocks can help bring certain issues to public attention, especially via the news media. These changes do not automatically place issues on the policy agenda, although they can help make conditions ripe for the advocacy groups who want to promote their policy goals and public officials who wish to respond—or must respond—to the altered circumstances.

Broad trends in the social environment regarding, in particular, conceptions of marriage and homosexuality have gradually made legalizing same-sex-marriage seem possible. Some advocacy groups and politicians have eagerly greeted these developments and endorsed policy change; others, recoiling in horror, have used the same changes to launch a vigorous counterattack against same-sex marriage.

Every day, advocacy groups toil away to define problems, identify remedies, and promote policy change.[3] Groups that advocate same-sex marriage seek to use the changing environment in ways that allow them to support their vision of a just society, one that accepts the practice as a matter of simple fairness, of full citizenship, of equal rights. Groups that oppose same-sex marriage see these same changes very differently and respond to them by calling for laws (or constitutional amendments) that preserve traditional conceptions of heterosexual marriage. Advocacy groups on both sides of the issue have responded to and shaped that environment in defining and promoting policy solutions to questions concerning the issue.

Public officials, especially elected politicians and judges, live in worlds with their own norms, incentives, and rules. Politicians seek election, power, and policy goals, among other things. They seek policy options that will allow them simultaneously to gain all three. Judges may have their own values, standards, and goals, but they cannot, by necessity, seek to promote them; instead, they must respond only to the policy questions brought before them. Both sets of public officials ultimately must address, in their own ways, the issues that arise from the social environment and from advocacy groups.

Kingdon argues that policy questions become part of the political agenda when the environment, advocates, and political actors intersect to open a window of opportunity. Such a window opened in 2004, though not for the first time. At least since the 1970s same-sex marriage has repeatedly appeared on the agenda, each time with increasing prominence. Moreover, the window that opened in 2004 has hardly slammed shut; the environment, advocates, and public officials have continued to change and adjust to the changes they face.

In many ways, the social environment has become more favorable to same-sex marriage. Changes in the social environment do not produce policy shifts, however, though they make it more possible for change to occur. Ultimately, policy change is made by political actors who are determined to create it. The exact form that change will take cannot be predicted—you will find no argument for historical inevitability here—and the outcome of the struggle for same-sex marriage is far from certain. Of this we can be certain: it will continue to remain on the policy agenda until it is either widely accepted or durably proscribed.

This chapter proceeds in four major sections. In the first I consider the broad trends in the social environment. Two major trends are especially noteworthy: the changing conceptions of marriage and the shifting views regarding homosexuality. In the second section I provide a preliminary assessment of the advocacy groups and their efforts to define and promote answers to the questions concerning marriage. The third section outlines the most important political actors and their role in the debate.[4] Finally, I trace the major developments concerning same-sex marriage, showing how environment, advocates, and officials interact to place marriage on the agenda and address it once it is there.

THE SOCIAL ENVIRONMENT

MARRIAGE

It is possible to view marriage as a monolith: a single, immoveable structure. It is possible but unwise. Marriage is an enormously malleable institution that varies across place and time (Coontz 2005).[5] Marriage is also, like love, a many-splendored thing, its splendor having sacred, social, and political dimensions. Marriage involves a set of legal rights and obligations, a way of living and, for many Americans, a consecrated vow.

The sacred and secular elements of marriage are conceptually distinct. A society could exist in which marriages are blessed but the blessing has no secular consequences. Alternatively, a nation could confer legal rights and obligations upon couples through contract (that is, "civil marriage") without reference to religious authority. If either of these conditions prevailed, then the disputes about whether same-sex couples could marry would likely be muted. If marriage were purely a religious matter, then same-sex couples, like many opposite-sex couples, could simply find a church that would marry them, or they could simply live together. If marriage were merely a secular contract, one might expect that homosexuals would not be barred from signing one.

Marriage's sacred and secular elements are tightly connected in the United States. This is an exceptionally religious country, and millions of Americans choose to have religious weddings. Marriage, in turn, yields a vast array of public benefits and protections; by one count, there are more than one thousand federal laws in which marriage is a factor (General Accounting Office 1997).[6] Many Americans believe that public policy should embrace a particular religious view of marriage and that any attempts to change the secular definition of marriage pose a threat to their spiritual beliefs. From this viewpoint, religious and secular marriage are virtually inseparable.

Religious Views of Marriage

The religious denominations with by far the largest memberships in the United States appear to be implacably opposed to same-sex marriage. The Catholic Church, with about fifty million adult adherents (Largest religious groups n.d.), emphatically rejects legalization (Congregation for the Doctrine of the Faith 2003). The Vatican goes further by indicating that politicians and lawmakers are "morally bound" to oppose "gravely unjust laws" intended to allow such unions. The U.S. Conference of Catholic Bishops Administrative Committee (2003) concurred in its statement concerning marriage. Echoing the Vatican's declaration, the committee noted that to force an equivalence between marriage of a heterosexual couple and a liaison between a same-sex couple "not only weakens the unique meaning of marriage; it also weakens the role of law itself by forcing the law to violate the truth of marriage and family life as the natural foundation of society and culture."

The various evangelical churches, with about forty million members, also are unequivocally opposed to same-sex marriage. As the Southern Baptist Church officially states: "The Bible condemns [homosexuality] as sin. . . . We affirm God's plan for marriage and sexual intimacy—

one man, and one woman, for life" (Southern Baptist Convention n.d.). Other mainline Protestant churches, such as the Methodist Church (fourteen million adult members) and the Presbyterian Church (five million), also affirm that marriage should only be between a man and a woman (Southern Voice 2005).

Not all religious faiths count themselves as defenders of this view of marriage, however. The Unitarian Universalist Association (1996) has called for fully legalizing same-sex marriage. Within American Judaism, the Reform and Reconstructionist movements have also endorsed same-sex marriage; the Orthodox and Conservative movements have not, though prominent voices in each have called for it (Powers 2004). In 2005 the United Church of Christ (1.3 million adult members) became the first mainline Christian denomination endorsing the right of homosexuals to marry, concluding that "[i]n the Gospel we find ground for a definition of marriage and family relationships based on affirmation of the full humanity of each partner, lived out in mutual care and respect for one another" (United Church of Christ 2005).

Other churches continue to struggle with the notion. The Episcopal Church (three million adult members), for instance, has not officially sanctioned full marriage rights, but its national leadership in 2003 approved a resolution stating that "local faith communities are operating within the bounds of our common life as they explore and experience liturgies celebrating and blessing same-sex unions" (Southern Voice 2005). Some of these local communities have gone further: the Diocese of Massachusetts accepted a resolution affirming that state's judicial ruling in favor of same-sex marriage (Sukraw 2004). The Evangelical Lutheran Church of America (five million members), for its part, has not yet resolved the issue; its most recent resolution called for members to "concentrate on finding ways to live together faithfully in the midst of disagreement" (Evangelical Lutheran Church of America 2005).

Though only a distinct minority of religious faiths in the United States approve of same-sex marriage, the crucial point is that at least some do. It is no longer possible for persons of faith to claim that there is universal religious hostility to such unions.

Secular Views of Marriage

Opponents of same-sex marriage argue that marriage has always been about the union of "one man and one woman." Although this is not universally true—polygamy has been common in many cultures and in various ages, and common-law same-sex marital bonds are hardly unknown—the union of man and wife has defined marriage in the United States. But if the definition of marriage in the United States has been a constant, views about marriage and practices within marriage have been constantly evolving. This evolution has had four elements.

1. *Marriage becomes a fundamental right.* At our nation's inception, formal marriage (as compared to the common-law variety) was not an institution open to all. Slaves, in particular, were not allowed to marry. Slaves might live as "man and wife," but neither a slave owner nor the broader society was required to honor these commitments: the marriage bond could be (and often was) broken at the auction block. Indeed, abolitionists "decried slavery's degradation of the marital relationship as one if its greatest moral failings," and the right to marry was one of emancipation's greatest moral accomplishments (Chauncey 2004, 62).

Prohibitions against marriage were not limited to slaves, however, nor were these proscriptions eliminated in the distant past. Various states had policies that forbade members of certain groups from marrying or doing so without explicit permission from the courts. For example, Wisconsin law forbade individuals with child support obligations from marrying unless they received permission from the court to do so (with the individual having to demonstrate that he would fulfill his support obligations). Some states barred felons from marrying, at least so long as they were serving their prison sentences. But these groups, as well as others, have gained the right to marry. In 1978 the Supreme Court struck down the Wisconsin law, ruling that it was unconstitutional under the Fourteenth Amendment's equal protection clause (*Zablocki v. Redhall*). Similarly, the Court ruled in 1987 that prisoners could not be denied this basic civil right (*Turner v. Safley*).[7]

That individuals of every group except homosexuals have a fundamental right to marry is now uncontroversial. Some of those who oppose same-sex marriage argue that homosexuals also have this right and that they simply choose not to use it ("You can marry anyone you want, so long as it is a person of the opposite sex"). Advocates reply that the right to marry is meaningless unless it allows individuals to wed someone they actually *want* to marry ("I cannot marry anyone I want, because anyone I want I cannot marry").

2. *Choice in marriage becomes a fundamental right.* The American experience has not only been about a broadening the right to marry to include every group; it has also been about expanding the ability of individuals within each group to wed the partner of their choice. That ability is

now a basic right. It has not always been thus. The choice of partners has historically been linked to religion, ethnicity, and class. These factors still count in practice, of course, but they count far less as matters of principle.

Marrying outside one's group was not limited only by custom. In particular, laws prohibiting interracial marriage have long been a part of the nation's history. Maryland enacted such a ban as early as the 1660s (Chauncey 2004, 62).[8] These laws did not disappear with the freeing of the slaves after the Civil War; if anything, as blacks gained additional legal and political rights, efforts to "preserve" marriage increased, with more states enacting antimiscegenation laws than repealing them.[9] By 1930, thirty states prohibited interracial marriage, either by statute or by constitutional amendment. No state repealed its laws between 1887, when Ohio did so, and 1951, when Oregon did so (Kennedy 2003, 258–59).

The constitutional argument in support of these laws was based, in part, on the idea that they did not violate the Constitution's equal protection clause because they applied equally to individuals of all races: individuals were free to marry so long as whites did not marry those of other races.[10] But those who supported bans on interracial marriage hardly rested their case on constitutional principles. Three other key arguments were commonly raised. First, interracial marriage violated "natural" (or divine) law: "Almighty God created the races white, black, yellow, malay and red, and he placed them on separate continents . . . the fact that he separated the races shows that he did not intend for the races to mix." [11] Second, interracial marriage allegedly produced negative outcomes such as social disorder and "inferior offspring" (Kennedy 2003, 263). Finally, such marriages abandoned "settled traditions."

These arguments ultimately crumbled in the face of sociological evidence and judicial decisions. In 1948 California became the first state to strike down its ban on interracial marriage. Though public opinion (apparently) still strongly supported such a ban, the California high court concluded in *Perez v. Sharp* that "the essence of the right to marry is freedom to join in marriage with the person of one's choice." As a result, the court struck down the state's law as contradictory to constitutional guarantees of equality. Following the *Perez* decision, more than a dozen states repealed their statutes (Kennedy 2003, 258). In 1967, the United States Supreme Court weighed in by striking down state bans against interracial marriage (*Loving v. Virginia*). The Court ruled unanimously that "the freedom to marry has long been recognized as one of the vital personal rights essential to the orderly pursuit of happiness by free men.

Marriage is one of the 'basic civil rights of man,' fundamental to our very existence and survival. . . . Under our Constitution, the freedom to marry, or not marry, a person of another race resides with the individual and cannot be infringed by the State."[12]

In striking down the same-sex marriage ban, the Massachusetts Supreme Judicial Court relied on its interpretation of *Loving:* "In this case, as in *Perez and Loving,* a statute deprives individuals access to an institution of fundamental legal, personal, and social significance—the institution of marriage—because of a single trait: skin color in *Perez and Loving,* sexual orientation here. As it did in *Perez and Loving,* history must yield to a more fully developed understanding of the invidious quality of discrimination." Although the *Loving* decision did not explicitly address the religious arguments opposing marriage equality, the Massachusetts court did. In *Goodridge* the court concluded that "many people hold deep-seated religious, moral, and ethical convictions that marriage should be limited to the union of one man and one woman, and that homosexual conduct is immoral. . . . Our concern is the Massachusetts Constitution as a charter of governance for every person properly within its reach. Our obligation is to define the liberty of all, not to mandate our own moral code."[13]

Claims about natural law, social consequences, and traditional values have not proved sufficient to halt the gradual increase in the freedom to marry the partner of one's choosing.

3. Procreation becomes separated from marriage. A key argument against allowing same-sex marriage is that, as one court put it, "[M]arriage exists as a protected legal institution primarily because of the societal values associated with the propagation of the human race."[14] Yet societal values regarding the link between marriage and procreation have changed substantially in recent decades, in practice, if not in opinion.

First, more and more children are born outside of marriage. Between 1960 and 2003, the proportion of births occurring in nonmarital relationships increased from a little over 5 percent to almost 35 percent (Child Trends n.d.). Marriage is not a prerequisite for childbearing.

Nor is childbearing a condition for marriage. The rising proportion of children born outside of marriage is due not only to the increasing number of unmarried women giving birth but also to the fact that fewer married women are giving birth. The proportion of women of childbearing age (defined by the Census a those between fifteen and forty-four years of age) who were childless approximately doubled between 1976 and 1995, and it appears to be continuing to increase. About 20 percent of married women in their childbearing years have chosen not to have children (Childless by Choice 2001). More married couples are choosing not to have children, or their marriages dissolve before they produce children. It is also increasingly common for couples who are unable to bear children—especially, but not exclusively, older couples—to marry. Society does not simply tolerate marriage for individuals who do not have children but, especially for individuals incapable of bearing children, celebrates it.

Whether married couples bear children is now generally seen as a matter of personal choice. The legal system agrees; heterosexual couples have no need to prove that they are willing and able to have children as a condition for obtaining a marriage license.

4. *Gender roles become less well differentiated.* A generation ago, gender roles were clear, and clearly differentiated, in virtually every way. Men worked; most women did not have paid employment. The women who did work typically did so in "feminine" jobs as nurses, teachers, secretaries, and so forth, while men dominated the legal, medical, scientific, and political professions, among many others. The gender roles within marriage were equally distinct. The man was master of the house—rhetorically, at least. Women did most of the cooking, cleaning, and childcare. When men cooked, it was over the grill; when they cleaned, it was by doing yard work. Their role in childcare consisted of discipline ("Wait until Father gets home!") and playing. These gender roles were stereotypes, but they did have a strong basis is fact.

Since at least the 1960s, gender roles have becoming increasingly blurred at work and at home. Progressively more women have had paid employment, and women have made large inroads into traditionally male occupations. To a lesser extent, men have moved into conventionally female jobs. The division of labor and authority have also become much more equally distributed in the homes of married couples. The earnings gap between husband and wife has greatly diminished. Men do more work around the house (though still much less than do women) and play a larger role in providing childcare (Morin and Rosenfeld 1998).[15] Marriage has become far more egalitarian than it used to be. Most Americans now believe that greater gender equity "enriches both sexes" (ibid., A1). If this is true, it is not clear that a successful marriage needs a husband and a wife as much as it needs two individuals capable of jointly fulfilling all the tasks for maintaining the household and the relationship.

The cultural shifts in gender roles have affected and in turn been reinforced by the legal aspects of marriage (and divorce). Gender is increasingly irrelevant, from a legal standpoint, regarding the rights and obligations of couples while they are married or concerning custody of children or division of property during divorce, as marriage has become more of an "economic partnership of autonomous individuals" (Behrman and Quinn 1994, 7).

HOMOSEXUALITY

Attitudes towards homosexuality, and policies and practices concerning it, have become considerably more liberal in the past few decades. This section focuses first on public opinion and then on how businesses and governments have altered their policies towards offering homosexuals various rights and benefits.

Public Acceptance of Homosexuality

Public opinion has become more sympathetic towards homosexuality in recent years. Since 1973 the National Opinion Research Center has sometimes included in polls the question, "What about sexual relations between two adults of the same sex—do you think it is always wrong, almost always wrong, wrong only sometimes, or not wrong at all?" Public opinion did not change much between 1973 and 1991 (though, if anything, it became slightly more negative during this period); on average, nearly 75 percent of the public thought such relations were always wrong, and only 14 percent said they were not wrong at all (see figure 1.1). In the next decade, however, the public became considerably more tolerant. By 2002, 55 percent of the public, still a solid majority, thought homosexual activity was always wrong, and 33 percent believed it was not wrong. The proportion answering "almost always" or "sometimes" was roughly constant (Bowman and O'Keefe 2004, 2).

Although a majority of the public believes that homosexual behavior is morally wrong, public opinion as to whether homosexual behavior should be legal is (and has been) more evenly split. In January 2004, 46 percent of the public believed that homosexual relations between consenting adults should be legal, and 49 percent believed they should not be legal (Bowman and O'Keefe 2004, 4). By a margin of almost two to one, however, respondents believed that homosexual activity between consenting adults in their own homes should be legal (5).[16] Americans have also become much more accepting of personal dealings with homosexuals. For example, a clear majority of the public appears to be willing

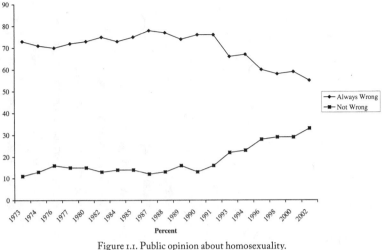

Figure 1.1. Public opinion about homosexuality.
Note: Data are not available every year.

to buy goods from homosexuals, receive treatment from a homosexual doctor, have their children taught by a homosexual schoolteacher, or allow a child to play in a household with a homosexual parent, among other activities (8–9). On a personal level, much of the public reports being personally comfortable dealing with gays.[17]

Views about same-sex marriage are also linked to the question of whether homosexuality is a choice or is innate. As Haider-Markel and Joslyn (2005) demonstrate, opinions regarding the acceptability of same-sex marriage (and interracial marriage) are closely tied to views about biology. An almost perfect linear relationship exists among popular support for interracial marriage and the opinion that blacks are not biologically inferior to whites: as biological prejudice diminished, so did bias against interracial marriage. Similarly, support for same-sex marriage is closely tied to opinions regarding whether homosexuality is innate or chosen. It appears that the more the public views homosexuality as biologically determined, the more support there is for same-sex marriage.

Acceptability to Businesses and Governments

It might be easy to imagine that the business community is conservative—and politically speaking, it often is—but regarding same-sex unions, corporations in many cases have taken the lead in providing benefits to domestic partners. Such benefits might include medical, accident, and

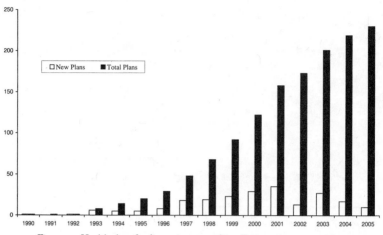

Figure 1.2. Health plans for domestic partnerships, Fortune 500 corporations.

life insurance, sick and bereavement leave, death benefits, parental leave (for a child whom the worker co-parents), and housing rights (Domestic partnership benefits n.d.).[18]

In 1992 the *Village Voice* was the first company to offer benefits to domestic partners. Since then, the number of companies offering such benefits has grown dramatically (see figure 1.2). By 2006, 263 of the Fortune 500 companies and 16 of the largest 20 corporations offered them (Human Rights Campaign Foundation n.d.a). The list includes old-line businesses: General Motors, Ford, General Electric, and Chevron Texaco. In all, almost 8,700 private companies offer domestic partner benefits. Most of the growth has occurred in recent years. Because companies have offered different benefits in different years, and the data are not all reported, the easiest way to show the adoption rate is to identify the year in which the firm began offering health insurance to domestic partners.

Why did so many companies adopt domestic partnership benefit programs? It seems unlikely that purely moralistic or legalistic concerns predominated. It is much more likely that firms award benefits because they have profit-oriented reasons for doing so. The profit motive can induce businesses to adopt benefit plans for a couple of reasons. First, the companies can be more attractive to potential employees, straight and gay. Providing benefits to domestic partners clearly benefit those who are eligible without imposing costs on those who are married. Second, it does not appear that consumers care much one way or the other. As the Human Rights Campaign (n.d.b) argues, "In 1996 the Southern Baptist

Convention, with 15.7 million members, voted to boycott Disney because of its gay-friendly policies. The results? Disney posted record earnings that year. Heterosexual consumers very rarely make purchasing decisions based on a company's gay employment policies, and if they do, such reaction will probably be short-lived. Also, there is probably just as much potential for gaining consumers who agree with a decision to implement [domestic partnership] benefits."

Some cities and counties have also enacted equal benefits ordinances (EBOs), which typically require that firms doing business with the jurisdiction offer benefits to domestic partners that are equal to those offered to married couples. Although a relatively small number of cities have EBOs, they are major ones: Los Angeles, San Francisco, Seattle, and Minneapolis.[19] As a result, firms wanting to obtain contracts from these cities must offer benefits to domestic partners (Equality Maryland n.d.). Business and governmental extension of domestic partnership benefits to same-sex couples has helped normalize the idea that gay couples deserve equal treatment and that equal treatment can be offered without calamitous consequences.

INTERESTS

Environmental changes surely bring hope to those who wish that same-sex marriage would be legalized. Marriage has increasingly come to be seen as an egalitarian partnership between two loving and committed adults and less as a patriarchal institution for the purposes of rearing children and maintaining property. Homosexuality has become increasingly normalized, with gays more open and visible and heterosexuals more understanding and accepting.

But environmental conditions do not by themselves produce policy change; political actors do. Two sets of actors are important: advocacy groups calling for policy change and governmental officials who are capable of producing it.

ADVOCACY GROUPS

Advocacy groups identify policy problems, develop policy solutions, and seek to mobilize other political actors in order to obtain their policy preferences. Their ability to succeed depends on a great many factors, of course. Environmental conditions are important: policies favored by the public have a greater chance of being enacted than do unpopular ones. Public opinion by itself is not a determining element, however, because even relatively unpopular policies can prevail given careful strategic activity by advocates.

Groups that seek to change policy normally operate at a distinct disadvantage compared to those that want to thwart change. To obtain legislative change, advocates must typically persuade subcommittees and full committees of both houses of a legislature to enact the change and convince the president (or governor) to sign it. Unless the advocates prevail at every step, they lose. Opponents, in contrast, must prevail in only a single institution.[20] Accordingly, those who resist policy change in general have a clear structural advantage over those who seek it. To overcome the legislative barriers to change, advocacy groups must be able to mobilize sufficient support among the public and elected politicians. As a result, we might normally expect only majority groups to seek to obtain their policy preferences through legislation.

The tables are turned somewhat when it comes to obtaining legal change. To prevail in court, an advocacy group need not have popular support, legislative patrons, or substantial resources. The requirements for success are relatively few: a strong case, skilled counsel, and sympathetic judges. A litigation strategy poses substantial risks, however.[21] The first is that the litigation might not, in fact, be strategic. Interest groups can be valuable in recruiting sympathetic plaintiffs and compelling cases, in providing skilled counsel, and in locating congenial courts.[22] But interest groups cannot *control* litigation and must worry about poor cases, weak counsel, or hostile courts; when such cases are brought, they potentially damage efforts to promote same-sex marriage. A more serious risk, for advocates of the practice, at least, involves backlash. Although it is understandable that advocates of equal marriage see a litigation strategy as the only viable means of obtaining full marriage rights, court rulings can and have motivated other political actors to mobilize to undercut judicial decisions.

GROUPS ADVOCATING SAME-SEX MARRIAGE

Group advocacy is neither necessary nor sufficient for an issue to rise to the political agenda and for policy change to occur, but absent such advocacy the prospects are not as good. When advocacy groups are unified and mobilized, the chances of success rise. Because a large majority of the population is either indifferent or hostile to same-sex marriage, it is difficult to imagine that it will become the law of the land without the committed advocacy of those most directly affected: gays and lesbians.

Homosexuals have hardly been unified in their support for same-sex marriage (Egan and Sherrill 2005). The division comes in two relevant forms. On one hand, many homosexuals, like many heterosexuals, do not personally aspire to become married. On the other, some homosexuals oppose marriage as an institution. Especially during the early years of the gay liberation movement, some voices "rejected everything they associated with heterosexuality, including sex roles, marriages, and the family" (Chauncey 2004, 89). For many men, gay liberation was about sexual experimentation, not monogamous coupling. For many lesbians, marriage was an "inherently patriarchal institution, which played a central role in structuring the domination of women" (93).

It seems likely that open opposition to the institution of marriage among homosexuals has weakened over time in matters of life as well as death. The same-sex baby boom, in which increasing numbers of openly homosexual individuals had or sought to have children, revealed the legal uncertainties they faced. Issues related to adoption, custody, childcare and support, and access to public benefits all made it abundantly clear that homosexuals faced huge barriers that heterosexuals simply did not have. Meanwhile, the AIDS epidemic starkly disclosed to those with the disease as well as their partners how precarious their legal positions were. As Chauncey notes, "couples whose relationships were fully acknowledged and respected by their friends suddenly had to deal with powerful institutions—hospitals, funeral homes, and state agencies—that refused to recognize them at all" (Chauncey 2004, 96). Individuals with sick partners often could not visit them in the hospital or authorize medical care; their health insurance rarely covered their partners. When one partner died, the other was routinely deprived of the partner's property or of the ability to help plan the funeral. For those with children, those who wanted them, and those who faced illness or death, the lack of access to the normal protections of marriage made it clear that the inability to marry deeply threatened their life, liberty, and pursuit of happiness.

The most prominent of the many groups that advocate on behalf of homosexuals include the Human Rights Campaign (HRC), the National Gay and Lesbian Task Force (NGLTF), and the Gay and Lesbian Alliance Against Defamation (GLAAD). Compared to the groups that oppose same-sex marriage, these groups are much smaller, poorer, and more politically divided. Moreover, the latter continue to face two difficult strategic choices. The first is whether to seek full marriage rights in one fell swoop or to broaden gradually the legal protections for gays so that they more closely resemble those available to married couples. The second is whether to proceed with a legislative or a litigation strategy. There is no unanimity among gay rights advocates concerning either of these issues.

Interest groups that oppose same-sex marriage—the Family Research Council, Focus on the Family, the Christian Coalition, and many others—have substantial strategic, structural and political advantages over groups that advocate full marriage rights. The first is that, in general, these groups merely need to preserve the status quo; that is, they do not necessarily have to advance legislation but only have to block it. The second is that the public continues to oppose same-sex marriage, and it appears that many voters are highly motivated by these beliefs. The final advantage is that these groups are often religion-based and so have ready access to a broad institutional network of individuals and resources that can be mobilized in opposition.[23]

Opponents of same-sex marriage have not been content with merely blocking policy change, however. They have also sought to preempt the issue by enacting federal and state laws and constitutional amendments that define marriage once and for all as exclusively the union of a man and a woman. Given the still (apparently) overwhelming public support for such measures, these efforts generally have thus far succeeded.

Groups that oppose same-sex marriage do have their own dilemmas. For example, given the increasing public acceptance of homosexuality, they find it increasingly difficult to defend marriage by openly attacking gays. As a result, opponents now are reluctant to demonize gays, at least publicly. As one essay posted on the Family Research Council's Web site notes, they oppose same-sex marriage "not because homosexuality is a greater sin than any other. It's not because we want to deprive homosexuals of their fundamental human rights. It's not because we are afraid to be near homosexuals, and it's not because we hate homosexuals. On the contrary, I desire the very best for them. And desiring the best for someone, and acting to bring that about, is the essence of love" (Sprigg 2004).[24]

Acceptance of homosexuality makes it more difficult for conservatives to oppose all legislation that expands the rights of gays. It is one thing for these groups to say "No marriage for homosexuals" and quite a different matter to argue "No hospital visitation rights or health insurance." Groups opposing same-sex marriage have a strong advantage in protecting marriage but a much weaker position in opposing the specific legal protections that marriage affords.

Rather than focusing on homosexuality per se, opponents of same-sex marriage have attempted to shift the frame of the debate, primarily to focus not on homosexual adults but on children. As the same author writes: "[M]arriage is a public institution because it brings together men and women for the purpose of reproducing the human race and keeping a mother and father together to cooperate in raising to maturity the children they produce. The public interest in such behavior is great, because thousands of years of human experience and a vast body of contemporary social science research both demonstrate that married husbands and wives, and the children they conceive and raise, are happier, healthier, and more prosperous than people in any other living situation" (Sprigg 2004).[25]

The second frame consistently used by opponents of same-sex marriage is the slippery slope.[26] "Advocates of same-sex marriage seek to remove the potential for procreation from the definition of marriage, making gender irrelevant in the choice of a spouse, and re-defining marriage only in terms of a loving and committed relationship. If that happens, then it is hard to see how other restrictions upon one's choice of marriage partner can be sustained. These include the traditional restrictions against marrying a child, a close blood relative, or a person who is already married" (Sprigg 2004).[27]

The major strategic choice that opponents of same-sex marriage face is whether to focus exclusively on marriage or to extend their opposition to civil unions, which provide some of the legal protections of marriage to same-sex couples. In the near term, the opponents can hold the political high ground by concentrating exclusively on marriage. As legal rights associated with marriage are extended to same-sex couples, however, it may become more difficult for these groups to defend marriage itself.

PUBLIC OFFICIALS

Judges and politicians are the public officials that are most important to this debate. Politicians can and do seek to place items on the political agenda. In contrast, judges cannot take the initiative, but their decisions can lead others to do so. Both sets of officials have different incentives and priorities.

POLITICIANS

Politicians seek election, power, and policy: they want to gain office and to put their favored policies into place. As a result, politicians have strong incentives to identify policy problems and promote policy solutions; in doing so, they both respond to and shape public opinion.

Among national politicians, there is virtually no support for same-sex marriage. All presidents have opposed it. In 1996, President Bill Clinton stated, "I remain opposed to same-sex marriage. I believe marriage is an institution for the union of a man and a woman. This has been my long-standing position, and it is not being reviewed or reconsidered" (Clinton t.k.). He pledged to sign the Defense of Marriage Act (DOMA), which he did later that same year (Moss 1996). President George W. Bush has gone further by calling for a constitutional amendment to ban same-sex marriage; the amendment would, however, allow states to make other legal arrangements for same-sex couples (Office of the Press Secretary 2004). Presidential candidate John Kerry also rejected equal marriage rights, though he did support state-sanctioned civil unions to provide legal rights to same-sex couples and voted against DOMA (Farhi 2004).

Members of Congress are almost as loath to support marriage rights for gays. In 1996 Congress overwhelmingly passed DOMA, which defined marriage for purposes of federal law as the legal union between one man and one woman as husband and wife ("An Act to Define"). The House vote was 342–67, with only 1 Republican (the openly gay Steve Gunderson of Wisconsin) voting against the bill. On the Democratic side, 65 voted against the bill and 118 voted for it (U.S. House 1996). In the Senate the tally was even more one-sided, with 85 members voting affirmatively and only 14 (all Democrats) in opposition (U.S. Senate 1996).

To the extent that politicians want to be elected and affect policy, nationwide the table is tilted decisively against same-sex marriage. Those who might be sympathetic to it have no incentives to promote it—in the near term, at least, favorable legislation has no chance of being enacted, and the vast majority of politicians potentially face retribution at the ballot box if they speak on behalf of same-sex marriage. Although most members of Congress have safe seats—in 2004, only 5 of the 401 incumbents running for reelection in the House were defeated, while 25 of 26 incumbent senators facing voters were reelected—they inevitably run scared. Elected officials know that reelection can never be taken for granted: making a highly unpopular decision on a salient issue can return to haunt one.

Opponents of same-sex marriage, on the other hand, can promote both electoral and policy goals by taking strong stances against marriage equality. Undoubtedly, many members of Congress truly believe that allowing the practice is bad policy; it is certain that opposing it is good for them in political terms.

One key interaction between the social environment and public officials must be noted: as society has become more tolerant of homosexuals and as homosexuals have become increasingly active politically, more and more have sought and won election to public office. More than 350 openly gay individuals have been elected to national, state, and local office, although this figure represents less than 1 percent of all elected officials (Gay and Lesbian Victory Fund 2006). These individuals may see themselves simply as representatives, not gay representatives, but it appears that their advocacy has been instrumental in sponsoring and promoting legislation to provide marriage rights to gays.

Two examples are especially noteworthy. When Vermont became the first state to authorize civil unions for same-sex couples, Bill Lippert was the only openly gay member of the state House, and he also served as the vice chair of the Judiciary Committee. A savvy political operator, Lippert spoke passionately on the House floor in support of the legislation: "There's something strange about sitting in the midst of a deliberative body that is trying to decide whether I and my fellow gay and lesbian Vermonters should get our rights now. . . . Don't tell me about what a committed relationship is and isn't. I've watched my gay brothers care for each other deeply and my lesbian sisters nurse and care. There is no love and no commitment any greater than what I've seen, what I know" (Moats 2005, 217). When Lippert finished, seventy-two-year-old Republican Robert Kinsey, a veteran of three decades in the legislature, a former Speaker, and an elder in the Presbyterian church, rose to tell his colleagues, "I just heard the greatest speech I've heard in thirty years" (218). The bill passed by a five-vote margin. It is hard to believe that the advocacy of an openly gay legislator was not essential to this outcome.

The case of California is similar. The lead sponsor of the legislation to legalize same-sex marriage was Mark Leno, one of six openly gay individuals in the California Assembly (Bee 2005). Carefully framing the issue, Leno stated: "It's not about gay marriage—it's about marriage equality. . . . [A]re all citizens in this country equal and first class, or are we not? That's the frame that should be established" ("Setting the Record Straight" 2005). Leno went on to argue: "The California state Senate embraced our common humanity. . . . This is about fulfilling the promise of our state constitution that all of our citizens should be treated equally and have full protection under the law" (Bee 2005).[28]

State-level elected officials have incentives similar to those holding national office, but they can face a different political environment. In some parts of the country, at least, politicians can support same-sex marriage without necessarily inviting electoral reprisal. Vermont and California again are instructive.

In Vermont, the highest court found in 1999 that the state was "constitutionally required to extend to same-sex couples the common benefits and protections that flow from marriage under Vermont law" (cited in Moats 2004, 11). The court left it to the legislature to find a solution; the legislature did so by enacting a measure authorizing "civil unions" but not marriage for same-sex couples. After extensive and heated debate, the Senate approved by the measure with all Democrats and two Republicans voting in the affirmative; the bill passed the House by a 79–68 vote (Moats 2004, 240–41).[29] Those voting in favor of the legislation realized that their votes were risky, as did Governor Howard Dean (presumably already gearing up for a presidential run). And risky the vote was: sixteen House incumbents who had supported the bill lost in the next general election, and Republicans gained control of the House (260–61). Still, the law has not been overturned, and it appears to be settled policy. When Republican James Douglas was elected governor in 2003, he noted that be believed that most Vermonters simply did not want to revisit the controversy: "I think most Vermonters have come to accept it, to live with it" (Banville 2004).

In California, the public overwhelmingly (by a vote of 61–39 percent) in 2000 approved Proposition 22 (Institute of Government Studies 2005), an initiative stating that "only marriage between a man and woman is valid or recognized in California" (Office of the Secretary of State 2000). Nonetheless, numerous state politicians have demonstrated strong support for extending the legal protections of marriage to same-sex couples. Prior to passage of Proposition 22, legislation was enacted in 1999 to establish a domestic partnership registry; it granted hospital visitation privileges to registered domestic partners equal to those of spouses and other immediate family members and gave health benefits to domestic partners of state employees (Legislative Council of California [1999]). The benefits of domestic partnerships were considerably expanded in 2003 with the passage of the Domestic Partners Rights and Responsibilities Act, which extended to registered domestic partners virtually all of the rights and responsibilities of marriage (Institute of Government

Studies 2005).[30] In 2004 the Assembly's Judiciary Committee, by an 8–3 vote (with all Democrats in favor and all Republicans opposed) approved a measure granting full marriage rights to same-sex couples. This was the first time that a state legislative committee had approved such legislation; the bill did not pass the full Assembly, however (ibid.).

The big political breakthrough came in 2005. On September 1, the full state Senate passed legislation that would legalize "gender neutral" marriage across the state; the measure passed by a 21–15 margin, with Democrats providing all the affirmative votes (Dignan and Argetsinger 2005).[31] Earlier that year, the Assembly had narrowly rejected a similar version of the bill by a 41–37 vote, but on September 5 the Assembly voted 41–35, a single vote more than the 40 necessary to approve the measure, to accept the Senate bill. As in the Senate, Democrats supplied all the affirmative votes, although four Democrats voted no and two abstained (Associated Press 2005). For the first time, an entire state legislature had voted to support full marriage equality for same-sex couples.

Several Democrats who had voted against the proposal earlier switched their votes. The decision to flip could not have been an easy one, and it seems likely that deeply personal concerns, rather than mere political calculations, provided the impetus. Tom Umberg (D-Anaheim) stated on the Assembly floor that he had been "cajoled, been harassed, been harangued and been threatened" by friends about the issue. But, he added, "This is one of those times when history looks upon us to see where we are. Ten years from now, there are a handful of issues that history will record where we stood, and this is one of those issues. History will record whether we pushed a bit, took the lead to encourage tolerance, to encourage equality to encourage fairness. The constituency I'm concerned about is a very small one, and that's the constituency of my three children, should they decide to look back on my record . . . and reflect on where I was when we could make a difference" (Vogel 2005).

Governor Arnold Schwarzenegger nonetheless vetoed the bill. A socially moderate Republican in a state dominated by liberal Democrats, Schwarzenegger's justification in issuing the veto seemed to be based less on principle than on political expediency: "If the ban of same-sex marriage is unconstitutional this bill is not necessary. If the ban is constitutional this bill is ineffective" (quoted in Lawrence 2005).

Politicians and advocacy groups on both sides of the issue seek first and foremost to define it in terms that will be most attractive to the public. Advocates of same-sex marriage emphasize certain themes (civil rights, citizenship, equality, and fair treatment), and opponents highlight different values (public sentiment, traditional values, protection of children, and religious belief).

Although public opinion remains solidly against same-sex marriage and few national politicians have come out in favor of it, one need not conclude that this status quo will prevail. Politicians pay close attention to public opinion, but not necessarily simply to learn what policies the public wants. Rather, politicians increasingly use polls to learn what messages the public wants to hear, and they use this information to create "crafted talk" to promote the policies the politicians favor (Jacobson and Shapiro 2000). So even when public opinion might seem to weigh strongly against the politicians' policy preferences, skilled politicians still seek to frame the issues in ways that can gain broader acceptance. They use information from public opinion polls and crafted talk to shift opinion in the direction they prefer.

Politicians do not necessarily pander to public opinion, but they can hardly afford to be indifferent to it. Public opinion can and does change, however. Though as recently as 2000 more than 60 percent of voters in California voted to preserve the concept of traditional marriage, the most recent polls by the Public Policy Institute of California revealed a dead heat between the two positions, with 46 percent of the public opposing same-sex marriage and an identical percentage supporting it (Skelton 2005). Moreover, Democrats who oppose same-sex marriage may potentially alienate their own base because nearly 60 percent of Democratic voters now support legalizing marriage for same-sex couples (Baldassare 2005). To the extent that politicians are influenced by public opinion, what is most important is not the opinion the public holds at the moment but what it thinks at the next election, and politicians can never be sure what this will be.

JUDGES

Judges operate under an almost totally different set of ideas and incentives than do politicians. The first key distinction is that judges—at least, federal judges—do not have to face the public in elections. Although politicians are almost always sensitive to electoral concerns, judges, in general, need not be. Accordingly, they need pay less attention to public opinion than do elected officials. But federal judges are not totally free from political pressures, for two reasons. First, all federal judges must be confirmed by the Senate, so any judge with preferences far outside the political mainstream faces dubious confirmation prospects. This is especially true at the high end of the judicial ladder. (For example, as of July 2004 the Senate had confirmed 93 percent [164 of 172] of President Bush's nominees for federal district courts and 67 percent [35 of 52] of his picks for federal circuit courts [Democratic Policy Committee 2004].) As a result, judicial nominees must be at least generally acceptable to a majority (actually, a supermajority of 60 percent) of elected Senators. In addition, the courts maintain their power and prestige to the extent that the public is willing to abide by their rulings. If the courts' opinions stray too far from public acceptance too often, then they risk loss of public confidence.

The matter is more complex in the states. In more than twenty states judges must face the voters at some point (Jacob 1996, 268). Although it appears that only in "special circumstances" are judicial elections hotly contested, it can happen if judges are on the wrong side of an unusually hot political issue (272–73).

Whether judges face the public in elections can have a substantial impact on the rulings they issue. Note that in the first three states with judicial rulings in favor of marriage equality (Hawaii, Vermont, and Massachusetts), the judges are appointed, not elected (Jacob 1996, 268). In these states, judges presumably have less to fear from making controversial decisions.

This is not quite true in California. Judicial selection in that state is such that judges are a political-judicial hybrid: they must be sensitive to public and legal concerns in deciding cases.[32] If they are not, they can face electoral punishment. In 1986 Chief Justice Rose Bird, as well as fellow justices Cruz Reynoso and Joseph Grodin, were voted off the state's high court after a vigorous campaign led by social conservatives (motivated, in part, by the justices' opposition to the death penalty) and business interests (which believed that the state's legal system had become too hostile). Governor George Deukmejian replaced the three with judges deemed to be more socially and economically conservative (Rose Bird n.d.).

In 2005 the legal issues concerning same-sex marriage were not yet resolved in California. In March, San Francisco Superior Court judge Richard Kramer ruled that the state's ban on the practice violates "the basic human right to marry the person of one's choice" and has no rational justification (Egelko 2005).[33] In October 2006 the First District Court of Appeal overturned this ruling, concluding that it was not the judiciary's role to define marriage. The state's Supreme Court is not obligated to review this decision, and it has ninety days to determine whether to hear a case. If it does not, the appellate court's decision will stand (Kravets

2006). How this court will rule is an open question. In 2004 the state Supreme Court did invalidate the same-sex wedding licenses issued in San Francisco after Mayor Gavin Newsom ordered that such licenses be granted. Rather than ruling on the merits of same-sex marriage, however, the court simply determined that Newsom had exceeded his authority in granting the licenses. It also explicitly noted that "[t]his stay does not preclude the filing of a separate action in superior court raising a substantive constitutional challenge to the current marriage statutes" (Judicial Council of California 2004).

A majority of the members of the California Supreme Court were appointed by Republican governors but, as Justice Kramer illustrates, this does not allow us to predict the outcome of the same-sex marriage dispute with confidence. As one experienced observer has commented, the court is "even more cautious than it is conservative." In assessing how it might rule, he predicted that the justices are likely to ask themselves, "Are we going ahead of society?" (Egelko 2005).[34]

The second important distinction between politicians and judges concerns the way they make policy decisions. Politicians are in general influenced by constituent, partisan, and ideological concerns. Judges, in contrast, are relatively free from constituent and partisan forces. They are, however, influenced by ideological as well as legal norms.

There is substantial debate as to whether courts "are primarily interpreters of the law or operate mainly as institutions though which judges follow their policy preferences" (Gerstmann 2005, 217). It is clear that legal doctrine has substantially increased the rights and benefits afforded to homosexuals (American Bar Association 2004, 8). Statutes criminalizing private sexual relations between consenting adults have been swept away, with all such laws overturned by the Supreme Court's 2003 ruling in *Lawrence v. Texas* (12). An increasing number of states have become neutral toward a parent's sexual orientation in assigning child custody or visitation rights, though some states continue to deny homosexual parents such rights (13). Many states now allow same-sex couples to conduct second-parent or joint adoptions; only a few states (such as Florida) continue to deny homosexual parents these powers (13–14). Courts in numerous states have issued rulings that protect homosexuals from discrimination in the workplace or in schools.

It seems clear that legal scholarship also has been strongly supportive of same-sex marriage. One scholar noted that, between 1990 and 1995, seventy-five law review articles were published on the subject, with a mere three making the case *against* such unions (Coolidge 1997). I have seen no similar compendium updating this count, but it appears that the vast majority of law review articles continues to be sympathetic to the claim that same-sex marriages are or should be legal if not constitutional.

EVOLUTION OF SAME-SEX MARRIAGE AND THE POLICY AGENDA

Understanding the social environment, advocates, and public officials and how they interact to influence each other provides us with strong hints as to how the politics of same-sex marriage has unfolded. A brief overview of the major developments surrounding the issue can highlight these interactions.

Same-sex marriage is now squarely on the political agenda, but it did not get there overnight. Events of the past three decades have gradually—and at times explosively—brought the issue to its current importance. As figure 1.3 demonstrates, media attention to the issue has waxed and waned over the past couple of decades.[35] The first surge in reporting occurred in 1996–97, when Hawaii was amending its constitution to prohibit same-sex marriage in response to a 1993 state Supreme Court ruling. The second swell was in 2000, when the Vermont legislature was making policy triggered by that state's high court ruling. The third peak began in 2003 following the Massachusetts Supreme Judicial Court decision. In each period, a state's high court ruled in favor of same-sex marriage, and then advocacy groups and legislatures mobilized in response.

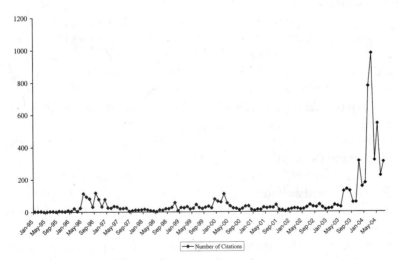

Figure 1.3. Same-sex marriage in the news.

At least seven times during the 1970s and 1980s homosexual individuals or couples sought to obtain the rights and benefits of marriage by filing cases in state courts. In each of these lawsuits the plaintiffs failed, and the cases generated little controversy. After the Supreme Court ruled in *Bowers v. Hardwick* (1986) that the states could criminalize homosexual activity, interest-group support for same-sex marriage vanished (Coolidge 1997).[36]

Same-sex marriage began to appear on the political agenda in 1990, when three same-sex couples applied for and were refused marriage licenses in Hawaii. The couples challenged this denial in state court. The state Supreme Court ruled in 1993 that same-sex couples did not have a fundamental right to marry but that the state's prohibition of marriage appeared to be sex discrimination and an unlawful denial of equal protection under the state constitution (*Baehr v. Lewin;* see also American Bar Association 2004, 20). The court indicated that the state must issue marriage licenses to same-sex couples unless it could demonstrate that prohibition of such marriages "furthers a compelling state interest and is narrowly drawn to avoid unnecessary abridgements of constitutional rights." Subsequently, a circuit court ruled that the state law prohibiting same-sex marriage was unconstitutional, but while the case was on appeal the state's constitution was amended to affirm that "the legislature shall have the power to reserve marriage to opposite-sex couples"[37] Because Hawaii statute provides that a "valid marriage contract . . . shall be only between a man and a woman" the state Supreme Court dismissed the appeal as moot.

It should come as no surprise that this key event took place in Hawaii. The social environment seemed supportive. Only a minority (34 percent) of the island state's residents identified themselves as Judeo-Christian, and close male societal and sexual relationships were an accepted part of ancient Hawaiian culture, at least until the arrival of the Christian missionaries. Although polls indicated that a majority of the public opposed same-sex marriage, opposition to it was not mobilized at first.[38] Public officials were also unusually sympathetic toward the practice. The Democratic Party dominated every level of state politics, and it in turn was dominated by liberal leaders. For example, the Hawaii congressional delegation voted uniformly against DOMA, and in 1996 it was the only state delegation to receive a 100 percent rating from the Human Rights Campaign (Coolidge 1997). After the high court's initial ruling, Governor Ben Cayetano formed two commissions to study the issue, and in 1995 the second commission issued a report in favor of marriage equality.

Still, the lawsuit was not part of a calculated strategy; the plaintiffs were neither recruited nor (initially) supported by advocacy groups (Coolidge 1997). Only when the case moved to the state appeals courts did national groups (the ACLU and the Lambda Legal Defense and Education Fund) intervene to support the plaintiffs. And only after the state Supreme Court issued its ruling did national groups that were sympathetic to the cause begin organizing to obtain favorable media coverage (ibid.).

Once the Hawaii Supreme Court made its initial decision, however, opponents of same-sex marriage, especially those from the mainland, mobilized to counteract the ruling, and resources quickly flowed to Hawaii in an effort to reverse it. The political battles played out in the public and the legislature.[39] Ultimately, two (partly) contradictory decisions prevailed. The legislature simultaneously enacted two measures. One bill (which became law without the governor's signature) created "reciprocal benefits" for same-sex couples, granting them some but not all of the legal rights of married couples.[40] The other called for placing a constitutional amendment stating that "the Legislature shall have the power to reserve marriage to opposite-sex couples" on the 1998 ballot (Same-sex marriage in Hawaii n.d.). In that year, the voters approved that amendment by a 69–31 margin. Because the legislature in 1998 had also enacted a bill stating that marriage consisted only of the union between a man and a woman, same-sex marriages were thus prohibited in the state.

The Hawaii decision unleashed a wave of political activity on the mainland. Fearful that other states would be forced to recognize same-sex marriages if Hawaii authorized them, opponents of such marriages mobilized to seek a federal defense of marriage act. Advocates of DOMA sought two goals: to define marriage as the union of man and woman at the national level and to prevent any state from being forced to recognize same-sex marriages performed in other states. The advocates won easily, and in 1996 Congress overwhelmingly approved DOMA.[41]

After the ruling in *Baehr v. Lewin* was handed down, many states also rushed to protect marriage. By 2004 thirty-eight other states had enacted their own DOMA or constitutional amendment barring same-sex marriage or the recognition of such marriages performed in other states, with most of the bills adopted between 1996 and 2000 (American Bar Association 2004, 30–32). The remaining states, concentrated in the Northeast but including a few others, had all considered DOMA-like bills, but as of 2004 had failed to enact them (32–33).

The next big surge of interest in same-sex marriage began in 1999, when the high court in Vermont ruled in *Baker v. State* (1999) that the state's constitution required that same-sex couples receive the same benefits and protections as married couples (see American Bar Association 2004, 20).[42] The court did not require that same-sex marriages be recognized but only that the state legislature provide them benefits equivalent to those of married couples. The legislature responded in 2000 by approving legislation to provide such benefits to all duly certified civil unions.[43]

As with Hawaii, it was no surprise that Vermont was the center of a legal and political battle. Like Hawaii, Vermont had a tradition of political and social tolerance. It also had a judicial system that was potentially responsive to the advocates of same-sex marriage; after all, in 1993 the Vermont Supreme Court was the first state high court to approve adoption by a homosexual partner (Moats 2004, 96).[44] Furthermore, in 1994 the Vermont legislature had approved certain benefits for domestic partners of state employees (American Bar Association 2004, 20). One key difference between Hawaii and Vermont, however, was that the plaintiffs in this case were actively recruited by the Vermont Freedom to Marry Task Force, an advocacy group formed to develop and promote a long-range strategy for obtaining full marriage equality (Moats 2004, 100).[45]

The decisions by the Vermont Supreme Court and the legislature did not engender the same amount of backlash as did the Hawaii case for a couple of reasons. First, the court required the state to authorize not same-sex marriages but only the legal benefits of marriage. Because the public is more sympathetic to extending the benefits of marriage than to changing its definition, advocacy groups opposing same-sex marriage found it more difficult to attack this decision directly. Moreover, because the legislature then acted, it stripped away the chance to call the action one merely of "unelected and imperial" judges although, as outlined above, some Vermont legislators were apparently punished for their support of the civil unions bill.

Political attention to same-sex marriage dramatically escalated in 2003 owing to both the *Goodridge* decision in Massachusetts and U.S. Supreme Court's ruling in *Lawrence v. Texas,* which declared state sodomy laws unconstitutional. These twin rulings had multiple political consequences. Fearing further judicial encroachment on the traditional definition of marriage, opponents of same-sex marriage were mobilized to seek a constitutional amendment to ban the practice.

The first consequence, again, was to nationalize the debate. Republicans introduced the Federal Marriage Amendment (FMA), which originally was drafted by the Alliance for Marriage, a conservative advocacy group, in the House and the Senate. The House voted 227–186 to approve the measure but fell well short of the two-thirds majority (290 votes) needed. The vote was largely along party lines; Republicans voted 191–27 in favor of the amendment, and Democrats voted 158–36 against it (Clerk of the House 2004).[46] In the Senate, supporters of the amendment did not obtain enough votes to invoke cloture (the vote was 48–50, with five Republicans voting against cloture and three Democrats voting for it), and so the measure died, despite President Bush's endorsement (U.S. Senate 2004).[47] Given the certainty that the FMA would not be approved by both chambers, it appears that supporters in each chamber forced a vote in order to put opponents on the political defensive.

The strategic calculations employed by politicians in their response to public opinion can be quite complicated. In early 2004 polls revealed the complexity (and fluidity) of public opinion regarding same-sex marriage. The public remained solidly against legalizing it (55 percent); 49 percent of those who oppose it voiced strong opposition, and 25 percent of those who favor it gave strong support.[48] But only 46 percent of the public favored a constitutional amendment, and 45 percent thought the matter should be left to the states.[49] Moreover, the public was much more closely split on the issue of civil unions ("all the rights, but none of the label"): 45 percent favored them, and 48 percent opposed them.

The second consequence was an electoral one. Same-sex marriage did not play a direct role in the 2004 presidential campaign; both Bush and Kerry came out in opposition, although both used equivocating statements to provide them with some flexibility.[50] The issue loomed large in state elections, however. Prior to 2004 only four states had constitutional amendments barring same-sex marriage, but in that year alone an additional thirteen states overwhelmingly approved such measures.[51] In 2006, eight more states voted on constitutional amendments banning same-sex marriage, and these measures passed in every state but Arizona (Johnson 2006).[52] In every case, the momentum for the amendments came not from elected politicians but from advocacy groups determined to forestall judicial interventions.

It is difficult to imagine that the Congress will approve a constitutional amendment banning same-sex marriage. The barriers to doing so appear to be too high. We can thus expect that most of the action in the near future will continue to take place at the state level, through legal challenges and legislative initiatives (or legislative responses to judicial rulings).[53] But surely state-level action will not be the end of the story. Ultimately, the U.S. Supreme Court will face the issue and will be forced to decide. Whatever decision it makes, we can expect politicians to respond. How they respond will depend, in part, on the actions of advocacy groups and the conditions in the broader social environment.

ENDNOTES

1. Eleven states—Arkansas, Georgia, Kentucky, Michigan, Mississippi, Montana, North Dakota, Oklahoma, Ohio, Oregon, and Utah—voted on the constitutional amendments on Election Day. Two other states also approved such constitutional amendments earlier in 2004. Each amendment passed by an overwhelming margin, with the closest race in Oregon, where 57 percent of the voters supported the amendment.

2. Kingdon labels these the problem stream, the policy stream, and the political stream.

3. The environment produces "conditions." Conditions become "problems" when political actors determine that the conditions should be addressed.

4. Environment, advocacy, and the work of public officials are inextricably linked: each influences, and in turn is influenced by, the others. Nonetheless, for the purposes of this chapter I simplify the matter by considering each separately, except where it is essential to show the interrelationships.

5. For a history of same-sex marriage, as well as arguments supporting and opposing it, see Eskridge (1993) and American Bar Association (2004).

6. Marital status affects pensions, taxes, health insurance and health care, and property rights, among a wide range of other benefits. A few examples might illustrate the matter. If a married person dies, Social Security will pay pension benefits to the survivor; the survivor in an unmarried couple (whether opposite-sex or same-sex) receives nothing. A married person can deduct from income taxes the health insurance costs of a spouse; an unmarried person gets no such deduction. A married person has automatic rights to visit a hospitalized spouse; an unmarried person does not does not have similar rights. A married person can take unpaid leave from a job to care for a spouse, but an unmarried person take similar leave.

7. *Zablocki v. Redhall*, 434 U.S. 374 (1978); *Turner v. Safley* 482 U.S. 78 (1987).

8. For a history of these laws and the controversies surrounding them, see Kennedy (2003).

9. Many of these laws prohibited whites from marrying people in other racial or ethnic groups as well. For example, the California law rendered "illegal and void" marriages between whites and Negroes, mulattoes, and people of Chinese, Japanese or Filipino ancestry (Kennedy 2003, 260).

10. The California law, for instance, did not forbid nonwhites of the various groups to intermarry.

11. *Loving v. Commonwealth of Virginia*, 388 U.S. 1 (1967), 3. Judge Leon M. Bazile, arguing for the Commonwealth of Virginia, is cited in Kennedy (2003, 274).

12. *Perez v. Sharp*, 32 Cal. 2d 711, 198 P.2d 17 (1948), 117; *Loving v. Virginia*, 12. The Court further noted that the ban was "designed to maintain White Supremacy" and therefore was constitutionally impermissible.

13. Goodridge et al. v. Department of Public Health et al., 440 Mass. 309 (2003). In regard to this matter the Court quoted Lawrence v. Texas, 539 U.S. 558 (2003), which itself quoted Planned Parenthood of Southeastern Pennsylvania v. Casey 505 U.S. 833, 850 (1992).

14. *Singer v. Hara*, 11 Wash. App. 247, 522 P.2d 1187, 1195 (1974).

15. Women still do far more work around the home than do men, though the differences have narrowed substantially. In the late 1960s, women did an average of thirty hours of housework each week, and men did only five hours; by 1998, the balance had shifted to twenty hours for women and ten hours for men (Morin and Rosenfeld 1998).

16. Results vary somewhat depending on the exact wording of the questions, the organization asking the questions, and the time the poll was administered. For further details, see Bowman and O'Keefe (2004).

17. It is possible that public opinion polls regarding these matters are subject to a "social acceptability" bias (i.e., political correctness), in which respondents are unwilling to give answers that are considered impolite.

18. A company might offer some or all of these benefits. If the benefits have monetary value, the recipient must pay taxes on them, because the IRS considers benefits awarded to unmarried partners taxable compensation.

19. California has adopted an EBO statewide; it will go into effect in 2007. In all, about 130 city and county governments provide health benefits to domestic partners. More than 40 percent began to offer benefits after 2000 (American Bar Association 2004, 34).

20. Given that there are three votes within each legislative body, and the executive's decision, the probability that a bill would be signed into law with a 50 percent chance of failing at any point is less than one in one million. Also, the U.S. Senate operates under rules that give determined minorities substantial powers to block legislation. Moreover, the structure of the Senate—two votes for every state, no matter how small—gives disproportionate power to rural and, presumably, more conservative voices. These features also exist, though at times to a lesser extent, in state senates.

21. For an extensive discussion of the costs and benefits of the litigation strategy, see Derthick (2004).

22. The conservative Center for Individual Rights actively recruited plaintiffs to challenge the affirmative action programs of the University of Michigan and the University of Texas, for example (Center for Individual Rights 1997).

23. See, e.g., You ain't seen nothing yet (2005).

24. To be sure, much of Sprigg's speech might be labeled "demonizing," as when he characterizes homosexuals as "transient, promiscuous, and unfaithful."

25. Politicians who oppose same-sex marriage have adopted this same frame. See, e.g., Liu and Macedo (2005) and Ponnuru (2003).

26. For a discussion of the slippery slope metaphor, see Stone (2002, 151–52).

27. Senator Rick Santorum (R-PA) made a similar arguments in more graphic terms, to harsh criticism (Liu and Macedo 2005, 214).

28. Leno clearly understood legislative procedures as well. After his bill was voted down in the Assembly, he used a controversial parliamentary tactic known as "gut and amend." Here's how it worked. An inconsequential bill (AB 849), dealing with the Department of Fish and Game, had passed the Assembly by unanimous vote. Before it was sent to the Senate, Leno convinced the bill's sponsor to strip out the existing text, replace it with his same-sex marriage proposal, and add his name as the sponsor. This was the bill approved by the Senate and then returned to the Assembly for its consideration (Right to marry bill resurfaces 2005).

29. The full text of the law can be found in An Act Relating to Civil Unions, 15 V.S.A. ch. 23, §§1201 et seq. (2000). http://www.leg.state.vt.us/docs/2000/bills/passed/h-847.htm.

30. The bill as approved can be viewed at Legislative Council of California ([2003].)

31. The bill as amended can be viewed at Legislative Council of California ([2005])

32. In California, each Superior Court serves a single county. Superior Court judges are chosen in nonpartisan elections by the voters of the county and serve six-year terms. Justices on the six Courts of Appeal and the Supreme Court are appointed by the governor and subject to approval by the commission on judicial appointments (American Judicature Society n.d.). These justices face "retention elections"—every four years, on a rotating basis, state voters can vote to retain or remove a sitting judge (Judicial Council of California 2005). The elections are uncontested, and the justices do not actively campaign. Supreme Court justices face statewide elections; lower courts face the voters in their particular jurisdictions.

33. Despite the name, the Superior Court is the court of initial jurisdiction. The full text of the ruling can be found at Superior Court of the State of California (2005). As an example of how unpredictable judicial rulings can sometimes be, Kramer is a registered Republican and Roman Catholic; he was appointed by Republican governor Pete Wilson (Finz and Derbeken 2005).

34. The quotations are from Dennis Maio, who spent twenty years on the high court's staff.

35. This figure shows the number of citations in East Coast newspapers and magazines based on the search term "same-sex marriage," according to Lexis-Nexis.

36. The marriage cases are summarized in Same-sex marriage: Developments in the law (2005). *Bowers v. Hardwick,* 478 U.S. 186 (1986).

37. *Baehr v. Lewin,* 852 P.2d 44, 68 (1993). After remanding it became *Baehr v. Miike.* Haw. Const. art. I, §23 (1998).

38. Actually, sources vary regarding this point. Wikipedia (Same-sex marriage n.d.) states that "polls at the time indicated that the majority of residents favored allowing same-sex marriage, possibly due to predominantly non-European demographics," though I have not been able to verify this information.

39. For one discussion of these battles, see Hull (2001).

40. Act 383, Relating to unmarried couples (1997). Summary available at http://www.hawaii.edu/ur/Gov/house.html#1. Ironically, "the Christian Coalition's chief lawyer, Jay Sekelow, campaigned vigorously in support of this bill—desperate to find anything that would prevent same-sex couples from gaining access to legal marriage" (Reciprocal beneficiaries 1997). For a summary of the law's provisions, see American Bar Association (2004, 24–25).

41. An Act to Define and Protect the Institution of Marriage. P.L. 104–199. 104th Cong., 2nd sess. http://frwebgate.access.gpo.gov/cgi-bin/getdoc.cgi ?dbname=104_cong_public_laws&docid=f:publ199.104.pdf.

42. *Baker v. State*, 744 A.2d 864 (1999).

43. An Act Relating to Civil Unions.

44. Denise Johnson, the justice who wrote the unanimous ruling, had been a civil rights lawyer championing women's rights before her appointment to the bench (Moats 2004, 97).

45. In 1997 the task force ultimately recruited three "ideal" (stable, long-term, "normal") couples to serve as plaintiffs.

46. One Independent also voted against the amendment.

47. It is one measure of the political sensitivity of the issue that neither John Kerry nor John Edwards cast a vote.

48. In addition, the overwhelming majority of Republicans opposed legalizing same-sex marriage, whereas Democrats were more evenly split.

49. As an indication of the fluidity of this issue, support for leaving it to the states declined from 58 percent one month prior to the survey, "an apparent backlash to the same-sex marriages now occurring in San Francisco" (Morris 2004, n.p.).

50. In an October 2004 interview, Bush stated, "I don't think we should deny people rights to a civil union, a legal arrangement, if that's what a state chooses to do. . . . I view the definition of marriage different from legal arrangements that enable people to have rights. And I strongly believe that marriage ought to be defined as a union between a man and a woman. Now, having said that, states ought to be able to have the right to pass laws that enable people to have rights like others" (Bush breaks with GOP 2004). For his part, Kerry opposes same-sex marriage but voted against DOMA and also supports civil unions.

51. An additional state, Kansas, enacted a constitutional ban in 2005. The constitutional bans in ten of the eighteen states also include civil unions (Peterson 2005).

52. The proposed amendment in Arizona not only would have banned same-sex marriage but also would have taken away all rights and benefits from heterosexual domestic partnerships and civil unions (Belge 2006).

53. It might appear that judicial challenges are off the table in the states with constitutional amendments barring same-sex unions, but this is not the case. In May 2005 a federal district court struck down the ban included in Nebraska's constitution, concluding that it denied same-sex couples fundamental rights guaranteed by the U.S. Constitution (Peterson 2005). Moreover, other state courts will likely rule on challenges that claim that there are inconsistencies

between the equal-protection clauses and same-sex marriage prohibitions within state constitutions.

REFERENCES

American Bar Association. 2004. *An analysis of the law regarding same-sex marriage, civil unions, and domestic partnerships.* White paper by the Section of Family Law Working Group on Same-Sex Marriages and Non-Marital Unions. http://www.abanet.org/family/whitepaper/fullreport.pdf.

American Judicature Society. n.d. Judicial selection in the states: California. http://www.ajs.org/js/CA_methods.htm.

Arce, Rose. 2004. Massachusetts court upholds same sex marriage. http://www.cnn.com/2004/LAW/02/04/gay.marriage/.

Associated Press. 2005. Assembly roll call on gay marriage bill. http://www.sfgate.com/cgi-bin/article.cgi?f=/n/a/2005/09/06/state/n210908D31.DTL.

Baldassare, Mark. 2005. Election: The growing polarization of California. San Francisco: Public Policy Institute of California.http://www.ppic.org/main/commentary.asp?i=478.

Banville, Lee. 2004. The battle over same sex marriage. *Online NewsHour.* April 30. http://www.pbs.org/newshour/bb/law/gay_marriage/vermont.html.

Bee, Clea Benson. 2005. Same-sex marriage gets state senate OK. *Sacramento Bee,* September 2. http://web.lexis-.nexis.com/universe/document?_m=7654192a75f 12f6a0e0482cabff44a53&_docnum=4&wchp=dGLzVzz-zSkVb&_md5=d6c295 aaeb70ee4105cbe81b6888302f.

Behrman, Richard E., and Linda Sandham Quinn. 1994. Children and divorce: Overview and analysis. *Future of Children* 4 (Spring): 4–14. http://www.futureofchildren.org/usr_doc/vol4no1ART1.pdf.

Belge, Kathy. 2006. Gay marriage Arizona. http://lesbianlife.about.com/od/lesbianactivism/a/Arizona107.htm (November 8).

Bowman, Karlyn, and Brian O'Keefe. 2004. Attitudes about homosexuality and gay marriage. Washington, DC: American Enterprise Institute. http://www.aei.org/publications/pubID.14882/pub_detail.asp.

Bush breaks with GOP on same-sex unions. 2004. *Washington Times,* October 26. http://washingtontimes.com/upi-breaking/20041026–121303–1337r.htm.

Center for Individual Rights. 1997. CIR sues to end use of racial preferences by University of Michigan. http://www.cir-usa.org/releases/20.html.

Chauncey, George. 2004. Why marriage? The history shaping today's debate over gay equality. New York: Basic.

Child Trends. n.d. Percentage of births to unmarried women. http://www.childtrendsdatabank.org/indicators/75UnmarriedBirths.cfm.

Childless by Choice. 2001. *American Demographics,* October. http://www.findarticles.com/p/articles/mi_m4021/is_2001_Oct_1/ai_79052844/print.

Clerk of the House. 2004. Final vote results for Roll Call 484. http://clerk.house.gov/evs/2004/roll484.xml.

Clinton, Bill. 1996. "Interview with Bill Clinton," by J. Jennings Moss. *The Advocate* 710 (June 25): 44–52.

Congregation for the Doctrine of the Faith. 2003. Considerations regarding proposals to give legal recognition to unions between homosexual persons. http://www.vatican.va/roman_curia/congregations/cfaith/documents/rc_con_cfaith_doc_20030731_homosexual-unions_en.html.

Congressional Budget Office. 1995. Characteristics of married and unmarried couples, 1995. http://www.cbo.gov/showdoc.cfm?index=7&sequence=9.

Coolidge, David Orgon. 1997. Same-sex marriage: As Hawaii goes . . . *First Things* 72:33–37. http://www.firstthings.com/ftissues/ft9704/articles/coolidge.html.

Coontz, Stephanie. 2005. Marriage: A history, from obedience to intimacy, or how love conquered marriage. New York: Viking.

Democratic Policy Committee. 2004. Bush judicial nominees confirmed at a rate better than or equal to recent presidents. http://democrats.senate.gov/dpc/dpc-doc.cfm?doc_name=fs-108-2-197.

Derthick, Martha. 2004. Up in smoke: From legislation to litigation in tobacco politics. 2d ed. Washington, DC: CQ Press.

Dignan, Joe, and Amy Argetsinger. 2005. California Senate passes gay marriage bill. *Washington Post*, September 2. http://www.washingtonpost.com/wp-dyn/content/article/2005/09/01/AR2005090102086.html.

Domestic partnership benefits. n.d. http://www.nolo.com/lawcenter/ency/article.cfm/ObjectID/86D4108D-25D1-498A-B38AF4AB25F14E84/catID/64C2C325-5DAF-4BC8-B4761409BA0187C3.

Egan, Patrick J., and Kenneth Sherrill. 2005. Marriage and the shifting priorities of a new generation of lesbians and gays. *PS: Political Science and Politics* 38 (April): 229–32.

Egelko, Bob. 2005. Court invalidates California's ban on same-sex marriage. *San Francisco Chronicle*, March 14. http://www.sfgate.com/cgi-bin/article.cgi?f=/c/archive/2005/03/14/samesexruling14.TMP.

Equality Maryland. n.d. Equal benefits ordinances. http://www.equalitymaryland.org/equalbenefits.htm.

Eskridge, William M., Jr. 1993. A history of same sex marriage. *Virginia Law Review* 79 (7): 1419–1513. www.jstor.org/.

Evangelical Lutheran Church of America. 2005. Recommendations from the ELCA Church Council to the ELCA Churchwide Assembly on Sexuality Studies. http://www.elca.org/faithfuljourney/050411churchcouncil.html.

Farhi, Paul. 2004. Kerry again opposes same sex marriage. *Washington Post*, May 15. http://www.washingtonpost.com/wp-dyn/articles/A28118-2004May14.html.

Finz, Stacy, and Jaxon Van Derbeken. 2005. Judge is Catholic and Republican—"A brilliant guy." *San Francisco Chronicle*, March 15. http://www.sfgate.com/cgi-bin/article.cgi?f=/c/a/2005/03/15/KRAMER.TMP.

Gay and Lesbian Victory Fund. 2006. Gay candidates win in record numbers across U.S. http://www.victoryfund.org/index.php?src=news&prid=183&category=News%20Releases (November 8).

General Accounting Office. 1997. The honorable Henry J. Hyde. http://www.gao.gov/archive/1997/og97016.pdf.

Gerstmann, Evan. 2005. Litigating same-sex marriage: Might the courts actually be bastions of rationality? *PS: Political Science and Politics* 38 (April): 217–23.

Haider-Markel, Donald P., and Mark R. Joslyn. 2005. Attributions and the regulation of marriage: Considering the parallels between race and homosexuality. *PS: Political Science and Politics* 38 (April): 233–39.

Hillygus, D. Sunshine, and Todd G. Shields. 2005. Moral issues and voter decision making in the 2004 presidential election. *PS: Political Science and Politics* 38 (April): 201–9.

Hull, Kathleen E. 2001. The political limits of the rights frame: The case of same-sex marriages in Hawaii. *Sociological Perspectives* 44 (Summer): 207–32.

Human Rights Campaign Foundation. n.d.a. Employers that offer domestic partner health benefits. http://www.hrc.org/Template.cfm?Section=Search_the _Database&Template=/CustomSource/WorkNet/srch.cfm&searchtypeid=3& searchSubTypeID=1.

———. n.d.b. Anticipating backlash. http://www.hrc.org/Content/Navigation Menu/Work_Life/Get_Informed2/The_Issues/Anticipating_Backlash/ Anticipating_Backlash.htm.

Institute of Government Studies. 2005. Same-sex marriage in California—Overview and issues. http://www.igs.berkeley.edu/library/htGayMarriage.html.

Jacob, Herbert. 1996. Courts: The least visible branch. In *Politics in the American states: A comparative analysis.* 5th ed, ed. Virginia Gray and Herbert Jacob, 253–85. Washington, DC: CQ Press.

Jacobs, Lawrence, and Robert Shapiro. 2000. Politicians don't pander: Political manipulation and the loss of democratic responsiveness. Chicago: University of Chicago Press.

Johnson, Ramon. 2006. 2006 GLBT ballot initiatives. http://gaylife.about.com/ od/gayrights/ig/2006-Election-Manual-for-Gays/2006-GLBT-Ballot-Initiatives.htm.

Judicial Council of California. 2004. California Supreme Court takes action in same-sex marriage cases. March 11. http://www.courtinfo.ca.gov/presscenter/ newsreleases/NR15-04.HTM.

———. 2005. Appellate retention elections: What they are and how to learn more about the appellate courts and the justices who serve on them. http://www .courtinfo.ca.gov/courts/courtsofappeal/1stDistrict/retention.htm.

Kennedy, Randall. 2003. Interracial intimacies: Sex, marriage, identity, and adoption. New York: Pantheon.

Kingdon, John W. 1997. *Agendas, alternatives, and public policies.* 2d ed. Upper Saddle River, NJ: Pearson Education.

Kravets, David. 2006. Gay marriage front in center before California Supreme Court. http://www.sacbee.com/114/story/76314.html (November 13).

Largest religious groups in the United States of America. n.d. http://www .adherents.com/rel_USA.html#families.

Lawrence, Steve. 2005. Schwarzenegger vetoes gay marriage bill. Associated Press. September 30. http://news.yahoo.com/s/ap/20050930/ap_on_re_us/gay _marriage.

Legislative Council of California. [1999]. Bill number: AB 26. State of California. http://www.leginfo.ca.gov/pub/99-00/bill/asm/ab_0001-0050/ab_26_bill _19991010_chaptered.html.

———. [2003.] Bill number: AB 205. State of California. http://www.leginfo.ca.gov/pub/03–04/bill/asm/ab_0201–0250/ab_205_bill_20030922_chaptered.html.

———. [2005.] Assembly Bill no. 849. State of California. http://www.leginfo.ca.gov/pub/bill/asm/ab_0801–0850/ab_849_bill_20050628_amended_sen.pdf.

Lewis, Gregory B. 2005. Same-sex marriage and the 2004 presidential election. *PS: Political Science and Politics* 38 (April): 195–99.

Liu, Frederick, and Stephen Macedo. 2005. The federal marriage amendment and the strange evolution of the conservative case against gay marriage. *PS: Political Science and Politics* 38 (April): 211–15.

Lochhead, Carolyn. 2004. Gay marriage: Did the issue help re-elect Bush? *San Francisco Chronicle*, November 4. http://sfgate.com/cgi-bin/article.cgi?file=/c/a/2004/11/04/MNG3A9LLVI1.DTL.

Moats, David. 2004. Civil wars: A battle for gay marriage. Orlando: Harcourt.

Morin, Richard, and Megan Rosenfeld. 1998. With more equity, more sweat. *Washington Post*, March 22. http://www.washingtonpost.com/wp-srv/national/longterm/gender/gender22a.htm.

Morris, David. 2004. Marriage amendments: Opinions split over amendment to ban same-sex marriages. http://abcnews.go.com/sections/us/Relationships/gay_marriage_poll_040224.html.

Moss, J. Jennings. 1996. Bill Clinton. *Advocate*, June 25. http://64.233.167.104/search?q=cache:7q47p_Bs7rQJ:www.advocate.com/html/stories/824/824_clinton_710.asp+&hl=en&lr=lang_en.

Office of the Press Secretary, Executive Office of the President. 2004. President calls for constitutional amendment protecting marriage. http://www.whitehouse.gov/news/releases/2004/02/20040224–2.html.

Office of the Secretary of State. 2000. Text of Proposition 22. [California.] http://primary2000.ss.ca.gov/VoterGuide/Propositions/22text.htm.

Peterson, Kavan. 2004. 50-state rundown on gay marriage laws. Stateline.org. http://www.stateline.org/stateline/?pa=story&sa=showStoryInfo&id=353058.

———. 2005. Same-sex unions—a constitutional race. Stateline.org (March 29; updated September 8). http://www.stateline.org/live/ViewPage.action?siteNodeId=136&languageId=1&contentId=20695.

Ponnuru, Ramesh. 2003. Coming out ahead. *National Review*, July 28, 24–26.

Powers, Amber. 2004. The major Jewish denominations, not surprisingly, have come to different conclusions about same-sex marriage. http://jewish.com/modules.php?name=News&file=article&sid=827.

Reciprocal beneficiaries: The Hawaiian approach. 1997. Partners Task Force for Gay and Lesbian Couples. http://www.buddybuddy.com/d-p-hawa.html.

Regan, Mark. 2002. Preserving marriage in an age of counterfeits: How "civil unions" devalue the real thing. Washington, DC: Family Research Council.

Right to marry bill resurfaces. 2005. *San Francisco Chronicle*, July 11. http://www.sfgate.com/cgi-bin/article.cgi?f=/c/a/2005/07/11/EDGBBDKKI61.DTL.

Rose Bird. n.d. http://en.wikipedia.org/wiki/Rose_Bird.

Same-sex marriage. n.d. http://en.wikipedia.org/wiki/Same-sex_marriage.

Same sex marriage: Developments in the law. 2005. http://www.nolo.com/article.cfm?objectID=6DF0766E-C4A3–4952-A542F5997196E8B5/118/304/190/ART/.

Same-sex marriage in Hawaii. n.d. religioustolerance.org. http://www.religious
tolerance.org/hom_mar5c.htm.

Setting the record straight. 2005. *San Francisco Chronicle*, August 23. http://sanfran
ciscosentinel.com/id48.htm.

Skelton, George. 2005. Debate brings clarity to gay marriage issue. *Los Angeles
Times*, September 5. http://web.lexis-nexis.com/universe/document?_m=7654
192a75f12f6a0e0482cabff44a53&_docnum=3&wchp=dGLzVzz-zSkVb&_md5
=ecb2d6cb017f6d1302436e4c60494832.

Southern Baptist Convention. n.d. Sexuality. http://www.sbc.net/aboutus/pssexu
ality.asp.

Southern Voice. 2005. Where other mainline churches stand on same-sex marriage.
July 8. http://www.southernvoice.com/2005/7-8/news/localnews/ucc.cfm#.

Sprigg, Peter. 2004. Homosexuality: The threat to the family and the attack on
marriage. http://www.frc.org/get.cfm?i=PD04F01.

Stone, Deborah. 2002. Policy paradox: The art of political decision making. Rev.
ed. New York: Norton.

Sukraw, Tracy. 2004. Diocese of Massachusetts affirms state court's ruling on civil
marriage. Episcopal News Service, March 19. http://www.episcopalchurch
.org/3577_32422_ENG_HTM.htm.

Superior Court of the State of California. 2005. Marriage cases. http://www.sftc
.org/Docs/marriage.pdf.

Unitarian Universalist Association. 1996. Resolution of immediate witness in support of the right to marry for same sex couples. http://www.buddybuddy.com/
church03.html.

United Church of Christ. 2005. In support of equal marriage rights for all. http://
www.ucc.org/synod/resolutions/gsrev25-7.pdf.

U.S. Conference of Catholic Bishops Administrative Committee. 2003. Calls for
protection of marriage. http://usccb.org/comm/archives/2003/03-179.htm.

U.S. House of Representatives. 1996. Final vote results for Roll Call 316. http://
clerk.house.gov/evs/1996/roll316.xml.

U. S. Senate. 1996. U.S. Senate roll call votes 104th Congress—2nd session. http://
www.senate.gov/legislative/LIS/roll_call_lists/roll_call_vote_cfm.cfm?congr
ess=104&session=2&vote=00280.

———. 2004. U.S. Senate roll call votes 108th Congress—2nd session. http://www
.senate.gov/legislative/LIS/roll_call_lists/roll_call_vote_cfm.cfm?congress=1
08&session=2&vote=00155.

Vogel, Nancy. 2005. Legislature OKs gay marriage. *Los Angeles Times*, September 7. http://www.latimes.com/news/local/politics/cal/la-me-gaymarriage7se
p07,1,5420306.story?coll=la-news-politics-california.

You ain't seen nothing yet. 2005. *Economist*. June 23. http://www.economist.com/
world/na/displayStory.cfm?story_id=4102212.

WILL THE COURTS SET US FREE?

REFLECTIONS ON THE CAMPAIGN FOR

SAME-SEX MARRIAGE

John D'Emilio

Sex laws are notoriously easy to pass. . . . Once they are on the books, they are extremely difficult to dislodge.
GAYLE S. RUBIN, "THINKING SEX"

In May 1993 the Hawaii State Supreme Court instructed one of its trial judges to reconsider a case involving same-sex marriage. Calling marriage "a basic civil right," the justices suggested that the prohibition against issuing licenses to same-sex couples violated state constitutional bans against gender-based discrimination. William Rubinstein, at that time the director of the American Civil Liberties Union's gay rights project, called the ruling "a major breakthrough."[1] This was the first time in U.S. history that a court came remotely close to approving "gay marriages," and it cracked open a nationwide debate that continues today. One can draw a straight line from this judicial instruction in Hawaii to the first same-sex marriages in Massachusetts in May 2004 and the raft of prohibitionist measures that graced many state ballots in November 2004.

By any logic, the Hawaii decision ought to have thrilled me. I study social movements. I think daily about collective efforts to achieve justice and about how disenfranchised groups act to redress their grievances. In particular, I have studied the gay and lesbian movement for the past three decades and at various points along the way have been not merely an observer but a participant in the cause. What could be more exhilarating than to witness history being made, to watch a campaign develop involving something as fundamental as marriage?

Instead, from the moment that the Hawaii courts put the marriage issue squarely on the political agenda, the unfolding of the campaign for same-sex marriage has left me distinctly uneasy. For the past dozen years, most new developments in the campaign have made this gnawing discontent ever more insistent.

Most of the time I have attributed this response to my own particular queer history. I am a member of what is often referred to as "the Stonewall generation." I belong to an exuberant radical subset of my age cohort. We were permanently influenced by the rebellious counterculture of the 1960s and the provocative writings of pioneering radical feminists.[2] Coming out publicly during the early and mid-1970s meant that we experienced being gay or lesbian as a worldview, a political orientation, a form of rebellion against social and cultural norms. To borrow the description of John Waters, the director of such camp films as *Pink Flamingo* and *Hairspray,* this was the generation of gay men for whom "one privilege of being gay was that we didn't have to get married."[3]

Rather than a lifestyle, being gay seemed an entry point to remaking society. By definition, we thought, queer life was subversive of marriage and the family. In a nation that was led by Richard Nixon and that was bombing Southeast Asia back to the Stone Age, any kind of subversion seemed a very good thing indeed. We imagined a world in which bonds of friendship, companionship, and sexual intimacy were knitting communities together with ties more durable than those that no-fault divorce could dissolve with a signature and a small fee.

Put aside for the moment any qualms about whether those views were little more than utopian fantasies. Instead, carry that consciousness forward into the 1990s. You might expect someone like me to be arguing thus: "Why are we campaigning for same-sex marriage? Why are we seeking the sanction of the state for our intimate relationships? Why are we expending scarce movement resources so that couples can walk

smilingly into the sunset? What about *urgent* issues like AIDS prevention, homophobic violence, and the safety of queer youth, issues that
legitimately might be termed matters of life and death?"

I lay this out for you—my personal history and where it might take
me a generation later—but I am not able to convince even myself that
this is why the marriage campaign has made me so disgruntled. Neither
my head nor my heart subscribes to the argument that I just articulated.
For instance, in my teaching, I regularly assign in my gay and lesbian
studies courses a pair of short readings that were published together in
1989.[4] Tom Stoddard and Paula Ettelbrick, two lawyers then working at
Lambda Legal took contrasting positions about marriage in order to foster community debate and reflection on this issue. Stoddard argued that
access to marriage was a basic civil rights issue. Whether one wanted it
for oneself was irrelevant. The denial of the right to marry a partner of
the same sex marked gay men, lesbians, and bisexuals as second-class
citizens. It excluded us from many of the rights and privileges of civil society. In contrast, Ettelbrick articulated a radical feminist position. She
saw marriage historically as an oppressive institution and she celebrated
the way that gays and lesbians stood outside conventional frameworks.
Why, she asked, would we seek inclusion in something old, tired, and
oppressive when, as a community, we could create something new and
visionary? However much Ettelbrick makes my queer soul sing, Stoddard has always made more sense to me. My head tells me that his argument has merit.

The research I did for a biography of Bayard Rustin only made the logic
of this civil rights reasoning more powerful. A gay man in the generation
before any kind of gay politics developed in the United States, Rustin was
a lifelong agitator for justice. A Quaker and a pacifist, he did more than
anyone to bring Gandhian methods of nonviolence to the black freedom
struggle in the United States. Rustin's pacifist convictions were so strong
that he willingly accepted prison rather than serve in the military during
World War II. Yet in the late 1940s, Rustin helped shape activist campaigns to desegregate the military and make it fully accessible to African
Americans. Whatever his own convictions about the immorality and
inhumanity of war, he knew that restricting military service because of
race diminished the status of black Americans.[5] Likewise, whatever one's
own views about the institution of marriage, to acquiesce in one's exclusion from it means accepting a diminished status in law and society.

Moreover, again and again I have seen evidence of how attaching gays
and lesbians to love, the emotion most closely associated with marriage,

loosens the grip of homophobia on heterosexuals and creates bonds of sympathy and identification across lines of sexual orientation. The first time I encountered this was at a roundtable on family issues that I organized for the National Gay and Lesbian Task Force in 1995. One of the participants, an African American activist in New York City, described the reaction in her workplace to the announcement that she and her female partner were planning a wedding. Suddenly an aspect of her life that her co-workers had assiduously avoided became the subject of animated conversation. Everyone wanted to share wedding stories, offer advice, see pictures, hear about the honeymoon. What had seemed like entrenched homophobia one day began to dissolve the next. Or take this example: many times I have observed the reaction of undergraduates to the documentary film *Chicks in White Satin*. Most students who enroll in gay and lesbian studies courses identify as heterosexual. Most of them, including many of the guys, become weepy by the end of the film. Apparently, love and weddings conquer all, including the stubborn sense that "they" are different from "us."

Finally, my own life experience makes me skeptical of the argument that gays and lesbians should take it upon themselves to remake the family and marriage as a step toward some hazily defined utopian future. With each passing year of my own intimate relationship, I find that the lack of legal recognition rankles more and more. The absence of marriage creates an endless series of awkward and stressful situations that heterosexual married couples never have to face. The absence of what marriage brings fosters a low-level discontent that is always simmering and that threatens, at any moment, to erupt into a rage. Any same-sex couple who has been together for a length of time can recount its own version of these situations.

The truth is that I would likely get married if marriage were available to me, just to be done with the annoyances and complications that the lack of marriage involves. I would not register at Bloomingdale's. I would not hold a reception for my four hundred closest friends. My partner and I would not purchase lavender tuxedos for the occasion. But I would leave campus early one afternoon, meet my sweetheart of twenty-six years at City Hall, and get the whole damned thing over with.

No. I'm grumpy about the campaign for same-sex marriage not because I'm philosophically opposed to marriage. It is not because I'm a descendent of the nineteenth-century free lovers who rejected the right of the state to intervene in their intimate lives. It is not a sign that I'm stuck in the sexual ethics of the Stonewall era, unable to reach gay maturity.

The source of my discontent finally became clear in the weeks after *Lawrence v. Texas*. On June 26, 2003, the Supreme Court issued a 6–3 decision in which it declared the remaining state sodomy laws unconstitutional.[6] These laws, as much as the often-quoted biblical passages from Leviticus and the Epistles of Paul, have been the grounding for the inferior status of gay men and lesbians. The criminalization of our sexual activities was the excuse for the thousands upon thousands of yearly arrests by local police forces. The criminal behavior that might erupt at any moment was an underlying rationale for why gay men, lesbians, and bisexuals should be excluded from government employment and other jobs that demanded moral probity. Our inherent criminality justified the denial of child custody and visitation rights after a divorce and a host of other restrictions on our rights and our lives. Although most states had already repealed these statutes by 2003, their survival anywhere linked the present to a long history of oppression. In that sense, *Lawrence* was profoundly important. It firmly closed a chapter in U.S. history that stretched back to the earliest years of English colonization of North America.[7]

Barely had Justice Anthony Kennedy finished reading the majority opinion than attention shifted away from sodomy laws and the story became, as *Newsweek* suggested, "Is Same-Sex Marriage Next?"[8] Print media, television journalists, and on-line commentators all seemed to converge around the assumption reflected in a Los Angeles *Times* headline: "Ruling Seen as Precursor to Same-Sex Marriage."[9]

Since the connection between sodomy laws and the right to marry is not immediately evident, why did it prove so easy to make this leap? One reason was coincidence. Earlier that month, the Court of Appeal in Ontario, Canada, had issued a decision clearing the way for same-sex marriage. Moreover, the national government in Ottawa quickly announced that it would support the ruling. There it was, just across the border. For many same-sex couples in the United States, marriage now seemed, metaphorically and literally, within reach, a short drive or a quick plane ride away.

Another reason for the easy leap from sodomy laws to same-sex marriage was that Justice Antonin Scalia, in his scathing dissent from the majority in *Lawrence,* said the leap was easy. Justice Kennedy's reasoning, he claimed, "leaves on pretty shaky grounds state laws limiting marriage to opposite-sex couples." In case a reader missed his point, Scalia repeated it four paragraphs later: "Today's opinion dismantles the structure of constitutional law that has permitted a distinction to be made between heterosexual and homosexual unions, insofar as formal recognition in marriage is concerned." [10]

It did not surprise me that Scalia leveled these accusations. The man is an unabashed ideologue. Scalia certainly was not speaking to his peers on the bench nor even to a community of constitutional law experts outside the courtroom. He wrote those passages for a much larger constituency. He meant to sound an alarm, to mobilize the armies of the Christian right, to alert conservatives to a danger in its midst and call them to action. How else to explain the ridiculous claim in his dissent that the Court "has largely signed on to the so-called homosexual agenda"? A phrase like that resonates not in the world of legal scholars but in the ranks of conservative Christian activists.

But it did surprise me when so many voices within the queer community and among its allies echoed that perspective. In the weeks and months that followed, lawyers, organizational leaders, journalists, and others all seemed intent on proffering the same spin: in the wake of *Lawrence*, same-sex marriage was close to a sure thing. The chorus of voices only grew more insistent when, in November 2003, the Supreme Judicial Court of Massachusetts swept away the legal barriers to same-sex marriage in the state. The prohibitions were "constitutionally suspect," said one prominent legal scholar. Same-sex marriage was "inevitable," said an activist lawyer. "It's not going to happen this year or next, but in the next decade," said another. Evan Wolfson, who, perhaps more than any other lawyer, has pressed for a court-based assault on the laws against same-sex marriage, even appropriated Scalia's language. The restrictions on the right to marry, he said, were on "very shaky grounds." [11] It is not often that one finds gay advocates and right-wing radicals in such close agreement.

Reading all this commentary crystallized why the marriage campaign of the previous decade had provoked such queasiness. Suddenly I understood the source of my discontent. As I encountered all these pronouncements about how *Lawrence* puts same-sex marriage within our grasp, I found myself thinking: "Oh, no. Oh no, no, no. You misapprehend the central lesson of *Lawrence*. If Justice Kennedy's opinion teaches us anything, it is this: *the Supreme Court follows rather than leads*. The Court does not boldly chart new directions. It does not venture on to new ground. Rather, it tends to consolidate change that has already occurred. The Supreme Court articulates a constitutional rationale that codifies these changes, that shapes them into a new consensus and then declares them, through its decision, to be right and good and just."

If *Lawrence* tells us anything, it is that same-sex marriage is still a long way off. In fact, in late 2006 we may have been farther away from attaining marriage rights universally in the United States than we were in 1993, when a court in Hawaii set in motion the contemporary campaign for same-sex marriage.

I take no joy in this assessment. I do not like being the bearer of bad news. But as a historian of social movements who is fascinated by the delicate interplay of activist forces with the larger cultural, social, and political environment, as one who believes that individuals and organizations have the freedom to choose among strategies and tactics and that those choices have profound consequences, I think it is best to write frankly.

Simply put, the marriage campaign has been a disaster. It is far better to assess the damage and learn from it, better to figure out if a course correction can be made, than to proceed down the current road blissfully in denial, claiming that night is day, stop means go, and defeats are victories.

To support this argument, I approach the contemporary campaign from three different angles. First, I offer a quick overview of how the freedom movement of gays and lesbians developed over the course of the past two generations and how marriage came to be on the community's agenda by the mid-1990s. Then I spend some time analyzing what I like to describe as "the ghosts of Supreme Court cases past." These have hovered silently over the campaign for same-sex marriage, impelling a strategy of litigation as the primary means of securing marriage rights. Finally, I assess the court-based strategy of the past decade to see what it has provoked. Despite all the cheering for the gains we have made, the attempt to achieve marriage through the courts has provoked a series of defeats that constitute the greatest calamity in the history of the gay and lesbian movement in the United States.

THE GAY AND LESBIAN MOVEMENT: HISTORICIZING THE ISSUE OF SAME-SEX MARRIAGE

The marriage debacle aside, the history of the gay and lesbian movement since its beginnings in the 1950s has been one of change so rapid and extraordinary that it can justifiably be described as progress. Fifty or more years ago, when the first gay and lesbian organizations in the United States were taking shape in California, every state had sodomy laws that criminalized homosexual behavior. Local police forces used them as warrant for making thousands and thousands of arrests every year. The federal government enforced a blanket ban against its employment of lesbians, gay men, and bisexuals, and many state governments and professional licensing agencies did likewise. Cold War rhetoric about perversion and sexual menace saturated the public domain. Christian religious teaching utterly condemned same-sex desires. The medical profession categorized homosexuality as disease, and many states allowed judges to send gays to asylums with indeterminate sentences and permitted parents to institutionalize their queer teenagers.[12]

The first cohort of pioneering activists had little room to agitate for justice. They tried, successfully, to secure de facto recognition of their right to assemble, a not insubstantial victory since police could argue that, when gays met together, it was prelude to criminal activity. They won from the courts acknowledgment that their publications were not obscene. Influenced by the nonviolent demonstrations of civil rights activists, a few of them in the 1960s braved public exposure by mounting picket lines outside government buildings and carrying signs that demanded fair treatment. Still, for all their effort, by the late 1960s there were fewer gay and lesbian organizations in the entire United States than exist today in the state of New Jersey alone.[13]

Then "the sixties" intervened. I use this as shorthand for the few years when the United States experienced at home a broad-based challenge to authority. Core institutions found themselves under assault. At least temporarily, bodies as diverse as the presidency, the medical profession, the military, the university, national political parties, and local police saw their legitimacy questioned, their exercise of power challenged.[14]

Gay liberation and lesbian feminism rushed into this vacuum. Like those who launched the sit-in movement in the South a decade earlier, activists were relatively young, many of them college students or not far removed. They were deeply influenced by the message of self-assertion that came from the black power movement; by the challenge to white middle-class values that came from the counterculture; and especially by the rethinking of gender norms, sexual ideology, and family structure that women's liberation put forward. Their radicalism impelled them to violate one of the central principles of gay life in the generation that preceded them. They refused to stay hidden and keep their identity secret. Instead, they turned the mandate to stay in the closet on its head. They made "coming out" a new imperative. Men and women who came out more easily became activists in a movement.[15]

In the course of the 1970s, the movement achieved a host of victories. The American Psychiatric Association removed homosexuality from its catalogue of mental illnesses. The Civil Service Commission dropped its blanket exclusion of gay men and lesbians from federal employment. A number of states eliminated their sodomy statutes. Almost three dozen cities enacted statutes banning discrimination on the basis of sexual orientation. Federal courts repeatedly affirmed the First Amendment speech and assembly rights of homosexuals. Of greatest significance, perhaps, activists in many cities succeeded in sharply curtailing the police harassment that had been endemic to queer life.

Measured by the expectations of the early twenty-first century, the gains provoked by gay liberation seem like just a few faltering steps on a very long road to the still-unreached destination of equality. Measured by what had preceded them, they seemed huge to activists at the time. The constraints on police behavior had especially profound consequences. In the 1970s a queer public life became visible. It was different from the queer worlds that existed earlier, less contingent on the whims of law enforcement, less contained and restricted. It was visible and accessible in a sustained and continuing way. Among men, it was highly commercialized, consisting primarily of bars, bathhouses, discos, and sex clubs. Among women it was more overtly oppositional, consisting of coffeehouses, music festivals, small presses and bookstores, and art and theater collectives.[16]

Stop for a moment and reflect on what I've described in the preceding few paragraphs. Where does "family" fit in this story? What kind of a policy agenda around family will a movement produce when the primary influences on this movement have been the hippie counterculture (think "communes, free love, Woodstock Nation") and radical feminism (think "Down with the patriarchy!")?

There was a bit of a family agenda in the 1970s. The one concrete plank in it was "defend the rights of lesbian mothers," though even here the meaning of that exhortation then was far different from what it might connote today. Defending the rights of lesbian mothers signified fighting to allow the lesbians who had become mothers when they were still living in heterosexual marriages to keep their children. It did not mean campaigning for the right of lesbians to choose to become mothers.

To the extent that family figured in the queer politics of the 1970s it did so in the form of slogans like "smash monogamy" and "smash the nuclear family" that helped mark these activists as oppositional, as radical.

Listen to what some of them had to say about the family and marriage. In "Gay Is Good," one of the earliest pieces of gay liberation literature, Martha Shelley described lesbians and gays as "women and men who, from the time of our earliest memories, have been in revolt against the sex-role structure and nuclear family structure." In "A Gay Manifesto," a widely circulated document of the gay liberation era, Carl Whitman called marriage "a prime example of a straight institution fraught with role playing. Traditional marriage is a rotten, oppressive institution." In New York City, an organization of radical gays of color asserted that "all oppressions originate within the nuclear family structure." Meanwhile, gay liberation groups in Chicago defined one of the key virtues of being gay as its contribution to breaking down the nuclear family.[17]

These were not the only sentiments in the gay and lesbian community, of course. During these same years, the Metropolitan Community Church, a Christian organization created by Troy Perry to provide a safe place of worship for gays, lesbians, and their allies, performed union ceremonies—weddings, in other words—for members in committed relationships. Indeed, almost everywhere that gay folk came together through religious affiliation, a yearning for marriage would surface. In West Virginia in the mid-1970s, Jim Lewis, an Episcopal minister, gained a reputation for being sympathetic to gays. Soon couples began approaching him and begging him to marry them, although the ceremonies would not have the force of law.[18] In the early 1970s, moreover, a few gay and lesbian couples—in Minnesota, Kentucky, Washington, and Colorado—made efforts, all unsuccessful, to have their unions recognized as legally sanctioned marriages.

But if a consensus in the gay community was absent, the radical voice was certainly the loudest and most evident. In this era, *family* and *homosexual* seemed mutually antagonistic. Here was a place where homophobe and homosexual seemed to unite. If straight America could not imagine queers in the family photo album, neither could lesbians and gay men imagine themselves within the family's bosom. In the work of novels as different as *Another Country* by James Baldwin and *Rubyfruit Jungle* by Rita Mae Brown, gay life took shape—indeed, could only take shape—through escape from the confines of family. Queers lived in exile from home and hearth, rejected by their families and rejecting family as well.

This, then, is where things stood in the early 1980s. Yet a mere decade later, not only had same-sex marriage emerged in Hawaii as a viable issue, but the gay and lesbian community had fashioned a full-fledged multiplank platform of family issues. Matters such as partnership recognition, spousal benefits at the workplace, parenting by same-sex couples, the place of queer youth, and gay-supportive public school policies had all become rallying points for activists.

What provoked the gay and lesbian community's relation to family to shift so profoundly in so short a time? A number of developments in the 1980s contributed to this reorientation.

One factor was the impact of the Sharon Kowalski case. In 1983 Kowalski was involved in an automobile accident that left her ability to communicate seriously impaired. The courts awarded guardianship to Kowalski's father rather than to her partner, Karen Thompson, who for years was denied access to Kowalski. Across the United States, lesbian communities hosted forums, organized fundraisers, and worked to raise public awareness about the case. After an eight-year battle the courts eventually made Thompson the legal guardian, but in the meantime "Free Sharon Kowalski" became a rallying cry among lesbians concerned about the lack of legal recognition for their relationships.[19]

If this one case could so powerfully affect so many lesbians, then multiplying it by the thousands can give one a grasp of the force of the AIDS epidemic in redefining the significance of family for gay men. In the course of the 1980s, sickness and death became part of the everyday experience of young and middle-aged gay men. Many of them faced situations where the phrase "next of kin" came into play: hospital visitation rights; decision making about medical care; choices about funeral arrangements and burials; the access of survivors to homes, possessions, and inheritance. The ugly dramas that in some situations played themselves out between gay partners and their friendship circles on one hand and families of origin on the other exposed the legal inconsequentiality of same-sex relationships.[20]

Another factor inducing a shifting politics of family was the emergence of newly organized constituencies, both nationally and locally, among gays and lesbians. Some, but not all, of this was provoked by AIDS. From the beginning, the epidemic disproportionately affected African Americans and Latinos. Gays and lesbians of color took the lead in battling the disease in their home communities, and the infrastructure generated by AIDS funding helped build organizations—such as the National Latino/a Lesbian and Gay Organization, founded in 1985, and the National Black Lesbian and Gay Leadership Forum, founded in 1987—that served as their platform in the movement. The disease also spurred the proliferation of queer organizing beyond metropolitan centers so that, by the late 1980s, the movement had an unprecedented national spread. One result was a subtle shift in the rhetoric of family away from tropes of exile and exclusion and toward themes of dialogue, engagement, and belonging. For gays and lesbians of color, family was a needed resource, a means of survival; for those in smaller cities and towns, life existed within a web of dense ties of kinship and neighborliness.[21]

The lesbian (and gay) baby boom was the fourth reason family issues came to the fore. Unbeknownst to a culture that had thoroughly associated gay life with sexual abandon and deadly disease (lesbians were largely erased from mainstream discourses), more and more individuals within the community were now choosing to become parents. The means varied—from the "turkey baster" babies conceived through the cooperation of gay men with the procreative desires of lesbian friends to the use of sperm banks, adoption agencies, surrogacy, and sex among friends—but the growing visible presence of children in the community made family less metaphorical and more descriptive of the contours of queer life.[22]

Generational change also played a role in the shifting priorities of the gay and lesbian movement. On one hand, as members of the Stonewall generation advanced into middle age, more of them were likely to be settled in long-term relationships. In every way except the legal, these partnerships had the texture of marriages. At the same time, a younger generation came of age and it had never known anything but the era of pride and visibility. Having come out to family and friends early, many had seamlessly integrated their sexual identities into every sphere of their lives. Why shouldn't they be able to get married, just like all their straight friends?

Finally, never underestimate the power of sheer orneriness in the evolution of a policy agenda. A politics of "traditional family values" took shape during the Reagan-Bush era. One of the first legislative proposals of the Reagan years was the draconian Family Protection Act; one of the last rhetorical engagements of the Bush White House was Vice President Dan Quayle's attacks on the unwed motherhood of Murphy Brown, a fictional newscaster on a popular network television series. As the Republican Party and evangelical Christians made family a cause that bound them together, was it any wonder that queers would respond "we are family too"?[23]

The embrace of family by lesbians and gay men was more than a self-defensive reaction to a homophobic opposition. It generated a platform of sorts, a cluster of issues loosely bound together conceptually under the heading of family. It provoked a decade's worth of creative organizational initiatives. It sparked an intriguing inventiveness from a community striving to extend understandings of family to include queer folk. Although AIDS may have overshadowed this at the time, the 1980s witnessed a widespread reclaiming of family among gays and lesbians.

One form of this creativity came from the National Center for Lesbian Rights. Lesbian couples raising children together faced a problem. The nonbiological parent had no legal standing as a parent, since no state laws and no courts had ever recognized as parents of a child two individuals of the same sex. In case of the death of the biological mother, legal challenges from the sperm donor, or the breakup of the couple, "the other woman" risked loss of access to the child, and the child risked loss of access to a woman who had filled the role of parent. In the early 1980s lawyers at NCLR fashioned the notion of "second parent adoption," and soon lesbian couples were petitioning courts around the country for the right to have two women declared the parents of a child. Confronted with real families with a real problem, some judges responded flexibly. By the early 1990s family court judges were creating, in effect, new law on the ground.[24]

Another imaginative response to the legal barriers to gay and lesbian family recognition was the invention of the concept of "domestic partnership." In the early 1980s, domestic partnership received its first incarnation as simple registries, created by municipalities, so that same-sex couples could achieve a modicum of legal recognition. Registration put couples on firmer ground if they confronted situations—in hospitals, for instance—in which the nature of their relationship needed confirmation. By the late 1980s, some municipalities were taking this a step further and extending spousal benefits, such as health insurance and family medical leave, to employees in same-sex domestic partnerships. Interestingly, many of these early measures were equally available to same-sex and opposite-sex couples.[25]

From my vantage point as a student of social movements, what made these policy innovations especially notable was that they were the tangible outcome of a much broader organizing impulse. By the late 1980s, one could find much evidence of community mobilizations taking shape around the concept of family. For instance, the National Gay and Lesbian Task Force (NGLTF) created a Families Project at the end of the decade. Because it was the national organization most committed to a philosophy of community organizing and with close ties to grassroots activists around the country, NGLTF's initiative in this area signaled that more change was on the horizon. The growing attention to the issue of children raised by gay parents provoked the formation in 1990 of COLAGE (Children of Lesbians and Gays Everywhere).[26] Its members functioned not only as a support group for one another but also as an advocacy organization campaigning for fair treatment for queer families. Most dramatically, perhaps, these years witnessed an explosion of activism within the corporate world. Gay and lesbian employees, and increasingly bisexual and transgender workers as well, formed organizations at the workplace where they campaigned for, among other things, domestic partnership benefits. These efforts led not only to major shifts in the policies of corporate America but to changes in workplace culture as well. The last bastion of the closet was fast becoming a site of queer visibility.[27]

Where was marriage in this story? It would be a mistake to say that marriage never surfaced in the 1980s. At the massive March on Washington in October 1987, one of the unforgettable moments was the mass "wedding" of same-sex couples on the steps of the National Cathedral. But the event was as much a public expression of love and commitment in the face of AIDS and American homophobia as it was a step in a campaign for the right to marry. Indeed, writing two years later in *Out/Look*, Tom Stoddard, the executive director of Lambda Legal, commented: "As far as I can tell, no gay organization of any size, local or national, has yet declared the right to marry as one of its goals." [28] In other words, marriage was a peripheral matter in the vibrant new family politics that lesbians and gay men had created by the early 1990s.

THE GHOSTS OF COURTROOMS PAST

By the time of the national elections in 2004, when the issue of same-sex marriage jockeyed for headlines with news about war and terrorism, it was hard to remember that the gay, lesbian, bisexual, and transgender movements had ever had a politics of family that was about anything except marriage. Beginning in the 1990s, litigation to win the right to marry had moved forward in four states. Cases brought in Hawaii and Alaska had resulted in judicial victories, but the state legislatures intervened to undo them. In 1999 the Vermont Supreme Court gave the state legislature the unambiguous instruction that it must extend the rights and privileges of marriage to same-sex couples, and the legislature responded by creating a new status called civil unions. In 2003, the Supreme Judicial Court of Massachusetts ruled that only marriage would do. The first weddings in May 2004 coincided with feverish debates in more than a dozen state legislatures about whether to adopt constitutional bans to forestall any possibility of same-sex marriage.

Why did the field of gay family politics shift—some might say narrow—so dramatically in the course of the 1990s? How did litigation for marriage become the magic bullet expected to deliver on the promise of equality? Why did one tactic and one goal replace many tactics and many goals?

Underlying the decision to pursue through the courts the right to marry is an unspoken belief that goes something like this: "The courts are the place to go for the redress of grievances. When elected officials and public opinion are lined up against us, the courts can be relied upon to protect minorities from the tyranny of the majority. In fact, through the mechanism of civil rights litigation the courts can be the engine of progressive social change." This assumption is so pervasive that it hardly needs to be articulated. It has been espoused by liberals and progressives, who endorse the idea, and by conservatives, who rail against it. The field of civil rights and public interest law has been constructed around it. Some of the best minds, some of the young people most committed to social justice, choose law as a profession out of the conviction that this is the way to change the world.

The source of this belief (a belief that would have been considered unusual for much of American history) is not difficult to identify. It emanates from popular understandings of two historic Supreme Court cases of the mid-twentieth century: *Brown v. Board of Education* (1954), in which the Court declared racially segregated public schools to be inherently unequal and hence unconstitutional, and *Roe v. Wade* (1973), in which the Court struck down state laws that banned abortion.[29] Each of these cases is closely associated with social movements—the African American civil rights movement and the second wave of feminism—that deeply changed America. In fact, each of them is seen as somehow central to the success of their respective movements.

To see these cases as provoking vast political upheaval on behalf of social justice badly misreads the historical evidence. The cases did not break new ground or map new territory. They did not take the law in new directions. Indeed, one could just as plausibly argue that these cases provoked the opposite of what they intended. Because of them, powerful reactionary movements had rallying points that allowed them to mobilize against racial and gender justice.

Take the *Brown* decision. When the Warren Court handed down its ruling, the forces already tending toward the demise of legally sanctioned
racial segregation were compelling. Here are only a few of them:

· Less than a decade earlier, the United States had fought a world
  war in which a major aim was the destruction of a Nazi regime
  that rested on an ideology of Aryan supremacy. Fighting a war
  against racism abroad weakened acquiescence to racial hierarchy
  at home.
· Cold War foreign policy impelled the United States to seek the
  support of Africans and Asians in its struggle against the Soviet
  Union. Racial apartheid in the American South seriously weakened diplomatic claims that the United States represented the
  pole of freedom in a global fight with communism.
· In 1947, a civil rights commission appointed by President Harry
  Truman released a report that outlined a comprehensive agenda
  to achieve racial equality. The White House itself seemed to be
  endorsing a racial justice platform.
· By the early 1950s, the Truman administration had committed
  itself to a thorough desegregation of the U.S. armed forces, thus
  establishing racial equality as a desirable goal in a key national
  institution.
· Many northern and western states had already enacted civil
  rights laws prohibiting racial discrimination in a wide variety of
  arenas. Racial equality rather than racial hierarchy was becoming the formal legal norm.
· Increasingly in the years after World War II, "Jim Crow" came
  to be perceived as a regional practice, an artifact of southern life
  that was discursively cordoned off as deviant, as un-American.

In this environment, the Supreme Court's declaration that legally mandated racial separation was unconstitutional did not suddenly chart a
new course for race relations. The Court aimed to consolidate a developing consensus, to add the force of the Constitution to powerful tendencies in American life. It declared its principles so unambiguously in
part because these tendencies already commanded judicial notice. As
Jack Greenberg, one of the lawyers involved in the litigation, phrased it,
"There was a current of history . . . and the Court became part of it." [30]
Notice also how the case had made its way to the Supreme Court.
Since the late 1930s, the National Association for the Advancement of

Colored People (NAACP) had litigated a series of cases designed to chip away at the edifice of white supremacist law. By the early 1950s the Supreme Court had provided civil rights forces with a number of victories. It had outlawed the exclusion of black voters from political primaries, court enforcement of racially restrictive housing covenants, separate seating arrangements in interstate transportation, and the denial of access to law school and graduate school education. Although none of these cases had been a sure thing, Thurgood Marshall, the chief legal strategist for the NAACP, employed rigorous criteria when deciding whether to take them on. According to one of his assistants, "Thurgood had to be convinced of victory beyond a reasonable doubt before he said yes." [31] Thus *Brown* was the last step in a carefully planned legal strategy that had moved forward one step at a time.

At first glance, the circumstances surrounding *Roe v. Wade* might appear very different from those attending *Brown*. As late as the mid-1960s, every state prohibited abortion. A law reform movement was slowly gathering force, but criminalization remained the norm. To some, the 1973 *Roe* decision seemed like "a bolt out of the blue," unexpected and without warning.[32] Thus the case might seem to prove that, yes, the courts will set us free.

Behind this decision, however, lay more than half a century of change. Change had proceeded along two fronts that were thoroughly germane to the issue in *Roe*. First, among American women, contraceptive practice had spread until it was almost universal. Second, in the two decades before *Roe*, the Supreme Court had delivered a series of decisions that took sexuality out of the Victorian era and placed it firmly within a modern sensibility.

By the time *Roe* was decided, Americans had already experienced a revolution in their practice of birth control. This was in part achieved by the radical agitation of militant advocates of contraceptive freedom, such as Margaret Sanger. Women and their male allies disrupted public events, gave fiery lectures, risked arrest, and went on hunger strikes in order to end restrictions on access to birth control information and devices. By the 1940s, with the rise of organizations such as Planned Parenthood, birth control became part of mainstream culture, a form of "family planning." Scientists investigated fertility control and entrepreneurs invested in it, provoking such innovations as the birth control pill. Controlling fertility had become so normative that even American Catholics, in the face of papal edicts against contraception, employed artificial methods of birth control at the same rate as other Americans.[33]

Meanwhile, beginning in 1957 with *Roth v. United States,* the liberal Supreme Court of Chief Justice Earl Warren pronounced on a number of cases involving sexuality. Many of these concerned the issue of obscenity. Federal statutes dating from the nineteenth century had placed tight restrictions on the representation of sexuality in literature, the arts, popular culture, and media. As understood by legislators, police, judges, and purity crusaders, these laws essentially equated sexuality and the erotic with obscenity. For decades, writers, artists, and publishers pressed against the limits of obscenity law; they changed social practice even as the laws constrained them. Finally, in the 1950s and 1960s, a string of cases challenging federal and state obscenity laws reached the Supreme Court. Although the Warren Court never declared the regulation of obscenity to be unconstitutional, it sharply attenuated the connection between sex and obscenity. Its rulings made the depiction and discussion of sexuality a commonplace in American culture and social life. So much changed in these decades that, in 1970, a presidential commission actually recommended the decriminalization of pornography.[34]

The Court's willingness to consider an issue such as obscenity made it unsurprising when, in the mid-1960s, it began to rule on state laws that restricted access to contraception. In *Griswold v. Connecticut* the Court not only invalidated a law that infringed on a married couple's ability to prevent pregnancy; it also framed its decision as a constitutional right to privacy. At least for married couples, the Court deemed fertility control—and, by extension, sexual expression—a liberty protected by the Constitution. In 1971 *Eisenstadt v. Baird* extended these principles to unmarried male-female couples.[35]

This was the environment in which the Supreme Court addressed the matter of abortion. By 1973, when the justices ruled on the constitutionality of state laws prohibiting abortion, contraceptive practice was normative, the Court had drawn some forms of sexual expression into the sphere of protected liberties, and sexual matters were an integral part of public culture in the United States. Add to these the fact that abortion had not always been criminalized in the United States (there were no antiabortion laws at the time the Constitution was written) and that a number of states were already revising their abortion statutes. One can then see *Roe* not as a ruling on the frontier of constitutional law but as firmly located within the realm of common social practice and cultural values.

To summarize: neither *Brown* nor *Roe* ought to be seen as decisions that placed the Supreme Court in the vanguard of social change. Instead, both decisions built on strong foundations in American society, culture, and law. They attempted to place a constitutional imprimatur on trends already well under way.

Although this interpretation is commonplace in scholarly writing about this era in American life, it is at odds with what we might call the "folk wisdom" about these decisions. For different reasons, both liberals and conservatives, the Left and the Right, have an investment in seeing these cases as radically innovative, as ruptures with the past. For progressives who in recent decades have seen themselves increasingly locked out of legislative majorities and the executive branch, the courts seem the last remaining hope for the survival of their political values. What the democratic process no longer seems to provide, the courts still promise. When prejudice, inertia, ideology, or electoral outcomes stand in the way, liberals can rely on the courts to extend personal liberties and nurture the impulse toward social justice. Liberals and the Left applaud this view of the courts, and thus they stake their political capital on defending the courts against conservative encroachments.

Adopting the same view of such cases as *Brown* and *Roe*, conservatives and the Right condemn what they describe as an activist judiciary. They have used the rhetoric of "judge-made law" as a mobilizing tool to rouse their constituencies and extend their political power. In the process, they have succeeded, far more than their rhetorical thrusts would suggest, in making the federal judiciary more conservative than it has been since the early 1930s.

But, to say it again, liberals and conservatives, the Left and the Right, have it wrong. Especially when one considers Supreme Court rulings in historic cases, it becomes clear that the Court cannot be relied on to push the nation in new directions. Instead, it moves, and by implication shifts, with the prevailing winds of history.

Interestingly, the decision in *Lawrence v. Texas* confirms both the prevailing misunderstanding of what the Court does and this more modest view of the Court's role as well. The gay community hailed the ruling as a breakthrough that paved the way for the approval of same-sex marriage. The Right denounced the ruling as a travesty that paved the way for the approval of same-sex marriage. Yet if *Lawrence* tells us anything, it is that the Court takes a measured approach to the cases before it and is reluctant to step far out in front of public opinion and social values. As Justice Kennedy took pains to point out in his opinion, most states had already repealed their sodomy laws; the legal profession had been calling for repeal for half a century; the European Court of Human Rights had already declared sodomy laws an infringement on basic human rights.

Eliminating the remaining ones might easily pass unnoticed in the daily life of Americans. The *Lawrence* case closed the books on sodomy laws. The Court was not ahead of its time but was catching up to its time.

WHAT POOR STRATEGY HAS WROUGHT

What happens when we apply to the topic of same-sex marriage this historical understanding of the relation of the courts to social movements and social change? What will we notice if we keep in mind that the Supreme Court rarely places itself far in front of public opinion, social practice, and cultural values?

One important thing to notice is that in April 1991, when *Baehr v. Levin* was initially filed in Hawaii, no foundation had yet been built for same-sex marriage. Sodomy laws still survived in American law. Fewer than half a dozen states included sexual orientation in their civil rights laws. One of the two major political parties in the United States had written antigay planks into its platform. The military excluded lesbians, gays, and bisexuals. Not one state legislature had approved domestic partnership benefits for public employees. Does this look like a society on the brink of accepting same-sex marriage?

Most of all, throughout the history of the United States, marriage had been understood, legislatively and in practice, as the union of a man and a woman. Yes, the institution of marriage had changed through the centuries. Yes, that change had been substantial. But this particular aspect of marriage, the gender and number of the partners, had remained fixed in law. Americans who challenged that, notably Mormons and various utopian communities in the nineteenth century, were viciously persecuted and scorned, and legislatures used the existence of deviations to ratify the norm of a man and a woman. This aspect of marriage—the "Adam and Eve, not Adam and Steve or Ada and Eve" part—has not budged, and in the popular imagination it has the quality of being fixed and eternal. The opposite-sex feature of marriage has seemed so rooted in history and nature that, in the early 1970s, when a few gay and lesbian activists mounted challenges to the ban on same-sex marriage in the states of Minnesota, Washington, Kentucky, and Colorado, judges dismissed their efforts as ludicrous.[36]

The second important thing to notice is that, although judges in Hawaii and Alaska opened the door to same-sex marriage by declaring the ban against it discriminatory, the state legislatures and the voters unambiguously erased those decisions by overwhelmingly approving an amendment to their state constitutions. Thus, the first court victories proved to be phantoms.

The third important thing to notice is that none of the above seemed to deter the gay and lesbian legal community. In fact, its commitment to pursue marriage through the courts only grew in the course of the 1990s, while resistance to a strategy of litigation crumbled.

But, a proponent of litigation might say, look at what our determined pursuit of marriage through the courts has accomplished. In Vermont in 1999, judges once again declared the ban on same-sex marriage discriminatory. This time the legislature responded not with new discriminatory laws but with the innovation of civil unions, a legal form that extended to same-sex couples in Vermont all the rights of marriage but without the name. In Massachusetts in 2003, the state's highest court went further. It said only marriage will do for same-sex couples. Since May 2004, same-sex couples there have been marrying, and the legislature has failed to come up with new measures to stop them. And in other states there are more court cases on the docket that promise additional gains. Bit by bit, we have made inroads; we are accumulating victories. "Why," such a proponent might say to me, "do you remain so crabby? Why are you attacking our campaign to achieve marriage rights in the face of these undeniable victories?"

I remain so crabby because of the fourth important thing that one should notice: the most significant outcome of litigation has been neither the existence of favorable court opinions nor the advent of same-sex marriage in Massachusetts. These have been phantom victories. Instead, the most significant outcome of litigation has been the negative legislative and voter response that the Hawaii case and its successors have elicited.

Before a trial court judge in Hawaii ruled that the prohibition of same-sex marriage violated the state constitution, in 1996 both the Senate and the House of Representatives passed by overwhelming majorities the federal Defense of Marriage Act. President Clinton, who fashioned himself a friend of the gay community, signed DOMA into law. The statute affirmed that, for the purpose of interpreting and implementing federal law, marriage was to be understood as the union of a man and a woman. No matter whether any individual state decided to approve same-sex marriages; the federal government would only recognize marriages between a man and a woman—for tax purposes, for the dispersal of such benefits as Social Security, for the determination of immigrant status, and for the many hundreds of other matters in which federal policy impinges on marriage.

Congress was not alone in its resolve. Beginning with Utah in 1995, at least thirty-eight states have passed "little DOMAs." That is, these state legislatures have declared that marriage is the union of a man and a woman and that their states will not recognize same-sex marriages performed elsewhere. The fear that so-called activist judges will try to impose same-sex marriage in their own states—as judges in Hawaii, Alaska, Vermont, and Massachusetts seemed to do—have led legislatures and voters in at least twenty-seven other states to go even further. Not only have these states declared that they will not recognize same-sex marriages from other states but, either through legislation or voter initiative, they have also amended their constitutions to include prohibitions against same-sex marriage.

This legislative onslaught has not yet ended. More states are considering little DOMAs. More states are considering amendments to their constitutions. Key Republican congressional leaders keep hauling out the threat of a federal constitutional amendment to prohibit same-sex marriage.

But, the cheerleaders for same-sex marriage might respond, why does this ultimately matter? Won't the Supreme Court eventually declare all these prohibitions unconstitutional when the same-sex marriages from a state such as Massachusetts are used to challenge them?

Cannot a strategy of targeted litigation lead us, state by state, to the promised land? Not likely. With the federal judiciary growing more conservative with each new appointment to it, we have only to look at the *Lawrence* decision to remind ourselves why. The Supreme Court will not set us free. It took until 2003 to declare sodomy statutes unconstitutional. *Lawrence* ruled on the fossilized remains of history. Same-sex marriage is an unprecedented innovation. As for the states, when even liberal courts such as those in New York and Washington vote against same-sex marriage, we have to see faith in judicial solutions as misplaced.

In 1984 the anthropologist Gayle Rubin published an extremely insightful and provocative article called "Thinking Sex: Notes for a Radical Theory of the Politics of Sexuality." She wrote it at a time when sexual issues had become deeply polarizing within feminism and when new forms of state intervention regarding sexuality loomed on the horizon. Rubin identified sex law as one of the chief—and most powerful—means of sustaining sexual hierarchies and enforcing sexual oppression. She elaborated the point in the passage that provides the epigraph to this chapter: "Sex laws are notoriously easy to pass. . . . Once they are on the books, they are extremely difficult to dislodge." [37]

Applied to the current battles concerning same-sex marriage, Rubin's point highlights how great a catastrophe for the gay and lesbian community the efforts to achieve marriage via the courts have provoked. Through the new legislation and state constitutional provisions it has instigated, the court-based campaign has ignited a firewall of protection against same-sex marriage that will burn for at least another generation. The homophobic reaction to this court-based campaign has provided an abundance of evidence that the restriction of marriage to a man and a woman is not an artifact from the ancient past but a long tradition that overwhelmingly majorities of elected officials and voters have reaffirmed in the present.

Rubin also made much of the idea of "sex panics," the power of issues related to sexual matters to stimulate intensely irrational reactions in society and the body politic. Long after the current homophobic panic is over, these DOMA statutes and state constitutional amendments will survive as a residue that slows the forward movement of the gay community toward equality. Contrary to the cheerleading from strategists for same-sex marriage who try to assure us that we are making progress, the promise of equal marriage rights for same-sex couples has disappeared beneath the horizon of reachable political change. Rather than a magic bullet, litigation to achieve same-sex marriage has morphed into a boomerang.

I can only hope that my understanding of social change and my skills of historical analysis will prove to be wrong.

ENDNOTES

I first presented these ideas in February 2004. Three years later, events seem to have confirmed the analysis. I thank Ellen Lewin, Nancy Hewitt, and Jonathan D. Katz, each of whom arranged visits for me to lecture at, respectively, the University of Iowa, Rutgers University, and Yale University, where my argument sparked lively debate and discussion.

1. Jeffrey Schmalz, "In Hawaii, Step Toward Legalized Gay Marriage," *New York Times*, May 7, 1993, 14.

2. See, e.g., such texts as Theodore Roszak, *The Making of a Counter Culture: Reflections on the Technocratic Society and Its Youthful Opposition* (Garden City, NY: Doubleday, 1969), and Shulamith Firestone, *The Dialectic of Sex: The Case for Feminist Revolution* (New York: William Morrow, 1970).

3. Terry Gross, interview with John Waters, on National Public Radio, *Fresh Air*, February 25, 2004. http://www/npr.org/templates/story/story .php?storyld51700561.

4. See "Gay Marriage: A Must or a Bust?" *Out/Look* no. 6 (Fall 1989): 8–17.

5. John D'Emilio, *Lost Prophet: The Life and Times of Bayard Rustin* (New York: Free Press, 2003), esp. chaps. 3–7.

6. *Lawrence v. Texas*, 539 U.S. 558 (2003).

7. For analyses of the *Lawrence* decision, see Harry Hirsch, ed., *The Future of Gay Rights in America* (New York: Routledge, 2005).

8. Evan Thomas, "The War over Gay Marriage," *Newsweek*, July 7, 2003, 38–45.

9. David G. Savage, "Ruling Seen as Precursor to Same-Sex Marriage," *Los Angeles Times*, A21.

10. *Lawrence v. Texas*.

11. Linda Greenhouse, "Supreme Court Paved Way for Marriage Ruling with Sodomy Law Decision," *New York Times*, November 19, 2003, 24 ("constitutionally suspect"); David G. Savage, "Ruling Seen as Precursor to Same-Sex Marriage," *Los Angeles Times*, June 28, 2003, A21 ("inevitable," "next decade"); Chad Graham, "Changing History," *Advocate*, January 20, 2004, 36–39.

12. See David K. Johnson, *The Lavender Scare: The Cold War Persecution of Gays and Lesbians in the Federal Government* (Chicago: University of Chicago Press, 2004).

13. On the homophile movement see John D'Emilio, *Sexual Politics, Sexual Communities: The Making of a Homosexual Minority in the United States, 1940–1970*, 2d ed. (Chicago: University of Chicago Press, 1998); Marc Stein, *City of Sisterly and Brotherly Loves: Lesbian and Gay Philadelphia, 1945–1972* (Chicago: University of Chicago Press, 2000); Elizabeth A. Armstrong, *Forging Gay Identities: Organizing Sexuality in San Francisco, 1950–1994* (Chicago: University of Chicago Press, 2002); and Nan Alamilla Boyd, *Wide-Open Town: A History of Queer San Francisco to 1965* (Berkeley: University of California Press, 2003).

14. For a recent account of the 1960s that captures how tumultuous the era was, see Maurice Isserman and Michael Kazin, *America Divided: The Civil War of the 1960s*, 2d ed. (New York: Oxford University Press, 2004).

15. There is not yet a satisfying book-length account of the gay liberation era. For aspects of it see Stein, *City of Sisterly and Brotherly Loves*; Armstrong, *Forging Gay Identities*; Dudley Clendinen and Adam Nagourney, *Out for Good: The Struggle to Build a Gay Rights Movement in America* (New York: Simon & Schuster, 1999). See also Terence Kissack, "Freaking Fag Revolutionaries: New York's Gay Liberation Front, 1969–1971," *Radical History Review* no. 62 (Spring 1995): 104–34; Justin David Suran, "Coming out against the War: Antimilitarism and the Politicization of Homosexuality in the Era of Vietnam," *American Quarterly* 53 (2001): 452–88. Important accounts from the era are Dennis Altman, *Homosexual: Oppression and Liberation* (New York: Avon, 1971), and Karla Jay and Allen Young, eds., *Out of the Closets: Voices of Gay Liberation*, 20th anniv. ed. (New York: NYU Press, 1992).

16. For aspects of the 1970s see Dennis Altman, *Coming out in the Seventies* (Boston: Alyson, 1981); Bonnie J. Morris, *Eden Built by Eves: The Culture of Women's Music Festivals* (Los Angeles: Alyson, 1999); and Karla Jay and Allen Young, eds., *Lavender Culture* (New York: NYU Press, 1994).

17. Jay and Young, *Out of the Closets*, 32, 333, 365, 258.

18. Keith Hartmann, *Congregations in Conflict: The Battle over Homosexuality* (New Brunswick: Rutgers University Press, 1996), 79–89.

19. On the Sharon Kowalski case see Karen Thompson and Julie Andrzejewski, *Why Can't Sharon Kowalski Come Home?* (San Francisco: Spinsters/Aunt Lute Press, 1988); Casey Charles, *The Sharon Kowalski Case: Lesbian and Gay Rights on Trial* (Lawrence: University of Kansas Press, 2003).

20. The literature on AIDS is vast. Some important works that discuss the impact of the epidemic in the 1980s and early 1990s are Cindy Patton, *Sex and Germs: The Politics of AIDS* (Boston: South End, 1985); Dennis Altman, *AIDS in the Mind of America* (New York: Anchor/Doubleday, 1986); Simon Watney, *Policing Desire: Pornography, AIDS and the Media* (Minneapolis: University of Minnesota Press, 1987); ACT UP/NY Women and AIDS Book Group, *Women, AIDS, and Activism* (Boston: South End, 1990); Martin P. Levine et al., eds., *In Changing Times: Gay Men and Lesbians Encounter HIV/AIDS* (Chicago: University of Chicago Press, 1997); and Cathy J. Cohen, *The Boundaries of Blackness: AIDS and the Breakdown of Black Politics* (Chicago: University of Chicago Press, 1999).

21. For writings by gays and lesbians of color from this era see Joseph Beam, ed., *In the Life: A Black Gay Anthology* (Boston: Alyson, 1986); Juanita Ramos, ed., *Compañeras: Latin Lesbians; An Anthology* (New York: Latina Lesbian History Project, 1987); Essex Hemphill, ed., *Brother to Brother: New Writings by Black Gay Men* (Boston: Alyson, 1991); Makeda Silvera, ed., *Piece of My Heart: A Lesbian of Color Anthology* (Toronto: Sister Vision Press, 1991); and Cherríe Moraga, *Waiting in the Wings: Portrait of a Queer Motherhood* (Ithaca, NY: Firebrand, 1997). For the perspective of gays and lesbians outside large urban centers, contrast Edmund White, *States of Desire: Travels in Gay America* (New York: Dutton, 1980) with Hartmann, *Congregations in Conflict*.

22. For discussions of the move toward parenting, see Kath Weston, *Families We Choose: Lesbians, Gays, Kinship* (New York: Columbia University Press, 1991); Mary Bernstein and Renate Reimann, eds., *Queer Family, Queer Politics: Challenging Culture and the State* (New York: Columbia University Press, 2001).

23. On the conservative family politics of the era see Didi Herman, *The Antigay Agenda: Orthodox Vision and the Christian Right* (Chicago: University of Chicago Press, 1997); Godfrey Hodgson, *The World Turned Right Side Up: A History of the Conservative Ascendancy in America* (Boston: Houghton Mifflin, 1996); and William Martin, *With God on Our Side: The Rise of the Religious Right in America* (New York: Broadway, 1996).

24. See Nancy D. Polikoff, "Raising Children: Lesbian and Gay Parents Face the Public and the Courts," in John D'Emilio et al., eds., *Creating Change: Sexuality, Public Policy, and Civil Rights* (New York: St. Martin's, 2000), 305–35; and http://www.nclrights.org/publications/2ndparentadoptions.htm.

25. David L. Chambers, "Couples: Marriage, Civil Unions, and Domestic Partnership," in D'Emilio et al., *Creating Change*, 281–304.

26. See its Web site, http://www.colage.org/.

27. On workplace activists see Kitty Krupat and Patrick McCreery, eds., *Out at Work: Building a Gay-Labor Alliance* (Minneapolis: University of Minnesota Press, 2001).

28. "Why Gay People Should Seek the Right to Marry," *Out/Look* no. 6 (Fall 1989): 12.

29. *Brown v. Board of Education,* 347 U.S. 483 (1954); *Roe v. Wade,* 410 U.S. 113 (1973).

30. Quoted in James T. Patterson, *Brown v. Board of Education: A Civil Rights Milestone and Its Troubled Legacy* (New York: Oxford University Press, 2001), 72.

31. Ibid, 13.

32. Kristin Luker, *Abortion and the Politics of Motherhood* (Berkeley: University of California Press, 1984), 126.

33. For histories of birth control activism in the twentieth century see James Reed, *From Private Vice to Public Virtue: The Birth Control Movement and American Society since 1830* (New York: Basic, 1978); Linda Gordon, *Woman's Body, Woman's Right: A Social History of Birth Control in America* (New York: Grossman, 1976).

34. *Roth v. United States,* 354 U.S. 476 (1957); Commission on Obscenity and Pornography, *Report* (New York: Bantam, 1970).

35. *Griswold v. Connecticut,* 381 U.S. 479 (1965); *Eisenstadt v. Baird,* 405 U.S. 438 (1970). For a detailed discussion of the legal history that led to *Roe,* see David J. Garrow, *Liberty and Sexuality: The Right to Privacy and the Making of* Roe v. Wade (New York: Macmillan, 1994).

36. Important historical analyses of marriage include Stephanie Coontz, *Marriage: A History; From Obedience to Intimacy, or How Love Conquered Marriage* (New York: Viking, 2005); Nancy F. Cott, *Public Vows: A History of Marriage and the Nation* (Cambridge: Harvard University Press, 2000); and E. J. Graff, *What Is Marriage For? The Strange Social History of Our Most Intimate Institution* (Boston: Beacon, 1999).

37. Gayle S. Rubin, "Thinking Sex: Notes for a Radical Theory of the Politics of Sexuality." In *Pleasure and Danger: Exploring Female Sexuality,* ed. Carole Vance, 267–319 (Boston: Routledge).

THE CONSEQUENCES OF MARRIAGE POLICY FOR SAME-SEX COUPLES' WELL-BEING

Ellen D. B. Riggle and Sharon S. Rostosky

The first hint of Nancy Walsh's shaky new status appeared just hours after the four planes crashed and the two towers crumbled. She knew her partner was on Flight 11. . . . As Carol Flyzik's partner of 12 years, she wasn't considered family. . . . Because Flyzik did not have a will, Walsh will not automatically inherit the rambling house they shared. She does not have the legal right to renew the car registration of Flyzik's car. . . . "It's really a slap in the face . . . to be told you're not the person we consider as the closest family member to this victim. We're not going to recognize your pain."

KATHLEEN BURGE

While the citizens of the United States compassionately grieved with the spouses of the victims of the tragedy of September 11, 2001, the same-sex partners of victims of this tragedy suffered the compounded consequences of a vulnerable (and often invisible) social and legal status. Was the loss of these committed relationships any less tragic because of the

65

lack of a civil marriage license? Was the grief of surviving partners any less deserving of a compassionate response because they were not labeled by the government as "spouse" or "family"? Did government policies denying civil marriage to same-sex couples exacerbate the pain and suffering of those who lost their same-sex partner?

The denial of the right of same-sex couples to enter into a civil marriage is an institutionalized form of stigma. This stigmatization, especially in the context of current public debates and actions, devalues the relationships of same-sex couples and ultimately greatly increases the risk of psychological harm. A public policy that induces harm by devaluing a group of citizens is a public health issue. To borrow Chief Justice Earl Warren's words from the decision in *Brown v. Board of Education* (1954), to separate same-sex relationships from others of similar circumstance solely because of their choice of intimate partner "generates a feeling of inferiority as to their status in the community that may affect their hearts and minds in a way unlikely ever to be undone."[1] Thus, the effect of current civil marriage policy is to exacerbate the negative psychological (and consequent physical) health effects of stigmatization through the sanction of law.

The culture of devaluation, including overt and subtle prejudice and discrimination, creates and reinforces the chronic, everyday stress that interferes with optimal human development and well-being. This form of chronic stress is referred to in the psychosocial literature as *minority stress* (Brooks 1981; Meyer 1995, 2003). We begin this chapter by reviewing this framework and its particular application to sexual minority individuals and same-sex couples. We then use this minority stress framework as the basis for our argument that current policy regarding civil marriage for same-sex couples negatively affects the health and well-being of families (1) by socially constructing a stigmatized family form composed of members who anticipate and experience discrimination; (2) by creating a legal status that induces and institutionalizes vulnerability, leaving couples open to financial and emotional crises; and (3) by reinforcing and perpetuating a rhetoric based on discriminatory attitudes and bias-based fears rather than democratic values and civility. We illustrate these points with findings from qualitative studies of relational commitment in more than same-sex couples. We conclude the chapter by suggesting that the inequity perpetuated by current civil marriage policy is a public health issue that needs to be addressed in policy and social context as a necessary step toward promoting well-being for all citizens.

MINORITY STRESS FOR SEXUAL MINORITIES

Minority stress is chronic stress associated with the prejudice and discrimination that accompany a stigmatized status (Brooks 1981; Meyer 1995, 2003). The concept of stigma has been applied to a wide variety of social groups, occupations, and characteristics. The conceptualization that we use is derived from Goffman's (1963) original definition of a stigma as an attribute that deeply discredits a person and reduces her or him "from a whole and usual person to a tainted, discounted one" (3). Crocker (1999) elaborated on this definition: "A person who is stigmatized is a person whose social identity, or membership in some social category, calls into question his or her full humanity—the person is devalued, spoiled, or flawed in the eyes of others" (89). A social identity may be either a self-identification or an identity that is attributed to a person because of certain characteristics and is located within a sociopolitical power structure. The stigmatized identity (attribute) is then used within the cultural power structure to discount a class of people by means of disapproval, rejection, exclusion, and discrimination, resulting in negative effects on an individual's health and financial and life opportunities (Link and Phelan 2000).

For the discounted class, the effects of stigmatization create a social stress that is chronic. This stress is uniquely related to the stigmatized social category and is in addition to the daily or ordinary stresses that are encountered in life. This type of chronic social stress as experienced by stigmatized groups within the sociopolitical culture has been called minority stress (Brooks 1981; Meyer 1995, 2003). Chronic stress, including minority stress, is associated with a decreased sense of well-being and increased mental and physical health concerns. Minority stress has been associated with elevated rates of anxiety, depression, substance abuse, eating disorders, and anger, as well as decreased self-esteem (Clark et al. 1999; Kessler, Mickelson, and Williams 1999; Swim et al. 2001; Meyer 2003; Cochran 2001).

Minority stress may be related to societal prejudice based on race, ethnicity, gender, disability, or sexual orientation (for example, Swim and Stangor 1998; Crocker, Major, and Steele 1998). Although gays, lesbians, and bisexuals experience much the same prejudice as do other stigmatized groups, there are also some unique features. For example, whereas belonging to a gender category of "female" or the racial category of "African American" is typically visible to others, belonging to the category of "gay" or "lesbian" is typically invisible to others. Invisibility results in the need to make decisions about disclosure or concealment of identity. Another unique factor involves experiences with the family of origin. Members of some stigmatized groups typically come from families of origin that are at least partly composed of members of the same group. For instance, Latino individuals typically come from predominately Latino families of origin. It is much less likely for a gay, lesbian, or bisexual (GLB) person to come from a family of origin with members identified as GLB. As such, sexual minority individuals are much less likely to receive support from and learn identity-specific resilience skills from their families of origin.[2]

Meyer (2003) has proposed a minority stress model that delineates the causal pathways between the stigmatization of a GLB identity and sources of stress. In this model, experiences of prejudice, expectations of rejection, higher levels of internalized homophobia, and concealment of sexual identity are related to negative mental health outcomes. Coping skills and social support, including having a partner and being in a committed relationship, help attenuate these negative effects.

Experiences and expectations of prejudice. For gays, lesbians, and bisexuals, overt experiences of prejudice and discrimination have long-term negative effects on well-being. And these experiences are common. Herek (1989) reported that 92 percent of a sample of self-identified lesbians and gay men reported being subjected to antigay verbal abuse. In another sample, 20 percent of lesbians and 25 percent of gay men reported at least one lifetime incident of criminal victimization related to their sexual identity, and 56 percent of respondents reported verbal harassment related to their sexual identity in the past year alone (Herek, Gillis, and Cogan 1999). These incidents, whether physical or verbal, personal or property-related, are perceived as based on the victim's sexual orientation and have a negative impact on the individual's long-term health and well-being (Otis and Skinner 1996; Herek et al. 1997).

Such individuals also commonly perceive discrimination against them based on their sexual orientation. More than 40 percent of GLB individuals report being victims of discrimination at some point in their work life, regardless of their level of disclosure about their sexual orientation, resulting in lower levels of psychological well-being and life satisfaction (Garnets and Kimmel 1993; Lane and Wegner 1995; Savin-Williams and Rodriguez 1993) and increased health risks, including higher levels of stress-sensitive mental health problems (Mays and Cochran 2001).

In addition to direct experiences, the expectation of prejudice and discrimination creates additional stress for members of stigmatized groups. Gays, lesbians, and bisexuals, relying on their personal experience or the experiences of friends or acquaintances, expect that others will stigmatize and subsequently discriminate against them. Anticipating that interactions with others who are not in a sexual minority will be nonaccepting or negative, regardless of the actual experience, creates a cognitive load of hypervigilance and defensiveness that is deleterious to health and well-being (Crocker et al. 1998; Meyer 2003).

Internalized homophobia. The internalization of negative societal attitudes about homosexuality is referred to as internalized homophobia. This process creates negative self-images and may result in self-destructive behaviors. Higher levels of internalized homophobia have been found to be associated with increased indications of psychological distress such as lower self-esteem (Shidlo 1994) and increased anxiety and depression (Stein and Cabaj 1996), as well as decreased success in intimate relationships, including decreased intimacy and commitment in relationships (Ross and Rosser 1996; Stein and Cabaj 1996; Meyer and Dean 1998).

Disclosure. The invisibility of sexual minority status creates the necessity for sexual minority individuals to make judgments and weigh decisions about concealing or disclosing their identity. A decision to disclose one's sexual orientation involves a cost-benefit analysis that may include issues of personal safety or livelihood. For instance, gay men and lesbians must weigh the costs of concealment at work (for example, taking energy away from creativity) against the costs of possible job discrimination (for example, losing a job or not getting a raise). Or, in regard to romantic relationships, same-sex partners must consider the benefits of disclosing the relationship to members of a family of origin and the risk of the turmoil of negative reactions. Limiting disclosure of sexual minority status is associated with lower levels of psychological well-being and life satisfaction (Garnets and Kimmel 1993; Lane and Wegner 1995; Savin-Williams and Rodriguez 1993).

SAME-SEX RELATIONSHIPS IN A MINORITY STRESS CONTEXT

Intimate relationships have been identified by gay men and lesbians as a primary source of social support (Kurdek 1988). Whereas same-sex couples report levels of relational satisfaction and relational longevity similar to those of heterosexual couples, same-sex couples must negotiate minority stress factors simultaneously with the developmental tasks of relationship formation and maintenance (Rostosky et al. 2006; Green and Mitchell 2002). The interdependent nature of couples' relationships suggests that any minority stress factors that are experienced by one member of a couple will also to some extent have an effect on the partner as well (Rostosky and Riggle 2002; cf. Kelley and Thibaut 1978).

Anticipation of prejudicial treatment or experiences of discrimination effects individuals and contributes to stress in couple relationships. For example, Murray et al. (2001) found a significant psychological and emotional impact of perceived racism within the marital relationships of African American couples. Similarly, Otis et al. (2006) found that an individual's perception of past discrimination was associated with the stress level of both members of same-sex couples.

Discrimination in the form of denied legal protections for a relationship can generate or exacerbate minority stress in several ways within same-sex relationships. Kuehlwein and Gottschalk (2000) note that when stressful events occur in the lives of couples, the lack of legal protections can compound problems and negatively affect relationships by increasing couples' awareness of their vulnerability. These pressures can compromise the sense of security and cohesion within a couple and create tension and conflict. The negative psychological effects of vulnerability can include feelings of helplessness to effect outcomes and feelings of anxiety resulting from perceived threats from external forces.

In an analysis of conversational data collected from forty same-sex couples in committed relationships, we found evidence of each factor of minority stress affecting the couple's relationship (Rostosky, Riggle, Gray, and Hatton in press). More than half of the couples discussed the lack of legal protections (including civil marriage rights) for their relationship as a source of stress. Although the couples had developed important coping strategies for dealing with other sources of minority stress (such as creating support systems to deal with experiences of prejudice or self-acceptance to cope with rejection by others), there were few effective coping strategies for dealing with the lack of legal protections. Some couples had created wills and powers of attorney, but the majority of couples had not (see Riggle and Rostosky 2005). Couples with legal documents recognized the limitations of such documents and the continued vulnerability of their relationship.

MINORITY STRESS AND MARRIAGE POLICY

The desire to form a long-term, committed relationship is a part of healthy development for most adults. Forming committed relationships always involves challenges. For opposite-sex couples, there is a culturally defined script for the development of a committed relationship that includes markers for significant events. In modern American culture these markers include dating, engagement, and marriage. For same-sex couples, the negotiation of a committed relationship includes dating (and even this is somewhat ill-defined), but the markers for engagement and marriage are virtually absent. In 2006, opportunities for civil marriage were limited to the Netherlands, Belgium, Spain, and Canada; several other countries have established versions of registered partnerships. In the United States, only the Commonwealth of Massachusetts extended civil marriage to same-sex couples, and the civil marriages conducted there were very rarely recognized outside the jurisdiction of Massachusetts and were not recognized by the federal government.

Our research with committed same-sex couples suggests that the lack of civil marriage creates a stressful sociopolitical context for these couples. In three separate studies, a purposive, local sample of more than one hundred same-sex couples have participated in structured conversations and interviews about their relationships. These couples have talked about the negative effects of the lack of marriage rights on their committed relationships, their ability to create legal rights and responsibilities in their partnerships, and, most recently, the psychological impact of the state constitutional amendment in Kentucky limiting the recognition of marriage to unions of one man and one woman. In the following sections we present the words of couple members to illustrate these negative impacts.

Relational commitment. As part of a study of relational commitment, we asked forty same-sex couples to define *commitment* and talk about what the concept means in their relationship. Analysis of these data revealed that couples defined their commitment to each other (1) in comparison to other relationships, (2) by noting the investments they make in the relationship and the costs associated with it, the rewards they received from being in the relationship, and their ability to negotiate intracouple differences and sexual boundaries, and (3) in relation to their relational values and ideals (Rostosky et al. 2006). Many of these definitional categories are similar to those used to define the commitment of heterosexual couples (for example, costs and investments, Rusbult 1980). Some of the categories are only fully understood within a minority stress framework, however. For instance, the decision to disclose the relationship to others, including members of a family of origin, represents an important marker of commitment. For many couples, this decision generates anxiety and stress as the couple anticipates possible reactions. The following is an example of a discussion between the members (A and B) of a couple (1).

> 1-A: It's definitely influenced my relationship with you . . . especially since I'm not out to my parents . . . and she [the mother of A] wouldn't speak to me for a month when she found out my friends were gay. . . . So, just all that hate, she has made me feel like, "What's the point in continuing (the relationship) if I could lose my mom or she would . . . "
>
> 1-B: Oh, yeah, 'cause you feel like your family's gonna disown you.
>
> 1-A: Right.

Even when couples have disclosed their relationship to families of origin and others, some couples perceive a difference in the treatment of their relationship and those of legally married couples.

> 2-A: I think they don't quite view us as married or anything; it's more like we're boyfriends. [Therefore,] there's not that solidification of a more permanent relationship and the rights that go with it. It's kind of something I get in my mind. It's more like they're still seeing how long we stay together.

Other couples who participated in the study talked specifically about the stigma involved in not being able to get married. Two examples illustrate this point.

> 3-A: I think it's the same thing but much more complicated, and there's the stigma of us not being able to get married in certain states, so that a lot of people don't take it as seriously.
>
> 3-B: I think the commitment is the same, but I think . . .
>
> 3-A: It should be the same.
>
> 3-B: Yeah, definitely. But I think that maybe the way we're viewed isn't the same. Like, we're not seen as having as much commitment, because it's like we could be together for two and a half years, but someone who's been a heterosexual couple who's been together for a year, they're already getting married.

> 4-A: Well, I think that straight couples also see our committed relationships differently because—since we can't legally get married—I think they [think] our relationships are more, umm . . . throw-away.

The psychological impact of not having access to civil marriage includes feeling a lack of social and community support for a relationship (illustrated below by the comments of 5-B) and, for some, feeling angry (as illustrated by the comments of 6-B).

> 5-B: Heterosexual relationships are of course the most visible norm of this world, so that's what people are most comfortable with, and the civil ceremonies are all legal, and that's expected and ok . . . [but] two women or two men can hardly find anyplace in the world to have a public legal marriage ceremony, and I think that's a real travesty. I think it's completely unfair and I think that contributes to same-sex partners feeling not enough support from the community.

> 6-B: I see so many people go through the same cycles when it comes to marriage. Like my sister, she marries a man who is abusive to her, she has kids by him, she divorces him, tells everybody what a horrible person he was. Six months later she's back out, she meets another man who [drinks] and is abusive to her and starts it all over again. And at the same time, then she turns around and says that I'm less than a human being because of my relationship with you. So that has made me on a certain level very angry.

Couples discussed the legal inequities they experienced and the lack of the social and legal support that are available to married (heterosexual) couples. The three examples below illustrate this point.

> 7-B: Well, we don't have the option of having it legal, and I think that . . . that marriage certificate legal stuff holds a lot of heterosexual couples together that might not stay together otherwise. It's such a pain to separate, it's such a long battle, especially with kids and property, etc. I think they stay together longer due to that, kind of "we're married, what would my family say or do if we separated"—there's more pressure to stay together, whereas in a same-sex relationship there's more pressure to pull apart. And they don't have all those legal bonds—I think that a lot of same-sex couples who separate might not separate if they had more social and legal mores holding them together.

> 2-A: For straight people . . . when they get married, there's this whole romance around the ritual act of marriage. The bridal magazines, the grooms-people, and the bachelor's party and everything. And they don't

really contemplate that you're also getting this enormous, complicated legal package. For gay couples, something we've discussed is, at what point do you move in? At what point do you get the other person's name on the mortgage? At what point do you combine some assets? . . . Power of attorney, health visitation, a lot of legal aspects that are elements of commitment.

8-b: You get no formal commitment ceremonies, the government doesn't grant you spousal benefits, your employers generally don't; some do, most don't. You got inheritance, as far as children are concerned, you're not even recognized as the other legal parent; you know, to this day if you were to go into the hospital or something, I wouldn't be considered a relative, so basically, in that sense, you get no support, you get no support as far as recognizing that there are same-sex couples who are in committed relationships from an institutionalized standpoint, like the government, the military, school systems, you know, all that. They just sort of ignore it.

Legal rights and advance planning. Same-sex couples have few options to cope with and counteract the legal vulnerabilities that result from the lack of civil marriage rights. They can create a limited set of legal rights for their partners by means of advance planning documents (for example, a will or power of attorney). They may also use contract law to create legal responsibilities and obligations (for example, a separation agreement or a joint ownership contract). These documents create, at best, a very limited set of rights, mostly for crises.

In an online survey of same-sex couples, we found that only approximately one in three had executed the major advance planning documents (a will, power of attorney, and health care surrogate; Riggle, Rostosky, and Prather 2006). The 37 percent of same-sex couples in this sample who reported having wills is much less than the 53 percent of married couples who report having a will (Findlaw 2002). In the current sociopolitical context, where every same-sex couple needs to have protective advance planning documents and this is one of the few legal strategies available to them, this disparity is cause for great concern.

We conducted an interview study of twenty-eight committed same-sex couples that lived together to ask why they had or had not executed advance planning documents. We analyzed the transcripts of these interviews to discover the motivations and barriers to advance planning (Riggle et al. 2006).

Couples who had not executed such documents cited a lack of priority or urgency in the matter, youth and good health (along with a general discomfort with talking about death or ill health), and a lack of resources as reasons for not having the documents. Although most of these reasons were similar to the reasons given by general population samples, there were also some barriers related to minority stress factors for same-sex couples. For example, some couples cited a lack of knowledge about how to find a "gay-friendly" attorney and a fear of a negative reaction or incompetent service by a nonaffirmative attorney. Other couples had little knowledge about the effects of advance planning documents or had misconceptions about their legal rights. For instance, many of the subjects stated that it was "understood" that their partner would inherit their property in case of death or make decisions in case of a medical emergency. Most of these couples had little understanding of the ramifications of their lack of legal status. One couple did vaguely recognize this and expressed their uncertainty.

> 9-A: If something were to happen to him, I think . . . he would expect me
> to step in and deal with those things. . . . I don't know how ignorant of a
> view that is in terms of our relationship as far as views from family and
> outside our relationship.

Couples that had executed advance planning documents had a more informed perspective on the consequences of the lack of marriage rights and the effects of trying to create legal rights and responsibilities for a same-sex relationship. These documents create a limited number of rights to property and decision making for persons who would not legally have those rights without a specification by the individual partner. Whereas legally married couples have many of these rights by law, same-sex couples must take proactive steps to declare their partners' rights, particularly in the event of a crisis.

All couples talked about executing advance planning documents to protect their relationship and their partner, typically from interference by the family of origin. One person stated, "You know, unless I write that down [in a will], I can see my family coming in and just saying, you know, . . . taking all this stuff away and that would really be disturbing." Couples also typically talked about advance planning as a concrete symbol of their commitment to the relationship and as a marital equivalent.

10-A: What went on [when executing the documents] was to try to make our relationship as legal as we could. Since we can't get married, we were thinking, how can we protect ourselves as best we can?

Other couples discussed the feeling of "validation" of their relationship that they experienced when signing the documents.

11-B: Well, I figured it was the closest we'd ever get to marriage.
11-A: It gave us legal status.
11-B: Just the ceremony of having it executed in the attorney's office. I'm like, "wow." It's not like it was any less real before. But it validated us.

Couples were also motivated by their prior experiences or the experiences of others. One persons' story of his prior experience with the death of a partner illustrates the legal vulnerability of same-sex couples.

12-B: I lost a husband of seven years. Luckily we had most of the documents we needed. Almost everything went off well. In the end it was one life insurance policy that was a benefit through his employment that he had signed when he had gotten his job, which was about six months before we had gotten together. And that was left to his next of kin. And that was never changed when [he] and I met . . . he never thought about it. And that was a $50,000 policy and that ended up going to his family, which in the end worked out okay. But if I had been a legal spouse it would have come to me. In addition to that there was about six to eight months of Social Security that he was entitled to, but I was unable to file it for him.

Constitutional amendments and minority stress. Forty-four states and the federal government have legislation that limits civil marriage to one man and one woman. As of this writing, nineteen states (with six more voting on the issue in November 2006) have amended their constitutions to limit the recognition of civil marriage to one man and one woman. Some of the amendments and laws include a prohibition on state recognition of statuses similar to marriage for unmarried couples. For example, the amendment to the Ohio constitution reads: "Only a union between one man and one woman may be a marriage valid in or recognized by this state and its political subdivisions. This state and its political subdivisions shall not create or recognize a legal status for relationships of unmarried individuals that intends to approximate the design, qualities, significance or effect of marriage" (art. XV, §11). This amendment, along with twelve others on state ballots in 2004, passed by an average of 71 percent of voters in those states.

Privileging heterosexual relationships socially and politically constructs an "outgroup" or "outsider" identity for nonheterosexual couples, whose devalued status becomes institutionalized. The debate over civil marriage for same-sex couples has activated negative stereotypes of gays, lesbians, and same-sex relationships, reinforcing their stigmatization. The debate has created an environment wherein an already stigmatized class is subjected to further social and political devaluation (Riggle, Thomas, and Rostosky 2005).

As a result, the public debate concerning the amendments and legislative action has created divisions in communities and families, as well as the larger body politic (Russell 2004). Russell argued that when members of a stigmatized group "[are] the subject of political debate, group members often exhibit a variety of negative outcomes including anxiety, depression, alienation, fear, and anger" (2004, 3). The dehumanizing and devaluing rhetoric negatively effects the well-being of all citizens who are exposed to the debate.

Russell conducted a study of the effects of the passage of Amendment 2 in Colorado in 1992 on lesbian, gay and bisexual Coloradoans (Russell 2000; see also Russell and Richards 2003). Russell noted that members of her sample attributed an increased level of anxiety and stress to several sources in the sociopolitical context. She found that sample participants felt stressed by their encounters with homophobia and felt an increased sense of internalized homophobia. They were also stressed by their sense of divisions within the GLB community and by the anger that they felt was directed at them by amendment proponents. In addition, they were demoralized by the failure of their families of origin and straight friends to support them.

Although Colorado's Amendment 2 eliminated sexual orientation from governmental nondiscrimination policies in the state (and was later nullified by a successful appeal to the U.S. Supreme Court in *Romer v. Evans*),[3] the marriage amendments target the committed intimate relationships of same-sex couples. In November 2004, Kentuckians passed an amendment to the state constitution with nearly 75 percent of the vote. It reads: "Only a marriage between one man and one woman shall be valid or recognized as a marriage in Kentucky. A legal status identical or substantially similar to that of marriage for unmarried individuals shall not be valid or recognized." As part of an interview study with ten same-sex couples in February and March 2005 and members of twenty-five couples in May 2005, we asked about their feelings about the amendment and how it had impacted them.

A member of one couple talked about how relationships with co-workers were affected, and another resigned from a job in response to the passage of the amendment.

13-A: And then I went to work and it seemed like everything just kind of was changing slowly. I went to work and I started being really suspicious and I'd look at my co-workers and the people I had lunch with and the people that I enjoyed talking to, and I was thinking, did you vote "no" [against the state constitutional amendment]? Even though they look like they're OK with me and they might be cordial, this might not be something that they believe in. You know, and then starting to think people that I felt like were really for me and my partner having a great life together, were maybe just tolerating us. And, you know, then I think it really hit home.

14-B: I worked up until [last Wednesday] for the legislature. . . . My job was to work for the legislators and their constituents. . . . When I left, with trembling hand I hit the "send" button because I wrote a letter to them all, to everybody in [the agency] and to all the legislators and told them [the] impact the last session had on me. Personally, it had broken my spirit and as a matter of conscience I could no longer work for them because they initiated that amendment and that they had to believe that I was less worthy than they and that they had taken away basic civil rights that they enjoy. Taken away from us, the same civil rights that they enjoy. And that I feel bad about that. And so, I think it made sort of a little stir there, but that's, so that's been something that's been very important to me that I decided to speak up.

Many subjects talked about the negative feelings that they had after the amendment passed. They used words and phrases such as "angry," "disheartening," "numbness," "settled down in our bones in a bad way," "like I'd been hit by a ton of bricks," "I'm really not welcome in this country," and "like somebody had just kicked me or punched me in the gut" to describe their feelings. Others talked at greater length about their feelings of being attacked and alienated.

15-A: You know, I believe that love is blind and [that] God's love is universal and that, and it killed me, I almost took it as a personal attack when

I saw one of those bumper stickers that said Marriage Equals Man Plus Woman, because that, to me, is saying that love is not blind. Love is selective, conditional. And that just didn't mesh with my personal beliefs. And so the marriage amendment, I won't say hurt but it was defeating in more ways than one.

16-B: And so when the day actually came, I mean a part of me wasn't really surprised. But then another was just like I was so stunned. I felt so alienated. I felt so invisible. I felt like everything we had worked for, they had just kind of flung us back against the wall and said, "You don't deserve this." You are less than . . . and [it] goes right back into [that] hatefulness and that inequality.

CONCLUSIONS

Institutionalized stigma creates obstacles and barriers for same-sex couples and their families. Couples must devise strategies to cope with these stresses. Resilient couples draw on their strengths as individuals and their commitment to the relationship to deal with the consequences of stigma. Even for highly resilient couples, generating and enacting strategies for overcoming institutionalized obstacles requires creativity, knowledge, and financial and psychosocial resources. Despite these efforts, many institutional barriers are insurmountable.

Research concerning heterosexual couples has found marriage to be associated with increased well-being for the partners. Obviously, marriage is no guarantee of good physical or mental health. Having a spouse with whom to share the stresses and concerns of life is, however, a protective factor for health. The legal status of marriage helps promote, assist, and support the relationship. Inasmuch as civil marriage policy creates a stigmatized status by excluding same-sex couples, these policies deny them full psychosocial benefits and create stress, with attendant health risks.

The Massachusetts Supreme Judicial Court, in *Hillary Goodridge v. Department of Public Health* (2003), affirmed the importance of civil marriage to individuals and the state:

Marriage also bestows enormous private and social advantages on those who choose to marry. Civil marriage is at once a deeply personal commitment to another human being and a highly public celebration of the ideals of mutuality, companionship, intimacy, fidelity, and family. . . . Because it fulfils yearnings for security, safe haven, and connection that express our common humanity, civil marriage is an esteemed institution, and the decision whether and whom to marry is among life's momentous acts of self-definition. . . . Tangible as well as intangible benefits flow from marriage. . . . Because civil marriage is central to the lives of individuals and the welfare of the community, our laws assiduously protect the individual's right to marry against undue government incursion. . . . The marriage ban works a deep and scarring hardship on a very real segment of the community for no rational reason. The absence of any reasonable relationship between, on the one hand, an absolute disqualification of same-sex couples who wish to enter into civil marriage and, on the other, protection of public health, safety, or general welfare, suggests that the marriage restriction is rooted in persistent prejudices against persons who are (or who are believed to be) homosexual.[4]

The court also issued an advisory opinion to the Massachusetts State Senate on February 3, 2004, in response to an official question from the Senate asking whether "civil unions" would comply with the original court ruling. The court answered that "the history of our nation has demonstrated that separate is seldom, if ever, equal" and further advised the Senate that civil unions would create an "unconstitutional, inferior, and discriminatory status for same-sex couples." In these opinions, the Massachusetts Supreme Judicial Court articulately made the link between the issue of civil marriage and the full exercise of citizenship.

Clearly, denying a group of citizens full participation in the institutions created to sustain a society is antithetical to the ideals of a just society. Action to equalize the opportunity for civil marriage is a necessary first step for equalizing the status of same-sex couples and their families. Although legalization of civil marriage would not erase all social discrimination or prejudice, it would send a clear message of institutional legitimation and equality. Evidence based on a study of same-sex couples in Scandinavian countries supports the suggestion of positive health benefits for couples in legalized relationships (Eskridge and Spedale 2006). Marriage creates a legitimate social status and couple identity for same-sex couples that provide a foundation and security for couples to come out and negotiate family and social support (see also Solomon, Rothblum, and Balsam's 2004 study of Vermont couples in civil unions). So although social stigmatization will not totally disappear (just as social stigmatization of interracial marriages did not disappear after *Loving v. Virginia*)[5] and minority stressors will still be an issue, the stress effects may be significantly decreased over time. This is an empirical question for future research to investigate.

So why do we call current discriminatory marriage policies a *public health* issue instead of simply a health issue for same-sex couples? Simply put, the devaluation of one group of citizens devalues all citizens. Stigmatizing a class of citizens actively devalues them. In creating, debating, and supporting the marginalization of a stigmatized class, citizens lose their compassion and empathy for others. And when the well-being of a class of citizens is compromised by such actions, all citizens feel the effects. The rights of all citizens are compromised by the restriction of opportunities to fully express their humanity and enact the rights and responsibilities of their citizenship.

A just society affirms the inherent worth and dignity of every citizen as a part of the public good. A just government promotes equality and supports human relationships in order to protect the expression of democracy. Civil marriage policies must extend these principles by extending the full support of the state to all of its citizens with equal opportunities for life, liberty, and the pursuit of happiness.

ENDNOTES

The authors would like to thank Barry L. Tadlock for his comments. Data were collected with the support of the American Psychological Foundation's Wayne E. Placek Award (Sharon S. Rostosky, PI, 2000) and grants from the Vice-President for Research at the University of Kentucky. Please address correspondence to: Ellen Riggle, Department of Political Science, University of Kentucky, Lexington, KY, 40506.

1. *Brown v. Board of Education,* 347 U.S. 483 (1954), 495.
2. We are not specifically addressing the complex stigma attached to transgender identity, although stigmatization and minority stress very much apply to transgender persons. Further, the application of civil marriage policy to transgender persons is even more complicated than for same-sex couples, and the health consequences are perhaps even more harmful.
3. *Romer, Governor of Colorado, et al. v. Evans et al.* 517 U.S. 620 (1996).
4. *Hillary Goodridge v. Department of Public Health,* 440 Mass. 309 (2003).
5. *Loving v. Virginia,* 388 U.S. 1 (1967).

REFERENCES

Brooks, Virginia R. 1981. *Minority stress and lesbian women.* Lexington, MA: Heath.

Burge, Kathleen. 2002. Sept 11 leaves same-sex partners adrift: Laws bar benefits, even recognition. *Boston Globe.* http://www.boston.com/globe (accessed March 18 2002).

Clark, Rodney, Norman B. Anderson, Vernessa R. Clark, and David R. Williams. 1999. Racism as a stressor for African Americans: A biopsychosocial model. *American Psychologist* 54 (10): 805–16.

Cochran, Susan D. 2001. Emerging issues in research on lesbians' and gay men's mental health: Does sexual orientation really matter?" *American Psychologist* 56 (1): 931–47.

Crocker, Jennifer. 1999. Social stigma and self-esteem: Situational construction of self-worth. *Journal of Experimental Social Psychology* 35 (1): 89–107.

Crocker, Jennifer, Brenda Major, and Claude Steele. 1998. Social stigma. In *The handbook of social psychology*, 4th ed., ed. Daniel T. Gilbert, Susan T. Fiske, and Gardner Lindzey, 504–52. New York: McGraw Hill.

Eskridge, William N., Jr., and Darren R. Spedale. 2006. *Gay marriage: For better or for worse? What we've learned from the evidence.* Oxford: Oxford University Press.

FindLaw. 2002. Most Americans still don't have a will, says new survey by FindLaw. http://company.findlaw.com/pr/2002/081902.will.html (accessed July 13, 2004).

Garnets, Linda D., and Douglas C. Kimmel. 1993. Lesbian and gay male dimensions in the psychological study of human diversity. In *Psychological perspectives on lesbian and gay male experiences*, ed. Linda D. Garnets and Douglas C. Kimmel, 1–51. New York: Columbia University Press.

Goffman, Erving. 1963. *Stigma: Notes on the management of a spoiled identity.* Englewood Cliffs, NJ: Prentice-Hall.

Green, Robert-Jay, and Valory Mitchell. 2002. Gay and lesbian couples in therapy: Homophobia, relational ambiguity, and social support. In *Clinical handbook of couple therapy*, 3d ed., ed. Alan S. Gurman and Neil S. Jacobson. New York: Guilford.

Herek, Gregory M. 1989. Hate crimes against lesbians and gay men: Issues for research and policy. *American Psychologist* 44 (6): 948–55.

Herek, Gregory M., J. Roy Gillis, and Jeanine C. Cogan. 1999. Psychological sequelae of hate-crime victimization among lesbian, gay, and bisexual adults. *Journal of Consulting and Clinical Psychology* 67 (6): 945–51.

Herek, Gregory M., J. Roy Gillis, Jeanine C. Cogan, and Glunt, Eric K. 1997. Hate crime victimization among lesbian, gay, and bisexual adults: Prevalence, psychological correlates, and methodological issues. *Journal of Interpersonal Violence* 12:195–215.

Kelley, Harold H., and John W. Thibaut. 1978. *Interpersonal relationships: A theory of interdependence.* New York: Wiley.

Kessler, Ronald C., Kristin D. Mickelson, and David R. Williams. 1999. The prevalence, distribution, and mental health correlates of perceived discrimination in the United States. *Journal of Health and Social Behavior* 40 (3): 208–30.

Kuehlwein, Kevin T., and Deborah I. Gottschalk. 2000. Legal and psychological issues confronting lesbian, bisexual, and gay couples and families. In *Handbook of couple and family forensics: A sourcebook for mental health and legal professionals*, ed. Florence Kaslow, 164–97. New York: Wiley.

Kurdek, Lawrence A. 1988. Perceived social support in gays and lesbians in cohabitating relationships. *Journal of Personality and Social Psychology* 54 (3): 504–9.

Lane, Julie D., and Daniel M. Wegner. 1995. The cognitive consequences of secrecy. *Journal of Personality and Social Psychology* 69 (2): 237–54.

Link, Bruce G., and Jo C. Phelan. 2001. Conceptualizing stigma. *Annual Review of Sociology* 27 (1): 363–85.

Mays, Vicki M., and Susan D. Cochran. 2001. Mental health correlates of perceived discrimination among lesbian, gay, and bisexual adults in the United States. *American Journal of Public Health* 91 (11): 1869–76.

Meyer, Ilan H. 1995. Minority stress and mental health in gay men. *Journal of Health and Social Behavior* 36 (1): 38–56.

———. 2003. Prejudice, social stress, and mental health in lesbian, gay, and bisexual populations: Conceptual issues and research evidence. *Psychological Bulletin* 129 (5): 674–97.

Meyer, Ilan H., and Laura Dean. 1998. Internalized homophobia, intimacy, and sexual behavior among gay and bisexual men. In *Stigma and sexual orientation: Understanding prejudice against lesbians, gay men, and bisexuals*, ed. Gregory M. Herek, 160–86. Thousand Oaks, CA: Sage.

Murray, V. M., P. A. Brown, G. H. Brody, C. E. Cutrona, and R. L. Simons. 2001. Racial discrimination as a moderator of the links among stress, maternal psychological functioning, and family relationships. *Journal of Marriage and the Family* 63 (4): 915–26.

Otis, Melanie D., Ellen D. B. Riggle, Sharon S. Rostosky, and Rebecca Hamrin. 2006. Stress and relationship quality in same-sex couples. *Journal of Social and Personal Relationships* 23 (1): 81–99.

Otis, Melanie D., and William F. Skinner. 1996. The prevalence of victimization and its effect on mental well-being among lesbian and gay people. *Journal of Homosexuality* 30 (3): 93–121.

Riggle, Ellen D. B., and Sharon S. Rostosky. 2005. For better or worse: Psycholegal soft spots and advance planning for same-sex couples. *Professional Psychology: Research and Practice* 36 (1): 90–96.

Riggle, Ellen D. B., Sharon S. Rostosky, Russell Couch, Carolyn Brodnicki, Jessica Campbell, and Todd Savage. 2006. To have or not to have: Advance planning by same-sex couples. *Sexuality Research and Social Policy* 3 (1): 22–32.

Riggle, Ellen D. B., Sharon S. Rostosky, and Robert A. Prather. 2006. The execution of advance planning documents by same-sex couples. *Journal of Family Issues* 27 (6): 758–76.

Riggle, Ellen D. B., Jerry D. Thomas, and Sharon S. Rostosky. 2005. The marriage debate and minority stress. *PS: Political Science and Politics* 38 (2): 21–24.

Ross, Michael W., and B. R. Simon Rosser. 1996. Measurement and correlates of internalized homophobia: A factor analytic study. *Journal of Clinical Psychology* 52 (1): 15–21.

Rostosky, Sharon S., and Ellen D. B. Riggle. 2002. "Out at work: The relation of actor and partner workplace policy and internalized homophobia to disclosure status." *Journal of Counseling Psychology* 49 (4): 411–19.

Rostosky, Sharon S., Ellen D. B. Riggle, Michael G. Dudley, and Margaret Laurie Comer Wright. 2006. Relational commitment: A qualitative analysis of same-sex couples' conversations. *Journal of Homosexuality* 51 (3): 199–223.

Rostosky, Sharon S., Ellen D. B. Riggle, Barry E. Gray, and Roxanna L. Hatton. In press. Minority stress experiences in committed same-sex couple relationships. *Professional Psychology: Research and Practice.*

Rusbult, Caryl E. 1980. Commitment and satisfaction in romantic associations: A test of the investment model. *Journal of Experimental Social Psychology* 16 (2): 172–86.

Russell, Glenda M. 2000. *Voted out: The psychological consequences of anti-gay politics.* New York: New York University Press.

Russell, Glenda M. 2004. The dangers of a same-sex marriage referendum for community and individual well-being: A summary of research and findings. *Angles: The Policy Journal of the Institute for Gay and Lesbian Strategic Studies* 7 (1): 1–3.

Russell, Glenda M., and Jeffrey A. Richards. 2003. Stressor and resilience factors in lesbians, gay men, and bisexuals confronting anti-gay politics." *American Journal of Community Psychology* 31 (3–4): 313–28.

Savin-Williams, Ritch C., and Richard G. Rodriguez. 1993. A developmental, clinical perspective on lesbian, gay male, and bisexual youths. In *Adolescent sexuality: Advances in adolescent development,* ed. Thomas P. Gullota, Gerald R. Adams, and Raymond Montemayor, 77–101. Newbury Park, CA: Sage.

Shidlo, Ariel. 1994. Internalized homophobia: Conceptual and empirical issues in measurement. In *Lesbian and gay psychology: Theory, research and clinical applications,* ed. Beverly F. Greene and Gregory M. Herek, 176–205. Thousand Oaks, CA: Sage.

Solomon, Sondra E., Esther D. Rothblum, and Kimberly F. Balsam. 2004. Pioneers in partnership: Lesbian and gay male couples in civil unions compared with those not in civil unions, and heterosexual married siblings. *Journal of Family Psychology* 18 (2): 275–86.

Stein, Terry S., and Robert P. Cabaj. 1996. Psychotherapy with gay men. In *Textbook of homosexuality and mental health,* ed. Robert P. Cabaj and Terry S. Stein, 413–32. Washington, DC: American Psychiatric.

Swim, Janet, and Charles Stangor. 1998. *Prejudice: The target's perspective.* New York: Academic.

Swim, Janet K., Lauri L. Hyers, Laurie L. Cohen, and Melissa J. Ferguson. 2001. Everyday sexism: Evidence for its incidence, nature, and psychological impact from three daily diary studies. *Journal of Social Issues* 57 (1): 31–53.

SAME-SEX MARRIAGE, GLBT ORGANIZATIONS, AND THE LACK OF SPIRITED POLITICAL ENGAGEMENT

Ronald G. Shaiko

Like many social movements in the United States, the gay and lesbian rights movement has evolved over the past several decades owing to the entrepreneurial efforts of organizational leaders as well as a series of catalytic events that have served to mobilize gays, lesbians, bisexuals, and transgendered people to political action (Berry 1978). Unfortunately for supporters of such rights, the catalytic events of late 2003 and early 2004 served not only to mobilize these groups but also to energize counter-movement organizations across the country, including secular and religious conservative organizations (Gale 1986). The Massachusetts Supreme Judicial Court ruling in November 2003 (upheld in February 2004) that legalized same-sex marriage in Massachusetts beginning in May 2004, followed by the granting of marriage licenses to gays and lesbians by San Francisco mayor Gavin Newsom in February 2004, set off a firestorm of controversy across the country. For gay and lesbian rights groups, these actions resulted in the elevation of same-sex marriage to the top of their agendas. For "traditional values" organizations and for conservative Christian groups, however, the prospect of legalized same-sex marriage was even more energizing. While gay and lesbian rights groups were working through federal and state courts to achieve equal rights, conservative organizations were quickly mobilized to stop what they believed was a dangerous pattern of encroachment on the institution of marriage. By August 2004, after filings by a variety of conservative groups, the California Supreme Court voided the more than four thousand same-sex marriage licenses granted in San Francisco.

Much to the chagrin of gay and lesbian rights groups, conservative and evangelical Christian groups quickly mobilized efforts to place the question of same-sex marriage before voters in eleven states in November 2004 elections. In each of these states—Arkansas, Georgia, Kentucky, Michigan, Mississippi, Montana, North Dakota, Ohio, Oklahoma, Oregon, and Utah—coalitions were formed to secure the marriage rights of gays and lesbians. In most cases these coalitions had some religious representation to combat the hard-charging conservative Christian denominations that were seeking to define marriage constitutionally as the union of a man and a woman only.

The Coalition for a Fair Michigan, consisting of more than eighty organizations, was formed as "a group of fair minded leaders and organizations committed to preventing an extreme and poorly written amendment from being added to Michigan's Constitution." More than one-third of the coalition's members were religious institutions that support gay and lesbian marriage rights (see table 4.1 for a list of such institutions). From the outset, this coalition, now known as Fair Michigan Majority, was in a defensive posture. Though many believed that the issue had died in March 2004 following the failure of the Michigan House to pass the constitutional amendment by the two-thirds vote required to place it on the ballot, Citizens for the Protection of Marriage, a volunteer group wishing to amend the state constitution to define marriage as the union of a man and a woman, managed to collect more than five hundred thousand signatures, thereby placing the amendment on the November ballot (Bell 2004).

Some of the debate dealt with specifically religious questions concerning the place of gays and lesbians in society and in religious faith, but the bulk of the coalition's effort was focused on the phrasing of the amendment, a more difficult message to deliver when the opposing side was sticking to the basics—Are you for or against same-sex marriage? In

TABLE 4.1. Religious institutions affiliated with the Coalition for a Fair Michigan.

American Apostolic Catholic Church	Paint Creek Unitarian Universalist
Ann Arbor Friends Meeting	Church
Birmingham Unitarian Church	Phoenix Community Church
Christ Community Church, Spring Lake	Plymouth United Church of Christ
Concerned Clergy of West Michigan	Quaker Friends of North Michigan
Douglas Congregational United Church of Christ	Religious Coalition for a Fair
Faith Action Network	Michigan
First Unitarian Universalist Church of Ann Arbor	Shalom Center for Peace and Justice
Freemont Friends Meeting	St. Paul's Episcopal Church
Full Truth Fellowship of Christ Church	Unitarian Universalist Church of
Grace Episcopal Church, Southgate	Flint
Metropolitan Community Church of Detroit	Unitarian Universalist Fellowship of
Metropolitan Community Church of Grand Rapids	Midland
Metropolitan Community Church of Ypsilanti	United Church of Christ, Kalamazoo
National Council of Jewish Women,	Unity Fellowship Church, Detroit
Greater Detroit	Wesley Foundation, United
New Covenant Community Church	Methodist Church
Northside Presbyterian Church	

Source: http://www.coalitionforafairmichigan.org.

the end, gay and lesbian rights groups lost the votes on ballot measures in Michigan and in ten other states on Election Day. Following this disastrous outcome, and pondering the prospects for more defeats of statewide propositions concerning the issue in 2005 and 2006, a number of GLBT organizations came together in January 2005 in an attempt to carve out a plan for support of gay and lesbian rights in the United States (see table 4.2 for the list of signatories). Although there was some degree of interaction among the participants, the bulk of the dialogue leading to the consensus document took the form of emails and faxes between group leaders. The end result of this enterprise involving the twenty-two groups and their leaders was an eight-point joint statement of purpose. The priorities identified in the statement are as follows:

1. equal employment opportunity, benefits, and protections
2. ending anti-GLBT violence
3. HIV and AIDS advocacy, better access to health care, and GLBT-inclusive sex education
4. safe schools
5. family laws that strengthen GLBT families
6. ending the military's ban on gays

TABLE 4.2.   National GLBT organizations adopting 2005 joint statement of purpose.

American Civil Liberties Union Lesbian and Gay Rights Project	National Black Justice Coalition
Equality Federation	National Center for Lesbian Rights
Freedom to Marry	National Center for Transgender Equality
Gay and Lesbian Advocates and Defenders	National Coalition of Anti-Violence Programs
Gay and Lesbian Alliance Against Defamation	National Gay and Lesbian Task Force
Gay and Lesbian Victory Fund	National Youth Advocacy Coalition
Gay, Lesbian, and Straight Education Network	Parents, Family, and Friends of Lesbians and Gays
Human Rights Campaign	Servicemembers Legal Defense Network
Lambda Legal	Sigamos Adelante—National Latino/ Hispanic LGBT Leadership
Log Cabin Republicans	Stonewall Democrats
Maunter Project	
National Association of LGBT Community Centers	

Source: Resnick 2005.

7. exposing the radical Right's anti-GLBT agenda and fighting its attempts to enshrine antigay bigotry in state and federal constitutions

8. marriage equality (Brandt 2005; Resnick 2005; Nieves 2005)

Although each of these priorities is of demonstrable importance to the gay and lesbian rights movement, the most controversial item on the list is the last—same-sex marriage. And it is with regard to this issue that the weaknesses of the movement and its component national organizations are most obvious. To date, these organizations have orchestrated a hodgepodge of offensive and defensive strategies and tactics that have left movement supporters puzzled and disheartened while they have emboldened opposition forces to continue their pursuit of additional anti–gay marriage statewide initiative victories across the country. That it took the debacle of the 2004 elections to force gay and lesbian rights groups to come together for the first time to reach simple consensus on the basics of an agenda is illustrative of the current state of the movement, such as it is. There is some degree of division of labor, with Lambda Legal, the ACLU Lesbian and Gay Rights Project, the National Center for Lesbian Rights, and a few other organizations focusing of litigation in the states and the Human Rights Campaign focusing on federal-level activities, but there is a distinct lack of a movement-wide strategic vision to guide such groups through the next decade.

TABLE 4.3. Members of the National Policy Roundtable.

ACLU Lesbian and Gay Rights Project	Log Cabin Republicans
Audre Lorde Project	Mautner Project for Lesbians with Cancer
BiNet USA: National Bisexual Network	National Association of Lesbian,
Children of Lesbians and Gays Everywhere	Gay, Bisexual, and Transgender
Dignity USA	Community Centers
equalityproject.org	National Black Justice Coalition
Family Pride Coalition	National Center for Lesbian Rights
Federation of LGBT Statewide Advocacy	National Center for Transgender Equality
Organizations	National Coalition for Anti-Violence
Freedom to Marry	Programs
Gay and Lesbian Alliance Against Defamation	National Consortium of Directors of
Gay and Lesbian Medical Association	LGBT Resources in Higher Education
Gay and Lesbian Victory Fund	National Lesbian and Gay Task Force
Gay, Lesbian, and Straight Education Network	National Stonewall Democrats
Human Rights Campaign	National Youth Advocacy Coalition
Immigration Equality	Parents, Families, and Friends of
Institute for Gay and Lesbian Strategic Studies	Lesbians and Gays
International Federation of Black Prides	Pride at Work
International Gay and Lesbian Human	Servicemembers Legal Defense Network
Rights Commission	Two Spirit Press Room
Lambda Legal Defense and Education	World Congress of GLBT Jews
Fund	

Source: Chibbaro 2006, 28.

This is not to say that the top national GLBT organizations have not been sharing information and insights over the years. In fact, a coalition of these groups, the National Policy Roundtable, met in its thirteenth bi-annual session in May 2006. This more formal conclave often takes place behind closed doors, with little media attention given to it. Many of the groups that signed off on the joint statement of purpose discussed above are members of the roundtable, but it also includes more than a dozen additional organizations (see table 4.3). Although this group meets every six months to discuss the current state of the movement, it is not entirely clear that it provides the collective focus and strategic planning necessary to give adequate direction to the movement in 2006 and beyond.

THE CURRENT STATE OF THE GLBT MOVEMENT

There are several reasons for this lack of vision, some particular to the gay and lesbian rights movement and others found more generally in all social movements. The first two reasons often pertain to social movements in the United States but are especially acute in the GLBT movement.

GROWING PAINS

The first difficulty is derived from *growing pains* associated with a rapid increase in the number and size of organizations affiliated with the movement. Two decades ago, gay rights groups had barely any institutional presence in Washington, DC, and, more important, in state capitals across the country. Even with the proliferation of such groups, the movement today, with collective wealth of more than $50 million, is about where the environmental movement was in 1970, prior to the first Earth Day (Shaiko 1999, 24). The resources of the GLBT movement are likely to reach the $1 billion mark far more rapidly than did those of the environmental movement, however. From 1997 to 2002 the movement doubled its collective wealth, thanks in part to the use of the Internet as a fundraising tool (Fox 2002). With more than twenty national organizations and hundreds of state and local groups, the movement has a growing multiplicity of voices, which at times seek similar goals as well as similar funding sources. Over time, the movement will be well served by a winnowing of groups and a consolidation of resources. An additional obstacle for the movement is the comparative paucity of philanthropic support. Whereas the major foundations (for example, the Ford and the Rockefeller Foundations) in the late 1960s and early 1970s provided crucial seed money and significant financial support to fledgling environmental groups, few of these prominent foundations have offered similar support to gay and lesbian rights groups. The Gill Foundation stands alone as the major philanthropic supporter of gay rights organizations as well as HIV/AIDS clinics and support groups across the country (Shaiko 2005, 11–12).

LEADERSHIP AT THE TOP

The second reason for the relative lack of focus in the contemporary gay and lesbian rights movement is *leadership at the top*. Again, this shortcoming is often identifiable in other social movements in the United States at various times. It may be a problem for a small cluster of leading organizations or it may be confined to a single group. In the case of the gay and lesbian rights movement, there is one organization that dwarfs all others—the Human Rights Campaign (HRC). Unfortunately for the movement in general, at the most crucial time in its history, leadership at the HRC has been lacking. It claims to have a national membership of more than six hundred thousand supporters, although the accounting process for "membership" was called into question when it was discovered that anyone who has ever purchased a single bumper sticker from HRC is included in that count (Koval 2005). The HRC currently has its third president in three years, Joe Solmonese, formerly executive director of EMILY's List, an organization dedicated to electing prochoice Democratic women. Apart from pouring significant resources into building its new Washington, DC, headquarters, it is difficult to discern a strategy for success at HRC in the past decade. According to Larry Kramer, founder of Gay Men's Health Crisis and ACT UP, "HRC is an ineffective organization and, apart from its palatial new building, it is more ineffective today than it was a decade ago" (Kramer 2005a).

Solmonese does recognize the problems that he has inherited at HRC and is attempting to chart a new course for the organization. To that end, he undertook a listening tour of "red" states across the country in order to get a better sense of the views of the GLBT communities outside of Washington, DC. He has also discussed the broadening of the HRC's agenda to deal with issues outside the purview of the federal government (Melzer 2005). Although it is too early to pass judgment on Solmonese, there are signs that he is moving in the right direction. It is crucial that HRC serve as the flagship of the gay and lesbian rights movement. It is too well invested with institutional resources simply to exist, to keep its doors open and little more.

THE ALL-OR-NOTHING STRATEGY

The next three reasons for the current difficulties within the gay and lesbian rights movement are particular to its current agendas, strategies, and tactics concerning same-sex marriage. First, the *all-or-nothing strategy* is and will continue to be a political loser (cf. Rauch 2004; Moats 2004). It is amazing to find such a lack of political pragmatism among the leaderships of the national organizations as well as an almost complete lack of understanding of their political opponents and their competing strategies. What is more important, the all-or-nothing strategy simply does not reflect the views of at least half of the gays and lesbians in the United States. In the first comprehensive survey of GLBT adults in the country conducted by Harris Interactive Market Research (2004) for the HRC Foundation in December 2003 (N=748), 51 percent of gay and lesbian respondents believed that "civil unions for same-sex couples are the same as civil marriage or a marriage license for heterosexual couples." Although 78 percent of the respondents preferred being legally married if they were in a committed relationship, it is significant that half of the respondents found no difference between civil unions and marriage. In scouring the HRC website, one cannot find a single reference to this finding.

Unfortunately for the movement, the political horse has left the barn. After the defeats in every state that placed gay marriage bans before voters in 2004, statewide initiatives held in 2005 and 2006 proved to be equally discouraging, with the exception of Arizona in 2006. The recent legislative success in Connecticut in gaining civil union rights should be built on, rather than pursuing the gay marriage strategy at this time. Unfortunately, this is a hard concept to sell, even after the Connecticut victory. According to Kevin Cathcart, executive director of Lambda Legal, "There may be places where it's a necessary political compromise. I don't know that that was the case in Connecticut, but it certainly was the compromise that was struck. I think it's important, though, that we always be focused on the problems with trying to have a separate but equal system, where you have one system for one set of people—that is, marriage for heterosexual people—and another system for another set of people—that is, civil unions or domestic partnerships for lesbians and gay men. Because separate but equal is inherently unequal and ultimately, we would be better served as a country if we had one standard for all families" (Suarez 2005).

THE WE-THEY MENTALITY

Cathcart makes a strong case, but it is not grounded in the political reality of the early twenty-first century. This all-or-nothing approach is derived from the second problem facing the contemporary gay and lesbian rights movement—the pervasive *we-they mentality*. There is an almost total lack of understanding of the political opponents of same-sex marriage and a resulting blanket vilification of all who stand in the way of equal marriage rights. Karl Jones, a former employee of the National Gay and Lesbian Task Force (NGLTF) and now employed by an anti-hunger foundation, aptly summarizes the gay rights organizational mindset: "[T]o work [at NGLTF], we had to kind of dehumanize the people we were working against—that happens all too often in identity politics. I was filled with so much hatred for people working against my cause that I couldn't even see people as human" (Fisher 2005). The result is an almost complete lack of political dialogue between competing interests in the debate.

THE SECULAR LIBERAL IDENTITY

This chasm is broadened by the final and most important problem facing the contemporary gay and lesbian rights movement: its *secular liberal identity*. The contemporary movement leadership is dominated by secular liberals who are unwilling and likely unable to engage their political opponents regarding the political and moral linchpin that divides Americans with respect to same-sex marriage—religion. Gay and lesbian rights groups have given religious conservative organizations and family values groups a free pass on the religious issues relating to gay marriage because they are constrained by their own identity politics, which defines the movement in overtly secular terms (for example, Blasius 2001; Phelan 1994; Rimmerman 2002). Too often the perception of their political opponents is simplistic or muddled. Solmonese offers the following characterization of religious opponents: "There is a right-wing Christian fundamentalist force that is against gay marriage because they truly believe that it is the breakdown of society. But there are a lot of people out there who are advancing this [antigay agenda] because it makes rich people richer and poor people poorer. Because if you buy the idea that voting against gay marriage is going to strengthen your family, you don't think a whole lot about the fact 'No Child Left Behind' has no money behind it, or that there's no money in your kids' school, or that you're not making enough money to have a stable, secure family. I think both things are at work" (Bugg 2005).

Beyond the less-than-clear thinking regarding the motives and strategies of opponents of same-sex marriage, there is a truly telling manifestation of the overarching secular liberal worldview in the construction of the Harris Interactive survey cited above. The Pew Research Center for the People and the Press conducted a national survey of 1,515 adults in October 2003 on the topic of same-sex marriage and published its findings a month before the HRC survey was conducted. Kohut and Dionne, authors of the Pew report, concluded that "opposition to gay marriage has increased since the summer and a narrow majority of Americans also oppose allowing gays and lesbians to enter legal agreements that fall short of marriage. Moreover, despite the overall rise in tolerance toward gays since the 1980s, many Americans remain critical of homosexuals—*and religious belief is a major factor in these attitudes*" (Kohut and Dionne 2003, 1; emphasis added). Yet neither researchers at Harris Interactive nor HRC leaders thought it important to ask any questions regarding the religious affiliations and religiosity of gays and lesbians.

As a result, religious conservatives are free to practice their selective biblical literalism without challenge. It is not clear that gay and lesbian rights leaders, for example, could correctly say whether the book of Leviticus is in the Old Testament or the New Testament, let alone critique the biblical cherry-picking that one finds prevalent in antigay religious rhetoric. It is in Leviticus that one finds reference to homosexuality as an abomination and as an act punishable by death. But also, according to Leviticus, adultery is punishable by death, as is cursing one's parents. Whereas perhaps a decade or two ago cursing one's parents may have resulted in corporal punishment, today children might receive a "timeout" or the loss of their iPods or MP3 players for a week, but certainly not death. Today, according to a recent nationwide Gallup survey, far more Americans find adultery more morally unacceptable than homosexuality; 44 percent of Americans find homosexuality to be morally acceptable, while only 5 percent of Americans find adultery to be morally acceptable. And the frequent result of adultery—divorce—has become commonplace in American society; 66 percent of Americans believe that divorce is morally acceptable (Harper 2005). The Catholic Church has even constructed a religious "do-over" in the form of annulment to push the problem further under the rug. Surely divorce is a far greater plague on American society than homosexuality, yet organized religion has done very little to address this overwhelming societal problem. In a sermon, George Evans of the Evangelical Lutheran Church in America captured the situation facing contemporary religious institutions: "We have swallowed a camel [divorce], and we are choking on a gnat [gay marriage]" (Evans 2005). These are just a couple of examples of ways in which gay and lesbian rights leaders could engage conservative religious leaders, but, unfortunately current leaders are ill-equipped for such a debate.

National gay and lesbian rights leaders must not jettison the grassroots connections made with religious institutions in Michigan and elsewhere during the failed efforts to block the same-sex marriage bans across the country. They should redouble their efforts to maintain and cultivate ties with allied religious groups, whether at the local level or at the national denominational level. One such effort, organized by the National Gay and Lesbian Task Force since 1998, is the National Religious Leadership Roundtable. The roundtable is currently composed of the leaders of three dozen organizations, most of which are faith-based groups (see table 4.4). In addition, the Human Rights Campaign operates the Religion and Faith Project, although it is now subsumed under the HRC Family Project.

TABLE 4.4.   Member organizations of the National Religious Leadership
              Roundtable.

Affirmation International (Gay and Lesbian Mormons)	More Light Presbyterians
Al-Fatiha (Muslim)	National Black Justice Coalition
American Friends Service Committee	New Ways Ministry (Roman Catholic)
Americans United for Separation of Church and State	Parents, Families, and Friends of Lesbians and Gays
Atlanta Interfaith AIDS Network	People for the American Way
Brethren Mennonite Council for Lesbian and Gay Concerns	Q Spirit
Center for American Progress	Reconciling Ministries Network (United Methodist)
Center for Lesbian and Gay Studies in Religion and Ministry	Religious Organizing Project of Kentucky
Christian Lesbians Out	River Fund NY/Majaya Kashi Ashram (Hindu)
Dignity USA (Catholic)	Seventh-Day Adventist Kinship International
Disciples Justice Action Network	Soulforce
Ecumenical Catholic Church	United Church of Christ Coalition for LGBT Concerns
Gay, Lesbian Affirming Disciples	
Human Rights Campaign	United Church of Christ Wider Church Ministries
Institute for Welcoming Resources	
Integrity (Episcopalian)	Women's Alliance for Theology, Ethics, and Ritual
Kashi Ashram (Hindu) Keshet	
Lutherans Concerned/North America	World Congress of GLBT Jews
Metropolitan Community Churches	

Source: National Gay and Lesbian Task Force (http://thetaskforce.org/ourprojects/nrlr/ index.cfm).

A CALL FOR SPIRITED POLITICAL ENGAGEMENT

The current state of the gay and lesbian movement as it relates to the issue of gay marriage is not very healthy. For the most part, GLBT organizations are on the defensive and have little in the way of a proactive agenda to counter the efforts of the religious conservatives and family values groups across the country. Unless and until movement activists and leaders are willing to engage their opponents in a spirited dialogue about the place of gays and lesbians in our society, they are destined, at least for the next few decades, to remain second-class citizens. Undertaking such a debate would require a significant retooling of the leaderships, infrastructures, and institutional mindsets of many GLBT organizations. The secular liberal approach to gay rights has failed; it is time to learn the lessons of social movements of the past. Jim Wallis, one of the few voices of the religious Left in America today, makes an important point: "The truth is that most of the important movements for social change in

America have been fueled by religion—progressive religion. The stark moral challenges of our time have once again begun to awaken this prophetic tradition" (Wallis 2005, 19).

FIRST, KNOW THY CONSTITUENCY:
GAYS, LESBIANS, AND RELIGION

I cannot overemphasize how glaring a mistake it was not to include survey questions about religious affiliation and religiosity on the 2003 HRC national survey of GLBT adults. At this point, there are virtually no systematic data about the religious affiliations or lack of affiliation of gays and lesbians in the United States. Without such data, one is left to make an educated guess about their religious activity.

If, as one might expect, there is a significant fall-off in religious affiliation among gays and lesbians, then the issue of same-sex "marriage" becomes less important. In my earlier research on the environmental movement I found a significant religious fall-off among environmentalists belonging to national environmental groups. Whereas national surveys typically identify 85 percent to more than 90 percent of respondents as having some religious affiliation (the 2003 Pew study found less than 9 percent of its survey sample to be unaffiliated; Kohut and Dionne 2003, 22), I found in a sample of more than three thousand environmentalists that only 60 percent were affiliated with an organized religion—a fall-off of more than 25 percent from the national average (Shaiko 1987; Shaiko 1999, 124–25). Given the less than welcoming attitude of many organized religious institutions toward gays and lesbians, one would expect to find an even greater fall-off among them.

If this is the case, then the religious institution of marriage is not likely to be a terribly attractive alternative to these constituents. Nonbelievers—gay, lesbian, or heterosexual—should be uninterested in marriage and should prefer civil unions, given the clear religious connotation that marriage has in contemporary American society. Therefore, it would seem to be quite important to understand the religious attitudes of gays and lesbians before drawing such sweeping conclusions regarding the all-or-nothing strategy toward same-sex marriage. The second issue that the potential fall-off in religious affiliation raises is the role of the states in marriage.

WHY IS THE RELIGIOUS INSTITUTION OF
MARRIAGE REGULATED BY THE STATES?

It is not clear why gay and lesbian rights organizations *as well as religious institutions* have not challenged the role of the states and the federal government in regulating marriage. From a governmental perspective, the joining of two people is a contractual obligation involving rights, privileges, and responsibilities that link the citizen with the state (for example, taxation and property rights). This union is and should be separate and apart from the religious institution of marriage and should not bear the label of marriage.

Ironically, the Catholic Church should be the most vocal ally in such a debate, because marriage in the Catholic Church is a sacrament. In most Protestant religions, only baptism and communion are sacraments. One can only imagine the outcry from Catholic parishioners on Sundays if they found the seal of the State of Texas or the Commonwealth of Virginia stamped into their communion wafer or if the holy water used in baptism had a state seal on the top as if it were a bottle of alcohol regulated by the states. Yet the Catholic Church, a global institution, allows the various states to dictate the definitions of marriage. Most organized religions, or at least the Judeo-Christian religions, are global phenomena; they know no territorial borders. I, for example, am a member of the Evangelical Lutheran Church in America, not *of* America. The Bible, translated at least in part into more than one thousand languages, is still the Bible, regardless of the language in which it is written. Why, then, should any of the states or any federal government dictate the definition of marriage? That most religions are content with the interpretation of marriage as it stands reflects laziness on their part regarding the intrusion of the government into religion.

The recent efforts to restart the Federal Marriage Amendment process shed light on the federal role in regulating marriage in 2006. A similar effort was made in the U.S. Senate in July 2004 to amend the Constitution to declare that marriage is limited to one man and one woman. It needed a two-thirds majority to pass but was defeated by a 48–50 vote. In 2006, not only were the GLBT organizations mobilized along with the National Religious Leadership Roundtable but, equally important, groups that are not usually viewed as closely aligned with the gay and lesbian rights movement were involved as well. Some of the strongest calls for defeat of the FMA came from such strange political bedfellows as the National Organization for Women (NOW) and the Cato Institute. Kim Gandy, president of NOW, condemned the Senate amendment as it passed out of committee on a straight party-line vote, saying, "The Federal Marriage Amendment is discriminatory, cruel, and contrary to the fundamental guarantees of the Constitution" (Gandy 2006). Later, on the NOW Web site, a call for action by members included the following: "The mis-named 'Marriage Protection Amendment" (S.J. Res. 1) is an attempt to etch discrimination into our Constitution and declare second-class status for LGBT individuals, especially those who want to marry the person they love" (NOW 2006).

Dale Carpenter, a law professor affiliated with the Independent Gay Forum, writing for the libertarian Cato Institute, declared the FMA to be "unnecessary, anti-federalist, and anti-democratic." He added, "Never before in the history of the country have we amended the Constitution in response to a threatened (or actual) state court decision. Never before have we amended the Constitution to preempt an anticipated federal ruling. Never before have we adopted a constitutional amendment to limit the states' ability to control their own family law. Never before have we dictated to states what their own laws and state constitutions mean. Never before have we amended the Constitution to restrict the ability of the democratic process to expand individual rights. This is no time to start" (Carpenter 2006, 16–17). Although the amendment failed in June 2006 to gain the two-thirds majority vote necessary to continue the amendment process, it gained the support of a majority of senators for the first time.

WHERE ARE THE RELIGIOUS LEFT AND THE CIVIL RIGHTS MOVEMENT?

Aside from the lack of a broad challenge to the role of the states in the institution of marriage, the religious debate concerning same-sex marriage is dominated by leaders of conservative religious institutions. Comparatively little is offered in support of gay and lesbian rights by more progressive Protestant denominations in the United States. That is not to say that there are not any progressive churches and synagogues that are welcoming of gays and lesbians—there are. The Episcopalian Church, the Lutheran Church, the United Church of Christ, and other denominations have issued doctrinal statements in support of gays and lesbians and opened communion to all who believe. The Episcopal Church offers blessings for the joining of gays and lesbians. The Lutheran Church recently choked on a gnat and rejected similar blessings this summer after five years of debate about the issue. Nonetheless, there is virtual silence in the policy domain on the part of progressive religious institutions.

Not a word has been uttered by the leader of the National Council of Churches (NCC), Bob Edgar, or his organization about same-sex marriage. When asked about the position of the NCC, a large umbrella group representing more than a dozen Protestant denominations, Brenda Girton-Mitchell, its associate general secretary for justice and advocacy, stated plainly, "[W]e are silent on the issue" (Girton-Mitchell 2005). What a sad commentary in the face of the antigay rhetoric offered by conservative religious clergy. Similarly, leaders of the contemporary civil rights movement in the United States have been strangely silent about the discrimination inflicted on gays and lesbians. Leaders of the GLBT movement need to hold the collective feet of the leaders religious Left and the civil rights movement to the fire and demand their support. Alternatively, they need to expose the hypocrisy of their collective silence.

At the same time, GLBT organizations need to jettison the all-or-nothing approach to religious institutions. A 2006 study conducted by the NGLTF titled "David v. Goliath: A Report on Faith Groups Working for Lesbian, Gay, Bisexual and Transgender Equality (and What They're Up Against)" is methodologically weak and reaches some less-than-nuanced conclusions by placing the Episcopal Church in the United States and the Evangelical Lutheran Church in America in the category of "anti-gay opponents" with the Roman Catholic Church and the Institute on Religion and Democracy (Lindsay and Stern 2006, 14–25). Some denominations are more open to and welcoming of GLBT individuals than are others. It is important to acknowledge those differences and to take advantage of the outreach by engaging in dialogue, rather than condemning actions or inactions of religious institutions.

Unfortunately, a prime opportunity for gay rights groups and progressive religious institutions to come together was missed when, in May 2005, the American Psychological Association announced at its annual meeting that it supports and urges "legal recognition of same-sex marriage" ("Top Psychiatric Group" 2005). The argument made by the APA is grounded in a basic biblical precept found in Genesis and elsewhere that humans on this earth are not meant to live apart. The response to this pronouncement from progressive religious organizations was silence.

THIS, TOO, SHALL PASS: AGE AND ATTITUDES
TOWARD GAYS AND LESBIANS

Failing any effort to bridge the gap between religious institutions and gays and lesbians, there is some small consolation that the future of the fight for gay and lesbian rights is potentially much brighter. Just as religion is a significant factor in public perceptions of gays and lesbians, so, too, is age. By virtually all measures, older Americans are more antigay than are younger cohorts. Education is also related to age in public perceptions of gays and lesbians (that is, undereducated elders are even more antigay than their educated age cohorts). In the 2003 Pew study, only 20 percent of respondents aged sixty-five and older had favorable views of gays and lesbians; conversely, more than half of respondents aged eighteen to twenty-four had favorable views. Regarding the issue of gay marriage, opposition peaks at 88 percent among seventy-year-olds in the survey; opposition to gay marriage remains below 50 percent among those aged eighteen to thirty-five (Kohut and Dionne 2003, 4, 11). In fact, among incoming college freshmen, support for gay marriage climbed from 51 percent to 59 percent between 1997 and 2004 (Saenz et al. 2004). If current trends continue, support for gay marriage will span all age groups in two generations. The question remains, is it necessary to wait that long?

TAKING A STAND FOR THE MOVEMENT

One would think that the leaders of gay and lesbian rights groups and progressive religious institutions will not let this become a war of attrition. They will win that war, but it will take forty years or more. Instead, it is time for these groups and institutions to take a stand, to call out organized religion for its shortcomings. But this stand must be preceded by some collective soul-searching on the part of gays and lesbians regarding the perceptions Americans have of them and why such perceptions are held.

Larry Kramer, founder of ACT UP, on November 7, 2004, took the podium at the Cooper Union in New York City and issued a damning indictment of the gay and lesbian rights movement but also, in essence, spoke truth to powerlessness. He concluded his remarks with the following advice, which should be taken to heart by all those concerned about the future of gay and lesbian rights.

And how do we claim the God that they have gobbled up for their own private reserve? If they have been able to convince this country that the Republicans are the party of the people, surely so many sons and daughters can be smart enough to find a way to sell our parents on the idea of permission to coexist, one nation, under their same God.

I do not know how to answer any of this. And I don't think anyone among us does either. To talk out loud about what our bodies have done and continue to do is asking for trouble. How do we admit our past, and for some of us our present, and own it, and evolve from it and move on? For we must do this. If, for one reason alone, to keep ourselves alive. We cannot afford to lose many more of us along the wayside.

I know some of you will immediately jump up to act. I caution [against] rushing off to form anything quite so fast until we decide how we want to deal with what I have raised tonight. I know many of you are prepared to tough it out and to say to them, "Fuck you, I am what I am." And point out quite rightly that they have simply pushed us too far and, no matter what we have done and continue to do, we simply cannot allow them to treat us this way any longer. We are human beings as much as they are, and their God is the same as everyone else's God and He simply cannot be allowed to be as punishing as they are requiring Him to be. . . .

These are the problems we must confront as we go forward. If you are going to fight in a united way, which I hope that you are convinced is the only way that can save us, we must find a platform that all of us can support without divisiveness and shame and guilt and all the other hateful weapons they club us with. (Kramer 2005b, 83–85)

There are some leaders in the gay and lesbian rights movement who are heeding some of Kramer's advice. In May 2005, Matt Foreman, executive director of the National Gay and Lesbian Task Force, took up the cause in an editorial in the *Washington Blade,* a gay newspaper in Washington, DC: "We must put others on the spot to stand up and fight for us. As the cascade of lies pours forth from the Ant-Gay Industry, morality demands that non-gay people speak out with the same vehemence as they would if it was another minority under attack. Ministers and rabbis must be challenged with the question, 'Where is your voice?' Elected officials who meet with and attend events of the Anti-Gay Industry must be met with the challenge, 'How can you do that? How is that public service?'" (Foreman 2005). Other leaders have received similar advice. Joe Solmonese would be wise to heed the recommendation he received during his tour of the red states—"a scriptural showdown in which alternative perspectives on the teachings of Jesus convince people that gay men and lesbians deserve equality" (Melzer 2005).

The contemporary gay and lesbian rights movement has reached a critical point in its existence. It is crucial that its leaders refocus their attention on new ways of engaging both their allies and their opponents. A more spirited approach by the leaders, combined with a more nuanced strategy that is open to compromise and middle-ground perspectives, will be more fruitful. Successful social movements are guided by a clear vision but are flexible enough to respond to changing political environments. According to Dale Carpenter, a law professor affiliated with the Independent Gay Forum, "[R]eform movements need both idealists and pragmatists. Without idealists, the pragmatists have no idea where to go. Without pragmatists, idealists have no idea how to get there." With regard to the issue of gay marriage, he calls for a more pragmatic approach. "Pragmatism means compromise. If we stamp our feet and demand marriage, and nothing less, we will get nothing" (Carpenter 2005).

What is desperately needed in the current situation is a healthy dose of pragmatism to match the idealism of the movement. In addition, there must be a broadening of the secular liberal mindset that is pervasive in the movement leadership today. The status quo will be a losing proposition for the gay and lesbian rights movement for at least the next forty years.

REFERENCES

Blasius, Mark, ed. 2005. *Sexual identities, queer politics*. Princeton: Princeton University Press.

Brandt, Doreen. 2005. Gay rights groups find common ground. www.365Gay.com. January 13, 1–3. http://www.365Gay.com/newscom05/01/011305rts.Statement.

Bugg, Sean. 2005. Finding common ground: Joe Solmonese takes the helm at HRC. (Washington, DC) *Metro Weekly*, May 12, 29–34.

Carpenter, Dale. 2005. Winning the right way. (Washington, DC) *Metro Weekly*, April 28, 16–18.

Evans, George. 2005. Sermon. Lutheran Church of the Redeemer, McLean, VA, 11:00 A.M. Service, April 17.

Fisher, Marc. 2005. A no-bash bash for gays and evangelicals. *Washington Post*, May 24, B1.

Foreman, Matt. 2005. Time to go for the gut. *Washington Blade*, May 12, 34.

Fox, Kara. 2002. Blade surveys smaller national gay rights groups. *Washington Blade*, April 12, 20–21.

Girton-Mitchell, Brenda. 2005. Telephone interview with the author, April 19.

Harper, Jennifer. 2005. Parties split on nation's morals: Survey looks at U.S. values. *Washington Times*, May 17, A4.

Harris Interactive Market Research. 2004. Strategic Insights Survey. Conducted for the Human Rights Campaign Foundation. February 18.

Kohut, Andrew, and Dionne, E. J. 2003. Republicans unified, Democrats split on gay marriage: Religious beliefs underpin opposition to homosexuality. Pew Research Center for the People and the Press. November 18.

Koval, Steve. 2005. HRC "members" include all who ever donated $1. *Washington Blade*, May 6, 1.

Kramer, Larry. 2005a. Interview and book signing, Lambda Rising Bookstore. Washington, DC, April 24.

———. 2005b. *The tragedy of today's gays*. New York: Tarcher/Penguin Group.

Melzer, Eartha. 2005. HRC leader wraps tour of "red states." *Washington Blade*, May 20, 12.

Moats, David. 2004. *Civil wars: The battle for gay marriage*. Orlando, FL: Harvest Books/Harcourt.

Nieves, Evelyn. 2005. "Gay Rights Groups Map Common Agenda." *Washington Post*, January 17, A3.

Phelan, Shane. 1994. *Getting specific: Postmodern lesbian politics*. Minneapolis: University of Minnesota Press.

Rauch, Jonathan. 2004. *Gay marriage: Why it is good for gays, good for straights, and good for America*. New York: Henry Holt.

Resnick, Eric. 2005. The gay agenda: 22 national groups adopt a joint statement of purpose with eight goals. www.gaypeopleschronicle.com, January 14, 1. http://www.gaypeopleschronicle.com/stories05/january05jan14-stl.htm.

Rimmerman, Craig. 2002. *From identity to politics: The lesbian and gay movements in the United States*. Philadelphia: Temple University Press.

Saenz, Victor, Silvia Hurtado, Nida Deason, Alexander Astin, Leticia Oseguora, and Angela Locks. 2004. Trends in political attitudes and voting behavior among college freshmen and early career college graduates: What issues drive the election? Higher Education Research Institute/UCLA. Research Report no. 1 (October).

Shaiko, Ronald G. 1987. Religion, politics, and environmental concern: A powerful mix of passions. *Social Science Quarterly* 68:244–62.

———. 1999. *Voices and echoes for the environment: Public interest representation in the 1990s and beyond*. New York: Columbia University Press.

———. 2005. Making the connection: Organized interests, political representation, and the changing rules of the game in Washington politics." In *The interest group connection: Electioneering, lobbying, and policymaking in Washington*, 2d ed., ed. Paul S. Herrnson, Ronald G. Shaiko, and Clyde Wilcox, 1–24. Washington, DC: Congressional Quarterly Press.

Suarez, Ray. 2005. Out in front on marriage. PBS *NewsHour with Jim Lehrer*. Transcript, n.p. April 14.

Top psychiatric group urges making gay marriage legal. *Washington Post*, May 23, A2.

Wallis, Jim. 2005. *God's politics: A new vision for faith and politics in America*. San Francisco: HarperCollins.

THEOLOGICAL PERSPECTIVES
ON GAY UNIONS

THE UNEASY MARRIAGE OF RELIGION AND POLITICS

Kenneth D. Wald and Graham B. Glover

It was April 2005. The caller was puzzled. The *Odyssey* program on Chicago Public Radio had been concerned with the politics of liberal Christians when the discussion veered to the controversial topic of same-sex marriage. The caller was floored by one speaker's claim that liberal Christians believed that gay marriage was entirely consistent with their religious tradition. He understood that believing Christians could legitimately take different positions with regard to many public issues because scripture was not always clear or definitive. But because the Bible is absolutely clear about the immorality of homosexuality, the caller asserted, no believing Christian could even pretend to consider marriage between two people of the same gender as somehow sanctioned by traditional religious beliefs. One could only find arguments to support gay marriage, he insisted, by dispensing altogether with religion.[1]

That caller is not alone. To judge by the rhetoric of American public life and polling data, many religious Americans do indeed believe that there is only one side to the debate about gay marriage (Saucier and Caw-man 2004). In this chapter, we take another look at the religious roots of attitudes toward the gay marriage controversy. The chapter is organized around two key themes. First we explore the theological underpinnings of attitudes toward gay marriage in a number of American religious traditions. In doing so, we emphasize that religion provides multiple perspectives on the question, not just one "authentic" position. The review demonstrates that supporters and opponents of gay marriage believe that their positions are consistent with biblical morality. The second part of the chapter examines the expression of such religious perspectives in the political conflict over same-sex marriage. Although theology may be the idiom of the debate, the question is resolved through the political process. Before religious values can be connected to certain political positions, congregants must both believe that law should reflect religious doctrine and accept the church's position as their own—neither of which is guaranteed. As we show, political elites play key roles in helping believers come to understand how to apply their faith to this policy question.

THEOLOGIZING SAME-SEX MARRIAGE

Although this question is ultimately resolved through the political process, many supporters and opponents of same-sex marriage ground their positions in their respective understandings of religion. To be sure, there are a number of factors that contribute to these understandings. This section of the chapter focuses primarily on one: namely, how various religious bodies and their elites utilize the authority of sacred scripture in articulating a theological position supportive of or opposed to same-sex marriage. But before we examine this factor, we offer a brief theoretical background to the normative issues surrounding same-sex marriage. Although the later part of this chapter illustrates the distinction between "church religion" and "lived religion," understanding the sacred scripture factor and the theoretical background of these issues remains critically important because they are regularly cited as key motivating factors in determining attitudes toward same-sex marriage (Pew Research Center 2003).

Determining the position of a sacred scripture on the issue of same-sex marriage is complicated by the very act of interpreting holy writ. Unlike mathematics, a field where concepts are expressed with great precision by unambiguous equations, religious codes are transmitted by the inexact vehicle of human language. Because many foundational religious documents were written in archaic languages and subsequently translated and retranslated into the vernacular, the meaning of words is subject to debate. As anybody who has ever attempted to translate a joke will understand, much can be lost when words and concepts from one language are forced into another tongue. Moreover, scripture often speaks through literary devices such as poetry, metaphor, and simile, making it necessary to render such rich and multifaceted concepts into prosaic prose. In the face of these challenges, religious bodies differ in how they go about extracting meaning from their most authoritative codes.

The contrasting approaches to scripture often parallel the various approaches used by judges and scholars to interpret the U.S. Constitution (original meaning versus current meaning, static meaning versus changing meaning). On one hand are those who believe that scripture means what it says, irrespective of historical or cultural circumstance, never changing or losing its original intent. The meaning is there in the words on the page, available to all who apply human reason and respect the text. On the other, there are those who believe that scripture doesn't always mean what it says, is contextualized within a specific historical and cultural experience, and always has the possibility of changing, never exclusively beholden to its original intent. Interpretation is inevitable.

Consequently, inquiries into what sacred scriptures say about same-sex marriage rarely yield a consensus. Within their traditions' frame of reference, theologians and others who attempt to apply religious values to policy debates do their best to offer reasoned and theologically coherent arguments about same-sex marriage, arguments that do in fact have a scriptural foundation. For an example of an argument that regards scripture as offering a clear, fixed meaning, we turn to a perspective offered in 2003 by the prefect of the Congregation for the Doctrine of Faith of the Roman Catholic Church: "The Church's teaching on marriage and on the complementarity of the sexes reiterates a truth that is evident to right reason and recognized as such by all the major cultures of the world. Marriage is not just any relationship between human beings. It was established by the Creator with its own nature, essential properties and purpose. No ideology can erase from the human spirit the certainty that marriage exists solely between a man and a woman." This argument by the future Pope Benedict XVI is rooted in the Roman Catholic Church's understanding of sacred scripture, a reading which suggests that homosexual acts are condemned "as a serious depravity" (cf. Romans 1:24–27; 1

Corinthians 6:10; 1 Timothy 1:10) and thus cannot become the legitimate basis for a sacred union (Ratzinger 2003, paras. 2, 4).

But if there is no single authoritative position among sacred scriptures on the issue of same-sex marriage, as many might originally be led to believe, where do religious bodies and elites garner scriptural support to educate their flocks about this contentious issue? Enter scriptural commentary on homosexuality. Most official statements about same-sex marriage made by religious bodies in the United States are intimately connected to the respective body's more explicit position concerning homosexuality (Siker 1994; Melton 1991). In other words, what various religious bodies say about same-sex marriage is often indicative of what they say about homosexuality. This is why statements about homosexuality are more readily and easily employed by clergy or religious elites in their discourses about same-sex marriage with their respective congregations or religious organizations (Olson and Cadge 2002).

Just as they differ with respect to same-sex marriage, American religious bodies part company in their understanding of homosexuality. Because those on both sides of the issue believe that scripture supports their position, the ultimate question for the religiously and politically active American citizen is how to interpret the numerous scriptural references used in the debate. There are any number of sources that summarize the varying interpretive means used in this debate and among religious traditions (for example, Via and Gagnon 2003; Balch 2000). Mirroring the different interpretive positions of constitutional scholars, theological interpretations of homosexuality and same-sex marriage often can be boiled down to either a traditional understanding of scripture (opposed to same-sex marriage) or a progressive one (supportive of it). As Olson and Cadge (2002) suggest, these understandings of scripture are important to grasp, because they often lead to even larger assumptions about religious attitudes. "Homosexuality is about scripture: How is the Bible to be read, interpreted, and understood? It is about creation: How ought the people that God creates behave sexually? Homosexuality is about families and reproduction: Who can be married? Bear children? Adopt children? Raise children? What lessons should those children be taught about sexual behavior? Homosexuality also raises important questions about who can serve the church and about how those people and the church are to act in the world" (155).

These questions explain why the interpretation of scripture and its use in forming religious and subsequent political positions with regard to homosexuality remain at the forefront of any discussion of same-sex marriage. Without understanding how religious bodies interpret their respective scriptures, one is hard pressed to fully comprehend their position on homosexuality and same-sex marriage.

This theoretical background sets the stage for examining the theological underpinnings that religious bodies use in interpreting sacred scriptures about homosexuality and same-sex marriage. For purposes of understanding how religious positions on same-sex marriage (typically either for or against) are effectively politicized, this chapter highlights some of the more commonly referenced scriptural arguments in American religious and political discourse. For the sake of simplicity, we organize our discussion of theological interpretations of homosexuality and same-sex marriage around two poles, one traditional, the other progressive.

THE TRADITIONALIST PERSPECTIVE

The Southern Baptist Convention (SBC), one of America's more conservative Christian denominations, has a brief yet succinct position statement on issues of sexuality. It notes, "We affirm God's plan for marriage and sexual intimacy—one man, and one woman, for life. Homosexuality is not a 'valid alternative lifestyle.' The Bible condemns it as sin. It is not, however, an unforgivable sin. The same redemption available to all sinners is available to homosexuals. They, too, may become new creations in Christ" (Southern Baptist Convention 2005).

This statement, in spite of its brevity, highlights some of the key assumptions about homosexuality and same-sex marriage among traditional interpreters of scripture. These include, but are not limited to, the following: (1) Sexual relations are to occur solely among persons who are married. Sex outside of marriage (homo-, hetero-, or bisexuality) is condemned as contrary to the word and will of God. (2) Marriage is at all times understood as occurring between one man and one woman. For the traditionalists, scriptural references are clear that marriage is never meant for those of the same sex or between more than two persons.[2] (3) Marriage is forever. In principle, divorce is understood to be a sin, and because most scriptural references concerning divorce are set in a context of man and woman, same-sex marriages are not assumed to be part of any legitimate conversation about marriage. (4) In practice, homosexuality is never accepted as a valid sexual lifestyle.[3] Neither are same-sex marriages. According to the traditionalists, the Bible is clear in its condemnation of such a lifestyle. Among those of a Judeo-Christian background, passages from the creation account in Genesis (chapters 1–2), the story of Sodom and Gomorrah (Genesis 19:1–28), the laws given in Leviticus (cf. chapters 18 and 20), and Paul's comments on sexuality in Romans, 1 Corinthians, and 1 Timothy are most often used in making their positions clear. (5) However sinful homosexuality and same-sex marriage may be, neither are unforgivable sins. This statement by the SBC and other traditionalists becomes important below when we show that political action among those with religious affiliation does not always correspond to the teachings of their religious organization. (6) Even though scripture condemns homosexuality (and consequently, same-sex marriage), there remains room for forgiveness, as noted above, and perhaps more important, conversion. The latter point becomes especially salient when discussing the distinction between religious and political positions and action regarding same-sex marriage.

In November 2003, a group of Baptist theologians sympathetic to the statement quoted above met at Midwestern Baptist Theological Seminary, where they prepared the "Kansas City Declaration on Marriage" (Land et al. 2003). Writing in response to the perceived threat of legalized same-sex marriages in the United States and elsewhere, these theologians further elaborated on their scripture-based opposition to same-sex marriage. Though authored by Baptists, the beliefs contained therein are commonly shared by those who oppose the practice within a Judeo-Christian background. First, they note that "marriage is the foundational institution of human culture," citing passages from Genesis 2:18–22, Matthew 19:3–9, Ephesians 5:22–23, 6:1, 1 Thessalonians 2:7, 11, and 1 Timothy 5:4. Recalling the words of Pope Benedict XVI, cited above, these traditionalists believe that any conversation about or understanding of marriage that does not assume one man and one woman runs the risk of destroying human culture through a deterioration of the family. The declaration continues, "The first social institution was marriage. As the foundation of the family, marriage is the foundational cultural institution. . . . A family established on the marriage between a man and a woman forces the cultivation of these characteristics in ways that other relationships do not." For the traditionalists, any interpretation of scripture that discusses family must begin with the creation story of Genesis and as such must only include a marriage between one man and one woman. Similarly, the General Assembly of the Presbyterian Church in America adopted a Declaration of Conscience in 1993 that read: "Mr. President, in this Declaration the General Assembly of the Presbyterian Church in America humbly declares its conscience concerning the moral legitimacy of homosexuality. God has spoken without equivocation through his Word declaring homosexuality to be perversion of his created order, his moral law, and the foundations of society" (Presbyterian Church in America 1993).

David Novak finds this same understanding in traditional Judaism. According to Novak, "There are few prohibitions that are more unambiguous than the traditional Jewish prohibition of male homosexual acts. . . . Furthermore, however different the respective penalties might be for homoerotic acts, the fact is that in Rabbinic Judaism any prohibited act is considered deserving of divine punishment" (Novak 1998, 12). He continues along the lines of the Kansas City Declaration. "As the Bible puts is, 'A man shall leave his father and his mother and cleave unto his wife, and they shall become one flesh' (Genesis 2:24). In traditional Jewish exegesis, 'one flesh' refers to the heterosexual couple themselves who intend to conceive a child by their union, and the child itself who results from their permanent, sustained union" (ibid., 15). Similarly, the Kansas City Declaration notes, "Marriage creates one unity out of two corresponding genders," citing Genesis 2:23–24, Matthew 19:4–6, Mark 10:6–9, 1 Corinthians 6:16, and Ephesians 5:22–23. In their interpretation of these scriptural passages, the traditionalists further maintain that this unity of one flesh is not possible among those of the same sex. Consequently, "By definition, homosexual marriage is incapable of achieving this 'one flesh' union. Therefore, we reject the notion that homosexual marriage is equal to heterosexual marriage."

These traditional scriptural interpretations and references to homosexuality are not unique to Christianity and Judaism but extend to Islam as well. Most Muslim clerics note the Koran's story of Lot and God's subsequent punishment of his homosexual behavior (7:80–84 and 26:160–75) as reasons to oppose same-sex marriages (Duran 1993). Such punishment, Muslims note, would not be found among righteous heterosexual believers.

By abandoning these beliefs, traditionalist interpreters of scripture contend, individuals abandon the word of God and society sanctifies actions contrary to sacred scripture. When the United States Congress took up the Federal Marriage Amendment in 2003, the president of the Lutheran Church's Missouri Synod summarized the traditionalists' outrage (Kieschnick 2003): "Incredible as it seems, if current trends and momentum continue, the day may be coming when the legal definition of marriage in our country is changed forever—when 'marriage' becomes whatever people want it to be, involving whatever sexes and

configurations of 'spouses' are desired. This, clearly, is not acceptable—
not to those who believe, teach and confess God's plan for marriage and
families as outlined in His Word."

THE PROGRESSIVE PERSPECTIVE

Though perhaps more commonly recognized as *the* religious understanding of homosexuality and same-sex marriage, the traditionalist interpretation is not the only means of evaluating sacred scripture concerning
these issues. Indeed, a respectable number of religious bodies and elites
subscribe to a more progressive interpretation of scripture.

Writing in November 1998, the former president of the United Church
of Christ, the Reverend Paul H. Sherry, noted, "When so many in our society would reject and exclude, it is critical that we of the United Church
of Christ bear witness to the conviction that it is possible to be deeply
faithful to the Bible, profoundly respectful of the historic faith of the
church and its sacraments, and at the same time support the full inclusion
and participation of all God's children in the membership and ministry
of the church. Likewise, there can be no compromise that all persons in
this society must enjoy equal protection under the law" (Sherry 1998).

Like the statement from the Southern Baptist Convention, the ideas
articulated by Sherry highlight some of the key assumptions that un-
derlie progressive interpretation of scripture about homosexuality and
same-sex marriage. These include but are not limited to the following:
(1) Homosexuality and same-sex marriage are compatible with passages from sacred scripture. (2) Such practices are not merely modern
interpretations but are historically supported by scripture and tradition.
(3) Supporting same-sex marriage and acceptance of homosexuals and
homosexual behavior is not only compatible but expected within a religious community. (4) Religious bodies and elites should support legislation that protects all persons, regardless of sexual orientation.

In recent years, a number of religious bodies have championed these
ideals. The Evangelical Lutheran Church in America (ELCA), which
continues to debate its official position on homosexuality and same-sex
marriage, adopted a resolution at its 1996 Church Council that shares
some of the ideas listed above. In 2005 the Task Force for ELCA Studies
on Sexuality left open the possibility of acceptance of homosexual behavior and the potential of ordaining homosexuals into the pastoral ministry.
The Episcopal Church, U.S.A., on the other hand, has not only reviewed
these issues and been willing to engage in theological conversation about

them but has enacted them in regular church practice. On November 2, 2003, only three months after the General Convention of the Episcopal Church approved such action, a New Hampshire diocese consecrated the Reverend Gene Robinson as the church's first openly gay bishop.

When progressive interpreters of scripture are pressed to offer a scriptural basis for their support of same-sex marriage, their responses are twofold: (1) a denial of the passages cited above by the traditionalists and (2) utilization of passages not cited by the traditionalists. With regard to the first point, Victor Paul Furnish notes, "It is sometimes argued that the creation accounts present heterosexuality as intrinsic to the created order, God's intention for humankind, and at least part of what it mean to have been created in the image of God. It has been concluded from this that any kind of a homosexual relationship is fundamentally evil, a perversion of the created order, and contrary to God's will. The texts themselves, however, do not support this interpretation" (quoted in Siker 1994, 22–23).

John Elliot notes that one of the New Testament passages regularly used by traditionalists is taken out of context. Commenting on St. Paul's first letter to the Corinthians, he says, "Paul employed this list in 1 Corinthians 6:1–11, not to make a point about sexual activity, but to respond to a legal problem that had social rather than sexual ramifications" (quoted in Siker 1994, 32). In other words, Paul's commentary had little, if anything, to do with one's sexual orientation, making homosexual activity morally acceptable to Christianity. Similarly, progressive interpreters are quick to point out that the passages from Genesis, Leviticus, Romans, and so on deal not with homosexuality per se but with homosexual rape, prostitution, and molestation. The passages from the Hebrew Bible, they argue, were intended to ensure that Jews refrained from practices common to the pagan communities in Canaan. Because the Israelites had encountered homosexuality only in these forms, they could not even imagine consensual, loving, and committed relationships among adult homosexuals. Hence, progressives believe these passages do not definitively condemn homosexuality or same-sex marriage but reflect the cultural values of a particular time and place.

Reform Jews share this progressive view of sacred scripture:

On the other hand, there are those, not all, who believe that the traditional laws against homosexuality originated in a more ritual context, since, for the most part, the word "abomination" was applied more in the ritual sphere of life than in the ethical. The Torah seems to see homosexual relations in a cultic context rather than something more parallel to the interpersonal context of heterosexual relationships.

Although the sin of Sodom and Gemmorah is apparently homosexuality, later Jewish tradition, including the Biblical prophets, makes no reference to homosexuality and see the sins of Sodom and Gemmorah as cruelty and lack of hospitality to the "stranger"—xenophobia, as it were. Reform Judaism, for the most part, seems to view the traditional prohibitions against homosexuality as mores from a bygone age, mores now replaced with clearer understandings of the reality of gender orientation. (Union of Reform Judaism 2005)

Lest we appear to be suggesting that the traditionalist and progressive perspectives are the only approaches to sacred scriptures, there are interpretations that take a nuanced middle ground. Although previously cited in the traditionalist camp, Roman Catholicism seems to take a mediated stand about homosexuality and same-sex marriage. On one hand, Pope Benedict XVI has referred to homosexuality as "an objective moral disorder," and the Catechism calls it "contrary to the natural law" (*Catechism of the Catholic Church*, 1998, para. 2357). On the other, homosexual inclinations do not become sinful until they are acted upon. In other words, celibate homosexuals do not, according to the Vatican's account, commit sin. Moreover, they stand the chance of perpetually resisting this inclination. The Catechism elaborates this point as well: "By the virtues of self-mastery that teach them their inner freedom, at time by the support of disinterested friendship, by prayer and sacramental grace, they can and should gradually and resolutely approach Christian perfection" (ibid., para. 2359).

The Presbyterian Church U.S.A., the United Methodist Church, and the Episcopal Church U.S.A. also acknowledge different viewpoints and arguments concerning homosexuality and same-sex marriage. Although these bodies tend to maintain official statements that condemn homosexuality as sinful, their congregational practices tend to be both accepting and supportive of persons who openly identify as homosexual.

Robert George suggested (2001, 259) that "[h]omosexual acts have long been condemned as immoral by the natural law tradition of moral philosophy, as well as by Jewish and Christian teaching" (259). Countless Christian and Jewish religious bodies concur with this statement, but such commentary cannot always be taken as the only interpretation of religious teaching among these groups. Although many Jewish, Christian, Muslim, and other sacred scriptures can be read to condemn homosexuality and, consequently, same-sex marriage, a number of religious bodies have recently interpreted these same scriptures differently, creating a variety of religious positions on the morality of these issues.

FROM RELIGION TO POLITICS

The conflict between advocates and opponents of gay marriage is often portrayed as a fundamentally religious controversy. Considering the religious doctrines we have just examined, it is perhaps inevitable that observers draw that conclusion. But if that is so, we need to consider how such an issue migrates from the religious sphere to the political. The translation of religious grievances into political movements is hardly automatic or unambiguous (Wald, Silverman, and Fridy 2005).

In explaining the controversy over issues such as gay marriage, many scholars have embraced the "culture war" model developed by James Davison Hunter (1991). This model asserts that political differences, at base, are about contending cultural values and that cultural values, in turn, are derived in the first instance from basic religious beliefs. In the United States, the argument goes, religious progressives and religious traditionalists are locked into fierce battle over a range of issues that include but are certainly not limited to gay rights or gay marriage. These lines of conflict split denominations internally and from one another.

There are gaping holes in this model. First, it has the nature of a black box: religion → culture → politics. The model is silent on how religious values become transmuted into cultural preferences and, eventually, become associated with political positions. Second, the model consigns politics to a subordinate position. In Hunter's view, the political world is a domain where cultural-religious differences are registered, not an autonomous sphere with some impact on the conflict. The culture war model takes the politics out of a profoundly political conflict.

To understand fully the religious basis of conflict about same-sex marriage, we must consider three other factors: the link between religion and law, the transmission of theology to congregants, and, finally, the way politicians mobilize such values for electoral purposes. The first two factors identify potential barriers between religious concerns and public policy; the last calls attention to the capacity of political entrepreneurs to overcome them by enlisting religious sentiment on behalf of political causes.

RELIGION AND LAW: THE GAP
BETWEEN BELIEF AND ACTION

Although the United States is a deeply religious society, "a nation with the soul of a church" in the words of one foreign observer, it is also a secular state. That status was conferred by the Constitution in Article VI (which outlawed religious qualifications for holding public office) and in the famous religion clauses of the First Amendment. Hence the relation between religious values and public law is problematic (Greenawalt 1993).

Although one can easily enough imagine two extremes, a completely secular state where religion is entirely a private matter and a theocracy where the law reflects religious codes, neither describes accurately how religion influences civil law in the United States. Very few Americans want a theocratic state where a particular religious tradition enjoys unfettered political and moral authority.[4] Americans have accepted the legitimacy of religious pluralism and differences of opinion, at least to some degree. Nonetheless, there remains considerable confusion about how moral values should be implemented via the law (Jelen and Wilcox 1995).[5]

Declaring "that which is morally wrong can never be politically right," the nineteenth-century English statesman William Gladstone sounded the motto of those who believe that law should reflect the basic moral beliefs of a people. The task of the law, Gladstone believed, was to provide rewards for good conduct and punishment for bad, enabling people to live righteously. The relevant moral standards were derived from religion and natural law. The state was properly an agent of moral regeneration and had an obligation to make people act better than their natures might otherwise have dictated. This set of assumptions often underlies opposition to same-sex marriage, considering the practice illegitimate because it contradicts the dominant moral order on marriage and sexuality.

Gladstone's perspective was never universally accepted, and some consider it hopelessly utopian. Some founders of modern political theory believe the state should be limited to providing the basic conditions of human order. Certain practices that disrupt society—for example, murder, rape, and theft—should be restricted by law not because they are necessarily immoral but because they undermine the very purpose of society. Beyond that the law should not go. From this point of view, immoral behavior not directly harmful to the state is the province of religion and conscience rather than government. The task of religion is to educate the conscience of humanity and try to promote behavior that is morally upright. But religion equipped with the coercive power of the state will only stray from its appointed task.[6] Because it separates religion and law, this perspective is more hospitable to gay marriage.

These rival perspectives on religion and law have powered many political conflicts (Kleppner 1979; Wald 1983). The positions are neither inherently liberal nor conservative because they have been adopted at different times by the same movement. Consider how evangelical Protestants have dealt with the issue of race in America. Many southern evangelicals once believed that slavery and racism were not the business of society. If the practices were evil, they would end when enough people were brought to salvation by belief in Christ.[7] Christianity should convert sinners one by one, not redeem society through legislation or collective action (Marsh 1997, chap. 3). Meanwhile, individuals should be free to act according to their own moral codes. So when northern churches and religious leaders condemned discrimination as inconsistent with scripture in the 1950s and 1960s, their southern counterparts objected to religious "meddling in politics." By the late 1970s, however, many of these same critics of religiously inspired political action had changed their tune. With the Supreme Court supposedly undermining the moral order in diverse ways—as they saw it, banning religion from the schools, promoting divorce, encouraging licentiousness—it was necessary for the churches to engage the public sphere. This wasn't "political action," they insisted, but "moral action" to uphold their deepest beliefs. Nonetheless, it required using the law as a means to enshrine morality in public policy, precisely their critique of the antislavery and civil rights movements.

We can view the debate about homosexuality through this lens. The animus against homosexuality was once reflected in laws that explicitly criminalized homosexual conduct. Physical intimacy between same-sex adults was punished by law, perceived by moral traditionalists as behavior that threatened the fundamental order of society. Traditionalists and progressives began sparring in the 1960s when gays and lesbians first pushed for the repeal of these antisodomy laws (Nice 1994, chap. 9), fought during the 1970s and 1980s over efforts to secure antidiscrimination protection for sexual orientation (Button, Rienzo, and Wald 1997), and moved onto new ground in 1990s when gays sought the legal benefits of marriage. In the conflict between law and conscience, traditionalists argued for society to impose legal sanctions against what they perceived as immoral behavior. Believing in the primacy of conscience, progressives contended that the state should take no notice of religious doctrine.

Theology may be consistent with a specific political stance, perhaps through what Tocqueville called an "elective affinity," but it does not guarantee that believers will seek legal status for scriptural morality. As long as some congregants believe that you can't legislate morality, religious values may remain outside the political sphere.

RELIGION: HIGH AND LOW

Even if religious people do believe that law should incorporate religious values, not all churches that condemn homosexuality necessarily mobilize against gay marriage. As we know, only a minority have taken such active steps. In some cases, the barrier results from slippage between churches' theology and members' beliefs.

Approaching religion in politics solely through theology overlooks the important division between "church religion" and religion as experienced in the lives of ordinary church members (Vrijhof and Waardenburg 1979; Sharot 2001; for an example from Catholicism, see Kennedy 1985). (The use of the word *church* is not meant to restrict the argument to Christianity; the difference between the two forms of religiosity extends to virtually all religious traditions.) The existence of multiple forms of religious traditions under a single common name affects the way religious values are brought into political conflict.

Scholars have given different names to the distinction between official and popular religion. Official religion is the product of a formally authoritative hierarchy, expressed in creeds of belief and authorized versions of religious literature, and often codified in religious law. From this perspective, "religion" is what the clergy say it is. Alongside official religion, scholars argue, popular religious commitment is sometimes consistent with and sometimes incompatible with official doctrine (Crapo 1987). It may be highly idiosyncratic and individualistic as each individual strains religious themes through the matrix of his or her personal life experience (Bellah et al. 1985). Popular religiosity, then, seems to be what ordinary people believe and practice, irrespective of church doctrine. Apart from informal or popular religiosity, this religion of the masses has also been called folk religion (Schneider and Dornbusch 1958), the little tradition (Redfield 1962), common religion (Towler 1974), and lived religion (Orsi 2003). In a related conception, Anne Swidler (1986) has urged scholars to treat religion as a cultural "toolkit" rather than a fixed entity with prescribed reactions to each and every eventuality. When faced with difficult issues or challenges, individuals can extract different cultural values from the arsenal of religious possibilities to make sense of what puzzles or upsets them.

Whatever name scholars have assigned to the religious perspectives of ordinary believers, they tend to agree that individuals do not simply absorb official doctrine as would automatons (Dillon 1999). Congregants consider church doctrine but may refine it, adapt it, connect it with other perspectives, and generally construct their own religious worldviews. Certainly, the theological tradition of the church is important, but parishioners do not invariably grant credibility to their spiritual leaders with respect to all issues. They may accommodate perspectives that theologians reject.

Parishioners often find their own way in matters of gender and sexuality. Although the Roman Catholic Church has long argued that artificial birth control is sinful, most Catholic laypersons have stopped listening (Westoff and Bumpass 1973). After all, one might imagine the voices from the pews saying, priests don't have to worry about paying food bills or driving in carpools or saving enough to provide for their children's college education. The same pattern operates in gender roles. On the basis of sermons that reiterate the headship of men and the duty of wives to submit to husbands, one might well imagine that the homes of evangelical Protestants are perfect patriarchies in which males make all the critical decisions. In fact, as studies of what is called gender negotiation reveal, that is not even close to reality. When making decisions about important household matters, husbands and wives in evangelical homes discuss, debate, and come to conclusions in a manner not all that different from the process in the homes of other families in similar social conditions (Bartkowski 2003). Similarly, evangelical women often find creative ways to reconcile strong religious faith with what amounts to feminist consciousness (Ozorak 1996).

In an ethnographic analysis of two United Methodist congregations struggling with the issue of homosexuality, Dawne Moon (2004, 13) emphasized "the mismatch between beliefs and doctrine" in discussions with church members. She wrote of the diverse "everyday theologies" that underlay the discussion. While much of the discourse in the churches drew on the Bible and denominational tradition,

beliefs about what God expects cannot always come directly from Scripture or tradition. Few members of these congregations accepted at face value the scriptural pronouncements that women must keep their heads covered and cannot teach men; none believed that slavery is a righteous and godly social order. Indeed, in these rapidly changing times, people ran into problems and other experiences that even their parents could not have imagined for them. . . . The quandaries that people find themselves in today are sometimes novel, and it took the church members I met a great deal of prayer, study, reflection and discussion to determine what their God expected of them, to determine the right thing to do—and they often came up with very different answers.

For one long-time member of Pullen Baptist Church in Raleigh, North Carolina, which was roiled by a debate about performing a same-sex union, the deciding factor was the discovery that some of the congregants he most admired were gays and lesbians. Explaining his support for the minister's decision to perform the ceremony, "Mike" reported, "It wasn't the scriptural arguments, or the arguments from medicine, or biology, or anything like that. It was seeing [gay] people that I really cared about, that I really respect. People who were intelligent human beings who obviously would not have chosen this way of life if they'd had any say so in the choice" (Hartman 1996, 36).

Armed with everyday theologies that often bear a limited relation to official doctrine, individuals negotiate the controversial waters surrounding the issue of homosexuality and gay marriage. Individuals who belong to religious traditions that regard homosexuality as immoral and gay marriage as an abomination may ignore such concerns, extracting from the tradition only the lessons relevant to their lives. All else may be seen as extraneous, marginal. Similarly, they might choose the strategy of "foregrounding" and "backgrounding," highlighting certain parts of the tradition while giving less attention to other components (Katz 1996). Clearly, they would still have views about what is right or wrong, but they would adopt a live-and-let-live orientation. Christian Smith (1998) found precisely that perspective in his discussion of sexual ethics with a Baptist: "There's nothing wrong with gay marriages. I know homosexuals from work who are married and their marriages lasted longer than mine did. I have also learned they have the exact same kinds of problems I had in my marriage. I know the Bible says homosexuality is wrong, but I just don't think so anymore. I just don't see it. God wants people to be happy. If that's what makes them happy, then fine" (54).

The genius of this comment is its reflection of both the traditional and the progressive interpretation of scripture, an approach that is increasingly played out in the political arena by those affiliated with religious organizations.

For many churchgoers, in sum, beliefs about homosexuality and gay marriage may well bear the imprint of factors outside the church and offer perspectives that clash dramatically with denominational positions. The autonomy of individual believers cautions against assuming that members of a religious community are passive receptacles of official doctrine. The slippage between official doctrine and everyday theology makes it important to consider exactly how religious values become engaged in overt political conflict, the subject of the next section.

POLITICIZING GAY MARRIAGE

Even if we assume that all believers absorb the formal theology of their religious tradition and have no hesitation about putting it into law, that still leaves unclear precisely how religious sentiments are translated into political positions.[8] How is it that some religious positions are politicized effectively? How, for example, did gay marriage become so central to religious traditionalists in the 2004 election?

As an alternative to the static and apolitical framework of Hunter's culture war theory, Leege et al. (2002) developed a model of cultural conflict that better accounts for the process by which religious differences and cultural orientations become grist for political alliances.[9] The critical actors in this process are political elites, primarily but not exclusively public officials. The argument unfolds as follows. Politicians are ambitious and creative power-seekers. They scan the political horizon for social and cultural tensions that have the potential to divide the electorate into competing blocs. In particular, they are on the lookout for what are sometimes called wedge issues, policy questions with the capacity to split off some voter blocs from the other party and thus increase their party's chances of victory. Politics is about convincing your supporters to vote ("stimulating the base") and persuading your opponents to stay home or to switch to your side. This is achieved by educating voters about how an issue position offends their deeply felt sense of moral order (Wildavsky 1987).

Fear and anxiety are the major tools in the effort to depress turnout among the opposition. Ambitious politicians identify issues that trouble key elements of the opposition party and package the issues ("framing," in the language of social science) in terms that arouse strong negative emotions among these potentially wavering groups. This approach rests on strong evidence that fear stimulates learning much more effectively than other emotions and that anxiety about one's favorite party often discourages political participation (Marcus, Neuman, and MacKuen 2000).

Fear and anxiety are best aroused by deploying symbols, shorthand devices that condense information in convenient packages; hence, much political rhetoric involves arresting images, powerful emotional stimuli designed to worry opposing partisans about where their party is going. In perhaps the most famous case of this strategy, the Republicans utilized the specter of Willie Horton, described by one key operative as a "big, black rapist," to paint the 1988 Democratic presidential nominee as soft on crime. The Democrats, one should note, do much the same thing, often likening Republican-oriented religious leaders to would-be ayatollahs eager to invade the private recesses of Americans' lives.

The conflict about homosexuality in general and same-sex marriage in particular is rife with such symbolism. The critics of gay rights have often used AIDS as a powerful symbol of God's antipathy to gays and called attention to the most bizarre examples of homosexual conduct as if they represented the lives of most gay people (Button, Wald, and Rienzo 1997, chap. 1). In the gay marriage debate, they warn of what could happen to American society if "Adam and Steve" displace "Adam and Eve" as the model of marriage. Barry Adam (2003) has called attention to the struggle surrounding gay marriage as a characteristic cycle of "moral panic" in which vivid images and dangers are routinely bandied about to encourage legislative action. The strategy appears to work well on the basis of persuasive evidence that symbolic issue frames dramatically affect how individuals think about policy issues (Sears et al. 1980; Wood and Bartkowski 2004).

Individuals may not realize that some government proposal or policy threatens the moral order until it is pointed out by ambitious politicians. A Florida congressman, Charlie Canaday, demonstrated how it works when he assigned the ominous label of "partial-birth abortion" to a very rarely used medical procedure.[10] He helped create a political movement by publicizing this procedure, hoping it would crystallize the anxieties of moderate Democrats about their party's prochoice position. Many of the women drawn into leadership roles in the Christian Right were tutored about the dangers of "secular humanism" by religious and political elites who tied together a variety of policies (liberalized abortion, gender equality, gay rights) as elements of a conspiracy that would undermine the essence of femininity (Andersen 1988). Conservative churches provided the venue where many religious traditionalists first came to see feminism as a challenge to their most cherished religious customs (Himmelstein 1986).

This may sound excessively cynical, as if politicians are merely engines of ambition without any redeeming values of their own. That judgment would be too harsh, but we do believe that politicians are ambitious office-seekers who capitalize on cultural tensions to advance their careers. They may indeed possess strong moral beliefs, but those beliefs are used instrumentally to advance political standing. The strongest evidence is that public officials often shift their positions on moral issues when it is politically advantageous to do so. Ronald Reagan signed the most liberal abortion law in the United States as governor of California but emerged as a vociferous advocate of the prolife movement when he later sought the Republican nomination for the presidency. Before he ran for the Democratic presidential nomination in 1988, the Reverend Jesse Jackson had been a critic of abortion, a position consistent with his denomination's position on the question. Aware that such a stance would damage his chances with the liberals who tended to dominate Democratic primaries, Jackson campaigned as a prochoice candidate. If their positions had been rooted in immutable religious values alone, such situational changes would not have occurred.

The same behavior has been on display in the gay marriage debate. Several state courts, local officials, and gay activists created a potential political fault line open to elite exploitation. On first seeking the presidency, George W. Bush made it clear he did not believe in punitive action against gays and rejected a constitutional amendment against gay marriage (Kirkpatrick 2005). During his 2004 campaign, however, when the issue became a hot-button concern for the social conservatives he needed to stimulate, he strongly supported such an amendment (Ireland 2003). The attorney general of Massachusetts, Thomas Reilly, one of the most public opponents of a state supreme court ruling that opened the gates to gay marriage in the Bay State, argued the state's case against gay marriage in the courts. When he began to take steps to enter the gubernatorial race in 2006, however, needing to appeal to a liberal Democratic primary electorate, Reilly reported that he no longer opposed gay marriage (Phillips 2005a). Reilly's potential opponent in the 2006 Massachusetts election, incumbent Republican Mitt Romney, portrayed himself as a moderate Republican in 2002 and indicated he would sign a domestic partnership law to forestall gay marriage. When he began a run for the Republican presidential nomination, Romney suddenly told audiences of Republican activists in conservative states that he was an uncompromising opponent of the very policy he had been willing to sign as governor (Phillips 2005b).[11]

It is not merely that politicians may change or modulate their positions in order ride a cultural wave; there is also evidence that they make short-term strategic calculations about what are supposedly immutable moral commitments. As Congress began to discuss legislation against gay marriage in the summer of 2004, House leader Tom DeLay was reportedly incensed by the timing. Discussing the issue in the summer was a waste of political capital because voters were not paying attention. Better to postpone congressional deliberation of the issue until the fall election season, when such activity would cross the radar screens of many voters (Babington 2004). There was an opportunity to capitalize on a cultural issue, but it would be better for the GOP to politicize it later in the electoral cycle.

Religious values pass through the prism of political competition. To surmount the barriers that separate religion and politics, political elites identify cultural tensions, excite voters by deploying vivid images, and enlist sympathizers as allies in political campaigns. Gay marriage became extremely important to many religious people, more so than other equally compelling moral concerns, because it was put on their agenda by political and religious elites in a profoundly political process.

CONCLUSION

As we hope this chapter demonstrates, the link between religion and politics in the gay marriage controversy is more complicated than it may first seem. We have demonstrated that, contrary to the notion that religious institutions and persons are invariably hostile to the idea of gay marriage, theologians have conflicting perspectives on the subject. Opponents and advocates of same-sex marriage find scriptural warrant for their positions. Translating these theological perspectives into political action requires at least three steps. First, members of religious communities must believe that their doctrine should become the foundation of public law rather than a matter for private conscience. Second, church members have to absorb the denominational doctrine as formulated by theologians. These steps may fail, undermining efforts to link religious worldviews with political positions. So, third, political entrepreneurs may step into the breach, activating religious sentiments in the political realm by developing powerful symbols that draw parishioners into political conflict.

We began this chapter with a vignette about one man, a caller to a radio program, who simply took for granted that his religious tradition could support no position other than opposition to gay marriage. As we have tried to show, that position itself reflects a long process involving the construction of one particular theology from many possibilities, the transmission of a particular religious worldview to a parishioner, and the effective linkage of a religious worldview to an issue on the political agenda. Every step along the path reflects the very human dimension of the process by which individuals come to understand and act politically on what they believe to be the word of God.

ENDNOTES

1. The radio call-in program, broadcast on March 18, 2004, is available for download from http://www.chicagopublicradio.org/audio_library/od_rama ro4.asp. The caller addressed his question to the senior author of this chapter.

2. Traditionalist Mormons who continue to support polygamous marriages in defiance of church authorities are clearly the outliers regarding this point. Concerning issues of homosexuality and same-sex marriage, however, they are in agreement with those who oppose such activity and that practice.

3. The very use of *lifestyle* to describe homosexuality is a controversial practice, and we are simply using the language that is customary among advocates of this position. Many gays and lesbians believe there is no lifestyle to homosexuality, that such a label implies that sexual orientation is both chosen and a matter of taste. Rather, they believe, gays are people who live their lives, just as heterosexuals do, with a sexual orientation fixed by birth or early socialization.

4. The principal advocates of theocracy, a school known as dominion theology, call for direct application of what they consider biblical law in the United States. The movement is small and sectarian, and it exerts little influence in American public life.

5. By conflating religion and morality we do not wish to suggest that religion alone provides a basis for a serious moral code.

6. Father John Courtney Murray (1960) offered a distinctive Catholic slant on this position in his doctrine of "civil peace." He noted that American Catholics achieved extraordinary freedom in the United States because the Protestant majority did not insist on a Protestant legal code. Catholics should not abuse the freedom they have enjoyed by demanding the imposition of a Catholic code. This position has been cited by contemporary prochoice Catholics to explain their reluctance to support the church's antiabortion position.

7. Ironically, northern evangelicals became the staunchest opponents of slavery, further emphasizing the ways common religious scriptures may engender divergent political paths (Hammond 1979). African Americans, who also embraced an evangelical style of religiosity, found the Bible to be a textbook on behalf of racial equality (Raboteau 2004).

8. The following discussion draws heavily on Leege and Wald (forthcoming).

9. Apart from explaining the role of politics in raising the salience of cultural conflicts, Leege et al. (2002) stress that cultural conflict has multiple domains. In addition to religion and gender issues, they discuss the moral orders surrounding race and nationalism.

10. The correct medical term for the procedure is "intact dilation and extraction." In the same way, prolife forces often speak of the fetus when they refer to what is scientifically an embryo. With its human form, the fetus is a much more compelling symbol than the mass of cells that is an embryo.

11. Reilly was defeated in the Democratic primary, and Romney chose not to run again for governor.

REFERENCES

Adam, Barry D. 2003. The defense of marriage act and American exceptionalism: The "gay marriage" panic in the United States. *Journal of the History of Sexuality* 12:259–76.

Andersen, Kristi. 1988. Sources of pro-family belief. *Political Psychology* 9:229–43.

Babington, Charles. 2004. GOP playing politics on gay marriage, Democrats say. *Washington Post*, March 24.

Balch, David L., ed. 2000. *Homosexuality, science, and the "plain sense" of scripture.* Grand Rapids, MI: Eerdmans.

Bartkowski, John P. 2003. *Remaking the Godly marriage: Gender negotiation in evangelical families.* Piscataway, NJ: Rutgers University Press.

Bellah, Robert N., Richard Madsen, William M. Sullivan, Ann Swidler, and Steven M. Tipton. 1985. *Habits of the heart.* Berkeley: University of California Press.

Button, James W., Barbara A. Rienzo, and Kenneth D. Wald. 1997. *Private lives, public conflicts: Battles over gay rights in American communities.* Washington, DC: Congressional Quarterly Press.

Catechism of the Catholic Church. 1997. 2d ed. Vatican City: Libreria Editrice Vaticana.

Crapo, Richley H. 1987. Grass-roots deviance from the official doctrine: A study of Latter-Day Saint (Mormon) folk-beliefs. *Journal for the Scientific Study of Religion* 26:465–86.

Dillon, Michele. 1999. *Catholic identity: Balancing reason, faith and power.* New York: Cambridge University Press.

Duran, Khalid. 1993. Islam and homosexuality. In *Homosexuality and world religions,* ed. Arlene Swidler, 181–98. Philadelphia: Trinity International.

Elliot, John H. 2004. No kingdom of God for softies? Or, what was Paul really saying? 1 Corinthians 6:9–10 in Context. *Biblical Theology Bulletin* 34:17–40.

George, Robert P. 2001. *The clash of orthodoxies—law, religion, and morality in crisis.* Wilmington, DE: ISI.

Greenawalt, Kent. 1993. The role of religion in a liberal democracy: Dilemmas and possible resolutions. *Journal of Church and State* 35:503–20.

Hammond, John L. 1979. *The politics of benevolence: Revival religion and American voting behavior.* Norwood, NJ: Ablex.

Hartman, Keith. 1996. *Congregations in conflict: The battle over homosexuality.* New Brunswick, NJ: Rutgers University Press.

Himmelstein, Jerome. 1986. The social bases of antifeminism: Religious networks and culture. *Journal for the Scientific Study of Religion* 25:1–15.

Hunter, James Davison. 1991. *Culture wars: The struggle to define America.* New York: Basic.

Ireland, Doug. 2003. Republicans relaunch the antigay culture wars—The GOP embrace of homophobia is more than simply a sop to the far right—Given the backlash against gay marriage, it's shrewd political strategy. *Nation.* November, 18–23.

Jelen, Ted, and Clyde Wilcox. 1995. *Public attitudes to church and state.* Armonk, NY: Sharpe.

Katz, Nathan. 1996. Understanding religion in diaspora: The case of the Jews of Cochin. *Religious Studies and Theology* 15:5–17.

Kennedy, Eugene. 1985. *Reimagining American Catholicism*. New York: Vintage.

Kieschnick, George B. 2003. Protecting marriage as instituted by God. Pastoral letter to Lutheran Church, Missouri Synod. www.lcms.org/graphics/assets/media/Office%20of%20the%20President/Protection%20of%20Marriage%20Statement.pdf.

Kirkpatrick, David. 2005. In secretly taped conversations, glimpses of the future. *New York Times*, February 20.

Kleppner, Paul. 1979. *The third electoral system*. Chapel Hill: University of North Carolina Press.

Land, Richard, Phil Roberts, Alan Branch, Barrett Duke, Terry Fox, Daniel Heimbach, Cindy Province, and Claude Rhea. 2003. Kansas City declaration on marriage. http//:churches.wcg.org/norwich-ct/sanctity_of_marriage.htm.

Leege, David C., and Kenneth D. Wald. Forthcoming. Meaning, cultural symbols, and campaign strategies. In *The affect effect: The dynamics of emotion in political thinking and behavior*, ed. Ann Crigler, George E. Marcus, W. Russell Neuman, and Michael MacKuen. Chicago: University of Chicago Press.

Leege, David C., Kenneth D. Wald, Brian S. Krueger, and Paul D. Mueller. 2002. *Politics of cultural differences: Social change and voter mobilization strategies in the post–New Deal period*. Princeton, NJ: Princeton University Press.

Marcus, George E., W. Russell Neuman, and Michael MacKuen. 2000. *Affective intelligence and political judgment*. Chicago: University of Chicago Press.

Marsh, Charles. 1997. *God's long summer: Stories of faith and civil rights*. Princeton, NJ: Princeton University Press.

Melton, J. Gordon, ed. and comp. 1991. *The churches speak on homosexuality*. Detroit: Gale Research.

Moon, Dawne. 2004. *God, sex, and politics—homosexuality and everyday theologies*. Chicago: University of Chicago Press.

Murray, John Court. 1960. *We hold these truths: Catholic reflections on the American proposition*. New York: Sheed and Ward.

Nice, David C. 1994. *Policy innovation in the American states*. Ames: Iowa State University Press.

Novak, David. 1998. Religious communities, secular society, and sexuality: One Jewish perspective. In *Sexual orientation and human rights in American religious discourse*, ed. Saul H. Oyland and Martha Nussbaum, 11–28. New York: Oxford University Press.

Olson, Laura R., and Wendy Cadge. 2002. Talking about homosexuality: The views of mainline Protestant clergy. *Journal for the Scientific Study of Religion* 41:153–67.

Olyan, Saul M., and Martha C. Nussbaum, eds. 1998. *Sexual orientation and human rights in American religious discourse*. New York: Oxford University Press.

Orsi, Robert A. 2003. Is the study of lived religion irrelevant to the world we live in? *Journal for the Scientific Study of Religion* 42:169–74.

Ozorak, Elizabeth Weiss. 1996. "The power but not the glory: How women empower themselves through religion." *Journal for the Scientific Study of Religion* 35:17–29.

Pew Research Center. 2003. Republicans unified, Democrats split on gay marriage—religious beliefs underpin opposition to homosexuality." Washington, DC: Pew Research Center for the People and the Press, November 18. http://people-press.org/reports/display.php3?ReportID=197.

Phillips, Frank. 2005a. AG backs legalizing same-sex marriage. *Boston Globe*, February 12.

———. 2005b. Romney's stance on civil unions draws fire. *Boston Globe*, February 23.

Presbyterian Church in America. Position paper: A declaration of conscience on homosexuals and the military; Adopted by the Twenty-first General Assembly, 1993, p. 129. http://www.pcanet.org/history/pca/2-399.htm.

Raboteau, Albert. 2004. *Slave religion: The "invisible institution" in the American South*. Updated ed. New York: Oxford University Press.

Ratzinger, Joseph. 2003. Considerations regarding proposals to give legal recognition to unions between homosexual persons. Vatican City: Congregation for the Doctrine of the Faith, June 3. www.vatican.va/roman_curia/congregations/cfaith/documents/rc_con_cfaith_doc_20030731_homosexual-unions_en.html.

Redfield, Robert. 1962. *Human nature and the study of society*. Chicago: University of Chicago Press.

Saucier, D. A., and A. J. Cawman. 2004. Civil unions in Vermont: Political attitudes, religious fundamentalism, and sexual prejudice. *Journal of Homosexuality* 4:1–18.

Sears, David O., Richard R. Lau, Tom R. Tyler, and Harris M. Allen Jr. 1980. Self-interest vs. symbolic politics in policy attitudes and presidential voting. *American Political Science Review* 74:670–84.

Schneider, Louis, and Sanford M. Dornbusch. 1958. *Popular religion: Inspirational books in America*. Chicago: University of Chicago Press.

Sharot, Steven. 2001. *A comparative sociology of world religions: Virtuosi, priests, and popular religion*. New York: New York University Press.

Sherry, Paul H. 1998. The rights of gay, lesbian, and bisexual persons in society and their membership and ministry in the church: A pastoral letter to the United Church of Christ. www.ucc.org/news/record/pastoral.shtml.

Siker, Jeffrey R., ed. 1994. *Homosexuality in the church—both sides of the debate*. Louisville, KY: Westminster John Knox Press.

Smith, Christian. 1998. *American evangelicalism—Embattled and thriving*. 1998. Chicago: University of Chicago Press.

Southern Baptist Convention. 2005. Sexuality. http//:sbc.net/aboutus/pssexuality.asp.

Swidler, Ann. 1986. Culture in action: Symbols and strategies. *American Sociological Review* 51:273–86.

Towler, Robert. 1974. *Homo religiosus: Sociological problems in the study of religion*. London: Constable.

Union of Reform Judaism. 2005. Ask the rabbi. urj.org/ask/homosexuality.

Via, Dan O., and Robert A. J. Gagnon. 2003. *Homosexuality and the Bible: Two views*. Minneapolis: Fortress.

Vrijhof, Pieter Hendrik, and Jacques Waardenburg, eds. 1979. *Official and popular religion: Analysis of a theme for religious studies*. The Hague: Mouton.

Wald, Kenneth D. 1983. *Crosses on the ballot: Patterns of British voter alignment since 1885*. Princeton, NJ: Princeton University Press.

Wald, Kenneth D., Adam L. Silverman, and Kevin Fridy. 2005. Making sense of religion in public life. In *Annual review of political science*, ed. Nelson Polsby and Ann Crigler, 121–43. Palo Alto, CA: Annual Reviews.

Westoff, Charles F., and Larry Bumpass. 1973. Revolution in birth control practices of United States Roman Catholics. *Science* 179:41–44.

Wildavsky, Aaron. 1987. Choosing preferences by constructing institutions: A cultural theory of preference formation. *American Political Science Review* 81:3–21.

Wood, P. B., and J. P. Bartkowski. 2004. Attribution style and public policy attitudes toward gay rights. *Social Science Quarterly* 85:58–74.

RELIGIOUS COALITIONS FOR AND AGAINST GAY MARRIAGE

THE CULTURE WAR RAGES ON

David C. Campbell and Carin Robinson

"We come here today for the audience of One," proclaimed the president of the Family Research Council, Tony Perkins. He stood before a cheering crowd gathered for the Mayday for Marriage rally on the National Mall in Washington, DC. "While our troops battle terrorists and tyrants abroad, a parallel battle rages here on our soil for the family and ultimately the future of our nation."[1] On October 15, 2004, more than two hundred thousand people gathered in Washington to defend what they see to be the traditional definition of marriage as being between one man and one woman. The Mayday for Marriage movement was organized in response to the rise of same-sex marriage on the national political agenda—on the West Coast the mayor of San Francisco had authorized the marriage of same-sex couples, on the East Coast the Supreme Judicial Court of Massachusetts had issued a ruling mandating gay marriages in the Bay State, and in between gay marriages were being performed in a handful of jurisdictions. A number of conservative pro-family groups such as the Family Research Council have since mobilized to host rallies across the country, attracting defenders of traditional marriage from a variety of denominations and faiths. To foreshadow the argument of this chapter—namely, that opposition to gay marriage unites religious traditionalists across the denominational spectrum—it is interesting to note that though the Family Research Council's constituency is predominantly white evangelicals, Mayday for Marriage was begun by an African American pastor.[2]

At the rally in Washington, the speakers included Rabbi Daniel Lapin, who encouraged attendees to "remember marriage at the voting booth." A Catholic group, the American Society for the Defense of Tradition, Family, and Property, waved banners and cheered following the rabbi's speech. An English-speaking Chinese pastor translated the message for members of his congregation, who stood holding a sign that read "Marriage = 1 Man + 1 Woman" in English and their native language. An Assemblies of God group joined hands to pray for the speakers. Members of a local African American church served as volunteers helping pass out programs, humming to the worship band playing "Great Is Thy Faithfulness" in the background. Gary Bauer, a prominent spokesperson for the Christian Right, proclaimed to the attendees, "You are not some small special interest group. You are America. You are the heart of America."

The religious and racial diversity present at the Mayday for Marriage rally is significant. Had there been any mention of welfare policy, the death penalty, or the Iraq War, the coalition would have dissolved. Their theological disagreements are even deeper; these groups are divided over such fundamentals as the divinity of Jesus Christ, speaking in tongues, and the afterlife. Groups with sharp disagreements about theology and in some cases a history of deep antagonism nonetheless stood side by side in opposition to same-sex marriage. Or, more accurately, people within these groups who hold traditional beliefs have found that they have more in common with other traditionalists, even those of other faiths, than members of their own religion who hold what are often called progressive beliefs.[3] For example, although many traditional Catholics attended the rally, their progressive counterparts stayed home. A similar divide is apparent within Judaism. The Union of Orthodox Jewish Congregations of America has joined white evangelical groups in calling for an amendment to the U.S. Constitution defining marriage as a union between a man and a woman. In contrast, the Union of Reform Judaism and the Central Conference of American Rabbis view gay marriage as a civil right and therefore support gay unions.

THE AMERICAN RELIGIOUS LANDSCAPE

The religious coalitions that have formed around the issue of gay marriage reflect a significant development in American religion and the way it shapes our politics. Only a few decades ago, the salient religious divide in American politics was defined by the boundaries between religious traditions, as famously summarized in the title of a well-known book by sociologist Will Herberg in 1955: *Protestant—Catholic—Jew*. Times have changed. Today, the salient divide is not *between* religious traditions but *within* them—in virtually every major religion in America, a split has developed between traditionalist and progressive factions. Although in each tradition the proximate sources of disagreement center on indigenous doctrinal disputes, at their roots these disputes all hinge on the source of ultimate authority. In the words of the sociologist James Davison Hunter, traditionalists believe in an "external, definable, and transcendent authority," whereas progressives are more willing to adapt their moral beliefs to "the prevailing assumptions of contemporary life" (1991, 44, 45). This fundamental division in the way moral questions are answered is not contained to arcane theological questions but spills over into opinions about politically relevant issues such as gay marriage. Thus, traditionalists from within various branches of Protestantism have joined forces with like-minded Catholics, Mormons, Jews, and Muslims to oppose gay marriage because they all share a belief in a transcendent authority, namely God, that holds the institution of marriage as limited to relationships between men and women. Although they have had a lower profile, some religious progressives have similarly allied with secularists in favor of same-sex marriages. Like the traditionalists, they, too, may appeal to God to justify their position, but in doing so they are more likely to speak of justice, equality, and inclusiveness than moral absolutes, having refracted their understanding of scripture through the prism of contemporary American society.

A common but often misused way to describe the intradenominational fissure we observe concerning gay marriage is as an example of the culture war in American politics. We use this term advisedly, aware that it borders on the hyperbolic. Nonetheless, its original usage aptly describes the coalitions that have formed regarding gay marriage. The term was popularized by James Davison Hunter, who used it to describe coalitions among traditionalists and progressives across denominational lines, especially with regard to issues of public policy such as abortion and pornography. The same development had also been carefully chronicled by Robert Wuthnow in *The Restructuring of American Religion* (1998), but *restructuring* does not have the same ring as *culture war*, and so it is the latter term that has gained wide usage. In 1992, when failed presidential candidate Pat Buchanan reached for a phrase to rally the moral conservatives who were increasingly congregating in the Republican Party, he declared that America was embroiled in a culture war. Interestingly, Buchanan himself exemplified what Wuthnow meant by the restructuring of American religion and what Hunter described as the culture war. Buchanan is a devout Catholic, but he found the most enthusiastic audience for his brand of red-meat conservatism among evangelical Protestants.

Since entering the public lexicon, the term *culture war* has morphed from the meaning Hunter assigned to it. Although it originally described the historically unusual development of religious coalitions that supersede denominational borders, it has come to be used as a short-hand description for the prominence of hot-button social issues such as abortion, gender roles, and homosexual rights. More recently, it has also been increasingly invoked as half-description, half-explanation of the perceived polarization within the American electorate. This latter usage has become so common among political pundits, in fact, that the political scientist Morris Fiorina (2005) has recently published a book in which he repudiates it. His book, however, only questions the term *culture war* as it is used to describe a highly polarized electorate, not Hunter's original definition. Indeed, Fiorina's thesis is quite consistent with Hunter's original formulation. Fiorina argues, convincingly, that Americans appear closely divided politically because when they go to the polls their choices are increasingly limited to political extremists. The general public is not as polarized as are political elites. Similarly, Hunter explicitly argues that the culture war he describes is most pronounced among social and political elites, in particular those within religious organizations.

In explaining how the culture war (or restructuring) framework illuminates the religious coalitions that have formed with regard to gay marriage, we begin with the attitudes in the general public. Because we would expect the lines between traditionalists and progressives to be blurrier among the mass public than among elites, public opinion data constitute a "hard case" for the culture war thesis. Nonetheless, we find patterns that reflect a divide between religious traditionalists and progressives regarding the subject of gay marriage that transcends denominational affiliation. We then turn to detailing the ways in which leaders of religious groups with a political dimension and political groups with a religious dimension have formed such coalitions, primarily in opposition. As we explain in greater depth, the anti–gay marriage movement reflects previous coalitions formed to deal with other cultural issues, such as abortion and opposition to the Equal Rights Amendment. Not only did those previous campaigns establish the institutional infrastructure for a campaign against gay marriage by forging a sense of shared purpose among religious traditionalists across denominational lines, but they also introduced culturally conservative groups to the strategies and technologies of modern political campaigns. The campaign against gay marriage thus represents the second generation of cultural conservatism, and it is far more politically sophisticated than the early stages of similar campaigns. In addition, this second generation is far more diverse than the first, both religiously and racially. Although the early leaders of the religious Right spoke of a big tent under which Protestants, Catholics, Jews, Mormons, and others would unite, in reality the movement was predominantly composed of white evangelicals.[4] The coalition against gay marriage, in contrast, is much more ecumenical and, consequently, more ethnically diverse.

THE CULTURE WAR IN THE TRENCHES

Although we would expect to see the greatest evidence of the culture war among the generals, the attitudes of the infantry are relevant also. Leaders must have someone to lead, and so political and religious elites cannot fall out of step with their constituencies. Is there evidence that the interfaith coalitions that characterize "culture war" politics describe attitudes about gay marriage? The strongest statement of the culture war hypothesis is that it predicts that divisions concerning gay marriage should be greater *within* than *between* religious traditions. Within religious traditions, we should see that adherents with divergent degrees of traditionalism differ in their attitudes regarding gay marriage to a greater extent than do people of different religious traditions. For example, a traditionalist Catholic should have more in common with a traditionalist evangelical Protestant than with a progressive Catholic.

To test whether this is the case, we turned to the 2004 National Election Study (NES), whose respondents were asked, "Should same-sex couples be allowed to marry, or do you think they should not be allowed to marry?" They were given the explicit option of indicating that gay marriage should or should not be allowed, and they could volunteer other responses, for example, expressing support for civil unions. For simplicity of presentation, we report the percentage of respondents who explicitly opposed any form of legal recognition for homosexual relationships. We divided NES respondents into four religious traditions based on a standard denominational classification system: White Evangelical Protestants, Mainline Protestants, Catholics, and Black Protestants (Steensland 2000; Kellstedt et al. 1996). Note that the category "Black Protestants" consists of all Protestants, either evangelical or mainline, who are African American, while Catholics can be of any race. Obviously, this is not an exhaustive list of religious traditions in America, but other groups such as Jews, Mormons, and Muslims, are too small to be adequately represented in a survey the size of the 2004 NES (roughly twelve hundred people).

To distinguish between progressives and traditionalists within each religious tradition we relied on an index of four questions, each of which taps into moral traditionalism. Respondents were asked the extent to which they agree with each of the following four statements:

1. The world is always changing and we should adjust our view of moral behavior to those changes.
2. The newer lifestyles are contributing to the breakdown of our society.
3. We should be more tolerant of people who choose to live according to their own moral standards, even if they are very different from our own.
4. This country would have many fewer problems if there were more emphasis on traditional family ties.

We used factor analysis, a statistical technique that compresses the four questions into a single index, and then divided the resulting scores into four quartiles.

Figure 6.1 displays the percentage of those within each religious tradition who oppose gay marriage,[5] dividing people within each tradition between those in the lowest and the highest quartiles of the moral traditionalism index. If the strongest version of the culture war hypothesis were to hold, we should see no difference in attitudes regarding gay marriage across religious traditions—people with the same score on the traditionalism index should share the same level of opposition to gay marriage, regardless of their religious tradition.

The strong version of the culture war hypothesis finds considerable support in figure 6.1. Among people in the lowest quartile of the moral traditionalism index, opposition to gay marriage is very similar regardless of religious tradition. Only 21 percent of Catholics and mainline Protestants, for example, oppose gay marriage. The figure for evangelicals is

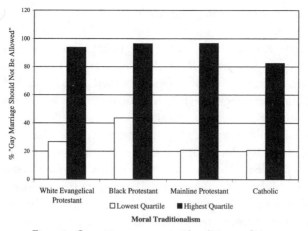

Figure 6.1. Opposition to gay marriage by religious tradition.

only slightly higher at 27 percent. The one group with noticeably stronger opposition to gay marriage is black Protestants, at 44 percent. At the high end of the traditionalism index, the similarities are even more apparent. The levels of opposition to gay marriage among evangelicals, mainline Protestants, and black Protestants are 94, 97, and 97 percent, respectively. In this case, Catholics are slightly less likely to oppose gay marriage, because "only" 82 percent are against it. A quick glance at figure 6.1 makes clear that, consistent with the culture war hypothesis, moral traditionalism is a far better way to predict opposition to gay marriage than religious tradition.

These data about general public opinion are suggestive, but they can only reveal the *potential* for interfaith coalitions to form to address the subject of gay marriage. The coalitions themselves are actually forged or not, as the case may be, among political and religious leaders. It is thus among the generals that culture war politics should be most evident, and so that is where we turn our attention.

WHO WORKS WITH WHOM, AND WHY DO THEY WORK TOGETHER?

As we trace the coalitions that have formed concerning the subject of gay marriage, the key test of the culture war hypothesis is whether they fulfill two conditions. First, as with the public opinion data, we should see divisions defined more by tensions within religious traditions than between them. Second, we should observe leaders of different religious traditions actually working together in the common cause of opposing gay marriage.

The story of the coalitions working against gay marriage begins long before this particular issue rose on the public agenda. The groups that are now mobilized against gay marriage have their roots in the New Christian Right movement, which began in the mid-1970s as white conservative Christians entered the political scene to speak out against feminism, the legalization of abortion, and the general decay of what they considered to be "family values." Originally the movement was ostensibly ecumenical, as evidenced by the names of two early members: the Religious Roundtable and the Moral Majority. These were groups with aspirations of assembling a broad, ecumenical membership as their leaders sought to attract religious conservatives from Protestantism, Catholicism, and Judaism alike. Notwithstanding a few notable Jewish and Catholic members, however, the awakening of religious conservatives in the 1970s and 1980s was largely an evangelical Protestant affair. In the early 1990s the Christian Coalition arose from the ashes of Pat Robertson's run for the presidency and inherited the institutional legacy of the Christian Right movement. Like its predecessors, it, too, sought to broaden its appeal to groups other than white evangelical Christians. And, also like its predecessors, the Christian Coalition was largely unsuccessful in trying to enlarge its tent (Robinson 2006).

Today, the religious coalitions that have formed to oppose gay marriage are far more ecumenical in their composition. Though having a narrow political focus, the range of participants has greater breadth than the original Christian Right, which was concerned with multiple issues. As was showcased at the Mayday for Marriage rally, participants come from a wider array of religions and races than was the case for the Christian Right movement in the 1980s and 1990s. Indeed, the presence of rabbis at the rally underscored that concern about gay marriage is not confined to Christianity. The old Christian Right laid the foundation, but the structure has taken a different shape.

Given the way the story is covered in the news media, it is easy to miss the interracial, transdenominational nature of the coalition against gay marriage. Because much of it is built on the preceding movement, it is tempting to assume that this is the Christian Coalition all over again. As a case in point, consider how coverage of the Mayday for Marriage rally fed that impression. Speakers at the rally included James Dobson, Gary Bauer, and Chuck Colson, all seminal figures in Christian Right circles. These are well-known, media-savvy figures, and so the news media gravitated toward them in their coverage. Consequently, the media portrayed the rally, and thus opposition to gay marriage generally, as dominated by white evangelicals. Scratch the surface of the movement, however, and you will find evangelical and mainline Protestants, conservative Catholics, orthodox Jews, and even Muslims. Because many of the spokespeople for these groups are relatively new to the political stage, they do not get the airtime afforded the familiar faces. Notwithstanding the way the movement is portrayed in the news, however, the denominational diversity that characterizes it is evidence favoring one criterion for culture war politics—a coalition that transcends denominational boundaries.

We have thus far focused on the rally as an exemplar of the anti–gay marriage coalition. But is it truly representative of the groups working against marriage for homosexuals? Far from being an isolated example, the rally fully reflects the cooperation across multiple denominations and religious traditions among gay marriage opponents. Other examples abound. Consider one of the earliest ballot initiatives against gay marriage, Proposition 22 in California, which was on the ballot in 2000. The campaign in favor of Proposition 22 featured cooperation among Catholics, evangelical Protestants, and Mormons, groups that had worked together previously, notably in opposition to pornography. Given the sharp theological disputes between these groups, especially the tensions between evangelicals and Mormons, this ecumenical partnership is remarkable (Campbell and Monson 2002).

Another case in point is the Arlington Group, a coalition of socially conservative supporters of the Marriage Amendment Project (MAP), an organization that serves as the nexus for groups working to pass an amendment to the federal Constitution that would define marriage as the union of one man and one woman. The Arlington Group is committed to defending traditional marriage in addition to addressing other issues of moral concern such as abortion and judicial activism. During the 2004 election cycle, the Arlington Group created another entity, MAP, to spearhead the work on the marriage issue specifically.[6] Although the Arlington Group is housed in the Family Research Council's facility in Washington, DC, and is associated with Christian Right groups such as Focus on the Family and the American Family Association, more than fifty religious or political organizations are members, and the list is anything but homogeneous. From denominational groups such as the Southern Baptist Convention and the Missouri Synod of the Lutheran Church to interest groups such as the Catholic Citizenship, Family, and Human Rights Institute and the Coalition of African American Pastors to state organizations such as Family First of Nebraska and the Center for Arizona Policy, the Arlington Group represents the breadth of the movement.

The number of groups that are under the Arlington Group's umbrella is actually a conservative estimate of the number of religious groups that oppose gay marriage because some gay marriage opponents do not favor a constitutional amendment and thus choose not to affiliate with the Arlington Group. Moreover, the Islam Society for North America, once part of the MAP, voluntarily left the project because of concern that any direct association with Muslims might tarnish the group's public image, owing to anti-Muslim sentiment following the terrorist attacks of September 11, 2001. Also, according to the coalition's staff, the Union of Orthodox Jewish Congregations of America has worked with MAP to pass the amendment but was never listed as a participating organization (Slatter 2004). Therefore, although the Arlington Group's supporters do not make up an exhaustive list of the organizations opposed to gay marriage, they are nonetheless evidence of the cooperation taking place across denominations, and the Arlington Group is on the front line of the culture war.

A similarly broad coalition characterizes the Alliance for Marriage, another group that opposes gay marriage but also seeks to defend traditional marriage more broadly by addressing issues such as divorce and social welfare policies that discourage marriage. Although it calls for an amendment to the Constitution to ban gay marriage, the Alliance for Marriage has worked less with interest groups associated with the Christian Right than with individual leaders within denominations. For example, the alliance's board of directors includes a rabbi, a Muslim, a minister from the African Methodist Episcopal church, a Hispanic pastor, and a Chinese minister, as well as a number of professors from Catholic universities.

Both the Arlington Group and the Alliance for Marriage provide evidence that opposition to gay marriage has brought together religious conservatives of varied backgrounds, fulfilling one criterion for culture war politics. The second criterion is evidence of tension within a given religious tradition between opponents and supporters of gay marriage. Nowhere has such tension been more apparent than within the black church. Most scholars of religion believe that predominantly African American denominations constitute a separate religious tradition within America because of their unique evolutionary path through the slavery, Jim Crow, and civil rights eras (Harris 1999; Lincoln and Mamiya 1990;

Steensland 2000). And within this tradition, there has been a pitched battle about gay marriage. Many African American clergy are theologically conservative and therefore oppose the practice. A number of conservative black ministers have aligned with white evangelicals to fight it. For example, the Traditional Values Coalition, a nondenominational grassroots church lobby that represents more than forty-three thousand congregations, has hosted a number of events specifically targeting the black churches within their constituency. "We're looking for African-American clergy members who have local authority, and we're getting them to hold a summit on marriage, just one issue," the chairman of the Traditional Values Coalition, Reverend Louis Sheldon, said in one media report (quoted in Banerjee 2005). A number of black leaders spoke at the Mayday for Marriage rally, including Bishop Harry R. Jackson Jr., the pastor of the Hope Christian Church in College Park, Maryland, who said the opening prayer. Jackson has said that blacks are especially attuned to the hardship of broken marriages, single parenting, and babies being born out of wedlock. Jackson said, "The bottom line is not about being anti-homosexual—it is about family reconstruction" (quoted in Chang 2005). Jackson and other African American clergy have joined with the Arlington Group, the Alliance for Marriage, or the Traditional Values Coalition to work against gay marriage.

Not all black clergy oppose gay marriage, however. Within the black church we observe the now-familiar split between traditionalists and progressives. In contrast to clergy members such as Harry Jackson, a number of the most prominent African American religious leaders have defined gay marriage as a civil rights issue and thus support the notion of granting marriage benefits to homosexuals. A common line of reasoning among this group is to draw a parallel with the bans on interracial marriage, which the civil rights movement worked successfully to end (Williams 2004). Former Democratic presidential candidate Al Sharpton shares these sentiments and has publicly endorsed same-sex marriage, going to great lengths to criticize the Republican Party for using the issue to target the religious black community (Finnegan 2004). After giving a sermon to Atlanta's Butler Street African Methodist Episcopal Church, Sharpton said, "George Bush manipulated a lot of religious feelings about marriage" and used gay marriage to draw attention away from Iraq and other policy positions that might not be as popular with the African American community (quoted in Plummer 2005). Perhaps the divide within the black church over gay marriage is best exemplified by the public split within the family of Martin Luther

King Jr. King's widow, Coretta Scott King, favored same-sex marriage, and King's daughter, Bernice King, opposes it. Coretta Scott King repeatedly compared homophobia with racism and was convinced that her husband would support granting rights to homosexuals if he were alive today. In contrast, King's daughter, who says homosexuality is a sin, is an elder at an Atlanta church that organized a march in opposition to gay marriage in December 2004. She led the march, which began at her father's grave (Barry 2004).

The divide between traditionalists and progressives is also apparent within Judaism. In 1996, when gay marriage had only begun to emerge on the nation's political agenda, the Reform movement within Judaism took a liberal position with respect to this issue. The Central Conference of American Rabbis (CCAR) within the movement passed a resolution opposing any government action that would prohibit same-sex couples from marrying. The congregational arm of Reform Judaism echoed this resolution a year later, saying that they would support legislation allowing same-sex marriage. Within the Conservative Rabbinical Assembly there is an endorsement of gay rights coupled with an intentional silence on the issue of gay marriage. In fact, a small number of Conservative rabbis have performed same-sex Jewish weddings. These groups stand in contrast to the Orthodox Jews who participated in the Mayday for Marriage rally and support the Arlington Group's agenda.

Many Catholic groups—but, pointedly, not all—have also joined with Jews and evangelical Protestants to oppose gay marriage. As a telling example of the fracture within Catholicism over the issue, we point to the divide between the two dioceses in the state of Virginia:[7] the Diocese of Arlington and the Diocese of Richmond. In 2004 the two dioceses jointly adopted a legislative agenda but then individually chose to give priority to various aspects of that agenda. The Arlington Diocese tends to focus on abortion and the traditional family structure, whereas the Richmond group focuses on issues relating to poverty and social justice. The Richmond Diocese has not come out in favor of same-sex marriage, but to our knowledge, it has not taken great strides in speaking out against the issue, either. Moreover, the diocese has taken more liberal positions when the issue of homosexuality has been addressed by the Virginia State Legislature. For instance, it supported amending the state's hate crimes law to include homosexuals. In contrast, the Arlington Diocese opposed the measure. The bishop of Arlington has been vocal about his opposition to same-sex marriage, addressing the subject in a homily to his congregants prior to the 2004 election. The differing orientation of the two dioceses is reflected in the religious coalitions in which they participate at the state level. The Richmond Diocese tends to cooperate with more progressive groups such as the Virginia Interfaith Center for Public Policy. The Arlington Diocese has worked closely with Focus on the Family and the Family Research Council's state affiliates to defend traditional marriage and other social conservative policies.

The tension over homosexuality within a number of mainline Protestant denominations echoes and amplifies the debate within Catholicism, the black church, and Judaism. For example, the United Methodist Church has been driven by an internal debate about gay marriage—as a matter not only of public policy but also church policy. In 1999, sixty-eight Methodist ministers presided over a lesbian couple's wedding as an act of protest of church law, which prohibits such ceremonies. The case brought against them was eventually dismissed, suggesting that there is substantial support for same-sex marriage within the church body. This support, though, was not enough to rescind the policy prohibiting same-sex marriage at the 2004 General Conference, where a spirited debate about the subject was conducted. The intensity of the debate is unsurprising; in a case that drew national attention, in March 2004 a jury of Methodist clergy members in Washington State acquitted a fellow minister of violating church law by being in a lesbian relationship. But then a few months later, a similar trial in Pennsylvania resulted in a guilty verdict issued against another lesbian minister, and as a result she was defrocked but was allowed to serve as a layperson in the church (Banerjee 2004). The lesbian minister appealed the ruling, and in May 2005 a committee reversed the decision made by the lower clergy court, citing technical grounds. (The church had never defined the term *practicing homosexual,* which was the basis of the charges brought against the minister.) In October 2005, however, the Judicial Council, the highest court in the Methodist Church, agreed with the original jury's verdict opposing "self-avowed practicing" homosexuals in ordained ministry (Cooperman 2005). The council also said that homosexuals have no immediate right to church membership and reinstated a Virginia minister who had been suspended by a bishop for not allowing a gay man to become a member of his congregation.

The Episcopal Church has been similarly divided about homosexuality, with the ordination of an openly gay bishop leading some Episcopal conservatives to threaten a schism within the church. Although there is obvious sympathy for gay marriage among some of the Episcopal hierarchy (Newman 2005), the Episcopal Church does not officially perform same-sex marriage ceremonies.

Although there are numerous examples of organizations that have united traditionalist denominations in opposition to gay marriage, examples of religious progressives who have banded together to support homosexual unions are few. The religious progressives who are in favor of allowing same-sex marriage are not mobilized to the degree that religious traditionalists are. They are smaller in number than the traditionalists, and either as a cause or as a consequence, they do not have an infrastructure comparable to the Christian Right's to bring their convictions into the political realm.

The group Clergy for Fairness is the exception that proves the rule. The interfaith group of religious leaders came together in 2006 to oppose a federal amendment to the Constitution that would ban same-sex marriage. In the summer of that year, the group maintained a regular presence in Washington, DC, as both houses of Congress debated the amendment. Representatives of Clergy for Fairness from numerous states visited congressional offices and hosted press conferences. The organization's Web site is perhaps the most sophisticated of its kind, providing links to sample sermons from various religious traditions and talking points about religious liberty and discrimination. Although united in their opposition to a federal amendment, the clergy do not necessarily agree on all issues related to homosexuality and same-sex marriage. Nor does the group take a position with respect to state constitutional amendments regarding same-sex marriage or civil unions.

Other religious groups that support civil marriage rights for same-sex couples are regionally based. The Religious Coalition for the Freedom to Marry, a small interfaith group of clergy, is limited to the New England states and thus a bit player at best in the national drama that is playing out. Similarly, the Colorado Clergy for Equality in Marriage (CCEM) is a group of 104 clergy members from across denominations, working in support of gay unions in the state. Again, there appears to be little coordination between CCEM and any groups on the national stage. The mobilization among religious progressives in support of same-sex marriage rights is hardly an analog to the interfaith organizations which oppose gay marriage.

It seems that the liberal mainline denominations, such as the Episcopal Church and the Methodist Church, are too consumed with the issue of homosexuality within the church to expend much energy on the issue beyond the church. And though there are individual denominations that support same-sex marriages, they represent a minuscule portion of the overall religious landscape. The Unitarian Universalist Association

(UUA), a representative body of UU churches, has showed support for same-sex marriage since 1970. Similarly, the United Church of Christ (UCC) officially came out in favor of gay marriage in a 1975 resolution and reasserted its commitment in 2005.[8] In an attempt to show its inclusiveness, in 2004 the UCC ran a television ad showing a same-sex couple being turned away by an unidentified church, only to be welcomed by a UCC church.[9]

Yet the UCC, one of America's most liberal denominations, is not immune from the traditionalist-progressive divide. Because the UCC is composed of autonomous local churches, the General Synod has little authority over individual church practices. So, for example, when the Western North Carolina Association of local UCC churches banned the ordination of openly gay clergy members in 2003, the General Synod had no authority to overrule the act. Other UCC churches have been critical of the governing body's support of same-sex marriage. The First Church of Christ in Wethersfield, Connecticut, the largest UCC church in New England, voted to become independent of the UCC denomination in 2004, explaining that its decision was largely due to the denomination's position regarding gay marriage and other social issues ("Largest UCC church in New England votes to become independent" 2004).

In reviewing the evidence given above, can we say that the religious coalitions surrounding gay marriage support the culture war thesis? Recall the two criteria for observing a culture war among elites: (1) cooperation among leaders of different religious traditions and (2) greater divisions within than between religious traditions. We have seen that both criteria are met, although perhaps the first to a greater extent than the second. Among gay marriage opponents we find a historically remarkable degree of ecumenism, exceeding the breadth of coalitions formed concerning other cultural issues such as abortion and the Equal Rights Amendment. Traditionalist Protestants, Catholics, and Jews alike have united in their opposition to gay marriage. On the other hand, although religious progressives are more naturally inclined toward interfaith cooperation, there are few examples of ecumenical action among gay marriage proponents. In this conflict, one side significantly outnumbers the other.

We also see some evidence for the other criterion, namely, divisions within religious traditions. Within Catholicism and various strains of Protestantism, religious leaders are split with regard to the question of gay marriage. One should not exaggerate the transdenominational nature of opinions about the issue, however. Certainly, the traditionalist-progressive split is salient, but this does not mean that denominations have ceased to matter. A Southern Baptist, regardless of her traditionalism, is more likely to oppose gay marriage than an Episcopalian, notwithstanding the Episcopalian's degree of orthodoxy. It would appear that when we look within denominations, the biggest fights over gay marriage occur inside liberal churches—whose congregants appear less unified in their progressivism than conservative church members are cohesively committed to traditionalism.

WHAT STRATEGIES HAVE THEY EMPLOYED?

The breadth of the coalition against gay marriage is interesting as an example of the fault lines that have formed with regard to cultural issues in American politics. Its significance is more than merely academic, however, because the transdenominational nature of the movement is an important element in its political success. The efforts to build a diverse coalition—in terms of race and religion—underscore the political sophistication of the religious activists who oppose gay marriage. They understand the fundamental rule in a participatory political system: numbers matter. Elected officials are more likely to listen to a large group representing more voters than a smaller group representing fewer voters; all else being equal, a broad coalition beats a narrow one every time. And for the battle over gay marriage, the coalition of opponents has been broad indeed.

Why is there such a broad coalition opposing gay marriage? Given the widespread opposition to the practice, as illustrated in figure 6.1, it may seem inevitable that the opposition to it would have a wide base. But there is nothing inevitable about the institutions that have been developed to lead the charge against gay marriage.

Although the widespread opposition to gay marriage is a necessary condition for a broad coalition, it is not sufficient. The breadth of the coalition is also the result of political experience gained over the previous generation of cultural battles and the political infrastructure that has been built to fight those battles. The coalition is in large part the result of a deliberate strategy employed by evangelical conservatives since the issue first gained national prominence in the mid-1990s, when the Defense of Marriage Act was passed in Congress and signed by Bill Clinton. The specific strategy in play consists of diversifying the coalition opposed to gay marriage, amending state constitutions to ban gay marriage, and, finally, creating the "perfect storm" so that the conditions will be right to pass an amendment to the U.S. Constitution defining marriage as the union of a man and a woman.

A good example of a Christian Right activist who has recognized the political advantage of a diverse coalition working against gay marriage is Matt Daniels of the Alliance for Marriage. Recognizing the limits of the prolife movement, which largely consists of white evangelicals and Catholics,[10] Daniels sought to create a multiracial movement in defense of heterosexual marriage. A Chinese pastor serving on the advisory board of the alliance notes that Daniels selected advisors and board members with the idea of bringing together people of diverse faiths and races (Wong 2004). As noted above, the Arlington Group is another example of Christian Right leaders' organizing an infrastructure composed of diverse religions and denominations to respond to gay marriage. After the groups were linked at the national level, the local and state affiliates came to coordinate with one another, an important development because the battle over traditional marriage has primarily been waged at the state and local levels.[11]

Examining one state in particular illustrates the political strategy of gay marriage opponents. On November 2, 2004, Ohioans voted to ban the recognition of same-sex marriage by amending the state constitution. The success of this ballot initiative was largely a result of coordination between Ohio affiliates of socially conservative advocacy groups and their national parent organizations. The leading figure in Ohio, Phil Burress, was a familiar face in local Christian Right circles, having run an antipornography group since the early 1990s.[12] When Hawaii's state supreme court issued a ruling in favor of allowing same-sex marriage in 1993, Burress began committing most of his time to fighting gay marriage in his own state. He started the Ohio Campaign to Protect Marriage, now a state affiliate of Focus on the Family and the Family Research Council. To assist Burress and his supporters, these and other national groups contacted their members in Ohio to mobilize them in response to the issue. The American Family Association, for example, sent out mass emails to sixty thousand supporters who live in Ohio to encourage them to sign the petition needed to get the issue on the ballot and then turn out to vote in November. Representatives from the Ohio group met with national leaders regularly. Part of the strategy involved discussing how to conduct outreach to leaders within other religious traditions in the state. As a result, staffers from the Ohio Campaign to Protect Marriage visited a large mosque in the greater Cincinnati area to encourage its members to support the state's ban on gay marriage (Miller 2005). The Ohio group also worked closely with African American churches to gather signatures for the petition. Further broadening the coalition, all twelve Catholic bishops in Ohio made a public statement in support of the state's marriage amendment. With these interfaith relationships in place, the Ohio Campaign to Protect Marriage was able to gather 575,000 signatures in fewer than ninety days to put a measure on the Ohio ballot. Sixty-two percent voted in favor, and thus a ban on same-sex marriage was written into the state constitution.[13]

The example of Ohio, like that of California, mentioned earlier, demonstrates that the religious diversity among groups opposed to gay marriage is not restricted to the national level. Although evangelical groups appear to be spearheading the cause, they depend on a larger community of religious believers to achieve political success. And we expect to see further interreligious cooperation because the success of the Ohio campaign now serves as a template for anti–gay marriage campaigns in other states. Soon after the 2004 election season, which resulted in bans on same-sex marriage added to the constitutions of twelve states,[14] Burress and other religious leaders met in Washington, DC, to discuss the following year's constitutional amendment battles in other states. By igniting support for traditional marriage at the grass roots, leaders at the national level hope to spur constituents to pressure their representatives and senators to support the amendment to the U.S. Constitution. To that end, they remain focused on the states.

As evidenced by the decision to build support for a gay marriage ban state by state, leaders in the movement against the practice have displayed a considerable degree of political sophistication (not to mention patience). This is nowhere more apparent than in their negotiations concerning the federal marriage amendment. Although it is certain to fail in the short term, it will be repeatedly introduced in the years to come. Conservative religious leaders do not expect success immediately. Years ago, prior to the first introduction of the amendment, leaders of the Christian Right met with members of Congress to determine a realistic strategy for enacting a constitutional amendment. They realized the limitations they faced in a contentious Congress and chose to work within those constraints, as illustrated by the wording selected for the amendment. A ban on civil unions, they were told, would never happen. And so instead of an amendment that would explicitly ban civil unions and gay marriage, they opted for one that would prohibit homosexual marriages only. The majority of groups represented by the movement to defend traditional marriage also oppose civil unions, but many of them were willing to focus their efforts on marriage as a political compromise. According to Allison Slatter of the Arlington Group's Marriage

Amendment Project, trying to outlaw civil unions would have been political suicide. Using a metaphor that resonates with our discussion of the culture war, she said, "Civil unions require a nuke and nuking is not popular. Restricting marriage to man and woman would require circular strikes, and those are acceptable. We pinpoint the area most troublesome and we stop that" (Slatter 2004). Focus on the Family, equally opposed to civil unions, agreed that pushing for an amendment to address civil unions would not be politically expedient. Instead, Focus on the Family believes that it must defend traditional marriage before attempting to outlaw civil unions as well. "Being an incrementalist is not an unprincipled approach," said Peter Brandt, the group's vice president of public policy (Brandt 2004). Brandt thinks it wiser to turn to the states to adopt the language necessary to ban civil unions.[15]

Contrast this flexibility with earlier incarnations of the Christian Right movement, which was characterized by absolutism with regard to moral issues. As it has become a more politically sophisticated movement, it has recognized the value of getting half a loaf when the whole loaf is out of reach. The evolving strategy of abortion opponents illustrates this change. When the Christian Right first appeared on the national political landscape, its leaders and organizations took a hard-line stand against abortion, supporting nothing less than an absolute ban on all abortions. In more recent years, however abortion opponents have adopted an incremental strategy by working to enact a prohibition on "partial-birth abortion" (known to abortion rights advocates as "intact dilation and extraction"), supporting parental notification laws, and the like (Saletan 2003). As applied to abortion, the incremental strategy appears to be working. Not only have numerous limitations and restrictions on abortion been successfully enacted, but recent years have seen a small shift toward prolife attitudes among the general public—two developments that are clearly related, although the direction of causality is unclear (Wilcox and Norrander 2002). Incrementalism with respect to abortion has served as a template for the strategy to oppose gay marriage. The half loaf of a gay marriage ban that permits civil unions is better than trying and failing to obtain the whole loaf of banning both.

CONCLUSION

We have seen that the religious coalitions that have formed around the issue of gay marriage—especially in opposition to it—are evidence of what James Davison Hunter memorably labeled "culture war politics."

The term is incendiary and perhaps misleading, but the interfaith cooperation it is meant to describe nonetheless includes the groups working to thwart gay marriage in the United States. In its current configuration, the debate about the practice pits opponents comprised largely of traditionalists spanning the religious spectrum against advocates who are predominantly secular but are joined by a small number of religious progressives. We stress that we are not saying that religious traditions are irrelevant in shaping opinions regarding gay marriage. To the contrary, members of different religious traditions vary systematically in their opposition to gay marriage. But the differences among religious traditions are surpassed by the differences within them. Your level of traditionalism within your church matters more than which church you go to.

At the moment, the opponents of gay marriage have the upper hand. Supporters of marriage among homosexuals are in the minority, as evidenced by public opinion polls and the overwhelming margins of victory for ballot initiatives to ban marriage between homosexual couples. As we look toward the future, however, should we expect to see the "culture war" continue? There are two ways to read the tea leaves. On one hand, attitudes toward homosexuality are becoming increasingly liberal, largely because young people are more accepting of homosexuals and gay marriage than their elders. Young people are also less likely than their elders to endorse morally traditionalist opinions. For example, 36 percent of Americans over the age of fifty-five are in the bottom half of the moral traditionalism index introduced above, compared to 72 percent of people under the age of thirty. As time marches on, those young people will come to occupy an ever-larger share of the population. It is thus tempting to say that we should expect to see a cessation of hostilities in the culture war—at least along the front line of gay marriage—in much the same way that racial attitudes changed dramatically over the course of a generation. It is also portentous, however, that the gap in attitudes toward gay marriage between young people at the bottom and at the top of the moral traditionalism index mirrors what we see among their elders. The former gap in is 28 percentage points. Among people over fifty-five, the gap is 32 points. In other words, we see that young people, taken as a whole, have more liberal attitudes about gay marriage than do their elders. Yet among young people, there remains a clear distinction between traditionalists and progressives. This sharp divide suggests that the most apt analogy for attitudes about gay marriage may be not public opinion regarding civil rights. Rather, perhaps a better comparison is with attitudes about abortion, which have remained sharply polarized for decades. If so, we can expect the battle over gay marriage to be with us for a long time.

ENDNOTES

1. Tony Perkins, president of the Family Research Council, in remarks made to attendees at the Mayday for Marriage rally in Washington, DC, on October 15, 2004, and printed in the event's program.

2. Ken Hutcherson, senior pastor at Antioch Bible Church in Kirkland, Washington, organized the first Mayday for Marriage Rally, in Seattle. It drew approximately twenty thousand people.

3. Terms such as *traditional* and *progressive* are contested. Since these are the terms Hunter uses in *Culture Wars,* we have adopted them. We prefer them to *conservative* and *liberal,* since these terms confuse theology with political ideology.

4. For an overview of the composition of the Christian Right, see Wilcox and Larson (2006), chap. 2.

5. This includes any other type of legal recognition for homosexual relationships. To keep things simple, we simply refer to "opposing gay marriage," which should be understood as including opposition to civil unions.

6. After 2005, MAP no longer existed as a separate entity, though the goal of barring same-sex marriage remains a prominent interest of the Arlington Group.

7. For a discussion of religious lobbying activity in Virginia, including a summary of its two Catholic dioceses, see Larson, Madland, and Wilcox (2006).

8. On July 4, 2005, at the Twenty-fifth General Synod of the United Church of Christ, delegates voted to adopt the resolution "In Support of Equal Rights for All." http://www.ucc.org/synod/resolutions/gsrev25-7.pdf (accessed October 17, 2006).

9. Both NBC and CBS refused to air the advertisement, deeming it too controversial.

10. For an overview of the composition of the prolife movement, see Luker (1985) and Maxwell (2002).

11. To understand the strategy one must have some understanding of the structural organization of Christian Right groups. Many national-level groups, such as the Family Research Council, Focus on the Family, and the Christian Coalition, have state affiliates that share the policy platform of the national body. When cooperation is taking place on the national scale, cooperation between state affiliates is likely to follow.

12. For a profile of Phil Burress and his work in defense of traditional marriage, see Dao (2004).

13. In 2004 the wording of state amendments went largely uncontested among the religious groups opposed to gay marriage. Burress, a staunch social conservative, was the original architect of the Ohio amendment, and he put forth a conservative text that banned same-sex contracts in addition to same-sex

marriage. Activists from other states chose to pursue a ban on same-sex marriage that did not include a ban on civil unions, possibly thinking that this additional stipulation might decrease the chances of the amendment's passage. In Oregon, for example, an amendment banning same-sex civil unions would have been asking too much from a liberal-leaning state. Oregon voters did pass an amendment banning gay marriage but by only 58 percent, the smallest margin of any marriage amendment proposed in 2004. To date, the text of state amendments has been left up to the discretion or conviction of local evangelical activists and evangelical groups.

14. Two states voted to amend their constitutions prior to Election Day. Missouri citizens voted to amend the state constitution in August 2004 to define marriage as a union of a man and woman. Louisiana voted in September to amend its constitution, outlawing gay marriage as well as civil unions. In November, however, a Louisiana lower court judge overturned the state amendment, saying it was flawed because it included two purposes, banning gay marriage and civil unions, within one amendment. At this point, it seems likely that the ban will eventually be reinstated, however, if only because Louisiana's supreme court is an elected body, and Louisianans voted overwhelmingly in favor of the ban (78 percent).

15. Not all socially conservative advocacy groups have been happy with this compromise. Concerned Women for America, for example, was so displeased with the failure of the amendment to address civil unions that it decided not to directly partner with the coalitions opposing gay marriage in April 2005.

REFERENCES

Banerjee, Neela. 2004. United Methodists move to defrock lesbian. *New York Times*, December 3, A18.

———. 2005. Black churches struggle over their role in politics. *New York Times*, March 6, 23.

Barry, Ellen. 2004. March clouded by stand on gay unions. *Los Angeles Times*, December 11, A18.

Brandt, Peter. 2004. Interview by Carin Robinson, December 30.

Campbell, David E., and J. Quin Monson. 2002. Dry kindling: A political profile of American Mormons. Paper presented at the Conference on Religion and American Political Behavior, Southern Methodist University, October 4.

Chang, Pauline. 2005. Interview posted January 17. The *Christian Post* online, http://www.christianpost.com/article/church/1841/section/interview.bishop .harry.s.jackson/1.htm (accessed March 30, 2005).

Cooperman, Alan. 2005. Lesbian minister defrocked by United Methodist Church. *Washington Post*, November 1, A3.

Dao, James. 2004. Flush with victory, grass-roots crusader against same-sex marriage thinks big. *New York Times*, November 23, A28.

Finnegan, Michael. 2004. The race for the White House; Jackson and Sharpton join Kerry on trail; Black voters are urged to focus on quality of life and not be diverted by GOP "hot button" issues. *Los Angeles Times*, October 11, A13.

Fiorina, Morris P., with Samuel J. Abrams and Jeremy C. Pope. 2005. *Culture war? The myth of a polarized America.* New York: Pearson Longman.

Goodstein, Laurie. 2005. Methodists reinstate defrocked minister. *New York Times,* April 30, A9.

Harris, Fredrick C. 1999. *Something within: Religion in African-American political activism.* New York: Oxford University Press.

Herberg, Will. 1955. *Protestant—Catholic—Jew: An essay in American religious sociology.* Garden City, NY: Doubleday.

Hunter, James Davison. 1991. *Culture wars: The struggle to define America.* New York: Basic.

Kellstedt, Lyman A., John C. Green, James L. Guth, and Corwin E. Smidt. 1996. Grasping the essentials: The social embodiment of religion and political behavior. In *Religion and the culture wars,* ed. John C. Green, James L. Guth, Corwin E. Smidt, and Lyman A. Kellstedt, 174–92. Lanham, MD: Rowman & Littlefield.

Largest UCC church in New England votes to become independent. 2004. *Boston Globe,* June 7. http://www.boston.com/news/local/connecticut/articles/2004/06/07/largest_ucc_church_in_new_england_votes_to_become_independent/ (accessed October 17, 2006).

Larson, Carin. 2004. From every tribe and nation? Blacks and the Christian Right. Paper presented at the Annual Meeting of the American Political Science Association, Chicago, IL. September 2–5.

Larson, Carin, David Madland, and Clyde Wilcox. 2006. Religious lobbying in Virginia: How institutions can quiet prophetic voices. In *Representing God at the statehouse: Religion and politics in the American states,* ed. Edward Cleary and Allen Hertzke, 55–72. Lanham, MD: Rowman & Littlefield.

Lincoln, C. Eric, and Lawrence H. Mamiya. 1990. *The black church in the African American experience.* Durham, NC: Duke University Press.

Luker, Kristin. 1985. *Abortion and the politics of motherhood.* Berkeley: University of California Press.

Maxwell, Carol. 2002. *Pro-life activists in America: Meaning, motivation and direct action.* Cambridge: Cambridge University Press.

Miller, David. 2005. Interview by Carin Robinson, March 22.

Newman, Andy. 2005. Connecticut Episcopalians defy bishop over gay issues. *New York Times,* April 14, B1.

Plummer, Don. 2005. Sharpton knocks Bush; Gays are used to duck real issues, he says here. *Atlanta Journal-Constitution,* January 10, 3B.

Robinson, Carin. 2006. From every tribe and nation? Blacks and the Christian Right. *Social Science Quarterly* 87:591–601.

Saletan, William. 2003. *Bearing right: How conservatives won the abortion war.* Berkeley: University of California Press.

Slatter, Allison. 2004. Interview by Carin Robinson, November 9.

Steensland, Brian, Jerry Z. Park, Mark D. Regnerus, Lynn D. Robinson, W. Bradford Wilcox, and Robert D. Woodberry. 2000. The measure of American religion: Toward improving the state of the art. *Social Forces* 79 (1): 291–318.

Wilcox, Clyde, and Carin Larson. 2006. *Onward Christian soldiers? The religious right in American politics.* Boulder: Westview.

Wilcox, Clyde, and Barbara Norrander. 2002. Of moods and morals: The dynamics of opinion on abortion and gay rights. In *Understanding public opinion,* 2d ed., ed. Barbara Norrander and Clyde Wilcox, 121–48. Washington, DC: CQ Press.

Williams, Sherri. 2004. Comparing gay, civil rights a divisive issue for blacks. *Columbus Dispatch,* July 2, A8.

Wong, David. 2004. Interview by Carin Robinson, November 12.

Wuthnow, Robert. 1988. *The restructuring of American religion: Society and faith since World War II.* Princeton, NJ: Princeton University Press.

THE ANTI–GAY MARRIAGE
MOVEMENT

Sean Cahill

INTRODUCTION

Since mid-2003, Americans have been inundated with images and claims about same-sex marriage. In the wake of the June 2003 U.S. Supreme Court ruling striking down archaic sex laws and the Ontario high court ruling in favor of same-sex marriage, the U.S. antigay movement seized on many Americans' discomfort with homosexuality in an attempt to make marriage equality for same-sex couples a major political issue in the 2004 elections. Although antigay bias has a long history in the United States, it is a mistake to understand it solely as a relic of our traditional past; in fact, antigay bias is amplified, mobilized, and deployed by the antigay movement for specific political objectives.

This chapter examines the anti–gay marriage movement in the United States and its role in electoral politics. The Christian Right—a political alliance of evangelical Protestants and conservative Roman

Catholics—spearheads this movement. Christian Right advocacy organizations articulate an across-the-board opposition to any form of legal equality for gay people. Antigay activism is central to its political project. Many Christian Right groups also advocate a much broader conservative, even reactionary, agenda. This includes opposition to no-fault divorce, teaching evolution, legal immigration, women in combat, affirmative action, and other issues.

Since the mid-1990s, the antigay movement has been focused overwhelmingly on banning marriage and other forms of partner recognition. The organizing strategies of the movement include advocacy at the local, state, and national levels. Antigay legislation and ballot campaigns have been major organizing strategies. Since 1988, when the televangelist Pat Robertson ran for president and then founded the Christian Coalition, the Christian Right has played an increasingly powerful role in national Republican Party politics and presidential elections.

This chapter also examines the arguments of the anti–gay marriage movement, including misrepresentations of who gay, lesbian, bisexual and transgender people are and what legalizing same-sex marriage would mean.[1] Finally, it reviews the functions of antigay ballot campaigns. In addition to banning legal protections and family recognition for gay people and same-sex couples, they play a myriad of other roles: they divert attention from other issues; they can have a "priming" effect by making gay rights a more salient issue in voter decision-making; they can mobilize the Christian Right's base of conservative voters; the mobilization of moderates and liberals to resist antigay ballot questions can starve such candidates of campaign funds; they can make gay rights issues politically radioactive; and they can serve as a hook to bring in new audiences to hear the Christian Right's broader conservative and theocratic policy agenda.

THE ANTI–GAY MARRIAGE MOVEMENT

The anti–gay marriage movement is an assemblage of national and local groups that generally reflect premillennarian Protestantism (Herman 2000, 140).[2] In some states, such as Massachusetts and Michigan, the Roman Catholic Church leadership has emerged as an equal partner in the anti-marriage movement alongside its traditional evangelical leaders. This alliance is ironic given the traditional tensions and divisions between the two currents of Christianity; many evangelical Protestants still consider Roman Catholicism a cult-like form of pagan idolatry.[3]

Among the leading Christian Right groups are Concerned Women for America, Focus on the Family, the Family Research Council and the Traditional Values Coalition. In addition, leaders of the Southern Baptist Convention, some Roman Catholic archdioceses across the United States, and the Christian Coalition play a leadership role.

Many local groups are also active at the state level. In Massachusetts, where the antigay movement has invested a great deal of resources to repeal same-sex marriage, local antigay groups include the Black Ministerial Alliance of Greater Boston, the Massachusetts Catholic Conference, the Massachusetts State Council of the Knights of Columbus, the Bay State Republican Council, and the Catholic Action League of Massachusetts. All these groups are members of the Coalition for Marriage, which also includes most of the large national Christian Right groups. The Massachusetts Family Institute, which has led the fight to repeal marriage for gay couples, is a local affiliate of the Colorado-based Focus on the Family.

About twenty-nine Christian Right organizations cosponsored the October 2003 "Marriage Protection Week,"[4] a series of political activities targeting marriage equality for gay couples as well as more limited forms of partner recognition, such as domestic partnership and civil unions.[5] The week of antigay prayer rallies and lobbying was endorsed by President George W. Bush.[6] Among the thirteen Marriage Protection Week co-sponsors for whom income data were publicly accessible, a total of $211 million in income was reported to the IRS in 2002. These groups range from Focus on the Family, with $126 million in revenue, to Citizens for Community Values, with a mere $89,000 in income. In comparison, the thirteen *largest* national gay political organizations reported a combined income of $53 million in 2002.[7]

Both the antigay and pro-gay forces active in the eleven statewide anti—gay marriage ballot campaigns in November 2004 appear to have spent about the same amount of money, according to an analysis of campaign expenditures compiled on the eve of the election by the National Gay and Lesbian Task Force. That analysis found that pro-amendment forces (those seeking to ban gay marriage) had spent $3.2 million, and opponents of the amendments (those seeking to prevent the banning of gay marriage) had spent $3.4 million (National Gay and Lesbian Task Force 2004).

If prostitution is the world's oldest profession, antigay politics is among the world's oldest obsessions. Although some cultures tolerated or even celebrated homosexuality, those that came to dominate the globe largely persecuted gay people, at least until recently (Trexler 1995). English and Spanish colonists in the Americas executed "sodomites," the Nazis persecuted homosexuals, and in the late 1940s Joe McCarthy attacked "sexual perverts" in the U.S. government before moving on to alleged political subversives (D'Emilio 1983, 40–53). Since the mid-1970s, Christian Right activists in the United States have increasingly turned to antigay political activism as a motivational, electoral, and fund-raising strategy. Almost as long as there has been a gay rights movement, there has been an antigay movement.

Antigay activism emerged as a major focus of the religious Right during the campaigns for the first antigay ballot measures of the mid- to late 1970s (Crawford 1980; Zwier 1982; both cited in Shaw 1997, 10). Green, an expert on the role of Christian conservatives in U.S. politics, notes that "[o]pposition to gay rights was one of the original pillars of the Christian Right" (Green 2000, 124).

A good example of the centrality of antigay politics to the Christian Right's project was Marriage Protection Week. This series of religious and political events did not focus on the most salient threats to the health and security of American families, such as the poverty affecting one in five U.S. children, the increasing prevalence of families without health insurance, domestic violence, or parents who do not pay child support. Instead, religious conservatives made it clear that they wanted to make same-sex marriage the key political issue in the 2004 election.

This focus on homosexuality to the detriment of other pressing social issues is reflected in a content analysis of the Web sites of key Marriage Protection Week sponsors. Of the thirty-three co-sponsoring organizations, nine had Web sites that allow users to search all of the documents available on the site. Searches using a few keywords found the following:[8]

- The Web site of the American Family Association, a $14 million-a-year nonprofit dedicated to "chang[ing] the culture to reflect Biblical truth," contains 334 documents referring to "homosexual" but only 13 about "health care," 29 that refer to "poverty," 17 that refer to "domestic violence," and a mere five that refer to "child support."
- Concerned Women for America, a $12 million-a-year "public policy women's organization," has 602 documents on its Web site that contain the word "homosexual" but only 97 referring to health care, 80 about poverty, 19 about domestic violence,

71 about rape, and 6 about child support—all important public policy concerns of American women.

- Focus on the Family, a $126 million-a-year religious Right behemoth, mentions homosexuality 740 times on its Web site but poverty only 212 times, domestic violence 85 times, and child support a mere 20 times.
- The Family Research Council, a $5 million-a-year spin-off of Focus on the Family, has 203 documents on its Web site about homosexuality but only 37 about poverty, 26 about domestic violence, and 2 about child support.
- Combined, the nine Web sites of co-sponsoring organizations mention "homosexual" a total of 2,369 times, but "child support" only 85 times, "domestic violence" 190 times, "poverty" 832 times, and "health care" 952 times.

A BROAD, REACTIONARY POLICY AGENDA

Many of the national and local Christian Right groups opposing marriage equality for same-sex couples also promote a broader, reactionary political agenda. They oppose any form of legal equality for gay people— including policies aimed at stemming harassment of public school students who are perceived to be gay. Several anti–gay marriage groups opposed services or benefits for the same-sex partners of gay victims of the 9/11 attacks. Many also oppose affirmative action, reproductive choice, immigration, the teaching of evolution, sex education, women in combat, and no-fault divorce. Of course, this is not true of all antigay leaders and organizations.

ACROSS-THE-BOARD OPPOSITION TO
LEGAL EQUALITY FOR GAY PEOPLE

The antigay groups portray themselves as representing a beleaguered middle America, but in fact they promote the development of a theocratic state and have a vision of an intolerant America that is out of step with the views of most Americans.

Opposing Sexual Orientation Nondiscrimination Laws

Most of the groups that oppose gay marriage also oppose sexual orientation nondiscrimination laws; one even encourages "intolerance" of homosexuals. All fifteen member organizations of the Massachusetts-based Coalition for Marriage, including four of the leading national antigay groups,[9] oppose such laws.

As of early 2006, nearly half of the U.S. population (48 percent) lived in a city, county, or state that outlaws sexual orientation discrimination (National Gay and Lesbian Task Force 2006). Seventeen states have sexual orientation nondiscrimination laws, as well as more than two hundred localities. Eight of these states also ban discrimination on the basis of gender identity or expression. In an additional eleven states, executive orders protect public-sector employees against sexual orientation discrimination (Human Rights Campaign 2003). Nondiscrimination laws usually ban discrimination in employment, housing, and public accommodations on the basis of real or perceived sexual orientation. Gay rights laws enjoy bipartisan support from U.S. voters. The 2000 National Election Study found that 56 percent of Republicans, 70 percent of Independents, and 75 percent of Democrats supported sexual orientation nondiscrimination laws (Yang 2001). According to a 2003 Gallup poll, nearly nine in ten Americans support the principle of sexual orientation nondiscrimination, if not the laws required to enforce this practice (Newport 2003).

Opposing Domestic Partner Benefits as "Special Rights" and "Sex Partner Subsidies"

The anti–gay marriage movement also opposes more limited forms of partner recognition for same-sex couples. During Marriage Protection Week, Christian Right groups proposed a sample "marriage protection" proclamation that Tony Perkins of the Family Research Council said "every federal and state lawmaker will be asked to sign." The proclamation stated that its signers would "oppose civil unions and domestic partnerships" as well as same-sex marriage (Wetzstein 2003).

The Massachusetts Coalition for Marriage also "opposes[s] the creation of civil unions or domestic partnerships" (Coalition for Marriage [2004a]). When in 2001 Acting Governor Jane Swift extended limited domestic partner benefits to some state employees, the Massachusetts Family Institute (MFI) denounced this as "special rights for a particular group" (Massachusetts Family Institute 2001b). The group also stated, "These are not equal rights since the decision is only for homosexual couples. . . . Our nation, as well as this commonwealth, was founded on equal rights as asserted through our founding documents. Allowing special rights for a particular group denies these principles and has damaging and far reaching consequences" (Massachusetts Family Institute 2001a). Of course, in 2001 gay couples could not marry in Massachusetts, so calling domestic partner benefits "special rights" is not accurate. This special rights theme was first used in the late 1970s antigay ballot campaigns, and it was amplified in the second wave of antigay ballot measures put forward in the late 1980s and early 1990s. It is examined in greater depth below. In 2003 the MFI ridiculed domestic partner health insurance—offered to employees in long-term, committed relationships—as "sex partner subsidies to homosexual employees" (Massachusetts Family Institute 2003).

Opposing Safe Schools Initiatives Based on Claims of "Homosexual Recruitment of Children"

Anti–gay marriage groups generally also oppose initiatives aimed at stopping antigay harassment and violence in schools, claiming that these are in fact a Trojan horse for the "recruitment" of children into "the homosexual lifestyle" (Dailey 2004). The claim that homosexuals are more likely to molest children has been definitively refuted by peer-reviewed social science research. A study reported in the *Journal of the American Medical Association* in 1998 found that 90 percent of pedophiles are men and that 98 percent of these individuals are heterosexual (Holmes and Slap 1998). In fact, the limited research indicates that gay men and lesbians are *less* likely than heterosexuals to sexually abuse children. Two studies that examined the sexual orientation of convicted child molesters found that less than 1 percent in one study and 0 percent in the other were gay or lesbian (Jenny and Roesler 1994, 44; Groth and Birnbaum 1978, 175–81).

Opposition to Parenting by Lesbian and Gay People and Same-Sex Couples

A related claim is that being raised by gay parents is bad for children. Focus on the Family (FOTF) claims that "same-sex parenting situations make it impossible for a child to live with both biological parents, thus increasing their risk of abuse" (Stanton 2003). In a full-page ad placed in the *Boston Globe* on January 23, 2004, FOTF implied that gay marriage would lead to gay parenting in the future, not that it would protect existing lesbian and gay families raising children: "Same-sex marriage advocates and the Massachusetts Supreme Judicial Court are asking our state and nation to enter a massive, untested social experiment with coming generations of children. We must ask one simple question: Is the same-sex 'family' good for children?" Given that at least eight thousand children are being raised by two lesbian or two gay parents in Massachusetts, according to the 2000 Census, parenting by same-sex couples is not some "massive, untested social experiment" (Ash et al. 2004). It's the lived reality for thousands of Massachusetts residents and many more families around the country.

Many same-sex couples are raising children. Estimates of the number of lesbian or gay parents in the United States range from two million to eight million (Patterson 1995; Casper and Schultz 1999, 4). These figures include many single parents who are lesbian, gay, or bisexual. Data from the 2000 Census indicate that 34 percent of lesbian couples and 22 percent of gay male couples[10] have at least one child under eighteen years of age living in their home (Simmons and O'Connell 2003). These figures may not seem very high, but when compared with parenting rates among married heterosexual couples (46 percent of whom are raising children), lesbian couples reported in the 2000 Census parent at about three-quarters the rate of married straight couples, and gay male couples parent at about half the rate. Many more are parents of children who do not live with them or are "empty nesters" because their children are away at college or living on their own as adults. Black same-sex couples are nearly twice as likely as white same-sex couples to be raising children (Dang and Frazier 2004, 23).

Claims that being raised by gay or lesbian parents disadvantages children go against a large body of social science research that confirms that children raised by gay or lesbian parents are not disadvantaged relative to their peers (Stacey and Biblarz 2001). The vast majority of children's advocacy organizations, including the American Academy of Pediatrics (Perrin et al. 2002), the National Association of Social Workers (Ferrero et al. 2002), and the American Psychological Association (Patterson 1995), recognize that gay and lesbian parents are just as good as heterosexual parents and that children thrive in gay- and lesbian-headed families. One APA publication reports that "not a single study has found children of gay or lesbian parents to be disadvantaged in any significant respect relative to children of heterosexual parents" (ibid.).

Although claims by Christian Right groups that gay parents put their children at risk are not backed by social science research, seven states ban or restrict parenting by gays in one way or another. Most of these bans were passed in the wake of debates about gay marriage and partner recognition. Frequently, claims by antigay leaders and politicians that children raised by gay and lesbian parents are hurt by such an upbringing encourage the passage of antigay parenting laws.[11]

Opposition to Benefits and Services for Gay Partners of 9/11 Victims

The leading national anti–gay marriage groups sought to prevent gay and lesbian survivors of those killed in the 9/11 attacks from getting benefits and services from the September 11 Victim Compensation Fund and the American Red Cross. Only a month after three thousand people were killed in the worst terrorist attacks in U.S. history—attacks that involved the simultaneous hijacking of four airplanes—Robert Knight of Concerned Women for America (CWA) accused "homosexual activists" of "trying to hijack the moral capital of marriage and apply it to their own relationships," which he characterized as "counterfeit marriage" (Johnson 2001). Leaders of the Traditional Values Coalition (TVC) and the Family Research Council (FRC) also joined in the criticism of surviving same-sex partners seeking benefits and services.

A REACTIONARY POLICY AGENDA IN
AREAS BEYOND GAY RIGHTS ISSUES

Although the anti–gay marriage Christian Right organizations claim to represent the people against "judicial tyranny" (as allegedly manifested in pro-gay, pro-abortion, and pro-secular court rulings), many member organizations advocate a reactionary political agenda that is not supported by a majority of Americans.

Opposition to No-Fault Divorce

The Family Research Council promotes an end to no-fault divorce and the requirement of mutual consent for divorce, as well as "covenant marriage" laws now in effect in Louisiana, Arizona, and Arkansas (Maher n.d.). Covenant marriages are much harder to enter into and harder to dissolve. Concerned Women for America's Jan LaRue also denounces no-fault divorce as a reason why many people support marriage equality for gay couples: "The biggest problem we have in getting people, especially younger ones, to understand why marriage is devalued by the existence of a counterfeit is that much of the public does not value marriage at all. Adultery is no big deal. No-fault divorce is tolerated. Absentee fathers and mothers devalue marriage" (LaRue 2003, n.p.).

Opposition to Feminism, Evolution,
and the Department of Education

Phyllis Schlafly, head of the Eagle Forum, is one of the founders of the
Christian Right. She helped defeat the Equal Rights Amendment in the
mid-1980s. A book titled *Feminist Fantasies* is linked at the bottom of
Schlafly's essay "Will Massachusetts Abolish Marriage?" posted at the
MFI's Web site. The book claims, "No assault has been more ferocious
than feminism's 40-year war against women, and no battlefield leader
has been more courageous than Schlafly. In a new book of dispatches
from the front, feminism's most potent foe exposes the delusions and
hypocrisy behind a movement that has cheated millions of women out of
their happiness, health, and security." [12] In August 2005 Schlafly spoke
at Justice Sunday II, a rally organized by Focus on the Family and other
Christian Right groups to oppose alleged judicial activism.

Other national antigay groups advocate the following reactionary
policies:

- The TVC, FOTF, CWA, and Eagle Forum oppose reproductive
choice, the teaching of evolution in public schools, and compre-
hensive sex education. They also promote prayer in public schools
(People for the American Way [2004c]; Concerned Women for
America 2004, 2002).
- The FRC supports a school prayer amendment to the U.S.
Constitution and would like to abolish the Department of
Education (People for the American Way [2004b]). Concerned
Women for America also seeks the abolition of Department
of Education (People for the American Way [2004a]). Christian Right groups oppose what they view as a secular humanist
conspiracy to indoctrinate America's children through the public
school system; hence the popularity of home schooling among
many evangelicals.

THE ANTIGAY MOVEMENT'S KEY ORGANIZING
STRATEGIES FROM THE 1970S TO THE PRESENT

Since its emergence in the 1970s, the antigay movement has engaged in
political and policy advocacy at the local, state, and national levels. The
promotion of legislation and the deployment of ballot campaigns have
both been major organizing strategies. A third major strategy has been

advocacy within the Republican Party. The Christian Right has played an increasingly powerful role in national Republican Party politics and Congressional and presidential elections. Today the polarization between the GOP and the Democratic Party with regard to gay issues is striking.

Fowler and Hertzke argue that in the early to mid-1990s the Christian Right "emerged as a leaner, more experienced, more locally based movement" (Fowler and Hertzke 1995, 142, cited in Shaw 1997, 12). Shaw notes that "[p]art of the strategy of the Christian Coalition . . . has been a concentrated focus on grassroots politics and local organizing." He cites former coalition executive director Ralph Reed: "Our goal was to transform the religious conservative community from a political pressure group to a broad social reform movement based in local communities. . . . States and localities would become the 'laboratories' for testing our policy ideas, and for building a 'farm system' of future candidates." (Reed 1996, 157, cited in Shaw 1997, 15).

A number of scholars in the early to mid-1990s noted the state and local focus of the Christian Right. Shaw, citing several scholars, notes that "the greatest impact of the New Christian Right on public policy has come at the state and local level" (Moen 1992; Wald 1992; Wilcox 1996, cited in Shaw, 1997, 16).

From the mid-1970s to the mid-1990s, the antigay movement focused on defeating or repealing sexual orientation nondiscrimination laws, opposing AIDS education and sex education, banning gays from teaching, and upholding the military ban on openly gay people, and it even advocated quarantining people with AIDS. Antigay ballot campaigns were a key tactic in these efforts.

ANTIGAY BALLOT CAMPAIGNS

Since 1974 antigay activists have deployed more than one hundred ballot referenda and initiatives.[13] The overwhelming majority were approved.[14] Following the first wave of antigay ballot measures in the late 1970s, a second wave swept the country in the late 1980s and early 1990s, in part in reaction to the widespread passage of gay rights laws at the local and state levels.[15] In the past few years antigay groups have sought the repeal of gender identity nondiscrimination laws—laws that protect transgender people against discrimination—as well as laws banning discrimination on the basis of sexual orientation.[16]

These initiatives and referenda were often promoted by local groups backed by significant outside support from national religious Right groups such as Focus on the Family. In 1994 antigay groups first promoted a ballot measure that would ban gay marriage as well as nondiscrimination laws and other policies. Today marriage is the frame through which the antigay movement talks about gay people and gay rights issues. Although the religious Right continues to promote opposition to gay parenting, school antihomophobia programs, and all forms of legal equality for gay people, for most of the past decade it has used marriage as the battering ram of its campaign. Since the turn of the new millennium an increasing number of antigay ballot campaigns have concerned marriage and other forms of partner recognition.

Hardisty argues that for three decades the national antigay movement has deployed ballot questions at the local and state levels as "its central strategy" in opposing legal equality for lesbian, gay, and bisexual people (Hardisty 1999, 98). Diamond, however, argues that "[n]ot until the late 1980s and 1990s . . . would the Christian Right make the prevention and reversal of gay rights initiatives a centerpiece of its activist program" (Diamond 1995 171, cited in Shaw, 1997, 15).

Most of these antigay ballot questions passed, especially those that were local (as opposed to statewide) and those that involved repealing a nondiscrimination law or pro-gay policy or program (Donovan and Bowler 1998). Referenda aimed at repealing existing gay rights protections, such as nondiscrimination laws, have been most successful. Green calls these referenda manifestations of "reactive opposition . . . the rejection or repeal of specific proposals regarding gay rights." Initiatives aimed at preempting gay rights provisions—which Green calls "proactive opposition"—were less likely to succeed (Green 2000, 127). Notable exceptions were the initiatives banning sexual orientation nondiscrimination laws in Colorado and Cincinnati.

ANTIGAY STATE LEGISLATION

Another key strategy of the antigay movement has been the promotion of its policies via state legislatures. Major legislative foci have included laws regulating mention of sexuality in schools, antigay parenting laws, and antigay family laws.

Parental notification laws in four states—Arizona, California, Nevada, and Utah—require students to obtain the written consent of their parents before they participate in classes in which topics such as sex, sexuality, and AIDS are discussed.[17] A number of states have also passed laws preventing teachers from mentioning the word *homosexual* in the classroom or mandating that homosexuality be presented in an exclusively negative way.[18] For example, South Carolina bans discussion of "alternative sexual lifestyles from heterosexual relationships including, but not limited to, homosexual relationships, except in the context of instruction concerning sexually transmitted disease." [19] Arizona law prohibits instruction that "promotes a homosexual lifestyle, portrays homosexuality as a positive alternative lifestyle, or suggests that it is possible to have 'safe' homosexual sex." [20]

At least seven states limit, in some fashion, the ability of gay men, lesbians, or same-sex couples to adopt or become foster parents. Four states have express restrictions on gay adoption: Florida, Mississippi, Nebraska, and Oklahoma. Thanks in part to Anita Bryant's "Save Our Children" campaign that overthrew Miami-Dade County's sexual orientation nondiscrimination law in 1977, Florida has explicitly banned adoptions by "homosexuals" for more than a quarter-century. In 1995 the director of Nebraska's Department of Social Services issued a directive banning "known" homosexuals and unmarried couples from adopting. Mississippi bans "same-sex couples" from adopting. Oklahoma passed an antigay adoption law in May 2004, banning recognition of joint or second-parent adoptions by same-sex couples who move to Oklahoma from another state.

A fifth state, Utah, has an implied, de facto restriction on adoption by same-sex couples: Utah bans adoption by "cohabiting" unmarried couples. A sixth state, North Dakota, passed a law in 2003 in the wake of a high-profile adoption by a gay male couple that allows adoption agencies that receive state contracts and licenses to refuse to place children with prospective parents to whom they object on religious grounds. This means adoption agencies could refuse to place children with gay individuals or couples, as well as unmarried opposite-sex couples, single mothers, divorced people, and many others.

At least three states prohibit gay and lesbian individuals or same-sex couples from serving as foster parents: Arkansas, Nebraska, and Utah. Since 1999 the Arkansas Child Welfare Agency Review Board has banned gays and lesbians from foster parenting. This ban was struck down in December 2004; the state is appealing the ruling to a higher court. Nebraska also prohibits gay men and lesbians from foster parenting. Arkansas and Utah prohibit foster parenting—explicit or implicit— by same-sex couples.

Even where lesbians and gay men are technically able to adopt or become foster parents as individuals in many states, judges sometimes intervene to prevent the placement of a child with a lesbian or gay parent. In addition, though no state expressly prevents parenting by bisexual or transgender people, if in same-sex relationships they may face the same obstacles that lesbian and gay parents face.

Laws prohibiting gay marriage swept throughout the United States starting in 1995 in reaction to a court ruling permitting it in Hawaii in 1993 and as a result of organizing by the national antigay groups in state legislatures and in Congress. Twenty-four anti–gay marriage laws were passed in 1996 and 1997 alone. As of August 2005, thirty-nine states had anti–gay marriage laws or state constitutional amendments. Fifteen of these states have laws or amendments banning or threatening not only marriage but also more limited forms of partner recognition such as civil unions and domestic partnerships. In the wake of the passage of nine broad antifamily amendments in 2004, local and state governments and public universities in Michigan, Missouri, Ohio, and Utah rescinded domestic partner benefits for public-sector employees (Albrecht 2005; Associated Press 2004; Human Rights Campaign 2005).

THE ANTIGAY MOVEMENT IN NATIONAL POLITICS

Although its primary focus has been on local and state grassroots activism, since the 1980s the Christian Right has played an increasing role at the national level, particularly within the Republican Party. The first antigay advertisements in a presidential campaign were used successfully by the Reagan campaign in 1980. During the 1980s the antigay movement put forth false claims about homosexuality and AIDS that stoked animosity toward gay people. Perhaps as a result of this, the Democratic Party, which had adopted pro-gay platform language in 1980, backed away from supporting legal protections for gays until the nomination of Bill Clinton in 1992.[21] Since 1992 the two major parties have become sharply polarized in relation to gay rights, with the Republicans portraying gay rights as a major threat to American civilization and opposing all forms of legal equality and the Democrats advocating for full equality for gay couples but not yet explicitly calling for marriage equality.

A FORK IN THE ROAD: 1992–2000

Televangelist Pat Robertson's run for president in 1988 was based on his opposition to the more moderate Republicans' alleged softness on the issues of homosexuality and abortion.[22] Although Robertson's campaign was ill-fated, the mailing list of donors to his 1988 campaign served as the core from which Robertson and Ralph Reed launched the Christian Coalition the following year. It soon became one of the largest right-wing religious political organizations in the country (Bull and Gallagher 1996, 32).

Hostility toward gays was a major theme of the Republican Convention in August 1992. Pat Buchanan denounced "the amoral idea that gay and lesbian couples should have the same standing in law as married men and women." He also ridiculed Clinton's support for gay equality to a receptive crowd, many of whom held signs reading "Family Values Forever, Gay Rights Never." Six others spoke against gay people, gay rights laws, and same-sex marriage (McElvaine 1992; Berlet and Quigley 1995, 15). The Republicans' strategy failed, however. Bill Clinton's mantra, "It's the economy, stupid," was a better indicator of the sentiment of voters still trying to escape the depths of a recession.

In 1993, the Hawaii Supreme Court ruled that it was impermissible gender discrimination under the state constitution to deny three lesbian and gay couples the right to obtain a marriage license.[23] This decision stated that Hawaii could only deny the marriage licenses if it could indicate a compelling reason to do so. In 1996 a Hawaii trial court found that the state had failed to justify its denial with a compelling reason, and so the couples had the right to marry under civil law.

In reaction to these developments, antigay activists and politicians tried to make gay marriage a key issue in the 1996 presidential campaign, holding a rally denouncing same-sex marriage just before the Iowa caucuses, the first primary election event. Nearly every Republican candidate attended and signed a pledge to "defend" heterosexual marriage against the threat allegedly posed by three same-sex couples in Hawaii. Gay marriage emerged as a wedge issue in the campaign. Throughout 1996 newspapers and talk radio hosts railed against gay marriage—including liberal editorial boards like that of the *Boston Globe*. For the second time in four years (the first being the "gays in the military" controversy), gay rights were debated among average Americans.[24]

Throughout the primary race for the 2000 nomination, which started in mid-1999, all ten of the Republican candidates opposed any form of legal protection for gay people, such as nondiscrimination laws. In August 1999, on the eve of the Iowa straw poll, six of the Republican candidates signed a document promoted by Christian Right groups pledging to oppose domestic partner benefits, education to fight antigay harassment and violence in the schools, adoption by gay people, and other issues (Log

Cabin Republicans 1999). In December 1999, the marriage issue arose again in the wake of the Vermont Supreme Court's ruling that the state must provide to same-sex couples every benefit and protection it provides to married heterosexual couples. Democratic candidates Bill Bradley and Al Gore, who sought the gay community's vote, applauded the decision, while the Republican candidates denounced it. Christian Right activist Gary Bauer called the ruling "worse than terrorism" (Ramer 1999).

Throughout 2000, Governor George W. Bush continued to articulate antigay positions when asked. In South Carolina, he told a Christian radio station that he probably wouldn't appoint gays to his administration because "[a]n openly known homosexual is somebody who probably wouldn't share my philosophy" (Keen 1999). As governor, Bush defended Texas's sodomy law as "a symbolic gesture of traditional values" (A sodomy law's last stand 2000), opposed sex education, and sought to tax condoms as a vice (Cahill and Ludwig 1999). Throughout 1999 and 2000 Bush spoke out against gay adoption, same-sex marriage, hate crimes legislation, nondiscrimination laws, and sex education. In a debate with Vice President Al Gore, Bush called the Employment Nondiscrimination Act, which Gore supported, a provision of "special rights." [25]

Despite Bush's adherence to antigay policy positions, the 2000 Republican Convention set a tone that was markedly different from that of its predecessors. Speakers eschewed antigay rhetoric, although language opposing marriage and other forms of partner recognition for gay couples, military service, and sexual orientation nondiscrimination laws remained in the party platform.

ARGUMENTS MADE BY THE ANTI-GAY MARRIAGE MOVEMENT

The antigay movement puts forth a number of reasons for opposing marriage equality for same-sex couples. One claim—that children of gay and lesbian parents are harmed by their parents' sexuality or gender—has already been addressed. Other arguments include the alleged mutability of sexuality, the claim that gay marriage is a "special right" and somehow threatening to the civil rights of people of color, the claim that gay people can already get married, the claim that religious conservatives will be forced to celebrate gay marriages, and claims that allowing same-sex marriage will open the floodgates to all sorts of perversions. In making these arguments, antigay activists often use intemperate language and falsely portray themselves as a David fighting a gay Goliath.

INTEMPERATE, VITRIOLIC ATTACKS

At least three of the antigay groups use intemperate, vitriolic language to promote intolerance and discrimination against gay people, including gay youth in the schools. Model sermons proposed by Marriage Protection Week organizers in October 2003 claimed that homosexuality constitutes the greatest threat to American society and that gay people have declared war against our culture.[26]

Several of the groups opposing marriage in Massachusetts have compared gay rights advances to terrorism. The Traditional Values Coalition's Lou Sheldon compared the June 2003 U.S. Supreme Court ruling striking down sodomy laws to the 9/11 terrorist attacks and likened gays or the Supreme Court to the terrorists who struck that day: "This is a major wake-up call. This is a 9/11, major wake-up call that the enemy is at our doorsteps. This decision will open a floodgate. This will redirect the stream of what is morally right and what is morally wrong into a deviant kind of behavior. There is no way that homosexuality can be seen other than [as] a social disorder" (Bluey 2003). Concerned Women for America warned in a September 2003 press release that same-sex marriage "pose[s] a new threat to US border security," calling a legally married Canadian same-sex couple trying to enter the U.S. as a married couple "the latest pair of 'domestic terrorists'" (Kimball 2003). The MFI, a state affiliate of FOTF, linked an essay by Dennis Prager to its Web site that portrayed gay marriage advocates and Democrats as a domestic version of Al Qaeda (Prager 2004).[27]

THE MUTABILITY OF SEXUALITY

Antigay groups have long argued that homosexuality is a choice and that homosexuals can choose heterosexuality if they try hard enough. For example, the executive director of Exodus International, Bob Davies, coauthored a 1993 book with Lori Rentzel titled *Coming out of homosexuality: New freedom for men and women.* The ex-gay movement started in the early years of the gay rights movement with the founding of the "Love in Action" ministry in 1973 (Burack and Josephson 2005, 1). In 1998 a coalition of Christian Right groups ran full-page advertisements in major U.S. newspapers claiming that homosexuals could be "cured" through religious conversion. The largest Christian Right group, Focus on the Family, still organizes "Love Won Out" conferences across the country on a regular basis (ibid.).

A statement on the Massachusetts Coalition for Marriage's Web site says it opposes sexual orientation nondiscrimination laws "because we do not believe that a person's sexual behavior is comparable to other protected categories such as race or sex—characteristics that are inborn, involuntary, immutable, innocuous and/or in the Constitution" (Coalition for Marriage [2004b]). Lou Sheldon of the TVC, a lead co-sponsor of Marriage Protection Week, wrote in early 2003: "We are not tolerant of behaviors that destroy individuals, families and our culture. Individuals may be free to pursue such behaviors as sodomy, but we will not and cannot tolerate these behaviors. . . . In short, we believe in intolerance to those things that are evil; and we believe that we should discriminate against those behaviors which are dangerous to individuals and to society" (Sheldon 2003).

Opponents of legal equality for gay people—whether in the form of nondiscrimination laws, safe schools programs, or access to the institution of marriage—claim that homosexuality is a choice, and a bad one at that. According to this logic, laws protecting gays against discrimination in employment, housing, and public accommodations and efforts to grant gay couples access to the institution of civil marriage reward bad choices by granting "special protections" or "special rights" based on sexual behavior (Hardisty 1999).

GAY RIGHTS ARE SPECIAL RIGHTS

Claims that homosexuality is a bad choice are closely linked to claims that gay rights are special rights. The upsurge in antigay ballot campaigns in the late 1980s was due in part to the success of the more explicit deployment of a unifying theme: that homosexuality is an individual choice, not a condition or status, and therefore different from race and undeserving of legal protection (Green, 2000, 133). Gay rights were portrayed as "special rights" and as a threat to the civil rights of "legitimate minorities," that is, African Americans and other people of color. Antigay groups increasingly put forward African American spokespeople to argue that gay rights threatened the civil rights of people of color, as the TVC did in its 1993 video *Gay Rights, Special Rights*. Civil rights struggles were presented as a zero sum game between blacks (presumed to be straight) and gays (presumed to be white). If gays get civil rights, the religious Right argued, Americans will have fewer rights.

Such arguments were deployed in support of the 1994 Idaho initiative that would have banned sexual orientation nondiscrimination laws, affirmative action for homosexuals, discussion of homosexuality in schools, domestic partner recognition, and marriage for gay couples. In October 1994 Idaho Citizens Alliance founder Kelly Walton said the "primary goal" of its initiative "is to prevent homosexuals from attaining special legal privileges. . . . Everybody ought to be protected on the basis of their constitutional rights, not some legal privilege that's granted when a group attains a minority-type status." (Pitman 1997, 78–80). In Idaho, Oregon, and elsewhere, antigay groups define special rights to include minority status, affirmative action, quotas, and special class status. This argument continues to be made in the context of the anti–gay marriage debate. In March 2004 CWA released a report titled "Homosexuals hijack civil rights bus" (LaRue 2004b).

As Goldberg notes, the concept of special rights" is legally meaningless: "no such 'rights' exist" (Goldberg 1995, 111). Antigay groups contend that gays are not eligible for "minority status and all the privileges thereof." This promotes another right-wing myth: that being a member of a racial minority group provides one with privileges (Nakagawa 1995, 280–281).[28]

Unfortunately, the incorrect view that sexual orientation nondiscrimination laws represent special rights has been shared by George W. Bush as well as many other conservative politicians. During the second presidential debate in October 2000, when asked if "gays and lesbians should have the same rights as other Americans," Bush responded, "Yes. I don't think they ought to have special rights. But I think they ought to have the same rights." When asked to elaborate on what he meant by "special rights," Bush responded, "Well, it'd be if they're given special protective status."[29]

During a press conference held on April 25, 2003, when asked about the president's beliefs about homosexuality in the wake of Senator Rick Santorum's comparing homosexuality to pedophilia and bestiality, Press Secretary Ari Fleischer responded, "The President has always said that when it comes to legal matters, that it's a question of different groups, homosexual groups, gay groups should not have special rights or special privileges."[30]

GAY PEOPLE CAN ALREADY GET MARRIED

Antigay groups insist that allowing gay couples to marry represents granting gay people a special right on top of the right they already have. "Homosexuals in Massachusetts have had the same right to marry as heterosexuals—the right to marry a person of the opposite sex," writes CWA's Jan LaRue (LaRue 2004a). The Family Research Council compares laws restricting marriage to opposite-sex couples to laws preventing cousins from marrying and laws preventing adults from marrying children: "every person, regardless of sexual preference, is legally barred from marrying a child, a close blood relative, a person who is already married, or a person of the same sex. There is no discrimination here, nor does such a policy deny anyone the 'equal protection of the laws' (as guaranteed by the Constitution), since these restrictions apply equally to every individual" (Sprigg 2003).

In other words, since a gay man could marry a woman and a lesbian could marry a man (as many gay people have done—often resulting in unhappy and dysfunctional marriages), they have the right to marry. But for a person who is only attracted to and capable of falling in love with someone of the same sex, such a freedom or right is pretty meaningless. In fact, these restrictions do *not* "apply equally to every individual" but limit the ability of gay people *only* to protect their life partner relationships.

People on death row, mass murderers, rapists, and child molesters can all get married as long as they are marrying someone of the opposite sex. Yet gay and lesbian people are denied this fundamental right because the people they love are of the same sex. Their right to marry someone of the opposite sex doesn't mean much; it doesn't allow them to marry the person they love.

THE HOMOSEXUAL LOBBY OUTSPENDS
THE ANTIGAY LOBBY

Antigay activists often portray gay people and activists as politically powerful, well-funded elites. For example, Ken Connor of the FRC wrote in a recent fundraising letter: "The Human Rights Campaign and the other groups in the homosexual lobby have very deep pockets. Big corporations, elite foundations, and Hollywood celebrities underwrite the homosexual lobby with tens of millions of dollars every year" (Connor 2003).

In an interview held about a month before the November 8, 1994, election during which a broad antigay question was on the ballot, Kelly Walton, founder of the antigay Idaho Citizens Alliance (ICA), said: [I]t's like the Alamo for the other side. . . . They feel their literal livelihood is at stake over this and for that reason they have been able to raise, I believe, $280,000 this year from forty-one different states around the nation. Our fund-raising efforts have been entirely in-state. . . . Frankly, we have not spent the kind of energies the other side has, and it's shown in the contribution and expense reports to the secretary of state" (Pitman 1997, 80).[31]

After proponents of the measure lost narrowly to a coalition of opponents, Walton again claimed that the ICA was a David taking on a homosexual Goliath: "We just had a few part-time volunteers taking on the entire homosexual political machine of the nation. The other side received contributions from over forty-one different states. It's very clear they have a network in place and that they're very good at raising money. We don't have to match the kind of money they are capable of raising and that's probably not possible" (Pitman 1997, 90).[32] Although it is unclear which group spent more in Idaho in 1994, it is clear that the Christian Right groups leading the charge against gay marriage today dramatically outspend groups promoting equal rights for lesbian, gay, bisexual and transgender people.

RELIGIOUS CONSERVATIVES WILL BE FORCED TO ACCEPT SAME-SEX MARRIAGE

In 1996 CWA's Beverly LaHaye warned, falsely, that the legalization of gay marriage could lead to the "imprisonment" of "parents who object to the homosexual agenda. . . . They could even have their children taken away from them because they are 'unfit parents'" (Concerned Women for America 1996). Yet parents' ability to hold conservative and even bigoted beliefs is not threatened in any way by gay couples seeking the family protections afforded by marriage.

The organization also warned, "Your church could be forced to hire or 'marry' homosexuals" if gay marriage is legalized. Churches that refuse to hire homosexuals "could be closed." In fact, the legalization of gay marriage under civil marriage laws would not in any way affect the religious freedom of conservative congregations to refuse to marry gay couples, just as the legalization of divorce does not prevent the Roman Catholic Church from maintaining its policy of not recognizing divorces or second marriages of divorced Catholics. Also, employment nondiscrimination laws usually exempt religious organizations, including hospitals and universities run by religious entities, from compliance.

LaHaye also warned that "every local, state and federal law will be changed to accommodate homosexual 'marriage'" and claimed that "homosexual 'marriage' would cause massive financial, legal and social upheaval as laws are revised to include same-sex partners. . . . Our entire system of government will be overhauled to include homosexuality as an approved and legal lifestyle" (Concerned Women of America 1996). Although changes clearly follow the legalization of gay marriage, as occurred in Massachusetts, no "massive . . . upheaval" occurred there or elsewhere in the United States, nor did this occur in Canada, Spain, or other countries that legalized same-sex marriage.

Like some antigay politicians, Supreme Court Justices, and pundits, at least two of the organizations that co-sponsored Marriage Protection Week argued that, once sodomy laws were struck down, it would be difficult to prohibit bestiality, polygamy, or incest. After the Supreme Court handed down its June 2003 *Lawrence v. Texas* ruling, which struck down thirteen state sodomy laws, former Nixon aide Chuck Colson, now head of Prison Fellowship Ministries, wrote: "If the Court is logical and consistent—and thank God they often aren't—then it's only a matter of time before the taboos and legal prohibitions against incest, polygamy, and bestiality fall. We will have to call it Santorum's Revenge—but don't hold your breath waiting for that" (Kennedy 2003). Colson was referring to Senator Rick Santorum's April 2003 comment that, if the court legalized consensual, adult gay sex, it would have to also legalize "man on child, man on dog relationships" (ibid). Family Research Council analyst Richard Lessner, reacting to the *Lawrence v. Texas* ruling, told the *Los Angeles Times:* "Once again the government has invented a right where no other existed before. Now [laws against] bigamy, incest, polygamy, bestiality, prostitution, and anything else you can think of . . . are now going to come under attack" (ibid).

Religious Right activists and politicians have long equated homosexuality with polygamy, bestiality, incest and pedophilia. Anti–gay marriage groups frequently assert the related claim that those seeking to legalize marriage for same-sex couples are also seeking the legalization of marriages among three or more people.[33] In fact, neither marriage equality advocates nor those promoting civil unions and domestic partnership are seeking recognition of marriages between more than two individuals.

The FRC (Sprigg 2003), Peter LaBarbera, the TVC, and others have long argued that gay people seek to abuse children. The TVC's report "Homosexuals Recruit Public School Children" claims that "homosexual militants" have an ongoing "campaign to legalize sex with children" and are "pushing for aggressive recruitment programs in public schools. . . . Sex with children—even grammar school kids—is a primary goal of homosexual activists." The report warns, "As homosexuals continue to make inroads into public schools, more children will be molested and indoctrinated into the world of homosexuality. Many of them will die in that world" (Sheldon n.d.). As noted above, the peer-reviewed, academic social science research indicates that there is no link between homosexuality and pedophilia and that homosexuals are no more likely to be pedophiles than are heterosexuals.

FUNCTIONS OF ANTIGAY BALLOT CAMPAIGNS

In addition to banning legal protections and family recognition for gay people and same-sex couples, antigay campaigns have a myriad of other functions. Such groups appeal to and amplify antigay bias and resentment to raise money, mobilize supporters, demonize gay people, and distract attention from other policy concerns.

Antigay ballot campaigns and legislative campaigns related to gay rights controversies are bitter and divisive. They usually involve defamatory, false claims about gay people and the impact of legal equality for gay people on other people's rights and freedoms.[34] When pro-gay forces defeat antigay ballot initiatives, gay rights issues often become politically radioactive in the process, and public opinion toward gay people and issues can become more polarized (Donovan and Bowler 1997, 116–17). Thus, even when pro-gay forces win an election, they may find themselves in a transformed political environment in which moderate politicians are reluctant to support pro-gay legislation.

Such fights can also divert attention from other issues. They can have a "priming" effect by making gay rights a more salient issue in voter decision making. Donovan et al. (2005, 8–9) analyzed an October 2004 survey of 1,307 registered voters conducted by the Pew Research Center for the People and the Press. Voters in the states facing an anti–gay marriage ballot question were more likely (36.4 percent) than not (30.3 percent) to state that gay marriage was "very important" in their choice of a presidential candidate (though both John Kerry and George W. Bush oppose marriage equality). That difference was statistically significant. Donovan et al. argue that "[s]tate level campaigns associated with the ballot measures banning gay marriage primed voters to consider gay marriage when making their choice for president" (ibid., 9).

Antigay ballot campaigns can also mobilize the Christian Right's base of conservative voters. Witt and McCorkle note that initiatives with little chance of passage can serve to mobilize supporters to turn out on Election Day and can generate media coverage of groups and issues (Witt and McCorkle 1997, 6). Donovan et al. find that "respondents [to the October 2004 Pew telephone survey] who reported being very motivated to vote because of the issues on the ballot in their state and supported the marriage ban were significantly more likely to vote for Bush in Ohio and Arkansas" (Donovan et al. 2005, 24). Although Kerry won two battleground states where gay marriage was on the ballot—Michigan and Oregon—the marriage controversy clearly played a role in Bush's winning of Ohio's key electoral votes. In Ohio Bush increased his support among four key voting blocs at rates higher than the national average of increase in support. The four blocs were black voters (a 7 percent increase versus 2 percent nationally), voters over sixty years of age (10 percent increase in Ohio versus 7 percent nationally), voters with a high school education (12 percent versus 10 percent), and frequent churchgoers (an increase of 17 percent in Ohio versus a 1 percent increase nationally; ibid., 26).

As moderates and liberals mobilize to resist antigay ballot questions, this mobilization can starve liberal candidates of campaign funds. After narrowly losing the 1994 ballot initiative fight, Idaho Citizens Alliance founder Kelly Watson noted that the mobilization against the antigay initiative "rob[bed] left-wing candidates of precious campaign money," the results of which, she claims, were visible on November 8, 1994, Election Day (Witt and McCorkle 1997, 6). Magleby points to another effect on electoral politics, noting that "gubernatorial candidates have begun backing initiative campaigns tailored to further policies complementing their run for office" (Magleby 1995, cited and described in Witt and McCorkle 1997, 6).

Finally, antigay campaigns can serve as a hook to bring in new audiences to hear the Christian Right's broader conservative and theocratic policy agenda. Polling data show that most Americans support sexual orientation and gender identity nondiscrimination laws, some kind of legal recognition for same-sex couples, an end to the military ban, comprehensive sex education, and other policy concerns (Cahill 2004, 74–76; Sherrill 2004). Marriage is one of the few issues left regarding which gay people do not enjoy majority support. By using this controversial issue as a hook, antigay groups can lure in fair-minded voters and hope to sway some of them to more antigay positions on other issues.

CONCLUSION

The anti–gay marriage movement, comprised of leading evangelical Protestant and Roman Catholic Christian Right organizations, has been widely successful in promoting an across-the-board opposition to any form of legal equality for gay people. Although it has not succeeded in stopping the passage of sexual orientation nondiscrimination laws, it has had great success in restricting marriage for gay couples by means of state and federal legislation and constitutional amendments. In addition to opposing any form of legal protections for gay people, the anti–gay marriage movement advocates a broad right-wing agenda that includes opposition to no-fault divorce, opposition to the teaching of evolution, an end to legal immigration, opposition to women in combat, among other things. In addition to achieving restrictions on the rights of gay people to form families and protect their bonds with their children and partners, the movement disseminates misrepresentations of who gay people are and what legalizing same-sex marriage would mean for America, particularly for heterosexual Christians. Since 1980, the two major parties have diverged widely on the issue of gay rights. Antigay campaigns serve a number of political functions that benefit both the Christian Right and conservative, usually Republican, candidates. Given the centrality of gay controversies in the "culture wars" in the United States since the 1970s and the intractability of differences in worldview between the Christian Right and gay rights activists, struggles about marriage and other legal protections for gay people are likely to remain a major fault line in U.S. politics for years to come.

ENDNOTES

1. Generally the antigay movement targets "homosexuals," i.e., gay men and lesbians, and ignores bisexuals and transgender people. Occasionally, however, it targets bisexuals and transgender people as well. Antigay politics certainly hurts these two groups, though gender identity differs from sexual orientation and thus many transgender people are heterosexual. In this essay the terms *gay* and *antigay* are used for brevity and readability. Usually *gay* refers to gay men and lesbians; *antigay* refers to attacks on gay men and lesbians. When bisexuals and transgender people are explicitly involved, this is noted.
2. Premillennialists are those who believe that the Book of Revelation prophesies the end of the world, at which time Christ will come for a second time and rule for a thousand years. They interpret radical social changes, crises, wars, and natural disasters as evidence of the "end times."
3. For examples of this belief, see Reaching Catholics for Christ (Bend, OR), www.reachingcatholics.org; Lamb and Lion Ministries (McKinney, TX), www.lamblion.com/articles/other/religious/RI-01.php; Chick Publications (Ontario), www.chick.com/default; Cutting Edge Ministries, http://www .cuttingedge.org/news/n1285.cfm.

4. http://www.marriageprotectionweek.com/purpose.asp (accessed October 8, 2003).

5. Antigay groups depict domestic partnership and civil unions as "counterfeit marriage," or a step down the slippery slope toward marriage. For the critical differences between marriage and more limited forms of partner recognition, see Cahill (2004), 4–5, 14–17.

6. Office of the Press Secretary 2003.

7. Financial information about these organizations was obtained from Guidestar.com, which posts the IRS Form 990s (or 990-EZs) for nonprofit organizations that may accept tax-deductible contributions. In turn, this information comes from the IRS Business Master File of 501(c) nonprofits. Those with $25,000 or more in annual revenue are required to file Form 990 with the IRS. I was not able to obtain financial data about sixteen of the twenty-nine organizations co-sponsoring Marriage Protection Week. There are a number of possible reasons: (a) some of the sponsoring organizations are not 501(c)(3) nonprofit organization eligible to accept tax-deductible contributions (religious organizations, for-profits such as Bott Broadcasting, and 501(c)(4) political advocacy organizations are not required to file Form 990; (b) the organization may be registered under a different name with the IRS; (c) the organization may be the program of a larger organization; (d) the organization may have lost its 501(c)(3) status; and (e) the organization may have been recently formed. These data were first published in Cahill, Cianciotto, and Colvin (2003), 6.

8. Web searches were conducted on October 2, 2003.

9. These are Concerned Women for America, Focus on the Family, the Family Research Council, and the Traditional Values Coalition.

10. Some individuals in these couples would not identify themselves as gay or lesbian but would use some other term for homosexual. Others would identify themselves as bisexual. Still others would not want to be categorized. But the critical point is that these individuals are in an amorous, long-term, committed, partnered same-sex relationship widely viewed as a "gay or lesbian" relationship.

11. For more on the seven antigay parenting laws and regulations, see below.

12. http://www.mafamily.org. Accessed March 2, 2004.

13. *Referenda* are popular votes on a law passed by a legislature or under consideration by a legislature. In some states, legislatures are required to subject certain bills to referendum approval, such as large budget expenditures for infrastructural improvement. Twenty-four states allow citizens to demand a referendum through the petition process. *Initiatives* are laws proposed directly by voters that don't require legislative approval or involvement to get on the ballot. Proponents of initiatives must gather a minimum number of signatures. Twenty-three states allow initiatives.

14. The first antigay ballot campaign occurred in Boulder, Colorado, in 1974. This referendum repealed a sexual orientation nondiscrimination ordinance. Anita Bryant's successful "Save Our Children" campaign, which repealed Miami-Dade County, Florida's sexual orientation nondiscrimination law in 1977, was the second antigay ballot measure but the first to reach national

prominence. Following Bryant's victory by more than a 2-to-1 margin, five antigay ballot questions ensued across the United States in 1978, three on the West Coast and two in the Midwest. The use of antigay measures continues to the present day. Most have been successful and resulted in the repeal of sexual orientation nondiscrimination laws (Vaid 1995, 112; Hardisty 1999, 98).

15. Coloradans passed Amendment 2 in November 1992 by a vote of 53 percent to 46 percent. This measure repealed existing local and state laws or policies protecting "homosexual, lesbian or bisexual" people against discrimination and prohibited the future adoption or enforcement of "any [such] law or policy." A year later, voters in Cincinnati, Ohio, Lewiston, Maine, and more than a dozen municipalities in Oregon passed similar ballot questions.

16. For more about transgender people and gender identity nondiscrimination laws, see Currah, Minter, and Green 2000.

17. Ariz. Rev. Stat. §15-716 (2003); Cal. Educ. Code §51550 (West 2003); Nev. Rev. Stat. 389.065 (2003); Utah Code Ann. §53A-13-101 (2003). These laws do not, however, require prior written consent if teachers want to discuss discrimination or harassment related to a student's sexual orientation or gender identity. State parental notification laws with opt-out provisions are also common. They allow parents to remove their children from classes or assemblies that include education about sexuality, HIV, sexually transmitted diseases, abortion, or even death. Such laws, which exist in several dozen states and the District of Columbia, vary in their provisions and scope (Alan Guttmacher Institute 2003).

18. Texas and Mississippi require any mention of issues related homosexuality to be followed by the admonition that homosexual conduct is a criminal offense in those states, and Utah prohibits the "advocacy" of homosexuality. Tex. Health & Safety Code Ann. §163.002(8) (Vernon 2003); Miss. Code Ann. §37-13-171(1)(e) (2003); Miss. Code Ann. §41-79-5(6)(d) (2003); Utah Admin. Code R277-474-3(A)(2) (2003); Utah Code Ann. §53A-13-101 (2003). State laws that require schools to teach that homosexual conduct is illegal will presumably be challenged and struck down in light of the 2003 U.S. Supreme Court ruling in *Lawrence v. Texas,* which abolished sodomy laws. *Lawrence v. Texas,* 123 S. Ct. 2472 (2003).

19. S.C. Code Ann. §59-32-30(A)(5) (Law. Co-op 2003).

20. Ariz. Rev. Stat. §15-716(C) (2003). Alabama requires any mention of homosexuality to be made within the context that "homosexuality is not a lifestyle acceptable to the general public and that homosexual conduct is a criminal offense under the laws of the state." Ala. Code §16-40A-2(c)(8) (2003).

21. Even as the gay and lesbian community struggled to resist the increasing number of antigay ballot campaigns spreading across the country, activists also sought support for legal equality from Democratic Party leaders. Gay rights language was proposed for the 1972 Democratic Party platform. Such language would not be adopted until 1980 (Shilts 1993). The 1980 presidential campaign was the first in which gay rights were directly addressed by presidential candidates or party platforms. Senator Ted Kennedy helped insert pro–gay rights language into the Democratic Party platform for the first time. The Republicans adopted antigay platform language in 1980, setting a

pattern of polarization that continues a quarter-century later. Ronald Reagan used the first antigay television ad against President Carter, claiming that he was the choice of gay voters (Vaid 1995, 115). Reagan's victory in 1980 swept leaders of the antigay Christian Right into positions of political and cultural power (Hardisty 1993). Reagan appointed Focus on the Family's Gary Bauer (later to lead the Family Research Council, a spin-off of Focus on the Family) as a domestic policy advisor and supported the Family Protection Act, which would have banned federal funds to "any organization that suggests that homosexuality can be an acceptable alternative lifestyle" (Bull and Gallagher 1996, 21). The advent of AIDS gave those on the religious Right the perfect justification for their condemnation of homosexuality. Because AIDS emerged in the United States first within the gay male community, where it was first known as Gay Related Immune Deficiency, antigay activists could seize upon this development and claim that homosexuality inevitably led to disease and death. Already viewed as a moral contagion, homosexuality was now redeployed by the Right as a practice associated with a physical contagion, a "deathstyle" that had to be prevented. The Moral Majority's Jerry Falwell, commentator Pat Buchanan, and others portrayed AIDS as God's retribution for sodomy. The televangelist Pat Robertson intoned, "AIDS is God's way of weeding his garden" (Kosofsky Sedgwick 1990, 129). In 1986 and 1988 Californians voted down propositions that would have quarantined people with AIDS (Donovan and Bowler 1997, 114–17). Even when the federal government finally provided funds for AIDS prevention and treatment, a 1987 amendment sponsored by Senator Jesse Helms (R-NC) and attached to many funding bills in the late 1980s and early 1990s banned the use of federal funds for AIDS education that "promotes or encourages homosexual behavior." This had a chilling effect on attempts to teach sexually active youth and adults how to avoid sexually transmitted diseases and unwanted pregnancy (Vaid 1995, 85). In 1984 and 1988 the Republican Party continued to oppose legal equality for gay men and lesbians. The 1984 Democratic ticket largely ignored gay issues, and the 1988 candidate, Massachusetts governor Michael Dukakis, was hostile to gay rights, having backed a state ban on gay foster parents in 1985 (ibid., 116–120). A version of this section first appeared in Cahill (2004), 66–69.

22. A version of this section first appeared in Cahill 2004, 79–80, 82–83.

23. *Baehr v. Lewin*, 852 P.2d 44 (Haw. 1993) (plurality).

24. In 1996 Congress passed the Defense of Marriage Act, which defined marriage in federal law as a "legal union between one man and one woman," thereby restricting federal protections such as Social Security survivor benefits to heterosexual couples. The act also told states that they did not have to recognize same-sex marriages should another state legalize such marriages. "No State . . . shall be required to give effect to any public act, record, or judicial proceeding of any other State . . . respecting a relationship between persons of the same sex that is treated as a marriage under the laws of such other State . . . or a right or claim arising from such a relationship." Defense of Marriage Act of 1996, Pub. L. No. 104-199, 110 Stat. 2419 (1996), cited in Lewis and Edelson (2000), 212–213. After it passed Congress, President

Clinton not only signed the Defense of Marriage Act, but he also bragged about doing so in ads run on Christian radio stations.

25. Commission on Presidential Debates 2000. Bush made that statement during the second presidential debate, October 12, 2000.

26. One model sermon was posted on the Marriage Protection Week Web site, and another was linked to it. Marriage Protection Week co-sponsors recommended that pastors and other clergy follow these models in their sermons on same-sex marriage Sunday, October 12, 2003. The first model sermon, by Ed Vitagliano, called homosexuality "an inverted, perverted love" and "a form of idolatry, whereby God is exchanged for the temporal and carnal pleasures of this life." Homosexuality was portrayed as "mere self-centered sensual enjoyment of the sexual faculties . . . in which one worships an image of oneself through same-sex copulation" (Vitagliano n.d.). In the second model sermon, Ronnie Floyd portrayed homosexuality as a fate worse than the death of a child. Floyd quoted a parishioner who told him, "Pastor Floyd, it would have been easier to have lost my child to death than to homosexuality. It is killing me." Floyd warned: "Satan has taken his tool of homosexuality, a gross and evil sin, and done a con job on the American culture, making it seem like all is okay when you are gay . . . what was once subtle has now turned into the rage of a lion as brazen and threatening as anything in our culture. . . . This is not a skirmish or a conflict or a disagreement, but it is a war. The war they have declared against our culture has an agenda and we need to be aware of it" (Floyd n.d.).

The American Family Association, one of the sponsors of Marriage Protection Week and a long-time leader in the Christian Right and antigay movements, recently criticized efforts to end widespread antigay harassment and violence in the schools: "What Would Jesus Do? Jesus never 'tolerated' or 'accepted' sin. While His response to sin was swift and sometimes harsh, His motive was always one of unconditional love. Jesus didn't 'pussy foot' around, fearful He may 'offend' someone or worried He may appear 'hate-filled,' 'intolerant' or 'bigoted.' No, Jesus called it like it was: sin is sin is sin. Many times He openly exhibited a holy, righteous anger and zeal for 'His Father's business.' Jesus rebuked and exposed. . . . It's high time Christians—followers and Ambassadors of Christ—did the same" (Bennett n.d.).

How should middle school and high school students who oppose homosexuality or dislike gay students interpret such comments? How would one "exhibit a holy righteous anger" or "not pussy foot around" in relation to a gay-straight alliance or a student whom everyone picks on for being gay? Given the already widespread harassment of gay, lesbian, bisexual and transgender students in the schools, such statements are irresponsible, at best. A 2001 national survey of such youth by the Gay, Lesbian and Straight Education Network found that 83 percent had been verbally harassed, 65 percent sexually harassed, and 42 percent physically harassed because of their sexual orientation (Kosciw and Cullen 2001).

27. The essay was titled "San Francisco and Islamists: Fighting the Same Enemy." Prager compared "secular extremism" to "religious extremism. . . . One enemy is led from abroad. The other is directed from home." He continued:

"The war over same-sex marriage and the war against Islamic totalitarianism are actually two fronts in the same war—a war for the preservation of the unique creation known as Judeo-Christian civilization." Claiming that "the Left" is ignoring the threat of anti-American terrorism from groups active in the Muslim world, Prager said this is because "the Left is preoccupied first with destroying America's distinctive values. . . . So, if the Islamists are fellow anti-Americans, the Left figures it can worry about them later." Warning that legalizing same-sex marriage represents "the beginning of the end of Judeo-Christian civilization," he concluded, "This civilization is now fighting for its life—as much here as abroad. Join the fight, or it will be gone as fast as you can say 'Democrat'" (Prager 2004).

28. In fact, affirmative action is a program aimed at rectifying the underrepresentation of women and members of some ethnic minority groups in higher education and the workplace. The Court struck down the use of rigid quotas in its 1978 *Bakke v. Regents of the University of California* ruling, except in cases—such as some urban fire departments—where a history of race-based exclusion can be proved. Race-based discrimination is subject to a higher standard of scrutiny because of the centrality of racism in U.S. history. Claims of voting rights abuses involving race, ethnicity, and language are given particular scrutiny because until the 1960s, people's voting rights were denied on the basis of race, ethnicity, and language. Also, racial nondiscrimination laws, like gender, religion, and sexual orientation nondiscrimination laws, protect everyone against discrimination on the basis of their race, sex, religion, or sexual orientation, not simply members of demographic minorities or women. In the process of allegedly protecting (presumably all straight) people of color against the alleged threat posed by (presumably all white) gay people, antigay activists reinforce misconceptions about nondiscrimination laws, affirmative action, and minority status that in fact hurt people of color (Nakagawa 280–81).

29. The 2000 Campaign; 2nd presidential debate between Gov. Bush and Vice President Gore. *New York Times,* October 12, 2000, A22.

30. Press briefing by Ari Fleischer, April 25, 2003. http://www.whitehouse.gov/news/releases/2003/04/20030425-4.html (accessed July 9, 2003).

31. Kelly Walton, interview by Harvey Pitman, October 12, 1994.

32. Kelly Walton, interview by Harvey Pitman, November 23, 1994.

33. The Traditional Values Coalition's Lou Sheldon predicted that the legalization of same-sex marriage would lead to marriages between "three women and two men, or two women and three men" (Sheldon 2003). The coalition's Web site claims, "Homosexual activists . . . don't want to marry just to have a normal home life. They want same-sex marriage as a way of destroying the concept of marriage altogether—and of introducing polygamy and polyamory (group sex) as 'families.' . . . Their ultimate goal is to abolish all prohibitions against sex with multiple partners" (Traditional Values Coalition n.d.). A flyer for Marriage Protection Week in October 2003 claimed that those seeking government recognition of same-sex marriages also want the government to recognize polygamous marriages: "Homosexual activists have made great progress toward redefining marriage to include two men, two women or a group of any size or mix of sexes." http://www.marriageprotectionweek.com/mpw_mini

poster.pdf. Marriage Protection Week's statement of purpose warned that if gays failed at legalizing group marriage by winning the right of two men or two women to marry, then gays would push for civil unions for three or more people. The FRC and CWA have made similar claims. The FRC's Robert Knight warned that if same-sex marriage is allowed, "[o]ther groups, such as bisexuals and polygamists, will demand the right to redefine marriage to suit their own proclivities. Once the standard of one-man, one-woman marriage is broken, there is no logical stopping point" (Knight et al. 2004). Knight et al. appear to equate bisexuality with promiscuity, a common misperception. Bisexuals are found in both heterosexual relationships and in homosexual relationships. Many people perceived to be straight or gay are in fact able to be attracted to both men and women. But most bisexuals describe themselves as monogamous in their committed relationships (Rust 2001, 57–65). As for polygamy, that issue was decided more than a century ago when it was banned in Utah by the federal government. Concerned Women for America warns that, in the wake of *Goodridge*'s injunction that the Massachusetts constitution "forbids the creation of second-class citizens," advocates of group marriage will argue that they are being treated like second-class citizens, too: "Polygamists now argue that limiting marriage to two people makes them second-class citizens. Bisexuals can now claim that they are second-class citizens because they cannot obtain fulfillment in marriage unless they're permitted to be married to a man and a woman at the same time" (LaRue 2004a).

34. Antigay activists, politicians, and commentators have constructed a gay menace in contemporary U.S. politics: they claim that gay rights are special rights, threatening individual freedoms. Gays are a group of ravenous pedophiles, a crafty, inscrutable minority pulling the strings of power from behind the scenes, bullies who intimidate and threaten violence. Gays are bearers of disease and death, hypersexed, criminal sodomites. Gays are active, aggressive; straights are passive, unwillingly dragged into divisive controversies. Gays threaten national security and Western civilization. These themes are evoked again and again in electoral and legislative antigay campaigns, damaging the social conditions of gay people even when the initiative or legislation in question fails (Cahill 1999). That paper was based on analysis of primary materials put out by antigay groups.

REFERENCES

Alan Guttmacher Institute. 2003. *State policies in brief.* http://www.guttmacher .org/pubs/spib_SE.pdf (accessed August 11, 2003).

Albrecht, B. 2005. Issue 1 conflicts with domestic abuse law, judge says. *Cleveland Plain Dealer,* March 24.

Ash, M., M. Badgett, N. Folbre, L. Saunders, and R. Albelda. 2004. *Same-sex couples and their children in Massachusetts: A view from Census 2000.* Amherst, MA: Institute for Gay and Lesbian Strategic Studies.

Associated Press. 2004. Michigan governor pulls same-sex benefits. *Bakersfield Californian,* December 1.

Bennett, S. n.d. Homosexual agenda: The deception and desensitization of America's youth. http://www.afa.net/homosexual_agenda/getarticle.asp?id=81 (accessed October 8, 2003).

Berlet, C., and M. Quigley. 1995. Theocracy and white supremacy: Behind the culture war to restore traditional values. In *Eyes right: Challenging the right-wing backlash*, ed. C. Berlet, 15–43. Boston: South End.

Bluey, R. 2003. Homosexuals push for same-sex marriage after sodomy ruling. *Christian News Service*, June 27.

Bull, C., and J. Gallagher. 1996. *Perfect enemies: The religious right, the gay movement, and the politics of the 1990s*. New York: Crown.

Cahill, S. 1999. Language struggles in gay rights controversies: The centrality of antigay discourse in contemporary US politics. Paper presented at "Politics, Rights and Representation: Achieving Equality across the lines of Gender, Race and Sexuality in the United States, France, and South Africa." Center for Gender Studies, University of Chicago, October 14–17.

———. 2004. *Same-sex marriage in the United States: Focus on the facts*. New York: Lexington.

Cahill, S., and E. Ludwig. 1999. *Courting the vote: The 2000 presidential candidates on gay, lesbian, bisexual and transgender issues*. New York: National Gay and Lesbian Task Force Policy Institute.

Casper, V., and Schultz, S. B. 1999. *Gay parents/straight schools: Building communication and trust*. New York: Teachers College Press.

Coalition for Marriage. [2004a.] Position statements: Civil unions. http://www.marriagepreservation.org/position.htm (accessed January 26, 2004).

———. [2004b.] Position statements: Homosexuals. http://www.marriagepreservation.org/position.htm (accessed January 26, 2004).

Commission on Presidential Debates. 2000. The second Gore-Bush presidential debate, October 11. http://www.debates.org/pages/trans2000b.html (accessed October 27, 2006).

Concerned Women for America. 1996. The drive to legalize homosexual "marriage." *Critical Issues Briefing*, April.

———. 2002. Georgia school board ponders creationism. September 12. http://www.cwfa.org/articledisplay.asp?id=2059&department=CWA&categoryid=education (accessed March 5, 2004).

———. 2004. Join CWA at the State Capitol! http://www.cwfa.org/articledisplay.asp?id=5290&department=FIELD&categoryid=misc (accessed March 5, 2004).

Connor, K. 2003. American renewal: The legislative action arm of the Family Research Council. www.frcaction.org (accessed November 3, 2003).

Crawford, A. 1980. *Thunder on the right*. New York: Pantheon.

Currah, P., S. Minter, and J. Green. 2000. *Transgender equality: A handbook for activists and policymakers*. New York: Policy Institute of the National Gay and Lesbian Task Force and National Center for Lesbian Rights.

Dailey, T. 2004. Homosexuality and children: The impact for future generations. *Homosexuality and Children* 15 (5). http://www.frc.org/get.cfm?I=FP02K&v=PRINT (accessed March 8, 2004).

Dang, A., and S. Frazer. 2004. *Black same-sex households in the United States: A report from the 2004 Census.* New York: National Gay and Lesbian Task Force Policy Institute and National Black Justice Coalition. http://www.thetaskforce.org (accessed January 30, 2005).

Davies, B., and L. Rentzel. 1993. *Coming out of homosexuality: New freedom for men and women.* Downers Grove, IL: InterVarsity.

D'Emilio, J. 1983. *Sexual politics, sexual communities: The making of a homosexual minority in the United States, 1940–1970.* Chicago: University of Chicago Press.

Diamond, S. 1995. *Roads to dominion: Right-wing movements and political power in the United States.* New York: Guildford.

Donovan, T., and S. Bowler. 1997. Direct democracy and minority rights: Opinions on anti-gay and lesbian ballot initiatives. In *Anti-gay rights: Assessing voter initiatives,* ed. S. Witt and S. McCorkle, 114–17. Westport, CT: Praeger.

———. 1998. Direct democracy and minority rights: An extension. *American Journal of Political Science* 42:1020–24.

Donovan, T., C. Tolbert, D. Smith, and J. Parry. 2005. Did gay marriage elect George W. Bush? Paper prepared for the 2005 State Politics Conference, East Lansing, MI, May 14–15.

Elliot, D. 1994. Bush promises to veto attempts to remove sodomy law. *Austin American Statesman,* January 22, B3.

Family Research Council. 2004. FRC president Tony Perkins reacts to State of the Union address. January 20. http://www.frc.org/get.cfm?i=PR04A07&v=PRINT (accessed March 8, 2004).

Ferrero, E., J. Freker, and T. Foster. 2002. *Too high a price: The case against restricting gay parenting.* New York: ACLU Lesbian and Gay Rights Project. http://www.lethimstay.com/pdfs/gayadoptionbook.pdf.

Floyd, R. n.d. First person: A biblical response to unholy gay "matrimony." http://www.bpnews.net/bpnews.asp?Id=16715. Linked at http://www.marriageprotectionweek.com/action.asp (accessed October 8, 2003).

Fowler, R., and A. Hertzke. 1995. *Religion and politics in America.* Boulder: Westview.

Goldberg, S. 1995. Civil rights, special rights, and our rights. In *Eyes right: Challenging the right-wing backlash,* ed. C. Berlet, 109–112. Boston: South End.

Green, J. 2000. Antigay: Varieties of opposition to gay rights. In *The politics of gay rights,* ed. C. Rimmerman, K. Wald, and C. Wilcox, 121–38. Chicago: University of Chicago Press.

Groth, A. N., and H. J. Birnbaum. 1978. Adult sexual orientation and attraction to underage persons. *Archives of Sexual Behavior* 7.3:175–81.

Hardisty, J. 1993. Constructing homophobia: Colorado's right-wing attack on homosexuals. *Public Eye* (March): 1–10.

———. 1999. *Mobilizing resentment: Conservative resurgence from the John Birch Society to the Promise Keepers.* Boston: Beacon.

Herman, D. 2000. The gay agenda is the devil's agenda: The Christian right's vision and the role of the state. In *The politics of gay rights,* ed. C. Rimmerman, K. Wald, and C. Wilcox, 139–60. Chicago: University of Chicago Press.

Holmes, W., and G. Slap. 1998. Sexual abuse of boys: Definitions, prevalence, correlates, sequelae and management. *Journal of the American Medical Association* 280 (21): 1855–62.

Human Rights Campaign. 2003. Statewide anti-discrimination laws and policies. December. http://www.hrc.org/Template.cfm?Section=Your_Community& Template=/ContentManagement/ContentDisplay.cfm&ContentID=1338 (accessed February 5, 2004).

———. 2005. *Truth or consequences: The effects of constitutional amendments on marriage in Ohio, Michigan, Missouri, and Utah.* Washington, DC: Human Rights Campaign. http://www.hrc.org. April (accessed May 4, 2005).

Jenny, C., and T. Roesler. 1994. Are children at risk for sexual abuse by homosexuals? *Pediatrics* 94 (1) : 41–44.

Johnson, J. 2001. Homosexuals seek survivor benefits intended for families. Cybercast News Service, October 22. http://www.dadi.org/homogred.htm (accessed February 9, 2004).

Keen, L. 1999. An about face for Bush? Opinion on appointing gays remains murky. *Washington Blade*, October 15.

Kennedy, D. 2003. Department of perverse logic: Doing it doggy-style on the homophobic right. *Boston Phoenix*, July 11–17. http://www.bostonphoenix.com/ boston/news_features/this_just_in/documents/03007023.asp (accessed August 24, 2005).

Kimball, J. 2003. Homosexuals pose new threat to U.S. border security. September 29. http://www.cwfa.org/printerfriendly.asp?id=4629&department=cwa&c ategoryid5family (accessed September 29, 2003).

Knight, R., et al. 2004. *Marriage: One man, one woman.* Washington, DC: Family Research Council. January 7. http://www.frc.org/get.cfm?i=IF03J01&v=PRINT (accessed January 15, 2004).

Kosciw, J., and M. Cullen. 2001. *The GLSEN 2001 national school climate survey: The school-related experiences of our nation's lesbian, gay, bisexual and transgender youth.* New York: Gay, Lesbian and Straight Education Network.

Kosovsky Sedgwick, E. 1990. *Epistemology of the closet.* Berkeley: University of California Press.

LaRue, J. 2003. *Talking points: Why homosexual "marriage" is wrong.* Washington, DC: Concerned Women for America.

———. 2004a. Why *Goodridge* is legally and constitutionally wrong. *Concerned Women for America Legal Studies,* January 27. http://www.cwfa.org/articledis play.asp?id=5150&department=LEGAL&categoryid=judges (accessed February 3, 2004).

———. 2004b. *Homosexuals hijack civil rights bus.* Washington, DC: Concerned Women for America. http://www.cwfa.org/articles/5395/LEGAL/family/ (accessed August 18, 2005).

Lewis, G., and J. Edelson. 2000. DOMA and ENDA: Congress votes on gay rights. In *The politics of gay rights,* ed. C. Rimmerman, K. Wald, and C. Wilcox, . Chicago: University of Chicago Press, 2000.

Log Cabin Republicans. 1999. Anti-gay pledge divides struggling far right from leading GOP candidates. August 25. http://www.logcabinwa.com/archive/ 19990825074i.shtml.

Magleby, D. 1995. Let the voters decide? An assessment of the initiative and the referendum process. *University of Colorado Law Review* 66:13–46.

Maher, B. n.d. *Why marriage should be privileged in public policy.* Washington, DC: Family Research Council. http://www.frc.org/get.cfm?i=IS03D1&v=PRINT (accessed March 4, 2004).

Massachusetts Family Institute. 2001a. Massachusetts Family Institute criticizes acting governor's decision to extend domestic partner benefits. August 16. http://www.mafamily.org/Press%20Room%20Folder/Press%20Releases/Press Release15.htm (accessed March 4, 2004).

———. 2001b. Massachusetts Family Institute criticizes Acting Governor Swift over the extension of special rights for homosexuals. September 10. http://www .mafamily.org/Press%20Room%20Folder/Press%20Releases/PressRelease20 .htm (accessed March 4, 2004).

———. 2003. Issue in focus: Same-sex marriage. http://www.mafamily.org/ samesexmarriage.htm (accessed December 16, 2003).

McElvaine, R. 1992. GOP "values"? Read their lip service. *Los Angeles Times,* October 12.

Moen, M. 1992. The Christian right in the United States. In *The religious challenge to the state,* ed. M. Moen and L. Gustafson, 75–101. Philadelphia: Temple University Press.

Nakagawa, S. 1995. Race, religion and the right. In *Eyes right: Challenging the right-wing backlash,* ed. C. Berlet, 279–82. Boston: South End.

National Gay and Lesbian Task Force. 2004. Expenditures in 2004 anti–gay marriage campaigns. New York: National Gay and Lesbian Task Force. November. http://www.thetaskforce.org/downloads/MarriageExpenditures2004.pdf (accessed August 22, 2005).

———. 2006. National Gay and Lesbian Task Force hails passage of Washington state bill prohibiting discrimination based on sexual orientation and gender identity. Press release. January 27. http://www.thetaskforce.org/media/release .cfm?print=1&releaseID=914 (accessed May 11, 2006).

Newport, F. 2003. Six out of 10 Americans think homosexual relations should be recognized as legal; but Americans are evenly divided on issue of legal civil unions between homosexuals giving them legal rights of married couples. Gallup News Service, May 15.

Office of the Press Secretary. 2003. Marriage Protection Week 2003: A proclamation. http://www.whitehouse.gov/news/releases/2003/10/20031003-12.html (accessed October 27, 2006).

Patterson, C. J. 1995. *Lesbian and gay parenting: A resource for psychologists.* Washington, DC: American Psychological Association. http://www.apa.org/pi/parent .html. Accessed November 1, 2002.

People for the American Way. [2004a.] Right wing organizations: Concerned WomenforAmerica.http://www.pfaw.org/pfaw/general/default.aspx?oid=3151& print=yes (accessed March 1, 2004).

People for the American Way. [2004b.] Right wing organizations: Family Research Council. http://www.pfaw.org/pfaw/general/default.aspx?oid=4211&print=yes (accessed March 1, 2004).

People for the American Way. [2004c.] Right wing organizations: Traditional Values

Coalition. http://www.pfaw.org/pfaw/general/default.aspx?oid=8992&print=yes (accessed March 1, 2004).

Perrin, E., and the Committee on Psychosocial Aspects of Child and Family Health. 2002. Technical report: Co-parent or second-parent adoption by same-sex parents. *Pediatrics* 109 (2): 341–44.

Pitman, Harvey 1997. In their own words: Conversations with campaign leaders. In *Anti–gay rights: Assessing voter initiatives,* ed. S. Witt and S. McCorkle, 77–93. Westport, CT: Praeger.

Prager, D. 2004. San Francisco and Islamists: Fighting the same enemy. March 2. Linked to the Massachusetts Family Institute website at http://www.mafamily .org/commentary.htm (accessed March 5, 2004).

Ramer, H. 1999. Bauer: Gay marriage is worse than terrorism. Associated Press, December 27.

Reed, R. 1996. *Active faith: How Christians are changing the soul of American politics.* New York: Simon & Schuster.

Rust, P. 2001. Two many and not enough: The meanings of bisexual identities. *Journal of Bisexuality* 31:57–65.

Shaw, S. 1997. No longer a sleeping giant: The re-awakening of religious conservatives in American politics. In *Anti–gay rights: Assessing voter initiatives,* ed. S. Witt and S. McCorkle, 7–16. Westport, CT: Praeger.

Sheldon, L. 2003. Discrimination and Tolerance. *Traditional Values Coalition Report* 21 (1): February.

———. 2003. Traditional Values Coalition fundraising letter. September 17. http:// www.traditionalvalues.org/defined.php (accessed October 27, 2006).

———. n.d. Homosexuals recruit public school children. Activists use issues of "safety," "tolerance," and "homophobia" as tactics to promote homosexuality in our nation's schools. *Traditional Values Coalition Special Report* 18 (11).

Sherrill, K. 2004. *Same-sex marriage, civil unions, and the 2004 presidential election.* New York: National Gay and Lesbian Task Force Policy Institute. http://www .thetaskforce.org/downloads/MarriageCUSherrill2004.pdf (accessed May 26, 2006).

Shilts, R. 1993. *Conduct unbecoming: Lesbians and gays in the U.S. military—Vietnam to the Persian Gulf.* New York: St. Martin's.

Simmons, T., and M. O'Connell. 2003. *Married-couple and unmarried-partner households: 2000.* United States Census Bureau. February. http://www.census .gov/prod/2003pubs/censr-5.pdf (accessed September 18, 2003).

A sodomy law's last stand. 2000. *Advocate,* July 18.

Stacey, J., and T. Biblarz. 2001. (How) does the sexual orientation of the parent matter? *American Sociological Review* 66 (2): 159–83.

Stanton, G. 2003. Is marriage in jeopardy? Focus on the Family: Marriage and Social Issues: Marriage and Family FAQs. August 27. http://family.org/cforum/ fosi/marriage/FAQs/a0026916.cfm (accessed October 3, 2003).

Traditional Values Coalition. n.d. *Do homosexuals really want the right to marry?* http://www.traditionalvalues.org (accessed January 22, 2004).

Trexler, R. 1995. *Sex and conquest: Gendered violence, political order, and the European conquest of the Americas.* Ithaca: Cornell University Press.

Vaid, U. 1995. *Virtual equality: The mainstreaming of gay and lesbian liberation*. New York: Anchor.

Vitagliano, E. n.d. One flesh: Why sodomy can never depict the relationship between Christ and his church. http://www.marriageprotectionweek.com/one _flesh.html (accessed 10, 2003).

Wald, K. 1992. *Religion and politics in the United States*. 2d ed. Washington, DC: Congressional Quarterly Press.

Wetzel, D. 2003. Senate approves measure to protect religious adoption agencies. Associated Press, January 29.

Wetzstein, C. 2003. Groups pledge to protect marriage. *Washington Times*, October 3. http://www.washtimes.com/national/20031002-114818-5707r.htm (accessed October 8, 2003).

Wilcox, C. 1992. *God's warriors: The Christian Right in twentieth-century America*. Baltimore: Johns Hopkins University Press.

Witt, S., and S. McCorkle, eds. 1997. *Anti–gay rights: Assessing voter initiatives*. Westport, CT: Praeger.

Yang, A. 2001. *The 2000 national elections study and gay and lesbian rights: Support for equality grows*. Washington, DC: National Gay and Lesbian Task Force.

Zwier, R. 1982. *Born-again politics: The new Christian right in America*. Downers Grove, IL: Inter-Varsity.

FRAMING THE ISSUE OF
SAME-SEX MARRIAGE

TRADITIONAL VALUES VERSUS EQUAL RIGHTS

Barry L. Tadlock, C. Ann Gordon, and Elizabeth Popp

SAME-SEX MARRIAGE EMERGES ON
THE NATION'S POLITICAL AGENDA

In the 1950s the Mattachine Society fought to have lesbians and gays treated as citizens with rights equal to those held by heterosexual individuals. Franklin Kameny, the society's Washington, DC, branch leader, argued that one necessary precursor to equality was for gay men and lesbians to emerge from their closets. Such "outings" did not occur in large numbers, however, at least not until the years following the June 1969 Stonewall riots in New York City (Eskridge 2002). The rioting is commonly seen as the flashpoint for the modern gay rights movement.

In the post-Stonewall years various other groups coalesced to form the National Coalition of Gay Organizations (NCGO). In 1972 the NCGO demanded several legal reforms, including equal marriage rights for all citizens. No state and virtually no municipal government acceded to this demand. In Boulder, Colorado, however, the court clerk issued marriage licenses to same-sex couples until the state's attorney general prevented further action. Owing in part to this setback, the NCGO's goals evolved. It set its sights on municipal rather than state governments, and it sought domestic partnership rights instead of marriage rights. In 1982, San Francisco—under Mayor Dianne Feinstein's leadership—became the first city government to acknowledge partnership rights. Few cities followed San Francisco's lead (Eskridge 2002).

The issue of same-sex marriage regained prominence in 1990 when three couples filed applications for marriage licenses in Hawaii. Once denied the licenses, the couples sued the state. In *Baehr v. Lewin* the Hawaii Supreme Court ruled that the state had no compelling interest in denying marriage rights to same-sex couples (Hull 2001).[1] Contemporaneously, the U.S. Congress passed the federal Defense of Marriage Act (DOMA, H.R. 3396, 1996). Thirty-seven state governments followed suit, passing so-called mini-DOMAs. Collectively these legislative acts permitted states to *not* recognize same-sex marriages performed in other states, thereby circumventing the U.S. Constitution's full faith and credit clause (Eskridge 2002).

In 1999 Vermont's Supreme Court ruled that the state had to grant same-sex couples the same benefits and protections that accrued to married heterosexual couples. Hence the nation's first civil union law was created (Jost 2003). Then, four years later, the Massachusetts Supreme Judicial Court ruled in the plaintiffs' favor in *Goodridge et al. v. Department of Public Health*, thereby legalizing same-sex marriage in that state.[2]

At the national level, U.S. Representative Marilyn Musgrave cointroduced H.J. Res. 56 in 2003. The constitutional amendment, if successfully proposed and ratified, would define marriage as being between one man and one woman. Although gay rights groups quite expectedly opposed Musgrave's proposal, somewhat surprisingly, some key gay rights opponents failed to line up behind it (Jost 2003). For example, Representative Bob Barr, DOMA's author, opposed Musgrave's proposed amendment on the basis that it gave too much power to the federal government (Darman 2004).

During the summer of 2004, the U.S. Senate voted on a Federal Marriage Amendment (FMA, S.J. Res. 40), and the U.S. House of Representatives enacted the Marriage Protection Act (MPA or H.R. 3313). Although the Senate failed to get a majority of that chamber's one hundred votes for the FMA, the successful House passage of MPA means that the federal courts cannot rule in same-sex marriage cases (Fitzgerald and Cooperman 2004).

In November 2004, citizens in eleven states supported ballot initiatives that banned same-sex marriage within their borders. These states joined Missouri, Louisiana, Alaska, Hawaii, Nebraska, and Nevada (Family Research Council 2003). Most states have joined their ranks, so that as of October 2006 only five states and Washington, DC, did *not* have laws or constitutional amendments prohibiting same-sex marriage.

Governmental action coincides with interest group action concerning this issue. In an article for the *Washington Post*, Alan Cooperman discusses the "institutionalized" nature of "the interest groups arrayed for and against" the issue of same-sex marriage. In other words, opposing forces are marshalling resources, establishing grassroots lobbying efforts, and hiring personnel in order to affect outcomes. Significantly, this has occurred "at lightning speed" as compared to the institutionalizing of forces surrounding the abortion issue (Cooperman 2004).

Why this issue, and why now? Although numerous groups and individuals have worked for years both in favor of and in opposition to gay and lesbian rights, some would argue that it was the U.S. Supreme Court's 2003 decision in *Lawrence v. Texas* that set the stage for the seemingly sudden emergence of same-sex marriage as a key battleground issue.[3] In *Lawrence* the Court threw out Texas's sodomy law and with it all sodomy laws nationwide. After the ruling, Justice Antonin Scalia said that laws limiting marriage to opposite-sex couples were on "pretty shaky ground" (Thomas 2003). A decline in public support for same-sex relationships was one immediate impact of the *Lawrence* decision (Jost 2003, 18).

The confluence of recent events—the Court's ruling in *Lawrence*, the Massachusetts Supreme Court ruling in *Goodridge*, President George W. Bush's announcement on July 30, 2003, that he favored limiting marriage to heterosexual couples, and the eleven ballot initiatives passed in November 2004—brought with it unprecedented activity by interest groups on both sides of the debate. The Human Rights Campaign (HRC), the largest of the gay-rights groups, created an Internet petition in support of gay marriage. By October 23, 2006, it had 762,636 signatures. The Traditional Values Coalition (TVC) reported that it was sending 1.5 million mailings a month in opposition to same-sex marriage. Of course, the actions of groups such as HRC and TVC are aimed at influencing the policy debate, and it is to that topic that we turn our attention.

FRAMING THE ISSUE OF SAME-SEX MARRIAGE

These interest groups attempt to frame issues in a way that is favorable to their position. They are successful to the extent that they are able to get the media to adopt their frame in reporting on the issue and also in getting the public to utilize their frame when thinking about the issue.

The essence of framing is that there exist many possible ways to present political and social issues. Those differences in presentation can influence the way in which individuals think about and evaluate those issues. Frames have been described as "the organization of experience" (Goffman 1974, 11), "linguistic windows" (Ball-Rokeach and Loges 1996, 278), and "*constructions* of the issue" (Nelson and Kinder 1996, 1057; emphasis in original). Nelson and his colleagues argue that "[f]raming is the process by which a communication source, such as a news organization, defines and constructs a political issue or public controversy" (Nelson, Clawson, and Oxley 1997, 567). With so much news and information available, individuals and the media use frames to organize and simplify their attitudes and evaluations of an issue (for example, Neuman, Just, and Crigler 1992). Frames are prevalent in mass communications, so it is important to understand framing effects and evaluate their impact on public opinion. Frames tell audiences what an issue is about, and communicators seek to establish the dominance of their frame. This desire to frame issues is particularly true of interest groups and political elites (Nelson and Oxley 1999). If one frame does become dominant in a competition among issue frames, it can eventually lead to one universally held understanding of an issue. The debate about that issue will then be limited within the parameters set forth by the dominant frame, restricting debate (Schattschneider 1960). Framing effects that originate from interest groups and political elites are of great interest when considering whether citizens have enough information and resources to make well-informed decisions and formulate opinions free of elite manipulation.

Interest groups and political elites have considerable influence within the media. Journalists' use of quotations, sound bites, and other input from such sources make the mass media the perfect vehicle for carrying their preferred frames (Nelson and Kinder 1996; Nelson, Clawson, and Oxley 1997; see also Nelson, Oxley, and Clawson 1997; Nelson and Oxley 1999). Frames "tell people how to weight the often conflicting considerations that enter into everyday political deliberations" (Nelson, Oxley, and Clawson 1997, 226). Such conflicting considerations often exist when "value words" are used to connect a policy position to an abstract value

(Brewer 2002). *Value-choice framing* is the presentation of an issue in terms of two or more conflicting values, each of which could justify an individual's issue position. For example, the health care debate of the mid-1990s centered around two core values: equality and freedom. In value framing, the frames are based on the personal values of individuals, which are theorized to be more accessible than specific political knowledge. Because these values should be accessible to most, if not all, individuals, it follows that value framing will be an expedient method for individuals to use when evaluating issues (Ball-Rokeach and Loges 1996).

Studies that examine the intersection between value frames and the debate about gay rights, including same-sex marriage and civil unions, have found that framing can have a significant impact on the ways individuals evaluate and judge the issues. Paul Brewer (2002) utilizes the concept of value framing to examine if, how, and when individuals borrow the language of the media to explain their own position regarding the issue of gay rights. The issue was presented using equality and traditional morality frames. Participants who received a particular frame in the experimental treatment were more likely to mention that frame explicitly in their explanation of their position on gay rights. The use of value words in open-ended responses, however, did not always endorse that particular value, demonstrating that individuals sometimes use a frame to challenge a particular value. Finally, when participants received both frames, the presence of the morality frame lessened the effect of the equality frame.

In a related article, Brewer (2003) argues that political knowledge gained from exposure to frames put forth by the media can help individuals connect their values with an issue, thereby affecting their positions regarding that issue. The study finds that as political knowledge increases, moral traditionalism and support for gay rights also increase. Furthermore, respondents were equally likely to link their egalitarian views with support for gay rights, regardless of their level of political knowledge. These results suggest that there are differences in public opinion depending on whether the media portray one undisputed interpretation or two competing interpretations of a value. Brewer concludes that framing effects are not based solely on the cognitive abilities of individuals; rather, effects are present when individuals are politically knowledgeable and receive undisputed value frames (Brewer 2003).

This brings us to the question of whether interest groups' framing of issues influences public opinion regarding an issue, in particular, such a volatile one as same-sex marriage. One can make an argument that citizens hold attitudes about this issue with such fervor that interest group frames do not matter. Furthermore, one could make the point that newspapers' utilization of the frames also does not influence public opinion. If public opinion is not influenced, then one must question whether legislative action is affected by framing of the same-sex marriage issue. Yet Haider-Markel reports that under "sub-optimal conditions of high conflict and low public and legislative support" interest groups can have an influence on congressional decision-making, if not legislative outcomes (1999, 138).

Those who have researched the framing of other lesbian and gay rights issues have found evidence that supports Haider-Markel's argument. Brewer reports that participants in an experiment who received an equality frame were likely to explain their opinions about gay rights in terms of equality, whereas those who received a morality frame from media coverage used the language of morality to explain their views (2002). Ott and Aoki (2002), in their study of media framing of the Matthew Shepard murder, find that the media's tragic framing of the event served to alleviate the public's guilt over Shepard's death. Furthermore, they argue that the frame hampered efforts to create public policy that would prevent a similar murder in the future. Finally, Meyers undertakes a discursive analysis of news coverage in the *Washington Post* that dealt with President Bill Clinton's attempt to repeal the ban on lesbians and gay men in the military. She argues that the coverage presented a male, heterosexist discourse that legitimated arguments against repealing the ban. She argues for a redefinition of gay men and lesbians as a minority group that has been denied basic civil rights (1994).

CONTENT ANALYSIS OF INTEREST GROUP WEB SITES

To study the ways in which political elites frame the same-sex marriage issue, we conducted content analyses of the Web sites of interest groups that are actively involved in the issue of same-sex marriage. Frameworks being put forth by political elites are important because of the possibility that the media will utilize them in stories about the issue.

Our sample of interest groups includes those that work most actively for and against same-sex marriage (see table 8.1). We selected ten groups on each side of the issue. We included in our sample only groups that had been cited in major newspapers' articles about this issue over a period of eighteen months (March 2003 to August 2004). The selection was a cross-section of major papers in all four regions of the United States

TABLE 8.1. Interest groups used in Web site analysis.

GROUPS THAT USE A TRADITIONAL VALUES FRAME	GROUPS THAT USE AN EQUAL RIGHTS FRAME
American Family Association	Soulforce
Traditional Values Coalition	Marriage Equality USA
Family Research Council	EqualMarriage.org
American Values	DontAmend.com
Christian Coalition of America	Freedom to Marry
Focus on the Family	Gay and Lesbian Alliance for Marriage
Eagle Forum	Love Makes a Family
American Center for Law and Justice	Lambda Legal Defense and Education Fund
Concerned Women for America	National Gay and Lesbian Task Force
Citizens for Community Values	Human Rights Campaign

(the *Boston Globe*, the *New York Times*, the *Chicago Sun-Times*, the *St. Louis Post-Dispatch*, the *Seattle Times*, the *San Diego Union-Tribune*, and the *Miami Herald*). We visited the Web sites of the selected groups and searched for information about their stance on and framing of the same-sex marriage issue. Where available we analyzed the mission statement for issue framing. If such a statement was unavailable we analyzed one of the following in order to discern a group's frame: the "frequently asked questions" (FAQs) page, media talking points, the issue position or statement, or in a couple of cases an article posted to the site about the issue. Note that some groups' sites, such as the American Family Association (AFA), directed users interested in the issue to a companion site. In the case of the AFA, users were directed to NoGayMarriage.com and ProtectMarriageRally.com.

It is evident that two frames stand out among these interest groups: a traditional values frame used by groups that oppose same-sex marriage and an equal rights frame used by groups that support it. For example, the Family Research Council opposes same-sex marriage. Its Web site states, "Gay marriage is not a moral alternative to traditional marriage" (2003). On the other hand, Marriage Equality USA supports same-sex marriage. Its Web site states, "The organization's sole purpose and focus is to end discrimination in civil marriage so that same-sex couples can enjoy the same legal and societal status as opposite-sex couples" (2002). Although these frames are used in opposition with respect to this issue, one could make the argument that these frames can be used in varying ways; after all, equality is a traditional principle of American political culture.

It is possible to discern other frames (see Hull 2002). One such alternative frame is, for lack of better terminology, a "majority rules" frame used by at least one of the groups opposed to same-sex marriage. This frame postulates that since the majority of Americans are opposed to the practice, legislative action is needed to further this belief. Among the groups supportive of same-sex marriage, at least one group used a tolerance frame. Yet no frames, including the two just mentioned, were used with the regularity that frames of equal rights and traditional values were used.

NEWSPAPER CONTENT ANALYSIS: FRAMING THE SAME-SEX MARRIAGE ISSUE

In order to construct a broad and thorough understanding of newspaper coverage of the gay marriage debate, we conducted a content analysis of twenty-six major, regional, and local newspapers for the year before the collection of our national public opinion survey data.[4] We selected six publications to represent major papers, and we randomly selected twenty papers, five from each geographic region, to represent regional papers (see table 8.2). Owing to the limitations of LexisNexis Academic, some of the desired major newspapers were not available, so substitutions were made to best preserve both geographic location and breadth of content.[5]

The "Guided News Search" feature of LexisNexis Academic was employed to collect newspaper articles containing the search terms "same sex marriage," "homosexual marriage," "gay marriage," or "civil unions" in the article headlines or lead paragraphs.[6] This procedure resulted in 411 articles, only 181 of which were suitable for this analysis. Articles were excluded if they were letters to the editor, only briefly mentioned the search terms without any substantive context, or were reports of candidate positions without any discussion of the search terms, among other reasons (see appendix A). The 181 remaining articles were coded for frames (see appendix B).

As discussed above, the same-sex marriage debate can be framed in terms of two potentially competing values: equality and traditional values (or morality). The equality frame is generally used to argue in favor of same-sex marriage on the basis of equal rights for all, and the morality frame is used to argue against it on the grounds of traditional moral values. The equality frame encompasses a broad range of discussion about rights, discrimination, fairness, and specific benefits that are afforded to married couples. For instance, one article cites a representative of the gay advocacy group Freedom to Marry: "The Supreme Court has said in the strongest possible terms that love and intimacy and family have deep

TABLE 8.2.   Newspapers used in article analysis.

Major Papers
    Boston Globe
    New York Times
    San Diego Union-Tribune
    Seattle Times
    Louis Post-Dispatch
    Washington Post
Northeast
    Connecticut Post (Bridgeport)
    Lowell Sun (MA)
    Portland Press Herald (ME)
    Post-Standard (Syracuse, NY)
    Union Leader (Manchester, NH)
Southeast
    Herald (Rock Hill, SC)
    Florida Times-Union (Jacksonville)
    Post and Courier (Charleston, SC)
    Star-News (Wilmington, NC)
    Winston-Salem Journal (NC)
Midwest
    Bismarck Tribune (ND)
    Columbus Dispatch (OH)
    Plain Dealer (Cleveland, OH)
    Omaha World Herald (NE)
    State Journal-Register (Springfield, IL)
West
    Argus (Fremont, CA)
    Daily Review (Hayward, CA)
    Las Vegas Review-Journal (NV)
    San Antonio Express-News (TX)
    Wyoming Tribune-Eagle (Cheyenne)

constitutional protection for all Americans and that gay people have an equal right to participate. This gives us a tremendous tool for moving forward to end discrimination" (Kershaw 2003). Articles that emphasize the rights being denied to gay and lesbian couples are also coded as containing an equal rights frame. For instance, one article discusses the financial burdens that same-sex couples face because they are not allowed to legally marry, such as taxes, health insurance, and lawyer fees for resolving special estate, custody, and medical issues. An article source then says that it is "a basic fairness issue" (Blanton 2003). The traditional values frame similarly encompasses a wide array of arguments against same-sex marriage, including arguments featuring religious and biblical elements, threats to the family structure, and threats to our traditionally held morals. The Roman Catholic Church is widely cited for its clearly stated belief that homosexual acts "go against the natural moral law," while at the same time traditional marriages are "holy" (Mahoney 2003). An article on the editorial page advocating in favor of the Federal Marriage Amendment argues that allowing same-sex marriage would "destroy marriage as a functioning social entity in America." The article also cites a source that says, "Losing this battle means losing the idea that children need mothers and fathers. . . . It means losing American civilization" (Harmon 2003).

The equality and the traditional values frames can appear in the same article. At times one frame is accepted and another rejected, and at times both frames are presented without the article or author favoring one or the other. The latter situation is common when journalists present arguments from both sides of an argument. For instance, an article about activities advocating same-sex marriage in the San Francisco Bay area included interest groups and sources involved in those activities who advocated "equality for same sex couples in California," but the article also included a quotation from a representative of the Bay Area Citizens for the Protection of Marriage and Family who declared that the activities constituted a "war on marriage" (Adamick 2003). One frame is often accepted while another is rejected in editorials or columns that clearly have a strong opinion about same-sex marriage or articles that feature an interest group evoking their opponents' argument in the course of discrediting it. For instance, a column in the editorial section of a Texas paper argued that gay and lesbian Texans are merely seeking "the legal protection granted to any legally married person," such as medical benefits and estate rights. It also evoked the traditional family and biblical arguments against same-sex marriage in order to argue against extending rights to lesbians and gays. For example, the author argued that Christian scripture provides contradictory accounts of marriage, citing the fact that Solomon had one thousand women and that Abraham's wife was also his half-sister (Rundin 2003). It is necessary to code articles as having both the equal rights and the traditional values frames in these situations, although sometimes frames are evoked simply to refute them, because any mention of a particular frame could potentially heighten the salience of that particular consideration for individuals.

RESULTS OF NEWSPAPER CONTENT ANALYSIS

Our content analysis demonstrates that the convergence of events related to same-sex marriage in the summer of 2003—the legalization of gay marriage in Canada, the *Lawrence* case, and the gay marriage issues

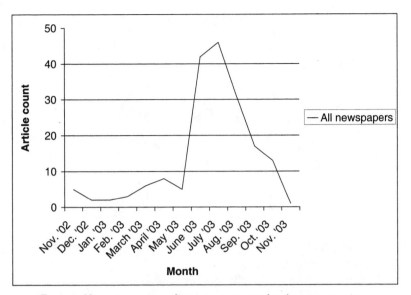

Figure 8.1. Newspaper coverage of same-sex marriage and civil unions across time.

argued before state supreme courts, particularly in Massachusetts—did result in a sharp increase in the attention paid to same-sex marriage and civil unions in our sample of newspapers (see figure 8.1). Although this content analysis did not follow additional issues with which to compare the same-sex marriage debate, a logical conclusion would be that many American citizens were at least exposed to the issue, if not to the values used to frame the debate.

This content analysis confirms the presence of equality and traditional value frames in newspaper coverage of the same-sex marriage debate and, to a lesser extent, the civil union and broader gay rights debates as well. More than 80 percent of the articles did not discuss civil unions in any sort of broader context apart from merely mentioning the term. But when framing of the civil unions issue did occur, the equal rights frame was used far more than either the traditional values frame alone or the equality and traditional values frames together (10 percent, 1 percent, and 3 percent of articles, respectively).[7] Similarly, when articles discussed general gay rights in a broader context, which occurred in only 10 percent of the articles used in this analysis, the equal rights frame dominated the traditional values frame used alone and the combination of the two frames utilized together (6 percent, 1 percent, and 2 percent, respectively). These framing effects for civil unions and gay rights are important; because they constitute such a small percentage of the articles

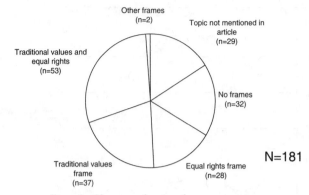

Figure 8.2. Newspaper framing of same-sex marriage.

in this analysis, however, we focus exclusively on how newspapers frame the same-sex marriage debate.

As expected, two distinct frames emerged in the newspaper coverage of same-sex marriage: equality and traditional values. Traditional values frames were slightly more common than equality frames (20 versus 16 percent); however, at 29 percent, the combination of the two was the most common framing condition (see figure 8.2). The dominance of this combination frame is likely due to the media's preference for presenting issues in an "objective" or "balanced" manner.

The same quest for objectivity that induces journalists to provide frames to represent both sides of a debate also drives them to avoid editorializing and providing their own views of a topic (of course, editorials and op-ed pieces are logical exceptions). The quotation of outside sources is a practical and necessary way for journalists to gather and convey information, but it can also be used (presumably inadvertently) to favor one frame or one argument more than another. Interest groups and political elites are eager, willing, and actively pursuing opportunities to provide journalists with such information. Journalists' use of quotations, sound bites, and other input from these sources make the mass media an attractive tool for the dissemination of their frames (Nelson and Kinder 1996). We focus on the utilization of input from interest groups in this analysis. In our sample of articles about same-sex marriage, thirty-five groups supporting it and twenty-six groups opposing it were quoted or referenced at least once (see table 8.3).

As discussed above, our parallel content analysis of interest group Web sites identified ten interest groups that promote an equal rights

TABLE 8.3.   Full sample of interest groups with number of newspaper citations.

NUMBER	PROPONENTS OF SAME-SEX MARRIAGE	TIMES CITED	OPPONENTS OF SAME-SEX MARRIAGE	TIMES CITED
1	Human Rights Campaign	18	Massachusetts Family Institute	9
2	Lambda Legal	13	Focus on the Family	6
3	Gay and Lesbian Advocates and Defenders	11	Family Research Council	5
4	Dignity USA	7	Alliance for Marriage	3
5	Freedom to Marry	6	Bay-Area Citizens for the Protection of Marriage and Family	2
6	Equality California	4	American Values	2
7	American Civil Liberties Union	4	Traditional Values Coalition	2
8	National Lesbian and Gay Task Force	3	Concerned Women of America	2
9	National Center for Lesbian Rights	3	Focus on the Family of Canada	1
10	Massachusetts Gay and Lesbian Caucus	3	Alliance Defense Fund	1
11	Love Makes a Family	3	Christian Coalition	1
12	Jacksonville Area Sexual Minority Youth Network	3	American Family Association	1
13	Log Cabin Republicans	3	Massachusetts Citizens for Marriage	1
14	Empire State Pride Agenda	2	League of American Families	1
15	Marriage Equality California	2	Pro-Family Law Center	1
16	International Gay and Lesbian Human Rights Commission	2	Family First	1
17	Egale-Canada	2	Mission America	1
18	Equality Alabama	1	Liberty Council	1
19	National Organization for Women	1	Coalition for the Protection of Marriage	1
20	Lesbian and Gay Immigration Rights Task Force	1	New Yorkers for Constitutional Freedoms	1
21	Stonewall Columbus	1	Christian Civic League	1
22	Equality Illinois	1	Christian Coalition of Alabama	1
23	Alliance for Full Acceptance	1	Eagle Forum	1
24	Triangle JAX Democratic Caucus	1	Faith and Action in the Nation's Capital	1
25	MassEquality	1	Arlington Group	1
26	Freedom to Marry Coalition of Massachusetts	1	Family Institute of Connecticut	1
27	Equal Rights Nevada	1		
28	Lesbian-Gay Rights Lobby of Texas	1		
29	Stonewall Syracuse	1		
30	Maine Lesbian-Gay Political Alliance	1		
31	Los Angeles Gay and Lesbian Center	1		
32	Religious Coalition for the Freedom to Marry	1		
33	Equality Virginia	1		
34	Legal Marriage Alliance of Washington	1		
35	Homosexual Community of Argentina	1		
	Article total	107	Article total	49

TABLE 8.4. Partial sample of interest groups with number of newspaper citations.

PROPONENTS OF SAME-SEX MARRIAGE	TIMES CITED	OPPONENTS OF SAME-SEX MARRIAGE	TIMES CITED
Freedom to Marry	6	American Family Association	1
Love Makes a Family	3	Traditional Values Coalition	2
Lambda Legal	13	American Values	2
National Gay and Lesbian Task Force	3	Christian Coalition of America	1
Human Rights Campaign	18	Focus on the Family	6
Soulforce	0	Eagle Forum	1
Marriage Equality USA	0	Concerned Women of America	2
EqualMarriage.org	0	Family Research Council	5
DontAmend.com	0	American Center for Law and Justice	0
Gay and Lesbian Alliance for Marriage	0	Citizens for American Values	0
Total	43	Total	20

Note: For a full listing of all interest groups cited in newspaper articles that were analyzed by content analysis, see table 8.3.

frame and ten that promote a traditional values frame. Table 8.4 displays those twenty groups and shows how many times the groups were cited in the content analysis of newspaper articles.

Overall, more of the groups were identified as employing the traditional value frame that were also discovered in the newspaper content analysis (eight of ten, compared to five of ten for the groups expressing the equal rights frame). Yet the groups expressing the equal rights frame were cited more frequently in newspaper coverage of same-sex marriage (forty-three instances of citation compared with twenty for the traditional frame). This pattern of nearly twice the number of citations of proponents is also present for the full sample of newspaper articles (see table 8.3). Despite this large discrepancy in the frequency of citation of each type of group, traditional value frames are more prominent than equal rights frames, contained in 20 percent and 16 percent of news coverage, respectively.

The traditional values frame dominates the equal rights frame, although the groups that promote the equal rights frames are referenced more often in newspaper coverage, suggesting that the traditional values frame is advanced by other groups in addition to those that oppose same-sex marriage. The first four sources for each newspaper article were identified and coded (see figure 8.3).[8] Interest groups that advocate same-sex marriage were cited most often in the articles, with politicians and candidates for all levels of elected office ranking an extremely close

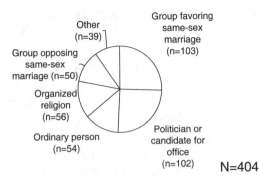

Figure 8.3. Newspapers' sources for stories about same-sex marriage.

second. Ordinary individuals, most of whom were quoted in the course of giving personal testimonials about the impact of same-sex marriage on their lives, interest groups that oppose it, and organized religions and their representatives were each present in approximately 12–14 percent of the newspaper articles. Organized religion include church organizations such as the Roman Catholic Church, various Protestant denominations, Jewish sects, and other religions. Individuals, in particular priests and ministers, who are affiliated with specific religions and speaking as their representatives were also coded in the "Organized religion" category. Many of these religions take hostile stances toward same-sex marriage, often evoking the same traditional values frame as the interest groups that oppose it. For instance, the Vatican issued a statement that evoked the terms "natural moral law" and "gravely immoral" when discussing the issue (Paulson 2003). When these groups and organized religion are combined, the total frequency of references to them exceeds that of the interest groups that support same-sex marriage (106 versus 103). More extensive research regarding the similarity of the frames of religions and interest groups is needed to confirm that the two groups are working together. Yet the disparity between how often each class of interest group is tapped for quotations and interviews is made clear in this content analysis. The numbers suggest that organized religions could possibly fill and exceed that source deficit.

This content analysis makes a number of contributions to our understanding of which frames are present in the media, the trends in newspaper coverage of same-sex marriage, and the sources tapped for interviews and quotations. We now turn to a discussion of public opinion about the topic, with particular attention to the extent to which frames used by interest groups and the media affect opinion about same-sex marriage.

PUBLIC SUPPORT FOR AND OPPOSITION TO
SAME-SEX MARRIAGE AND CIVIL UNIONS

In a November 2003 national survey (n = 1054) conducted by Ohio University's Scripps-Howard Survey Research Center, 42.5 percent of respondents said they strongly oppose same-sex marriage and 9.5 percent said they oppose it somewhat. It is strongly or somewhat favored by 26.7 percent of those surveyed. Although the issue has generated enormous controversy and media attention, fully 20.5 percent of respondents said they do not know whether they favor or oppose it (see table 8.5).

More respondents were in favor of civil unions than marriage, with 35.8 percent saying they strongly favor or somewhat favor them and 43.6 percent saying they strongly or somewhat oppose unions. As with same-sex marriage, 20.2 percent said they do not know how they feel about civil unions.

Respondents were also asked whether they consider same-sex marriage and civil unions to be matters of traditional moral values or equal rights (see table 8.6). Regarding the issue of marriage, 43 percent felt it was about moral values. Nearly the same number (42.4 percent) saw the issue as one of equal rights. Civil unions were somewhat more likely to be seen as a matter of equal rights (48.7 percent); 36.0 percent said it was about traditional moral values. Only about 11 percent of respondents said they did not know whether same-sex marriage was about moral values or equal rights, and 12.4 percent did not have a value frame in mind for civil unions.

TABLE 8.5.   Attitudes toward same-sex marriage and civil unions.

ATTITUDE	SAME-SEX MARRIAGE (%)	CIVIL UNIONS (%)
Strongly favor	13.9	18.3
Somewhat favor	12.8	17.5
Subtotal	26.7	35.8
Somewhat oppose	9.5	7.7
Strongly oppose	42.5	35.9
Subtotal	52.0	43.6
Don't know	20.5	20.2

Note: N = 1054. Entries do not total 100% owing to rounding or nonresponse.

TABLE 8.6. Respondents' values and attitudes toward same-sex marriage and civil unions.

BASIS FOR OPINION	SAME-SEX MARRIAGE (%)	CIVIL UNIONS (%)
Moral values	43.0	36.0
Equal rights	42.4	48.7
Don't know	10.7	12.4

Note: N = 1054. Entries do not total 100% owing to rounding or nonresponse.

TABLE 8.7. Predictors of support for same-sex marriage.

	B	STANDARDIZED COEFFICIENTS
Ideology	.111	.019*
Education	.145	.123**
Church attendance	.219	.081*
Party identification	.056	.058
Income	.004	.005
Values	.864	.320**

*$p < .05$
**$p < .01$

We now turn to the question of how important values are in predicting support for or opposition to same-sex marriage and civil unions. With respect to both, the more liberal and well-educated the respondent, the more supportive he or she is of same-sex marriage and civil unions. Those who regularly attend church were less supportive of both same-sex marriage (see table 8.7) and civil unions (see table 8.8). The issues seem to cut across party lines because a respondent's party identification had no impact. Income also did not play a role. When we controlled for all of these factors, the single best predictor of attitudes was whether the respondent attached the value of morality or equality to the issue. A review of the standardized coefficients reveals that those who think in terms of morality were more likely to oppose both practices.

Although the majority of Americans have formed an opinion on the issues of same-sex marriage and civil unions, a significant number (20 percent) do not know how they feel. It would seem as though efforts by

TABLE 8.8. Predictors of support for civil unions.

	B	STANDARDIZED COEFFICIENTS
Ideology	.141	.113[*]
Education	.195	.156[*]
Church attendance	.461	.159[*]
Party identification	.003	.003
Income	.007	.009
Values	.887	.305[*]

[*]$p < .01$

interest groups to frame the debate and influence media coverage could potentially have the greatest impact on this segment of the public.

CONCLUSION

Interest groups are concerned with framing issues in ways that further their positions. They do this in hopes that the media will utilize those frames when reporting on the issues and also in hopes that the public adopts the frames when evaluating the issues. Although there are several potential frames that groups on each side of the same-sex marriage debate could use, it is clear that groups in opposition use a traditional values frame and groups in support use an equal rights frame.

Our content analysis of newspaper coverage demonstrates that some interest groups have been more successful than others in getting newspapers to adopt their frame. Although 29 percent of the coverage used traditional values and equal rights frames, some groups were more successful than others. Groups opposed to same-sex marriage succeeded in having their frame adopted 20 percent of the time, whereas groups in favor of it succeeded 16 percent of the time.

Given our scholarly interest in this subject, we watched with keen interest as the issue of same-sex marriage played out in the 2004 campaign and election. Instant analyses done after the election often mentioned polling data that suggested that the so-called values voter propelled President Bush to his 51 percent electoral share (Hess and Dial 2004). More detailed analyses conducted in the months that followed the election, however, argued the opposite point. For example, Ken Sherrill, citing an analysis by Stanford University's Simon Jackman, noted that when one compares the electoral performance of President Bush in 2000 and 2004, one finds that his 2004 performance was *better* in states *with–*

out a gay marriage initiative on the ballot than it was in states *with* a ballot initiative. For instance, in the key battleground state of Ohio, where there was a ballot initiative, the "data suggest that mobilization for the same-sex marriage initiative had no net effect on the outcome of the presidential election" (Sherrill 2004).

Given the ongoing high-profile status of the same-sex marriage issue, it is unlikely that either side is likely to accept the other side's assessment of the 2004 election outcome. For the authors, this suggests that there will continue to be evidence of framing effects as we have discussed them in this chapter. Why is that? Issue framing affects public opinion. As we have demonstrated, the value (whether morality or equality) that one attaches to the issue is the single best predictor of support for or opposition to same-sex marriage and civil unions. As Ball-Rokeach and Loges (1996) point out, "The eventual winner . . . will be the contesting group that succeeds in having its value choice frame adopted by the mass media" (286).

APPENDIX A

APPENDIX A.   Breakdown of exclusions by region.

	MAJOR PAPERS	MIDWEST	SOUTHEAST	WEST	NORTHEAST	TOTAL
No Exclusions, Usable article	128	16	8	12	17	181
Letter to the Editor	66	3	1	5	7	82
Candidate Position (no context)	20	2	2	5	1	30
Other exclusions	87	14	1	8	8	118
Total	301	35	12	30	33	411

APPENDIX B

APPENDIX B.   Breakdown of frames by issue.

	SAME-SEX MARRIAGE	CIVIL UNIONS	GENERAL GAY RIGHTS
Topic not mentioned in article	29	147	162
No Frames	32	8	3
Equal rights frame	28	18	10
Traditional values frame	37	2	1
Both Traditional values and equal rights	53	6	4
Other frames	2	0	1
Total	181	181	181

ENDNOTES

Thanks to Justin Barasky and Chris Gohlke for assistance with various parts of this chapter. An earlier version of this chapter was prepared for delivery at the 2004 Annual Meeting of the American Political Science Association, September 2–5, 2004. Copyright by the American Political Science Association. For further information contact Barry L. Tadlock at 740.593.4610 or tadlock@ohio.edu.

1. *Baehr v. Lewin*, 74 Haw. 645, 852 P.2d 44 (1993).
2. *Goodridge et al. v. Department of Public Health*, 440 Mass. 309 (2003).
3. *Lawrence v. Texas*, 539 U.S. 558 (2003).
4. The specific dates were November 4, 2002 through November 4, 2003.
5. The *St. Louis Post-Dispatch* was substituted for the *Chicago Tribune*, and the *San Diego Union-Tribune* and the *Seattle Times* substituted for the *Los Angeles Times*.
6. The article search was originally conducted by searching for the terms in the full text of articles. This method produced a prohibitively large number of articles, many of which contained the search terms without any context or discussion. Therefore, the headline and lead paragraph search produced a sample that was both reasonably sized and as relevant as possible to this study.
7. These results are presented in appendix B.
8. For the sake of simplicity and clarity, only the first four sources were coded. A total of 404 sources were identified and coded by this method.

REFERENCES

Adamick, Mike. 2003. Same-sex partners demand rights. (Fremont, CA) *Argus* (online), February 15. http://www.lexisnexis.com/universe (accessed August 4, 2004).

Ball-Rokeach, Sandra J., and William Loges. 1996. Making choices: Media roles in the construction of value-choices. In *The psychology of values: The Ontario Symposium*, vol. 8., ed. Clive Seligman, James Olson, and Mark Zanna, 277–98. Mahwah, NJ: Lawrence Erlbaum Associates.

Blanton, Kimberly. 2003. Exclusionary costs: Legal marriage could ease gay couples' financial inequalities. *Boston Globe* (online), July, 29, F1. http://www.lexisnexis.com/universe (accessed August 4, 2004).

Brewer, Paul R. 2002. Framing, value words, and citizens' explanations of their issue opinions. *Political Communication* 19 (3): 303–16.

———. 2003. Values, political knowledge, and public opinion about gay rights: A framing-based account. *Public Opinion Quarterly* 67:173–201.

Cooperman, Alan. 2004. Gay marriage as "the new abortion": Debate becomes polarizing as both sides become better organized, spend millions. *Washington Post* (final ed.), July 26, A03.

Darman, Jonathan. 2004. "The federal government should not be stepping in": One of gay marriage's staunches opponents thinks amending the Constitution is a bad idea. *Newsweek* (Web exclusive), February 27. http://www.msnbc.msn.com/id/4401144/site/newsweek/ (accessed August 9, 2004).

Entman, Robert M. 1993. Framing: Toward clarification of a fractured paradigm. *Journal of Communication* 43 (4): 51–58.

Eskridge, William N., Jr. 2002. *Equality practice: Civil unions and the future of gay rights.* New York: Routledge.

Family Research Council. 2003. *FRC applauds Missouri voters on passage of marriage amendment.* Washington, DC: Family Research Council. http://www.frc.org/get.cfm?i=PR04H01 (accessed August 4, 2004).

Fitzgerald, Mary, and Alan Cooperman. 2004. Marriage protection act passes: House bill strips federal courts of power over same-sex cases. *Washington Post* (final ed.), July 23, A04.

Goffman, Erving. 1974. *Frame analysis.* New York: Harper Colophon.

Haider-Markel, Donald. 1999. Redistributing values in Congress: Interest group influence under sub-optimal conditions. *Political Research Quarterly* 52 (1): 113–44.

Harmon, M. D. 2003. Defend marriage by passing the Federal Marriage Amendment. *Portland* (Maine) *Press Herald* (online), July 21, A9. http://www.lexisnexis.com/universe (accessed August 4, 2004).

Hess, Tom, and Karla Dial. 2004. Year of the values voter. http://www.family.org/cforum/citizenmag/coverstory/a0035019.cfm (accessed July 19, 2005).

Hull, Kathleen E. 2001. The political limits of the rights frame: The case of same-sex marriage in Hawaii. *Sociological Perspectives* 44 (2): 207–32.

Jost, K. 2003. Gay marriage. *CQ Researcher Online* 13 (30): 721–48. http://library.cqpress.com/cqresearcher/cqresrre2003090500 (accessed July 27, 2004).

Kershaw, Sarah. 2003. Adversaries of gay rights vow state-by-state fight. *New York Times* (online), July 6, A8. http://www.lexisnexis.com/universe (accessed August 4, 2004).

Mahoney, Dennis M. 2003. Vatican reiterates: No gay marriage. *Columbus Dispatch* (online), August 1, E3. http://www.lexisnexis.com/universe (accessed August 4, 2004).

Meyers, Marian. 1994. Defining homosexuality: News coverage of the "repeal the ban" controversy. *Discourse and Society* 5 (3): 321–44.

National Gay and Lesbian Task Force. 2005. Voting tallies: State anti–gay marriage ballot initiatives. http://www.thetaskforce.org/downloads/StateBallotPollingData2004.pdf (accessed July 19, 2005).

Nelson, Thomas E., Rosalee A. Clawson, and Zoe M. Oxley. 1997. Media framing of a civil liberties conflict and its effect on tolerance. *American Political Science Review* 91 (3): 567–83.

Nelson, Thomas E., and Donald R. Kinder. 1996. Issue frames and group-centrism in American public opinion. *Journal of Politics* 58 (4): 1055–78.

Nelson, Thomas E., and Zoe M. Oxley. 1999. Issue framing effects on belief importance and opinion. *Journal of Politics* 61 (4): 1040–67.

Nelson, Thomas E., Zoe M. Oxley, and Rosalee A. Clawson. 1997. Toward a psychology of framing effects. *Political Behavior* 19 (3): 221–46.

Neuman, W. Russell, Marion R. Just, and Ann N. Crigler. 1992. *Common knowledge: News and the construction of political meaning.* Chicago: University of Chicago Press.

Ott, Brian L., and Eric Aoki. 2002. The politics of negotiating public tragedy: Media framing of the Matthew Shepard murder." *Rhetoric and Public Affairs* 5 (3): 483–505.

Paulson, Michael. 2003. Papal report: Vatican warns on same-sex marriage; broad edict has message for Catholic politicians. *Boston Globe* (online), August 1, A1. http://www.lexisnexis.com/universe (accessed August 4, 2004).

Rundin, John. 2003. Marriage act puts Texas in backwater. *San Antonio Express-News* (online), 24 June, B7. http://www.lexisnexis.com/universe (accessed August 4, 2004).

Schattschneider, E. E. 1960. *The semisovereign people: A realist's view of democracy in America*. New York: Holt, Rinehart, and Winston.

Sherrill, Kenneth. 2004. Same-sex marriage, civil unions, and the 2004 presidential election. http://www.thetaskforce.org/downloads/MarriageCUSherrill2004 .pdf (accessed July 19, 2005).

Thomas, Evan. 2003. The war over gay marriage. *Newsweek* (U.S. edition), July 7, 38–45.

IF I BEND THIS FAR
I WILL BREAK?

PUBLIC OPINION ABOUT SAME-SEX MARRIAGE

Clyde Wilcox, Paul R. Brewer, Shauna Shames,
and Celinda Lake

Fiddler on the Roof, set in pre-revolutionary Russia, tells the story of how the Jewish milkman Tevya confronts a series of challenges to his traditional conception of marriage. He arranges his eldest daughter's betrothal to a middle-aged butcher, but his daughter rejects her father's choice in favor of a much younger but poor tailor. Tevya's internal dialogue is voiced in a memorable song: in a rich, deep voice he loudly proclaims his commitment to tradition, and then in quieter tones he acknowledges that his daughter and the tailor love one another. In the end, his desire to make his daughter happy conquers his commitment to traditional marriage, and he allows them to wed.

Tevya is internally divided again when his second daughter seeks not his permission but merely his blessing for her marriage to a radical student; again, he bends tradition to make his daughter happy. When his third daughter seeks his blessing to marry a Christian, Tevya is torn yet again, but ultimately sides with tradition. "If I bend this far, I will break" he declares, turning his back on his pleading daughter and walking away.

In 2004 many Americans appeared to have voiced a similar sentiment in considering same-sex marriage. During the preceding decade, public attitudes toward gay rights issues had become dramatically more liberal. Many Americans had changed their minds about issues such as antidiscrimination laws and military service on the part of gays and lesbians; a sizable number had discovered that a friend or relative was gay or lesbian.

Yet when same-sex marriage burst onto the national agenda, a majority of Americans appeared to believe that policy had moved too far, too fast. Surveys showed that a majority of Americans opposed same-sex marriage and that many favored an amendment to the U.S. Constitution that would bar states from allowing same-sex marriage. Voters in thirteen states approved amendments to their state constitutions defining marriage as an institution involving one man and one woman. Some surveys suggested a short-run decline in support for other gay rights policies, as well.

Although several media-salient events that occurred throughout the 1990s brought attention to issues of civil unions and domestic partnerships, full same-sex marriage rights did not become a major issue for most Americans until a few years ago. Even for gays and lesbians, marriage rights were a relatively low priority until quite recently. A 1994 *Newsweek* poll of self-identified gay and lesbian respondents found that 91 percent thought equal rights in the workplace very important, 88 percent said equal rights in housing were very important, and 77 percent identified health and Social Security benefits for partners as very important. Only 42 percent said the same of "legally sanctioned gay marriage," and fully 17 percent called it not important at all (Kushner 1994, 46). By 2002, a Zogby/GL Census poll had found that 83 percent of gays and lesbians called marriage "one of the top three goals of the gay-rights movement," and 47 percent called it "*the* most important goal of the gay rights movement." The percentage calling protection against employment discrimination the most important goal of the gay rights movement had dropped to 16 percent (Same-sex marriage tops priorities for gays 2002, 1A). Obtaining the legal right for same-sex couples to marry had rocketed to the top of the agenda for the movement.

In light of these rapid changes, we seek to better understand public attitudes toward same-sex marriage. It is a new issue for many Americans, one that involves conflicting sets of values and beliefs about the nature of sexual orientation. This creates ambivalence on the part of citizens, allowing elites a larger role in framing the public debate (see Alvarez and Brehm 2002; Nelson, Clawson, and Oxley 1997; Zaller 1992). Over time, however, elite frames will not necessarily predominate as everyday experiences also help mold citizens' thinking.

We begin, therefore, with an exploration of the ways in which the public decides about new issues such as same-sex marriage. We consider partisan cues, core values, evaluations of groups (and especially of gay men and lesbians), and attitudes toward related issues. Next, we examine what the polls show about public attitudes toward same-sex marriage, drawing on many polls using a variety of questions for a number of years.

Using data from the National Election Studies, we explore what the sources of attitudes toward same-sex marriage are and how they differ from the sources of attitudes toward other gay rights issues such as employment discrimination, military service, and adoption. Finally, we consider factors that might influence the dynamics of opinion about gay marriage in the coming years.

SAME-SEX MARRIAGE IN THE PUBLIC DEBATE

Same-sex marriage has been an element of public debate for a number of years. In 1993 the Hawaiian Supreme Court ruled that a compelling state interest must exist in order for the state to bar same-sex couples from marrying, and in 1996 a trial court ruled that no such reason existed. In 1998, however, Hawaii voters approved an amendment to their state's constitution to allow (but not to require) the state's legislature to bar same-sex marriage. In 2000, California voters passed a resolution that defined marriage as being between one man and one woman. The federal government also reacted to the Hawaii case, with both Congress and President Bill Clinton making the defense of traditional marriage an election-year issue in 1996. Congress passed and Clinton signed the Defense of Marriage Act, legally defining marriage, as far the federal government was concerned, as the union of one man and one woman. The public opinion polls, which had shown a clear rise in support for same-sex marriage through the early 1990s, began to dip around 1996 as support receded in the face of election-year hype.

Still, the Hawaii and California cases were not salient to the average American voter, nor was the 1999 Vermont case that led to a civil union law in that state. For most Americans, the issue was thrust on the political agenda in the fall of 2003, when the Massachusetts Supreme Court ruled that the state had no grounds to deny same-sex couples the right to marry. Within a few months, public officials in a number of cities across the country were marrying same-sex couples in defiance of state laws. Thousands of couples flew to San Francisco, where hundreds of couples were married every day. Eventually, these marriages were halted and invalidated, but by then there was widespread public interest in the topic of same-sex marriage—and an increasingly heated political debate. By August 2003, Pew surveys showed that nearly half of the public was following the issue at least somewhat closely, with 19 percent following it very closely. By March 2004, nearly two in three were following the issue, with 29 percent following it very closely.[1]

Thus, most citizens found themselves interested in a new political issue about which they had not yet formed an opinion. In some ways, same-sex marriage was an "easy issue" regarding which anyone could form an opinion without careful study. Many Americans had strong religious objections to same-sex marriage; others had gay or lesbian friends and family members who helped them form opinions. Moreover, the institution of marriage itself was already quite familiar to the typical citizen, as were the values invoked in the debate about same-sex marriage.

Yet the issue had complexities as well. If a state were to forbid same-sex marriage, should it honor the marriages performed in Massachusetts if a couple moved there? If marriage is not permitted, should couples be allowed to form domestic partnerships or civil unions that confer many or most of the benefits of marriage? Is there—and should there be—a distinction between religious and civil marriage?

Moreover, many Americans found themselves pulled in different directions by conflicting values, emotions, and beliefs. How, then, will the public respond to the issue in the years to come?

HOW THE PUBLIC DECIDES ABOUT NEW ISSUES

When citizens are faced with new policy questions, they must rely on preexisting predispositions to form opinions. Partisan cues can provide important information to those who support a political party. Likewise, core values can help some voters decide. Others may consider their basic predispositions toward social and political groups that are involved in the issue, and still others may consider their attitudes about other related issues. Many may rely on some combination of these predispositions.

PARTISAN CUES

Partisan cues can be critical; if party elites send clear and distinct signals, partisans often are persuaded. When Republican and Democratic party leaders take opposite positions concerning key issues, many party supporters line up behind them. Persuasion is greatest with issues about which the public knows the least, such as foreign policy and highly technical, "hard" issues such as how to reform Social Security (Zaller 1992). But partisan cues can be influential in social and moral issues. In 1992 Bill Clinton "spent" some of his popularity on his support for gays and lesbians in the military, but he also persuaded some culturally conservative Democrats (Bailey, Sigelman, and Wilcox 2004).

Regarding same-sex marriage, however, party leaders did not take distinct positions. Leaders in both parties publicly opposed the practice with George W. Bush somewhat hesitantly backing a constitutional amendment to "protect" marriage and Vice President Dick Cheney indicating that he opposed the amendment. Bush's public statements focused more on "activist judges" than on the merits of the issue, and Bush seldom mentioned the amendment during the 2004 campaign. John Kerry also opposed same-sex marriage, and though he also opposed an amendment to the federal Constitution, he endorsed an amendment to the Massachusetts state constitution that would ban same-sex marriage but permit civil unions. In short, the Republican candidate favored a national amendment to ban same-sex marriage, and the Democratic candidate favored an amendment to the state constitution to do so. Thus, leaders from both parties sent consistent (if sometimes half-hearted) signals of opposition to same-sex marriage, a situation that one might expect to have produced greater opposition among the public (Zaller 1992).

Though there were no distinctive partisan cues regarding same-sex marriage, Christian conservatives sought to portray the 2004 election as a referendum on the issue. They seized on Bush's endorsement of the federal amendment as evidence of his stronger commitment to "protect" conventional marriage. In special mailings to pastors and activists, they sought to convey a distinctly partisan cue, and indeed conveyed the impression that without a victory by George Bush, same-sex marriage would be certain to follow. The Republican National Committee also sent mailings in morally conservative states such as West Virginia implying that Democrats supported same-sex marriage. This pseudo-partisan division lasted only until the voting was done. Since the election, Bush has done little to promote the amendment (Larson and Wilcox in press).

CORE VALUES

Citizens also rely on their core values to decide about new political issues (Feldman 1988). Two key values seem likely to lead to increased support for same-sex marriage, and two key values seem likely to work against such support (Brewer 2003a, 2003b; Wilcox and Wolpert 1998, 2000). Because most citizens hold each value to some extent, there is natural ambivalence among many Americans (Craig, Martinez, Kane, and Gainous 2005).

Liberal groups sought to frame the discussion in terms of equality. In the courts and in the public sphere they argued that bans on same-sex marriage discriminated against gay and lesbian couples. When San Francisco's mayor began performing same-sex marriages in 2003, the throng of long-term couples who lined up for their long-awaited chance to exchange vows and slices of wedding cake served as a powerful symbol of that equality claim. Yet the Massachusetts court victory and subsequent rush to marry in San Francisco and other cities seemed to catch gay rights groups by surprise, and few were ready to mount a substantial campaign to help frame the issue around equality values. Polls show strongest support for legal recognition of same-sex unions when the question wording includes a comparison with heterosexual marriage, implying an equality issue.

The second value that can lead to increased support for same-sex marriage is individual freedom. Vice President Dick Cheney, speaking of the proposed federal constitutional amendment to bar the practice, stated, "With respect to the question of relationships, my general view is that freedom means freedom for everyone. People . . . ought to be free to enter into any kind of relationship they want to" (Kaufman and Allen 2004, A1). Libertarian organizations have supported same-sex marriage, arguing that the state has no business interfering in private relationships.

Conservatives sought to frame the discussion in terms of traditional morality. Many argued that marriage was traditionally limited to a man and a woman in all societies. In a widely quoted interview with the Associated Press on April 7, 2003, Senator Rick Santorum noted, "Every society in the history of man has upheld the institution of marriage as a bond between a man and a woman. . . . That's not to pick on homosexuality. It's not, you know, man on child, man on dog, or whatever the case may be." He also linked his notion of traditional marriage to the goal of childrearing. Christian conservatives argued that God had created "Adam and Eve, not Adam and Steve" and that the Bible limited marriage to a single man and a single woman, ignoring in the process a number of cases of polygamous marriages found in the Old Testament.

Conservatives, primed and ready for the Massachusetts court decision, rapidly sought to define the issue for the public. Proclaiming a need to defend marriage, Christian conservative groups rallied and provided materials to local activists and churches. The "defense of marriage" frame was powerful in the short run, for most Americans value marriage and many think that it is a fragile institution. Moreover, the picture in most people's minds of a wedding involves a church, a white dress, and a man and a woman. It is not clear that the frame will be effective in the longer run, however. The argument that heterosexual marriage would be devalued by allowing gay and lesbian couples to marry is not particularly compelling, especially in light of the high rates of failure of heterosexual marriages (one *New Yorker* cartoon published during the same-sex marriage media frenzy of early 2004 depicted two blue-collar workers drinking in a bar, with one telling the other, "Allowing gays to marry would ruin traditional marriage, I was saying to my ex . . . "). Then again, the belief that allowing same-sex marriage would hasten the devaluation of heterosexual marriage is common and may prove to be resilient.

Religious values constitute a related but distinct set of values that might lead citizens to oppose same-sex marriage. Most religious bodies in the U.S. oppose the practice, and many teach that homosexual relations are inherently sinful. Deeply religious citizens, or those who regularly attend worship services and take guidance from religious elites, may well oppose same-sex marriage not because it deviates from traditional morality but because they believe that it is against God's will. An overwhelming majority of heterosexual couples who marry do so at a place of worship (even if they rarely attend there otherwise) or at least in a service performed by a religious figure.

Many large Christian and non-Christian religious bodies joined in a coalition to press for a federal amendment to bar same-sex marriage and to amend state constitutions as well. Though there was some disagreement among participants as to how far these amendments should go, the coalition was broad and included actors who often support Democratic candidates, including African American Protestants and white Catholics.

Most Americans hold all of these values to a certain extent. In the 2004 National Election Studies, for example, 75 percent of respondents agreed that there should be more emphasis on traditional family ties, and 62 percent agreed that newer lifestyles are causing societal breakdown.

But nearly two in three agreed that there would be many fewer problems if we treated people equally. Fully 39 percent agreed both that we would have fewer problems if we treated people equally and that newer lifestyles are causing societal breakdown.

Polls also show that Americans value individual liberty in sexual decisions. In Roper polls conducted from 1995 to 2000, 80 percent or more of Americans consistently said that the government should stay out of private matters such as sex, and surveys by PSRA/Kaiser and PSRA/Pew in 2000 and 2003 showed similar numbers of people who agreed that society should not put any restrictions on sex between consenting adults in the privacy of their own homes. But a majority of Americans also believe that gay marriage violates their religious beliefs, and nearly half say that if their church performed same-sex marriages then they would find another church.

EVALUATIONS OF GROUPS

Many Americans form policy opinions based on their feelings toward groups that they associate with the policy. When citizens especially dislike a social or political group, they may adopt political positions to maximize the difference between their position and that of the group. The "likeability heuristic" is used especially frequently by those with higher levels of education and knowledge (Sniderman, Brody, and Tetlock 1991). A sizable body of research has shown that attitudes toward homosexuals affect issue positions regarding gay rights (Brewer 2003a; Wilcox and Wolpert 2000).

At one time, many Americans held very negative evaluations of homosexuality and of gays and lesbians. Early surveys about gay issues reveal clear evidence of homophobia—a strong visceral reaction of fear and disgust toward homosexuality. In the 1993 National Election Study Pilot survey, nearly half of all respondents indicated that they were disgusted by the thought of homosexuality, and more than a third were strongly disgusted (see table 9.1). Although only one in six feared disease when working with gays and lesbians, nearly half believed that homosexuality is against God's will (almost all of whom strongly held this position), and nearly half believed that homosexuality is unnatural (most of whom strongly believed this). Few believed that gays and lesbians try to seduce heterosexuals, and the public was almost evenly divided on whether homosexuality was a lifestyle choice or a fixed trait.

TABLE 9.1. Affective and cognitive sources of evaluations of gays and lesbians.

Emotional reaction to gays and lesbians		Fear disease when working with gays	
Strong disgust	36	Strong worry	8
Mild disgust	6	Worry	6
Discomfort	13	Confidence there is no danger	32
No emotional reaction	46	Strong confidence	55
Homosexuality is against God's will		Homosexuality is natural to gays and lesbians	
Strongly against God's will	46	Strongly think it is natural	39
Against God's will	4	Think it is natural	6
Nothing to do with God	34	Think it is unnatural	15
Acceptable to God	5	Strongly think it is unnatural	40
Strongly acceptable	11		
Gays and lesbians try to seduce heterosexuals			
		Homosexuals can change	
Strongly agree	13	Strongly think they choose to be gay	36
Agree	5	They choose to be gay	12
Disagree	19	They cannot change	14
Strongly disagree	63	Strongly think they cannot change	38

Source: National Election Study Pilot 1993.
Note: Figures represent percentage of respondents.

Over time, however, attitudes toward gays and lesbians have become less negative. The National Election Study has since 1984 asked respondents to rate homosexuals on a scale of 0 to 100 degrees, with 0 being the coldest possible evaluation. In 1988, fully 35 percent of respondents rated homosexuals at 0, a higher figure than that for any other social or political group named in the survey. These especially negative evaluations have declined: by 2002, only 8 percent of respondents indicated similarly negative evaluations of gays. Meanwhile, positive evaluations (ratings of 60 degrees or more) of gays and lesbians have increased from only 10 percent in 1988 to 30 percent in 2000. In 2004, evaluations polarized somewhat, with 13 percent rating gays and lesbians at 0 degrees and 34 percent rating them at more than 60 degrees (American National Election Studies 2005). The trends are shown in figure 9.1.

Figure 9.2 shows the percentage of respondents to the General Social Survey who think that homosexual relations are always wrong and, for comparison, the percentage who think that extramarital sexual relations are always wrong. The public has not become more accepting of extramarital sex—if anything, the public has become more convinced in recent years that it is always wrong. The percentage thinking that homosexual relations are always wrong has dropped sharply since the early 1990s,

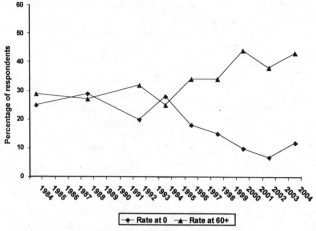

Source: American National Election Studies, 1984-2004.

Figure 9.1. Feeling thermometer ratings of homosexuals.

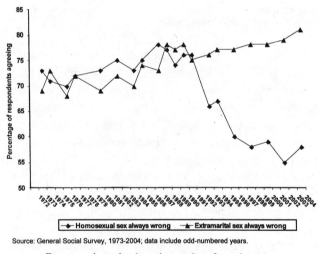

Source: General Social Survey, 1973-2004; data include odd-numbered years.

Figure 9.2. Attitudes about the morality of sexual activity.
Note: Data include odd-numbered years.

however. A majority in every survey say that gay and lesbian sex is always wrong, but there is also a clear trend toward more liberal attitudes.

Why have attitudes toward gays and lesbians become so much more positive over time? Three factors appear to have been at work. First, media portrayals of gays and lesbians became more positive and more prominent beginning in the early 1990s, with famous movie stars such as Tom Hanks,

Tom Selleck, and Kevin Kline playing sympathetic gay characters in major films, television personalities such as Ellen DeGeneres coming out, and a number of popular television shows featuring positive (if often stereotypical) gay and lesbian characters. This, in turn, may have led many Americans to come out to their friends and associates. Two *Los Angeles Times* polls showed that between 1985 and 2000, the percentage of the public who said that they knew someone who was gay or lesbian increased from 25 percent to 74 percent (Wilcox and Norrander 2002). Surveys by *Newsweek* magazine reveal a similar if less dramatic change. Such a realization puts a human face on both homosexuality and on policy issues relating to gays and lesbians. Suddenly the question is no longer about a nameless person in San Francisco but a co-worker, classmate, personal friend, or a family member (Wilcox and Wolpert 2000).

Second, beliefs about the nature of homosexuality itself have changed. In 1977, Gallup polls revealed that only 13 percent of the public believed that homosexuality was something inherent, and an additional 3 percent credited both genes and environment. By 2002, 40 percent of Gallup respondents believed that sexual orientation was in the genes, and an additional 12 percent thought that it was a combination of genes and environment. Thus, half of all Americans now believe that homosexuality is at least partly due to genes. This belief has two consequences. First, it makes it more difficult to justify unequal treatment of gays and lesbians, since their sexual orientation is at least partially fixed at birth. Support for same-sex marriage has increased over time in direct proportion to the percentage of the public who believe that sexual orientation is fixed at birth (Haider-Markel and Joslyn 2005). Second, the belief lessens fears that gays and lesbians will seduce heterosexual children and teens. This probably helps explain why Gallup polls show that support for allowing gays and lesbians to teach in elementary schools has increased from 41 percent to 54 percent since 1992 and that support for allowing them to teach in secondary schools has increased from 47 percent to 62 percent in the same period.

Finally, President Clinton's inept but consistent support for allowing gays and lesbians to serve in the military, as well as his support for anti-discrimination laws, appears to have moved public opinion somewhat. As noted above, analysis of surveys of the same individuals before Clinton assumed office and after the explosive fight over gays in the military in 1993 revealed that Clinton lost some of his popularity but also that he persuaded some Democrats to change their minds (Bailey, Sigelman and Wilcox 2004).

Although public attitudes have become more positive toward gays and lesbians, there remains a residual discomfort with homosexuality on the part of many heterosexuals. A majority of respondents to a 2004 *Los Angeles Times* poll professed not to feel uncomfortable around gays and lesbians, but a sizeable minority admitted to being uncomfortable. Almost half said that they would feel uncomfortable having a gay or lesbian baby-sit their children. Moreover, a majority of those polled by Gallup that same year reported being offended by depictions of homosexuality on television.

OTHER RELATED POLICY ISSUES

For some Americans, the easiest way to decide about new political issues is to think of other issues that resemble the new one and use their previous decisions as a basis for judging those issues. Table 9.2 shows the attitudes of Americans between 1992 and 2004 toward various gay rights issues. It reveals a marked liberalization over time, with support for antidiscrimination laws rising from less than one-half to three-fourths of all citizens, support for gays in the military increasing from slightly more than one-half to more than four in five, and support for allowing gays and lesbians to adopt children rising from a little more than one in four to one-half of all citizens in 2004. The table also shows that slightly more than one in three respondents supported same-sex marriage in 2004. This is a higher level of support than was voiced for adoption in 1992 but is well below the level for all other gay rights.

Supporters of same-sex marriage hope that Americans will come to view one other policy question as relevant to their opinions about same-sex marriage. At one time, many states banned mixed-race marriages—especially marriages between African Americans and whites. Data from the GSS show that as late as 1972, nearly 40 percent of Americans favored

TABLE 9.2.   Support for gay rights policies in NES surveys.

POLICY	1988	1992	1996	2000	2004
Allow gays and lesbians to serve in military		56	67	72	81
Favor antidiscrimination laws	48	59	61	65	75
Allow gay and lesbian couples to adopt		27		42	50
Allow same-sex marriage					34

Source: National Election Studies 1988-2004.
Note: Figures represent percentage of respondents who agree with the policy.

such laws, but by 2002 the figure had dropped to 10 percent. For most Americans, laws against mixed-race marriages were racist policies that are best forgotten; if some of these citizens come to see laws against same-sex marriage in the same way, then support for it should increase. Yet this analogy has not met with widespread acceptance among the American public as a whole or African Americans in particular.

SUPPORT FOR SAME-SEX MARRIAGE: WHAT THE POLLS SHOW

Many media polls asked questions about same-sex marriage in 2004, and some asked such questions in earlier years as well. Not surprisingly, the way the questions were worded sometimes influenced the results (Brewer and Wilcox 2005). In general, however, opposition to same-sex marriage was relatively unaffected by question wording. Support was lowest for questions that asked for personal evaluations (Do you support gay marriage?) and higher for questions that asked about laws, especially if they carried hints of equality issues (Do you think that marriage between homosexuals should or should not be recognized by law as valid, with the same rights as traditional marriages?). Polls showed that support for same-sex marriage varied between a little more than a quarter of the public to slightly more than 40 percent, depending on question wording, with a related increase or decrease in the percentage not stating an opinion.

The history of public opinion about gay rights policy over the past few decades is a story of increasing liberalization (see, for example, Bowman and O'Keefe 2004; Wilcox and Norrander 2002; Yang 1997). Polling data from the late 1980s puts support for same-sex marriage somewhere between 11 percent (GSS/NORC 1988) and 23 percent (Gallup 1989; *Time/* Yankelovich 1989). By the end of the 1990s, similarly worded polls found support hovering between 29 percent (*Time/*Yankelovich 1998) and 35 percent (Gallup 1999). Beginning in 2003—the year the Supreme Court's *Lawrence v. Texas* decision reversed *Bowers v. Hardwick* and therefore invalidated state anti-sodomy laws and also the year that the Massachusetts Supreme Judicial Court upheld the right of gay and lesbian people to marry in Massachusetts—one bipartisan poll found support for same-sex marriage as high as 49 percent (Hart/American Viewpoint 2003). Other polls, though not finding quite this level of support, did find that opinion shifted after *Lawrence;* immediately afterward, Gallup and Pew found support at 39 and 38 percent, respectively, and a CBS/*New York*

Times poll conducted in July (one month after *Lawrence*) found 40 percent in support.

The General Social Survey asked a same-sex marriage question in 1988 and again in 2004, and this trend line shows a substantial increase in support, from 11 percent to 30 percent, and a decrease in opposition from 69 percent to 54 percent. Among those with strong feelings on the issue, support increased from 3 percent to 12 percent, and opposition declined from 44 percent to 34 percent.

This latter comparison highlights something shown in most polls—those who oppose same-sex marriage show far more intensity than those who favor it. Indeed, in most polls conducted in 2004, there were more who intensely opposed same-sex marriage than who favored it even slightly. This intensity gap may have been an important factor in the way the same-sex marriage issue played out in the 2004 presidential elections.

Though polls showed the public to be opposed to same-sex marriage by a ratio of three to two or even two to one, polls also showed the public to be evenly divided by the issue of civil unions. One of the most interesting conclusions we can draw from the polling data is that support for civil unions seems to rise significantly when civil unions are viewed as a middle ground between no legal recognition and full marriage rights for gay and lesbian couples (see Brewer and Wilcox 2005). Civil unions, which were so controversial in Vermont and Hawaii, are now supported by nearly half of the public, and more in some polls (see Gallup 2004, where support reached 57 percent). Some polls that have experimented with question order, such as one conducted in 2004 by Gallup, have found higher support for civil unions when the question was asked after a question about same-sex marriage; in other words, once people can voice opposition to full marriage rights, they tend to be more supportive of civil unions. In every poll conducted in 2004, there was greater support for than opposition to some sort of legal recognition of gay and lesbian unions. For example, a CBS News/*New York Times* survey conducted right after the election showed that 21 percent favored marriage and 32 percent favored civil unions, with only 44 percent favoring no legal recognition. By February 2005 support had increased further. A *Los Angeles Times* survey done in July 2004 showed 26 percent supporting marriage, 37 percent supporting civil unions, and only 31 percent favoring neither.

A post-election survey by Lake Snell and Perry for the National Gay and Lesbian Task Force showed that a majority of those who were not strongly supportive of or opposed to same-sex marriage chose to support civil unions when offered the three-way choice. The data also showed a surprising level of inconsistency in responses across questions, suggesting that respondents were either uncomfortable with talking about the issues or were conflicted about their values.

Surveys that asked about specific marriage-type benefits for same-sex couples showed overwhelming support. *Newsweek* surveys conducted from 1994 to 2004 found consistent majorities for providing health insurance and other employee benefits, Social Security benefits, and inheritance benefits to same-sex spouses. In each case the margin of support was substantial, mirroring the magnitude of opposition to same-sex marriage.

Overall, then, there is widespread support for providing same-sex couples with many of the legal benefits that come with marriage for heterosexual couples, but the public is divided on how to deal with legal recognition of same-sex couples. Large majorities oppose same-sex marriage, but approximately one-half of the public supports civil unions, and that number rises to a significant majority when the public is allowed to choose between marriage, civil unions, or no legal recognition. The public is more supportive of civil unions when it appears to be the moderate option between no recognition and marriage than when it is posed without the marriage option. In short, a significant minority of the public is uncomfortable with providing no legal recognition for same-sex marriage but also uncomfortable with the idea of same-sex marriage.

This ambivalence is evident in a survey conducted by Peter D. Hart Research Associates in July 2003 for the Human Rights Campaign. In that survey, majorities agreed with the following policy goals:

Making sure that gays and lesbians receive the same rights and protections under the law as other Americans

Making sure that we maintain marriage as a legal union between a man and a woman only

Protecting our traditional family values from the gay lifestyle

Reconciling these diverse positions is not easy, and many Americans do not try. They are drawn to the goal of equality but rooted in a view of marriage that involves a man and a woman marrying in a church, blessed by a religious community.

Focus groups conducted by Hart Research for the Human Rights Campaign in September 2003 concluded that most participants were torn between the desire to provide equal rights to gays and lesbians and the acknowledgment of their right to be happy, on one hand, with concern about the label *marriage*, with how children would be raised by gay and lesbian couples, and with how they would discuss gay and lesbian couples with their children, on the other. The focus groups also revealed considerable residual discomfort with the idea of homosexuality on the part of participants, as well as deep and visceral reactions to a proposed advertisement that showed gay and lesbian couples kissing.

SOURCES OF ATTITUDES TOWARDS SAME-SEX MARRIAGE

To understand the sources of attitudes toward same-sex marriage, we analyzed 2004 NES data. The survey included one question about same-sex marriage. Sixty percent of respondents opposed it, 34 percent approved of it, and the remaining 6 percent indicated other intermediate positions including support for civil unions. It also included two four-point scales measuring attitudes toward antidiscrimination laws and gays and lesbians in the military, as well as a dichotomous item asking about adoption. Except for the marriage question, these items had been used in previous surveys (see table 9.2).

To capture religious observance, we used a measure of frequency of church attendance. We also used a measure of subjective religious salience and one of religious doctrine—the belief in the authority of the Bible. We experimented with dummy variables to identify those who belonged to various faith traditions, including evangelicals, Catholics, Jews, and those with no religious affiliation, but none of these variables proved significant in any model and so they are excluded from the final models.

The survey included a number of items that allowed us to measure two of the key values at play in the same-sex marriage debate: moral traditionalism and equality. We had no measures of the value of individual liberty, however. The survey also included a feeling thermometer for "gay men and lesbians—that is, homosexuals." We estimated the models with a variety of demographic variables, but only gender and education proved to be significantly related to any of the dependent variables.

We predicted liberal positions on all four gay rights policies, coding each dependent variable as a liberal position versus all others (see table 9.3). The table shows unstandardized logistic regression coefficients and Wald values, which are similar to T statistics in regression analysis. The results reveal considerable differences across the four policies in the mix of predictors, as well as some commonalities.

TABLE 9.3. Sources of attitudes toward gay rights.

GAY RIGHTS	ANTIDISCRI-MINATION		GAYS IN THE MILITARY		ADOPTION		MARRIAGE	
	B	WALD	B	WALD	B	WALD	B	WALD
Equality values	.56	14.28***	.19	1.45	.25	3.04*	.25	2.19
Moral traditionalism	−.21	1.82	−.36	4.29*	−1.01	40.77***	−1.08	39.16***
Religious salience	−.11	.82	−.20	−.2.11	−.01	−.01	−.46	12.91***
Church attendance	−.01	.04	−.06	−.67	−.16	−5.00**	−.05	.28
Believe that the Bible is inerrant	−.51	−8.98***	−.45	−4.85**	−.27	−3.69**	−.49	−9.43***
Effect toward gays	.03	47.08***	.03	34.24***	.04	68.69***	.04	49.18***
Female gender	.11	.24	1.01	18.34***	.64	9.80***	.30	1.69
Higher education	.06	1.87	.11	4.62**	.12	6.85***	.11	5.03**
Liberal ideology	.08	.59	.01	.00	.06	.33	.31	7.06***
Democratic partisanship	.07	1.38	.08	1.41	.08	1.96	.03	.19
Constant	−3.62	9.26***	−3.76	8.14***	−8.23	43.80***	−.25	−.86
N	747		746		739		755	
Nagelkerke R²	.34		.33		.52		.62	
Percent predicted								
Conservative	34		29		79		91	
Liberal	93		95		79		72	
Overall	79		83		79		84	

Source: National Election Studies 2004.
*$p \leq .10$
**$p \leq .05$
***$p \leq .01$

Equality values were very important in predicting attitudes toward antidiscrimination laws, but they were not significant sources of attitudes toward other public policies. The failure of equality values to predict attitudes toward gays in the military was somewhat surprising, but it is clear that liberal groups did not successfully frame same-sex marriage as an equality issue. In contrast, moral traditionalism played no role in predicting attitudes toward antidiscrimination laws, but it was a significant predictor of attitudes toward gays in the military and played a powerful role in explaining attitudes toward marriage and adoption.

Among the three religious measures, attitudes toward the Bible were consistent predictors of opposition to gay rights. Those who believe that the Bible is the inerrant word of God were more likely to oppose all four policies than were those who believe that it is God's word but contains human errors. The effect was less substantial for gays in the military or for adoption, but it was especially large for antidiscrimination laws and for same-sex marriage. It may seem surprising that one's view of the Bible would be such a robust predictor of opposition to antidiscrimination laws, but evangelical activists have argued that such laws would force religious institutions (and small businesses run by evangelicals) to hire gays and lesbians.

Those who attend church regularly were more likely than nonattenders to oppose gay and lesbian adoption. It is religious salience, however, that predicts opposition to same-sex marriage. Those who get a lot of personal guidance from religion were particularly likely to oppose same-sex marriage.

Effect toward gays and lesbians was a significant predictor of all four policies; it was especially important in predicting attitudes toward adoption and least important in predicting attitudes toward gays in the military. In general, feelings toward gays and lesbians were the strongest predictors in all four policy areas, but they were relatively more important for issues such as adoption and marriage than for antidiscrimination laws and military service. Put another way, even those who were uneasy with gays and lesbians now favored allowing them access to jobs and housing free of discrimination and allowing them to serve in the military, but they were less willing to support allowing them to adopt children or to marry.

Only two demographic variables had any impact on attitudes on gay rights, once we hold constant values and evaluations of gays and lesbians. Women were far more likely to favor allowing gays and lesbians to serve in the military than were men, and they were also significantly more likely to favor allowing gays and lesbians to adopt children (but not discernibly more likely to favor allowing them to marry). Citizens with higher levels of education were more likely to favor gay rights with respect to military issues, adoption, and marriage.

Finally, ideology and partisanship were generally not significant predictors of attitudes about gay rights, once the values and evaluations that are associated with partisan and ideological divisions were held constant. The exception is that liberals were far more likely to favor same-sex marriage than were conservatives. One of the striking results is that equality values did not predict support for same-sex marriage, whereas ideology did. This may serve to limit support for it, for many moderates and conservatives support equality and are thereby led to support antidiscrimination laws, gays in the military, and adoption.

TAKING THE MARRIAGE LEAP

Taken together, the data showed considerable support for gay and lesbian civil rights and also considerable momentum in favor of those rights. Yet among those who favored antidiscrimination laws, nearly 60 percent did not favor marriage. And among those who favored allowing gays and lesbians to adopt children, nearly 40 percent opposed marriage. Though gay rights groups have pointed to Christian fundamentalists and homophobic citizens as being responsible for the passage of so many state constitutional amendments in 2004, there is clearly something more going on.

To better understand attitudes about gay rights issues, we identified clusters of individuals with particular patterns of attitudes. Among all respondents who answered these questions, 88 percent fit into one of the categories shown in table 9.4. Roughly 11 percent opposed gay rights positions with respect to all four policies. An additional 18 percent favored either antidiscrimination laws (shown in the table as ENDA, after the Employment Non-Discrimination Act considered by Congress) or allowing gays and lesbians in the military but not both. Another 21 percent favored

TABLE 9.4. Attitude clusters on gay rights issues.

	OPPOSE ALL RIGHTS	FAVOR ENDA OR MILITARY	FAVOR ENDA AND MILITARY	FAVOR ALL BUT MARRIAGE	FAVOR ALL RIGHTS
Mean value					
Equality	3.21	3.32	3.47	3.52	3.89
Moral traditionalism	3.72	3.77	3.67	3.22	2.49
Rate gays at 0 (%)	48	31	13	3	0
Mean rating for gays	19	32	43	57	69
Republican (%)	57	55	53	39	17
Democrat (%)	29	40	38	53	73
Liberal (%)	18	11	14	25	47
Conservative (%)	67	62	68	43	29
Believe Bible is inerrant (%)	72	57	51	27	9
Attend church at least weekly (%)	45	35	32	20	9
Find religion very important (%)	54	49	46	34	14
Black (%)	12	20	21	12	10
Female (%)	47	44	51	62	56
Aged 30 years or younger (%)	14	17	16	16	30
Aged 60 years or older (%)	30	34	28	27	13

Source: National Election Studies 2004.
Note: ENDA, Employment Non-Discrimination Act.

both of these policies but not adoption or marriage, and yet another 16 percent favored all policies except marriage. Fully 33 percent favored all four policies, primarily because nearly everyone who favored marriage favored all three other policies.[2]

The data given in table 9.4 show selected characteristics of the individuals who held each policy position. Note that this table shows the composition of each issue bloc, so that each number is not the percentage of a group (say, women) holding a particular position, but rather the percentage of those holding a particular position who fit that description (for example, they are women).

Nearly half of those who opposed all gay rights policies rated gays and lesbians at 0—the coolest possible rating. Clearly, homophobia is at the heart of blanket opposition to gay rights policies. Those who opposed all gay rights policies were also more likely than others to be evangelical Christians, with nearly three in four believing that the Bible is the inerrant word of God. Though many evangelical leaders argue that they urge their followers to hate the sin but not the sinner, in fact evangelicals were more likely than non-evangelicals in this group to rate gays at 0 degrees. Note, however, that some evangelicals supported gay rights. Nearly 20 percent favored adoption, marriage, or both, and nearly 50 percent favored both ENDA and military service.

Those who favored either ENDA or gays in the military were mainly distinct from those who opposed all gay rights in their lower levels of homophobia and evangelical religious doctrine, their greater level of Democratic identification, and their greater odds of being African Americans. Those who favored *both* policies were distinctive in showing stronger levels of equality values and somewhat lower levels of moral traditionalism, much lower levels of homophobia, and greater likelihood of being women.

Those who also supported adoption had slightly higher levels of equality values and much lower levels of moral traditionalism, as well as very low rates of homophobia. They were less Republican and more Democratic than those who favored ENDA and military service but not adoption, as well as more liberal and less conservative. They were far less likely to hold evangelical religious doctrine and to attend church regularly. They were less likely to be black, indicating that African Americans tend to support some gay rights policies but stop before adoption, and they were very likely to be women.

Who takes the leap and supports marriage? Here the data showed markedly higher levels of equality values and considerably lower levels of support for traditional moral values. Marriage supporters were not distinctive in their lack of homophobia because those who supported adoption but not marriage also showed little dislike of gays and lesbians. Supporters of same-sex marriage did rate gays and lesbians more "warmly," however, significantly above the midpoint of the 100-point feeling thermometer scale. Indeed, fully 13 percent rated gays and lesbians at 100 degrees, the warmest possible rating.

Marriage supporters were far more likely to be liberals and Democrats and less likely to be conservatives and Republicans, than those who supported adoption and, especially, those who supported ENDA and military service. Those who supported marriage were a largely secular group, with only 9 percent holding evangelical doctrine, 9 percent attending church weekly, and 14 percent saying that religion provides much guidance in their lives. Note that these numbers are low but they are not zero; there are some deeply religious individuals who favor same-sex marriage and full gay rights, but religion is clearly a major barrier to support for marriage. The proportions of blacks and women were lower among those who favored all four policies than among those who stopped short of marriage, suggesting that African Americans and, especially, women find something distinctive about policy toward marriage.[3] Finally, there were important generational differences, with the proportion who were under thirty increasing dramatically and the proportion that was more than sixty years of age dropping just as dramatically.

Taken together, these data show that many people favor a variety of gay rights policies but stop short of marriage. Those who are unwilling as yet to take the plunge—those who support antidiscrimination laws and military service and adoption but not marriage—include significant numbers of moderates, conservatives, Republicans, women, African Americans, and those who place a moderately high value on equality. They feel warmly toward gays and lesbians but not extremely so. They are also moderately religious but not extremely so.

YOU DON'T NEED A WEATHERMAN TO KNOW WHICH WAY THE WIND BLOWS

Predicting the political future is dicey business, as the Las Vegas odds makers who made George McGovern a thousand to one underdog to take the Democratic nomination in 1972 discovered. Often social and political systems go unchanged for long stretches of time, only to reach a tipping point when rapid change occurs. Political scientists are good at predicting the "normal weather" of presidential elections and budgetary spending but not so adept at predicting major social changes such as the collapse of communism or the end to apartheid in South Africa.

Segura (2005, 189) suggests that the 2004 Bush victory and concurrent constitutional amendments against same-sex marriage in many states portend "the beginning of what may be a long period of defeat for gay and lesbian causes." Further research into changes in public opinion in the past decade, however, belie Segura's gloomy prediction. We may be in a period of initial backlash against gay and lesbian advances (and in particular to Massachusetts's bold step of legalizing same-sex marriage), but the data indicate that such a phase need not last long. The issue's impact in the 2004 presidential election may have been exaggerated (for further discussion, see Burden 2004; Hillygus and Shields 2005; Lewis 2005), and its long-term rewards for the Right may be limited. George W. Bush seems to have realized this, as his support for a federal constitutional amendment prohibiting same-sex marriage dissipated almost immediately after the election.

Surveys show that a plurality of Americans expect same-sex marriage to be legal in their lifetimes. This belief is much stronger among those who are young and those who know someone who is gay or lesbian. It does not necessarily translate into support for same-sex marriage, however. The Peter Hart report on the 2003 focus groups for the Human Rights Campaign quotes one Omaha voter who commented on a provocative *Newsweek* magazine cover that asked "Is Gay Marriage Next?": "Yes, it is next, but I do not want to see it happen" (Peter D. Hart Research Associates 2003).

It seems likely that support for same-sex marriage will build over time. The pace of change in gay rights policies has been surprising even for gay rights activists. Recall the data shown in table 9.2: since 1988 public support for antidiscrimination laws protecting gays and lesbians has increased from 48 percent to 75 percent. Support for gays in the military has gone from a close split in 1992 to near consensus, with 81 percent in favor in 2004.[4] And even support for gay and lesbian adoption increased from 27 percent in 1992 to 50 percent in 2004, a doubling in little more than a decade. When the issue of military service broke in 1993, Clinton suffered significant losses of support among southern white men because of his support for equality. Yet in 2004, fully 76 percent of southern white men favored allowing gays and lesbians to serve.

Part of this change has occurred as people have discovered that they know someone who is gay or lesbian. Although surveys vary as to the number of Americans who do, all show a powerful impact on attitudes. In one survey by Lake, Snell, and Perry just prior to the 2004 election, 65 percent of those who knew someone who was gay or lesbian favored same-sex marriage or civil unions, compared with only 35 percent of those who did not. Knowing someone well has the strongest impact, but knowing anyone who is gay or lesbian can change attitudes.

One recent study by the Freedom to Marry Project and LLEGO, a national nonprofit organization dedicated to public education about gay Latin Americans, found that discussion of gay and lesbian family members and friends makes an important difference. Focus group and survey participants were much more supportive of same-sex marriage rights when the questioner first asked them to talk about the gay or lesbian people they knew. Also, in the 2003 survey by Peter Hart discussed above, respondents were asked to agree or disagree that allowing gay marriage would undermine the morals of the country and encourage homosexuality. Only 13 percent of those who had close friends or family members who were gay and lesbian agreed, compared with 45 percent of those with casual acquaintances and 63 percent of those who said that they knew no one.

In addition, surveys show that the belief that homosexuality is not a personal choice but, rather, is fixed at birth or in early childhood has become more common. This belief is another powerful predictor of attitudes toward gay rights. In the same Lake, Snell, and Perry survey, fully 44 percent of those who strongly believed that sexual orientation is fixed at birth favored same-sex marriage, and an additional 40 percent favored civil unions, for a remarkable 84 percent supporting some kind of legal recognition. Those who believed this less strongly were less supportive of marriage, with 19 percent supporting marriage and 50 percent favoring civil unions. Among those who strongly believed that sexual orientation is a choice, however, only 6 percent favored marriage and 10 percent favored civil unions, leaving nearly 80 percent who oppose all legal recognition.

Young people are far more likely to know someone who is gay or lesbian, as well as to believe that sexual orientation is fixed at birth. In the Lake, Snell, and Perry poll, 68 percent of those who were thirty or younger knew someone who was gay or lesbian, compared with only 26 percent of those over seventy-five. And 63 percent of those under thirty believed that sexual orientation was fixed at birth, compared with 45 percent of those over seventy-five.

Small wonder, then, that only 2 percent of the older cohort favored same-sex marriage, with 30 percent favoring civil unions, whereas

28 percent of the younger group favored same-sex marriage, with another 34 percent favoring civil unions. Over the next several years, many of those over seventy-five will leave the voter rolls, and the numbers of those who were born in an era more accepting of gay rights will increase. In the 2004 NES, with no option offered for civil unions, half of those under thirty supported same-sex marriage.

Yet generational replacement alone will not create a majority for same-sex marriage, because a majority of even the youngest citizens do not yet support it. Moreover, generational replacement is a very gradual process. Over time, it may well be that more citizens will discover that they know gay men and lesbians, though the most homophobic citizens may never have an associate come out to them. And over time, more Americans may come to believe in the existence of a "gay gene," though the results of future scientific research are always uncertain.

In the short run, many Americans will continue to strongly oppose same-sex marriage. For those whose opposition is based in moral traditionalism, exposure to same-sex marriage—and to friends and associates who support same-sex couples—may ease opposition in the longer term. Our traditional notion of marriage may involve a bride and a groom in a church with a white gown, but over time traditionalists have come to grudgingly accept brides who live with grooms before marrying, as well as brides and grooms of different races. So ideas of traditional marriage can change over time. As other countries legalize same-sex unions, the idea will seem less shocking. In *Fiddler on the Roof*, Tevya eventually shows signs of breaking down his barriers to his youngest daughter's marriage, telling another daughter to shout after her to "go with God."

The numerous surveys analyzed for this chapter suggest that public opinion about same-sex marriage is extremely sensitive to education, salience, and framing. Large majorities of the public routinely tell pollsters that they support the principle of equal rights and protections for gays and lesbians; when polls frame marriage as part of such equal rights and protection, support for same-sex marriage rises. Focus group research shows that even for people who are initially opposed to same-sex marriage, discussion and education can be effective in increasing support levels among some.

Among others, opposition to same-sex marriage may never dissipate. The intensity of opposition among devout evangelical Christians is built on deeply held religious doctrine and other associated beliefs.[5] With major Christian bodies mobilized to oppose the practice, there will remain strong cues for conservative Christians to oppose it. Yet it is important to remember that many conservative Christians support other gay rights positions, when only ten years earlier they opposed them based on their interpretation of church teachings.

In the short run, the label "marriage" is a major impediment for many Americans. They are torn between a desire to treat gay men and lesbians with equality and respect, on one hand, and core beliefs that marriage is a sacred institution designed by God, on the other. This suggests that it would be more profitable for gay and lesbian rights activists to focus first on building additional support for civil unions. The public is ready now to support civil unions in many states, and if state constitutions do not ban them it is possible to imagine moving rapidly in that direction in a short period of time. Some states will not adopt civil unions voluntarily for many years, if at all, but many have significant majorities in favor. If significant numbers of citizens come to know people who have entered into civil unions, then this may lower barriers toward marriage. Perhaps a few states might then adopt "civil marriages," and public support might continue to grow.

Politically speaking, the most important task for gay rights activists is to prevent the passage of a federal constitutional amendment and limit the passage of state constitutional amendments. Federal amendments can be repealed—the nation sobered up after passing Prohibition, after all—but it is not easy to repeal one; a few states could block that repeal. Repealing state amendments is easier, but as more states pass them by large margins a federal amendment may become easier to pass.

For gay marriage opponents, the political logic behind the push for constitutional amendments is equally clear. At present, public opinion is on their side in one key sense: nearly all surveys show significant majorities opposed to same-sex marriage. Amendments provide mechanisms to lock in public policy now, making it harder to change if the political landscape shifts from majority opposition to majority support. Foes of gay marriage can also point to polls showing majority support for a national amendment defining marriage as being between a man and a woman.

Other surveys, however, show majorities opposed to amending the federal constitution. One Pew survey conducted in March 2004 asked the 59 percent who disapproved of same-sex marriages whether a constitutional amendment to ban them was a good idea. Support for an amendment was 36 percent and opposition was 21 percent, with 2 percent undecided. In open-ended questions that followed, those who opposed same-sex marriage but also opposed an amendment indicated that they believed that the Constitution was a stable document that should not be changed, that this was a matter for state governments to decide, that it was an issue of individual freedom, and that it was too trivial to amend the constitution because of such an issue. More generally, the responses to questions on the topic seem quite sensitive to question wording, suggesting that elite framing could play a key role in any large fight over a national amendment.

In the longer term, gay rights activists might succeed by framing the issue more powerfully in terms of equality, stressing the rights and benefits that committed same-sex couples do not receive. Opponents of same-sex marriage would be happy for this to be an ideological issue of the culture war, pitting liberals against conservatives, Democrats against Republicans. Supporters should seek to portray it as a matter of equality—and fairness as well—that lies beyond ideology.

Regarding the 2004 elections, our conclusion is that the 2003 legalization of marriage for gays and lesbians in Massachusetts caught the general public by surprise. The right wing was able to capitalize on the shock factor to pass the state constitutional amendments, which can be read as an electoral slamming on of the brakes. Yet it does not appear that opposition to same-sex marriage is high enough to fuel a federal constitutional amendment campaign or to keep the issue near the top of the public agenda in the wake of the 2004 election. In addition, it is still unclear how much of the opposition was to same-sex marriage itself and how much was public anger about what Bush and other Republican politicians called "activist judges" in Massachusetts. Public resistance to judicial lawmaking could be clouding the issue, and it may be that as these issues are sorted out by state legislatures over time, resistance to same-sex marriage rights may not be nearly as high or as salient in the media. Segura's prediction of a sustained antigay backlash implies the kind of "massive resistance" seen in the South after the Supreme Court decision in *Brown v. Board of Education*, but this is actually not consistent with a careful examination of the public opinion evidence.

The evidence that we have presented suggests that the public's initial, gut-level reaction may be more in line with the conservative position of opposing same-sex marriage, which is true in the early phases of many, if not most, social reform movements. Public opinion often tends to reflect a distrust of large-scale rapid change. Same-sex marriage, however, is an issue regarding which discussion, education, and contextualization of the issue as relating to friends and family can all move people from one side to the other. Thus, support levels for marriage rights for same-sex couples will probably continue to rise within the public at large, even as a minority segment mobilizes to oppose it.

"Every successful social movement eventually moves from the unthinkable to the impossible to the inevitable," says Laura Liswood, founder of Women World Leaders. For the issue of same-sex marriage, recent developments have accelerated this process. What was unthinkable merely decades ago is now being discussed as not only possible and legal for some, but perhaps inevitable. Taken as a whole, the public opinion data indicate that we may be in a period of initial backlash, but they also suggest that opposition to same-sex marriage rights will probably not be sustainable in the long run.

ENDNOTES

1. Except where indicated, all poll results reported in this chapter are from the Roper Center for Public Opinion Research at the University of Connecticut (www.ropercenter.uconn.edu).
2. The exception is adoption. Of those who favor all but one gay rights policy, 21 percent favor marriage and not adoption.
3. In general, men were less supportive of gay rights overall, but among men and women who favored all three of the other gay rights policies, men were more likely to also favor same-sex marriage.
4. Of course, in 2004 the war in Iraq was under way, and the military badly needed soldiers—a practical concern that some Americans may have weighed.
5. For example, few evangelicals believe in the existence of a "gay gene" because they believe that gay sex is sinful and that God would not create a being who is innately drawn to sin. For Catholics, in contrast, the notion that God has made people gay but wants them to be celibate is less foreign.

REFERENCES

Alvarez, R. Michael, and John Brehm. 2002. *Hard choices, easy answers: Values, information, and American public opinion.* Princeton: Princeton University Press.

American National Election Studies. 2005. The 1948–2004 ANES cumulative data file [data set]. Stanford University and the University of Michigan [producers and distributors].

Bowman, Karlyn, and Bryan O'Keefe. 2004. *Attitudes about homosexuality and gay marriage.* Washington, DC: American Enterprise Institute Studies in Public Opinion.

Brewer, Paul R. 2003a. The shifting foundations of public opinion about gay rights. *Journal of Politics* 65:1208–20.

Brewer, Paul R. 2003b. Values, political knowledge, and public opinion about gay rights: A framing-based account. *Public Opinion Quarterly* 67:173–201.

Brewer, Paul R., and Clyde Wilcox. 2005. Trends: Same-sex marriage and civil unions. *Public Opinion Quarterly* 69:599–616.

Burden, Barry C. 2004. "An alternative account of the 2004 presidential election." *Forum* 2 (4): n.p. http://www.bepress.com/forum/vol2/iss4/art2/.

Craig, Stephen C., Michael D. Martinez, James G. Kane, and Jason Gainous. 2005. Core values, value conflict, and citizens' ambivalence about gay rights. *Political Research Quarterly* 58:5–17.

Feldman, Stanley. 1988. Structure and consistency in public opinion: The role of core beliefs and values. *American Journal of Political Science* 36:268–307.

Haider-Markel, Donald P., and Mark R. Joslyn. 2005. Attributions and the regulation of marriage: Considering the parallels between race and homosexuality. *PS: Political Science and Politics* 38:233–39.

Hillygus, D. Sunshine, and Todd G. Shields. 2005. Moral issues and voter decisionmaking in the 2004 presidential election. *PS: Political Science and Politics* 38:201–9.

Kaufman, Marc, and Mike Allen. 2004. Cheney sees gay marriage as state issue; vice president details differences with Bush. *Washington Post*, August 25.

Kushner, Tony. 1994. Fireworks and freedom. *Newsweek*, June 27.

Larson, Carin, and Clyde Wilcox. In press. The faith of George W. Bush: The personal, practical, and political. In *Religion and the American Presidency*, ed. Mark J. Rozell and Gleanes Whitney. London: Palgrave Macmillan.

Lewis, Gregory B. 2005. Same-sex marriage and the 2004 presidential election. *PS: Political Science and Politics* 38:195–200.

Nelson, Thomas E., Rosalee A. Clawson, and Zoe M. Oxley. 1997. Media framing of a civil liberties conflict and its effect on tolerance. *American Political Science Review* 91:567–83.

Peter D. Hart Research Associates. 2003. Report to the Human Rights Campaign. Washington, DC: Peter D. Hart Research Associates.

Same-sex marriage tops priorities for gays. 2002. *USA Today*, June 19.

Segura, Gary M. 2005. A symposium on same-sex marriage: An introduction and a commentary. *PS: Political Science and Politics* 38:195–200.

Sniderman, Paul M., Richard A. Brody, and Philip E. Tetlock. 1991. *Reasoning and choice: Explorations in political psychology.* New York: Cambridge University Press.

Wilcox, Clyde, and Barbara Norrander. 2002. On moods and morals: The dynamics of opinion on abortion and gay rights. In *Understanding Public Opinion.* 2d ed., ed. Barbara Norrander and Clyde Wilcox, 121–47. Washington, DC: CQ Press.

Wilcox, Clyde, and Robin Wolpert. 1996. President Clinton, public opinion, and gays in the military. In *Gay rights, military wrongs: Political perspectives on lesbians and gays in the military,* ed. Craig Rimmerman, 127–45. New York: Garland.

———. 2000. Gay rights in the public sphere: Public opinion on gay and lesbian equality. In *The politics of gay rights,* ed. Craig A. Rimmerman, Kenneth D. Wald, and Clyde Wilcox, 409–32. Chicago: University of Chicago Press.

Yang, Alan S. 1997. Attitudes toward homosexuality. *Public Opinion Quarterly* 61:477–507.

Zaller, John. 1992. *The nature and origins of mass opinion.* New York: Cambridge University Press.

SAME-SEX MARRIAGE
IN THE 2004 ELECTION

DeWayne L. Lucas

In politics, framing the issue is often the most important component of the electoral campaign.[1] Setting the terms of the campaign allows one side to present its issues in the most favorable light and places the opposing side on the defensive. In the 2004 elections, the ability of Republicans to frame the issue of same-sex marriage as an attack on traditional values was a major asset to the party's electoral armory. Republicans were successful in framing the election as a defense of the institution of marriage rather than providing equivalent support for life partners, as many same-sex marriage advocates had hoped. The party presented itself as the defender of the institution of marriage and portrayed the Democratic Party as part of the movement to change the meaning of marriage. Republicans thus were able to appeal directly to their socially conservative constituents and place Democrats at odds with American tradition and values.

Although Democratic-leaning groups such as Gays and Lesbians Advocates and Defenders (GLAD) and the Human Rights Campaign (HRC) had made substantial advances on behalf of same-sex marriage in the judiciary, Democrats were less effective at making that argument in the races of 2004. In state courts, same-sex marriage advocates had the advantage of unbiased and nonpartisan arbitrators in determining that their intention was simply to acquire equal treatment for same-sex couples before the law. In the electoral arena, supporters of same-sex marriage had to present their best arguments to a more conservative and traditional electorate, not bound by legal precedent or the principle of equal treatment before the law. Adoption of an equal treatment approach in the campaign process would not be easy. Although polls suggested considerable support for providing same-sex couples with many of the benefits of marriage, the ability of the Republican Party to focus the campaign on the redefinition of marriage and the failure of the Democratic Party to counter that question were clear electoral advantages for the Republicans.

THE ELECTORAL LANDSCAPE: THE VOLATILITY OF PUBLIC OPINION

Both sides of the debate faced a major force: the American public. Americans have never been strong supporters of homosexual rights, and that opposition had come to light well before the 2004 elections in terms of sodomy laws, military service, and adoption. Nevertheless, as early as the 1990s, signs were beginning to emerge that this opposition may be waning and, depending on the issue, was advancing in favor of extending civil rights to homosexuals. For elected officials, staying ahead of this movement was essential to their electoral strategies.

THE INFLUENCE OF MODERN SOCIAL CONSERVATISM: IDEOLOGY IN AMERICAN ELECTIONS

The American political and electoral landscapes show signs of the increasing division of the major parties along conservative-liberal lines. Unlike the early political parties, the electoral base and partisan makeup of the parties have become more ideologically polarized. Social and economic liberals collectively are far more likely to identify with and vote for the Democratic Party, and social and economic conservatives are more likely to align with the Republican Party.[2] Whereas in previous decades Democratic and Republican campaigns had to attract varying degrees of liberal, moderate, and conservative voters, elections in the early twenty-first century required Republicans to appeal directly to their conservative base and to fight with Democrats for the moderate vote.

This partisan polarization has had particular effects on the actions of the two parties within Congress, but it has had an equally significant impact on the voting patterns of the electorate and thus the campaign strategies of the two major parties. The polarization has compelled Democrats to seek the endorsement of a more liberal primary group and Republicans a more conservative one, instead of the broad electoral coalitions that both sought in prior decades.[3] Without a liberal Republican cohort to appeal to, for instance, the Republican Party has been free to pursue strategies designed to mobilize its conservative base.

For Republicans, the biggest component of that conservative shift has been the increased mobilization and empowerment of religious groups. The Christian Right, in particular, has been aggressive in its approach to and demands on elected officials. Less concerned with the economic and global role of the United States, the Christian Right has focused its demands on government as a return to traditional moral and family values for the country. It evaluates candidates on the basis of their commitment to restoring the proper role of God and the Bible in the direction of the nation.[4] It has opposed teaching evolution in schools, abortion, and homosexual rights.[5] Its involvement in the 1990s accentuated its impact on the 2004 election. Republican candidates pursued the policies and issues that would draw this highly desired electoral constituency to the ballot box and guarantee its support on Election Day.

Nevertheless, as early as 2003, social conservatives began to show signs of dissatisfaction with the Republican-controlled government. The talk of their revolt impressed on the president and Republican Party leaders the need to show their continued support for issues that concern the Christian Right. In 2003 Ken Connor, president of the Family Research Council, questioned the Republican commitment to fighting for the socially conservative policies that defined the group. Summarizing his concerns, Connor stated: "If Republican leaders cannot mount a vigorous defense of marriage, then pro-family voters perhaps should begin to reconsider their loyalty to the party." [6] He expressed similar thoughts in radio messages and open letters to the Family Research Council's members. He echoed similar concerns voiced by like-minded groups.

Republicans would need to stand up for socially conservative policies, in particular, marriage, or a significant proportion of their electoral constituency would stay home on Election Day.

Conservatism had united the party in past elections, but now members of the Christian Right began to wonder what Republicans were doing to address their needs in the current administration. Tax cuts, terrorism, and the war in Iraq showed the nation and other conservative groups the commitment of the Republican Party to economic conservatism and global leadership but did not speak to its commitment to defending and restoring family values, moral values, and religion to the daily lives of the American public. To encourage social conservatives to turn out at the polls, the Republican Party needed to highlight its commitment to their concerns.

PUBLIC OPINION AND HOMOSEXUAL RIGHTS: ASK THE RIGHT QUESTION

Although at the forefront of the Christian Right's fight, the homosexual rights movement had seen considerable progress. Television sitcoms, newspaper articles, and local community activities increasingly highlighted homosexuals in society, and Americans were becoming more accepting of their presence and lifestyle. Social conservatives perceived the advances in homosexuals' military service, adoptions, and employment rights as signs of the nation's abandonment of traditional values and of God. The country appeared to be slowly embracing many of these rights, and social conservatives and their elected leaders would need a way to direct the country back to the right path.

Social conservatives, however, were also cautious about their approach and about the issues that they would undertake. In the early 1990s they took on the issue of military service by homosexuals and noted the changes in public opinion that followed. Shortly after the enactment of President William Clinton's 1993 executive order regarding the "Don't ask, don't tell" policy, a NBC–*Wall Street Journal* poll reported that a substantial number (40 percent) of Americans favored "allowing openly gay men and lesbian women to serve in the military" whereas a slight majority (52 percent) opposed the proposal. A year later, the Pew Research Center reported that 52 percent of the public supported military service in 1994.[7] By the end of 2003, a Gallup poll reported that the number of supporters had grown to 79 percent and the share of opponents had dropped to 18 percent; the majority of all major social groups, according to the Gallup poll, found service by homosexuals in the military acceptable.[8] Likewise, a Pew Research Center poll stated that whereas age, gender, racial, and ideological groups had come to accept military service, Republicans were evenly split (46 percent to 46 percent) with regard to the issue.

The public's opposition to such service was changing in the wake of efforts to curtail homosexuals' rights. Acceptance of military service for homosexuals had crossed social lines and thus party lines. For campaign strategists in 2004, restricting military service would prove a difficult electoral message, especially as the demands of the military increased. The American public apparently had become more supportive of homosexuals in the military. The Republican Party and social conservatives needed to be cautious in their approach to the issue because electoral defeat might await them.

Same-sex marriage, however, presented different opportunities for the nation. Though yet to reach the levels of support reported by Gallup for military service, the public showed considerable support for spousal benefits for homosexual couples. National polls conducted shortly after 2000 repeatedly showed that an ever-increasing majority of Americans supported granting the legal benefits of marriage (hospital visitation rights, health care benefits, and inheritance rights) to same-sex couples, but the majority of the country remained opposed to permitting them to wed. A 1989 *Time* poll of the American public reported that just as majorities of respondents supported adoption rights (75 percent), inheritance rights (65 percent), and health care benefits (54 percent) for same-sex couples, a significant majority (69 percent) opposed same-sex marriage and a small minority (23 percent) supported it.[9] Later, in a 1992 *Newsweek* poll, less than one-third of those surveyed approved of same-sex marriage and two-thirds supported inheritance rights and health benefit for same-sex couples.[10]

These studies suggested a general acceptance by Americans of homosexual rights in terms of employment, spousal benefits, and discrimination but continued resistance to the idea of same-sex marriage.[11] The American public would be willing to accept an expansion of a number of rights to same-sex couples, but they still wanted a limit to that expansion. With the events of 2003 and 2004 showing that same-sex marriage could become a reality, conservatives wanted to protect moral and family values by curtailing these advances.

Moreover, same-sex marriage divided the country along both ideological and partisan lines. According to 2,527 Gallup Poll interviews conducted in February 2004, 65 percent of conservatives and 66 percent of Republicans favored a constitutional amendment to ban same-sex marriage while 65 percent of liberals and 54 percent of Democrats opposed such an amendment.[12] Same-sex marriage provided both parties with the ability to appeal to their political and ideological base to ensure turnout. The issue provided a basis for mobilizing and uniting the Republican Party's base, the conservative base, and potentially the moderate base without alienating large majorities of the American public.

With this political landscape before them, Republican strategists recognized that same-sex marriage advocates could win public support if the debate was focused on the benefits or the equal treatment argument. The public showed mixed opinions toward same-sex marriage, unlike military service, and that could benefit the party. Same-sex marriage represented an issue that would rally social conservatives and Republican partisans, and, if framed properly, would present the Republican Party in a favorable light to a majority of the American public. Allowing the Left to define the issue as equal treatment before the law, as advocates did before the courts, however, posed a real threat to social conservatives and to the Republicans' electoral hopes. To stave off such an event, the Republican Party needed to focus the electoral discussion on same-sex marriage. They also needed to demonstrate to likely voters that this would directly impact their daily lives—that it was an issue they needed to turn out and vote for.

LAYING THE GROUNDWORK: THE THREATS TO MARRIAGE

Although focusing on the defense of traditional marriage would be beneficial to the party's electoral aspirations, Republicans also needed to highlight the threat of marriage to individuals' daily lives. They wanted to make sure that same-sex marriage was an issue that motivated voters. To do so, Republicans continued portraying the question as a challenge to the very institution of marriage. To social conservatives, same-sex marriage threatened the building blocks of marriage, and the political apparatus was ill prepared to contain the threat. Without action, they would argue, the courts would force the nation to accept same-sex marriage.

By the beginning of the twenty-first century, the Republican message highlighted this threat to Americans. Many Republicans and conservatives saw the advances in Massachusetts and Vermont as a heightening of the threat to marriage. State courts had decided that civil unions should be recognized and were constitutionally mandated. During the Clinton administration, it was argued that the federal government's main defense against civil unions and same-sex marriage, the Defense of Marriage Act (DOMA), would be ineffective in containing the actions of state courts, which might overturn the act. Social conservatives argued that the threat was even more apparent when city and town mayors, following the lead of San Francisco mayor Gavin Newsom, violated their state laws to wed same-sex couples.[13] The federal government was unable to restrain the actions of the judiciary in this arena.

With the DOMA and other state and federal efforts to limit same-sex marriage in 1996, the Republicans laid the groundwork for portraying the same-sex marriage movement as the redefinition of marriage. The party presented the movement as an attempt to change the culture of the nation. In 1996, while President Clinton and fellow Democrats argued that DOMA only ensured that states would have the right to determine their own definitions of marriage, Republicans asserted that the act was a necessary step for limiting the same-sex marriage movement.

State courts in Vermont and Massachusetts would also play a significant role in framing the argument. Same-sex marriage advocates had been successful in advancing an equal treatment argument in northern state courts and had led to the creation of civil unions in Vermont and same-sex marriage in Massachusetts. The core argument was that marriage provided legal, financial, and social protections and responsibilities to heterosexual couples that homosexual couples could not enjoy. Massachusetts Chief Justice Margaret Marshall summarized the argument in the majority opinion:

Marriage is a vital social institution. The exclusive commitment of two individuals to each other nurtures love and mutual support; it brings stability to our society. For those who choose to marry, and for their children, marriage provides an abundance of legal, financial, and social benefits. In return it imposes weighty legal, financial, and social obligations. The question before us is whether, consistent with the Massachusetts Constitution, the Commonwealth may deny the protections, benefits, and obligations conferred by civil marriage to two individuals of the same sex who wish to marry. We conclude that it may not. The Massachusetts Constitution affirms the dignity and equality of all individuals. It forbids the creation of second-class citizens. In reaching our conclusion we have given full deference to the arguments made by the Commonwealth. But it has failed to identify any constitutionally adequate reason for denying civil marriage to homosexual couples.[14]

This denial would be a severe violation of the equal protection clauses of the state's constitution. Given that state constitutions historically have granted far more civil rights and protections than does the federal Constitution, same-sex marriage advocates were able to justify their claims solely within the state's legal framework. Ideally, by adopting a selective state-by-state approach, advocates would be able to ensure the advancement of their rights in various states and build national support slowly.

To social conservatives, however, the events in Vermont and Massachusetts highlighted the threat before them. Ignoring the equal protection arguments of the court and the same-sex marriage advocates, they immediately challenged the Massachusetts court's action as a sign of the inability of DOMA and the federal government to prevent a redefinition of marriage and as a direct threat to the institution. Moreover, on televisions across the country, Americans saw thousands of same-sex couples flocking to San Francisco to wed. Although many same-sex marriage advocates saw this as an advance for their movement, opponents were upset further and felt even more threatened by the impending changes. They demanded action from Republicans.

Republican congressional leaders brought up for debate two measures designed to protect the institution of marriage. The Senate considered the Federal Marriage Amendment (FMA) but failed (48 to 50) to invoke cloture on the legislation; the House did not take up the bill. The House passed (233 to 194) the Marriage Protection Act to prevent the courts from considering cases about the interpretation of DOMA; the Senate did not act on the bill. With control of both chambers of Congress, social conservatives were unable to further protect marriage. Republican strategists and leaders stressed the need for a stronger majority to do so. The threat represented by the Massachusetts courts and activist local officials could not be defeated without more Republican senators and representatives dedicated to defending marriage.

Whether intentionally or not, political events were used to set up the argument that the sanctity of marriage was threatened and that a strong defense of the institution was needed. The desire of social conservatives to give voters a reason to vote for the Republican Party, the public's willingness to defend marriage but accept spousal benefits for same-sex couples, and the advances in the same-sex marriage movement at the state level presented a prime opportunity for the Republican Party and conservative activists to focus on same-sex marriage as a major campaign issue in the 2004 election.

THE REPUBLICAN ADVANTAGE: A UNITED VOICE

Over the course of the past two decades, the success of the Republican Party owed much to its unprecedented levels of party unity and cohesion. In 1994 the ability of Newt Gingrich and the Republican Party to rally around a single plan for the future of the country, the Contract with America, provided a significant advantage to the party in taking control of and framing the electoral debate. In the wake of major legal battles to present same-sex marriage as a question of equal treatment, the Republicans sought to use this solidarity to portray the same-sex marriage movement as an attack on traditional marriage. Although the issue may have played only a minor role in the final electoral outcomes, it provided Republicans with a key opportunity to strengthen their connection with conservative voters and to portray Democrats as extremists to mainstream and moderate voters.

By presenting same-sex marriage as an attack on the traditional definition of marriage, Republicans signaled to their conservative base that the party was committed to the protection of its views and values and showed moderate, middle-of the-road voters that the party was not a radical conservative group. The former approach allowed the party to unite and secure its base, and the latter helped build connections with crucial voters. Instead of attacking the provision of spousal benefits to same-sex couples, Republicans were able to focus the debate on the less controversial and more popular task of defending the definition of traditional marriage.

THE NATIONAL REPUBLICAN CAMPAIGN

The effort to describe the events of 2004 as a threat to the institution of marriage began long before the 2004 election. Republicans had attempted to define the movement toward same-sex marriage as an attack on marriage as early as the 1993 debates about DOMA. Whereas social conservatives and many Republicans continued to make this connection, the Bush administration largely ignored the issue during his first term. Though he never denied his support for a constitutional amendment to ban same-sex marriage or opposition to such marriage, Bush rarely discussed the issue in his first three years in office.

In October 2003, a month prior to the expected Massachusetts decision concerning same-sex marriage, Bush proclaimed the week of October 12 to 18 "Marriage Protection Week" and pledged the support of the administration for counseling, tax relief, and education to help married couples.[15] Nonetheless, as the issue achieved greater national prominence, the president and Republicans became more aggressive. By February, three months after the Massachusetts ruling was released and at the height of San Francisco and other local movements to wed homosexual couples, Bush declared his support for a constitutional amendment, saying, "Yet there is no assurance that the Defense of Marriage Act will not, itself, be struck down by activist courts. In that event, every state would be forced to recognize any relationship that judges in Boston or officials in San Francisco choose to call a marriage. Furthermore, even if the Defense of Marriage Act is upheld, the law does not protect marriage within any state or city." [16]

Bush affirmed the concern of many conservatives that the courts and local governments would readily overturn DOMA and open the doors for the union of gay and lesbian couples. His first major response was to charge the courts with judicial activism. Blaming the judiciary ideally would not directly antagonize gays and lesbians or moderates supportive of gay rights. It would, however, resonate with social conservatives opposed to court actions relating to abortion, gun ownership, and other social issues and would shift responsibility away from the legislative and executive branches. It was a reminder to the influential conservative base that the administration was fully behind them, even if it did not directly attack same-sex marriage.

Less than a year from Election Day 2004, Bush called for a constitutional amendment to define marriage as a union between a man and a woman. Without addressing the equal treatment argument or the relevant issues at stake in the state courts, Bush advanced for the Republican Party and social conservatives a "defense of marriage" argument. The goal was simple: make the terms of the campaign about the meaning of marriage. Doing so presented the opposition (social liberals and Democrats) as opposed to traditional marriage and placed the Republican Party, Bush, and conservatives closer to the center.

In his February 2004 State of the Union address, the president reasserted the necessity for federal action in the same-sex marriage debate and underscored the threat posed by the judiciary to the checks and balances of the American political system:

A strong America must also value the institution of marriage. I believe we should respect individuals as we take a principled stand for one of the most fundamental, enduring institutions of our civilization. Congress has already taken a stand on this issue by passing the Defense of Marriage Act, signed in 1996 by President Clinton. That statute protects marriage under federal law as a union of a man and a woman, and declares that one state may not redefine marriage for other states. Activist judges, however, have begun redefining marriage by court order, without regard for the will of the people and their elected representatives. On an issue of such great consequence, the people's voice must be heard. If judges insist on forcing their arbitrary will upon the people, the only alternative left to the people would be the constitutional process. Our nation must defend the sanctity of marriage.[17]

Bush avoided the issues that had been argued before the Supreme Judicial Court of Massachusetts as well as its ruling. Whereas the focus in the courts was on whether the state under its constitution could deny spousal benefits and marriage to same-sex couples, Republican political leaders had already began to frame the issue as the redefinition of marriage by activist judges.

The president and the vice president said little else about the issue of same-sex marriage throughout the campaign season, but they stayed true to their conservative roots. In the only question asked at the presidential debates about homosexual rights, Bush asserted his desire to be tolerant and respectful of all consenting adults and his mistrust of the judiciary to ensure the proper protection of marriage. Unsure of the cause of homosexuality, the president said he believed that: "as we respect someone's rights, and as we profess tolerance, we shouldn't change—or have to change—our basic views on the sanctity of marriage. I believe in the sanctity of marriage. I think it's very important that we protect marriage as an institution between a man and a woman." [18] Still cognizant of the national implications of his statement, Bush attempted to portray his position as sympathetic to the homosexual rights movement but still committed to the proper defense of marriage. He asserted his support of same-sex individuals but opposition to their marriage. Vice President Richard Cheney would give a similar response in his debate with Democratic nominee John Edwards.

Social conservatives would nonetheless take another step to protect the institution of marriage at the Republican National Convention. Although the details are often ignored by individual politicians, the party platform establishes the general direction of the party in the years to come. In 2004 the Republican National Convention adopted the official agenda of the party as it regarded same-sex marriage. The 2004 platform stated that (1) marriage was between a man and a woman, (2) marriage benefits should be reserved only for married couples, (3) the judiciary and local officials have threatened the sanctity of marriage, and (4) a federal constitutional amendment was needed to protect the benefits and sanctity of marriage. The platform read as follows:

We strongly support President Bush's call for a Constitutional amendment that fully protects marriage, and we believe that neither federal nor state judges nor bureaucrats should force states to recognize other living arrangements as equivalent to marriage. We believe, and the social science confirms, that the well-being of children is best accomplished in the environment of the home, nurtured by their mother and father anchored by the bonds of marriage. We further believe that legal recognition and the accompanying benefits afforded couples should be preserved for that unique and special union of one man and one woman which has historically been called marriage.[19]

Not committing any Republican to a particular position on same-sex marriage, the platform laid out the party's general approach to the issue. As a whole, the party was committed to a strong defense of the institution in line with its social conservatism. Nonetheless, Log Cabin Republicans, gay rights advocates in the Republican Party, challenged the platform's language but failed to garner the majority support in six different state delegations needed to bring such a challenge to the floor. The group would later withhold its endorsement of Bush's reelection, citing his support for the Federal Marriage Amendment.[20]

Faced with an increasingly polarized electorate and the need for greater electoral maneuverability, the national Republican campaign wanted an issue that would rally conservative voters without mobilizing the Left. Same-sex marriage provided the party with that issue. Conservative voters recognized the threat before the country and could easily be mobilized by a call to protect the institution of marriage. Although many American voters were prepared to support spousal benefits for same-sex couples, most were less accepting of same-sex marriage. Bush and other national-level Republicans used the issue to rally their conservative base and reassure moderates that they were not extremists.

PICKING UP THE REPUBLICAN MANTRA

Republican congressional candidates adopted the defense of marriage approach in their congressional campaigns. The presidential elections as well as the events of 2004 made the issue salient in the minds of most voters. The president and the national party had laid out the party's message for many voters. Republicans thus were able to spend less time defining their conservative roots and simplified their message to basic statements that they opposed gay marriage and believed that marriage is the union of a man and woman. The message expressed the candidates' support of traditional values without requiring them to overtly appeal to their conservative base. They could, for instance, present more moderate positions and use the defense of marriage argument to maintain conservative support. Their conservative connection was implied in the message; it was a reminder that the opposition—the Democratic Party—was not on the side of tradition.

From campaign advertisements to political debates to interest group activity and support, Republican strategists needed to effectively use the defense of marriage argument to mobilize their conservative base. Often the message was sent subtly and in passing; occasionally, it was a blatant attack on the opponent. In many party and individual political advertisements the defense of marriage argument simply scrolled across the screen, was printed in the background, or was briefly stated in a lengthy list of major topics.

Republican candidates effectively used these advertisements to tout their commitment to social conservatism without highlighting their positions for moderate and liberal voters. There was little discussion or explanation beyond the basic statement of opposition to same-sex marriage. No mention was made of the candidate's position in terms of the equal treatment argument of the Left. No explanation of their position on homosexual issues was given. The candidate simply was against same-sex marriage. The campaign was not intended to be about the merits or demerits of the issue or the expansion or suppression of homosexual rights. It was a statement about the candidate's defense of tradition. The message was seen as enough to connect the conservative and moderate wings of the electorate.

A popular Republican approach to using the issue of same-sex marriage was to join the issue with other popular "American" images to appeal to conservative voters. Representative Todd Akin of Missouri's Second District ran a direct defense of marriage ad. Without stating his opponents' position, Akin's television commercial showed a picture of the American flag with a gavel in the background fading from view. While a just-married bride and groom exited their church, Akins spoke out against activist judges trying to rewrite the definition of marriage as well as the words of the Pledge of Allegiance. He concluded by stating his intention not to allow the courts to undermine the framework of this country.[21] The image made powerful mental connections between patriotism and opposition to same-sex marriage. Akin won the election with 65 percent of the vote.

Likewise, Virginia Foxx of North Carolina's Fifth District, an open seat, used a television advertisement to establish her conservative credentials. Foxx began by asserting her pride in being a conservative and listed as her first major accomplishment in the state senate her sponsorship of a bill to prevent same-sex marriage; below, the phrase "Led the Fight against Gay Marriage" scrolled across the screen.[22] Foxx's primary challenger, Republican Vernon Robinson, used a similar approach to attract Republican support for the party's nomination.[23] Along with tax cuts and abortion, opposition to same-sex marriage became a mechanism by which candidates could express their conservative values to their constituents. Foxx and Robinson were engaged in one of the fiercest primary competitions in 2004, and both were able to use their position regarding same-sex marriage to shore up the conservative vote.

The Foxx-Robinson primary contest, one of the most expensive in the 2004 election, highlighted another plus of the same-sex marriage issue for the Republican Party. It kept party members from engaging in hostile intraparty policy debates; it kept the members united. In contemporary politics, primaries have become the major battlegrounds for elected office. As the increasingly polarized American electorate has aligned itself ideologically with the two parties—liberal voters support Democrats, conservative voters support Republicans—winning the primary and thus the party nomination has become an automatic step to elected office. The similarity between Foxx and Robinson in the primary reduced the possibility of moving too far to the right or to the left (center) for the Fifth District's voters. Though a nasty campaign, the focus of the primary was on the ideological and stylistic differences rather than the policy differences between the two candidates.[24] After winning the Republican primary nomination, Foxx easily shifted to a right-of-center general election campaign against Democrat Jim Harrell; she won 58 percent of the vote.

Some candidates portrayed a more flexible image early in the campaign, but for strictly political reasons. Despite his brewing company's support of expansive homosexual rights, Colorado Senate candidate Peter Coors was hesitant in asserting his position on same-sex marriage early in the election and was attacked by his primary opponent Bob Schaffer for not being conservative enough. Though Coors opposed same-sex marriage, Schaffer attempted to use the issue to paint Coors as too liberal to represent the Colorado Republican Party.[25] After winning the primary in this traditionally moderate state, Coors narrowly lost to Democratic candidate Ken Salazar.

In a few races, the attacks were more aggressive. In Arkansas, the challenger for the Republican Senate seat, Jim Holt, a state senator, made the issue of same-sex marriage a central piece of his campaign against Democratic senator Blanche Lincoln. Although Lincoln defended her vote against the Federal Marriage Act on the ground that it was an issue of protecting state's rights and that the federal Constitution "should only be [amended] as a last resort," during their debate Holt questioned her commitment to protecting the sanctity of marriage.[26] He repeatedly attacked Lincoln for her opposition to the FMA, saying that it was the equivalent of supporting same-sex marriage. Despite raising a fraction of Lincoln's $6 million, Holt was able to carry an impressive portion of conservative voters and 44 percent of the entire state.[27]

The Senate race in Kentucky took an even more aggressive tone when Democratic challenger Daniel Mongiardo was accused of being gay by the campaign of the incumbent, Senator Jim Bunning. At a Rotary Club meeting, two surrogates of Bunning—Kentucky Senate president David Williams and state senator Elizabeth Tori—questioned Mongiardo's masculinity and called him a "limp wrist." [28] Given Mongiardo's opposition to the FMA, he was questioned about his sexuality and had to defend his position against other Republican charges.

In 2004 Republicans were able to use the issue of same-sex marriage to establish their conservative credentials and cast doubts on their opponents' commitment to traditional values. The vast majority of Republicans ran campaigns that merely described the same-sex marriage movement as seeking to redefine traditional marriage and relied on the national role of the issue. The strategy allowed them to frame the issue in terms favorable to the party. It assisted them in connecting to conservative and moderate voters in moderate electoral districts and in mobilizing voters in heavily conservative districts. Framing the issue as a defense of marriage was important in shaping the campaign.

HESITATION FROM MODERATE REPUBLICANS

The general response of the moderate voices of the Republican Party was that the effort to confine the definition of marriage to a man and a woman was an overreaction to the situation. They attempted to portray the issue at hand as simply a matter of federalism. Faced with a constituency that was more ideologically diverse than those that other Republicans faced, these Republicans needed to downplay their socially conservative connections in the primary and general elections. They also faced the challenge of explaining their congressional votes and actions with regard to same-sex marriage.

During congressional efforts to strengthen DOMA and limit the possible effects of state recognitions of same-sex marriage, moderate Republicans were hard pressed by the party and by primary voters to stand up in defense of marriage. Only six Republican senators opposed the vote to end debate and call for a vote on the Federal Marriage Amendment. Senator John McCain was the only one of the six who was up for reelection in 2004.[29] Likewise, no Republican voted against the Marriage Protection Act, though five did not vote at all. Republican unity in these efforts was an important reminder to social conservatives in moderate and conservative districts.

Representative Jim Kolbe of Arizona's Eighth District expressed the strongest opposition within the party to a constitutional amendment to ban same-sex marriage. Kolbe, the only openly gay Republican in the House of Representatives, made an argument a line that many Democrats would echo: "Never before has it been proposed that our Constitution should be used to limit the rights of citizens rather than expand those rights."[30] Although he grounded his opposition in the Constitution, he remained mildly supportive of same-sex marriage and civil unions. He was disheartened at times by his party's failure to recognize the federal issues at stake in the defense of marriage approach.

It is important nonetheless that few of the Republican opponents of federal regulation of same-sex marriage were supportive of gay marriage. Representative Mary Bono of California's Forty-fifth district refused to attend the Republican National Convention because of its portrayal of same-sex marriage and other issues in a divisive manner. "Although I do not support gay marriage, I do believe that our party's focus should be on issues of greater concern to most Americans such as national security and improving our economy," she stated.[31] Bono, who represented a large homosexual constituency in western Coachella, was faced with balancing the concerns of that constituency with the Republican Party's message. Nevertheless, the moderate Republican's position regarding gay marriage included opposition to the FMA, support for homosexual rights, and opposition to same-sex marriage. In her campaign, Bono attempted to minimize her position regarding same-sex marriage and her connection to the Republican Party.

Likewise, prominent Republican leaders not running for office, such as former New York City mayor Rudy Giuliani, California governor Arnold Schwarzenegger, and New York governor George Pataki, also expressed support for the rights of homosexual couples. Yet neither Schwarzenegger nor Giuliani spoke about the issue in his address to the convention. The number of Republican leaders who publicly supported same-sex marriage was extremely small in the 2004 election. The number that would actively challenge the Republican Party's position would be even lower.

One of the biggest advantages to the Republican effort was the party's unity. This agreement allowed party leaders such as the president to convey to the conservative base the importance of banning same-sex marriage and defending traditional marriage. Recognizing the considerable amount of public support for spousal benefits for same-sex couples and the potential for such support to gain momentum, Republicans quickly portrayed the issue as an attack on traditional marriage and culture. They were able to use the issue to establish a strong link with their conservative base in such a manner as not to offend many moderate and liberal voters. A unified majority party with a relatively silent minority amongst a polarized electorate would easily frame the issue for the election. With the advantages of the presidency and the majority party status, Republicans were able to set the agenda on same-sex marriage in the 2004 election as a question of whether to change the definition of marriage.

The challenge for the Democratic Party was to find a way to counter the message and the unity that the Republican Party had spent decades building. An ideologically diverse minority party would find this to be no easy task.

THE DEMOCRATIC CHALLENGE: CORE CONSTITUENTS AND THE MEDIAN VOTER

For years the Democratic Party has been an ally of the gay rights movement. Yet as gay rights advocates heralded the decision of the Massachusetts court on same-sex marriage as a promising sign of future advancements, party leaders hesitated. Despite the success of homosexual rights advocates in the courts, the party struggled to articulate a message that resonated with its core constituency and mainstream America's vision of a cultural war about same-sex marriage.

With the Republicans focused on defending traditional marriage, the Democratic Party was in the position of showing support for their homosexual allies and constituents and offsetting allegations that they supported changing the definition of marriage. For a party with a history of support for the homosexual minority in an increasingly conservative country where marriage is valued, this was a difficult position to be in. Democratic leaders had to find ways of maintaining their commitment to diversity and respecting individual rights and had to acknowledge that they were not prepared to change the definition of marriage.

TOO MANY DEMOCRATIC COOKS

For many gay rights advocates, this was not perceived as a challenge: simply make the debate about the Democratic Party's support for providing spousal benefits to same-sex couples. At best, this was an opportunity to build momentum and support for their civil and political rights. Being the minority party, however, gave Democrats limited opportunities to make the case and curtail the Republicans' ability to set the agenda. Every vote mattered to their ability to regain control of either chamber of Congress. With control of both chambers of Congress, the presidency, and a mobilized conservative constituency, Republicans easily were able to call for votes on same-sex marriage, portray judges as overreaching, and define the court decision in Massachusetts as a threat to marriages everywhere. Democrats lacked the ability and the willingness to stand firm in defense of same-sex marriage.

Instead of debating the issue as the provision of health care benefits to same-sex partners, Democrats faced a vote on the Federal Marriage Amendment and had to defend to their constituents their opposition to defining marriage as between a man and a woman. Instead of a national platform to discuss the advantages of allowing homosexual couples to share inheritance rights, they had to counter the president's assertion that activist judges were rewriting the norms of society in fifty states and 435 congressional districts. Instead of a single message that united all party members, the Democrats struggled to differentiate themselves from the Republican Party. The Republican agenda-setting ability was critical to their success in the electoral process.

The result was that Democratic congressional candidates were far more nuanced with their message than Republicans were. They were often responding to the actions of Republicans. As a whole, the Democratic message supported the traditional definition of marriage but varied with regard to same-sex marriage. Unlike the Republican compliance with the defense of marriage argument, Democratic leaders, incumbents, and challengers were compelled to express their belief in same-sex marriage and their varying degrees of support for the equal treatment of same-sex couples. Although Democratic party cohesion was higher than in previous campaigns, it fell far short of the Republican norm.

Because the presidential election had framed much of the same-sex marriage debate for Republicans and the country, Democrats faced the need to be united in a single message that articulated their party's position on the issue. Lacking an incumbent president or a national leader, party members waited until one emerged. By that time, the issue had been framed by the Republican Party and social conservatives as an attack on marriage.

In the Democratic presidential primary, nine candidates sought the party's nomination. They would highlight the range of positions of the Democratic Party in 2004. During the primary season, all nine Democratic contenders voiced support for homosexual rights and equal treatment. The range of positions offered by the Democratic primary candidates did little to solidify the Democratic base but did outline the contours of its electoral message.

DEMOCRATS FIGHT FOR SAME-SEX MARRIAGE?

Though heralded by gay rights advocates as the most gay-friendly group of primary challengers ever, only three of the nine individuals expressed support for same-sex marriage.[32] Citing marriage as a civil right that should not be denied to any American, Reverend Al Sharpton, former Illinois senator Carol Moseley-Braun, and Ohio representative Dennis Kucinich expressed complete support for gay marriage.[33] Presenting the civil rights argument for the practice, the three asserted that marriage was a right that everyone held and should be able to share with the person of their choice. Every person, they argued, was entitled to choose a spouse to share marriage benefits, regardless of their sexual orientation. Sharpton, Moseley-Braun, and Kucinich believed that allowing gays and lesbians to marry was the one way to ensure the true sanctity of marriage and to acknowledge their equality as Americans.

Unfortunately, the three were considered the "long-shot" candidates in the Democratic pool. Their positions garnered little additional support, and they stood in stark contrast to the Democratic frontrunners and other Democratic candidates at the federal level. Though few Democrats picked up the idea that this was basically another civil rights movement and should be defended, they did demonstrate the will of the party to accept as nominees advocates of same-sex marriage. Nevertheless, few Democrats with realistic chances of winning their districts would emerge as strong proponents of same-sex marriage.

DEMOCRATIC PRONG I: CIVIL UNIONS,
CIVIL RIGHTS, BUT NO MARRIAGE

The official position of the Democratic Party showed the influence of its leading supporters of homosexual rights and a return to the equal treatment argument of the same-sex marriage advocates. In its platform, the Democratic National Convention stated: "We support full inclusion of gay and lesbian families in the life of our nation and seek equal responsibilities, benefits, and protections for these families. In our country, marriage has been defined at the state level for 200 years, and we believe it should continue to be defined there. We repudiate President Bush's divisive effort to politicize the Constitution by pursuing a 'Federal Marriage Amendment.' Our goal is to bring Americans together, not drive them apart."[34] Though supportive of the rights of gays and lesbians and of guaranteeing that marriage benefits are available to same-sex families, the platform reflected both prongs of the Democratic effort. The first was an acceptance of and commitment to the full inclusion of homosexuals in the nation. The second focused on the primacy of state governments and not federalism in setting marriage policy for the country.

Senator John Kerry, the eventual Democratic presidential nominee, adopted a federal approach to the issue of same-sex marriage, based on the first prong. Like Bush, Kerry believed that marriage was a sacred institution between a man and a woman, but unlike the president he thought that same-sex couples should have the legal protections of civil unions. Though opposed to the creation of same-sex marriage, he appeared opened to the idea of some states' allowing such an institution.

In the 2003 Human Rights Campaign Democratic Forum, Kerry expressed his strong support for protecting the rights of gays and lesbians but withheld support for same-sex marriage.

I believe I come to you with the broadest, strongest and longest record of support on issues of concern to this community of any of the candidates running. . . . I was the only United States senator in 1996 who was running for reelection to vote against DOMA, and to go to the floor of the United States Senate and say that it was gay-bashing and it was beyond the dignity of the Senate to engage in that at the time. . . .

Well, I think it's important to do first of all what we can do, and that is hopefully try to pass civil unions, which give all the rights—some 1,000 benefits within the government—of taxes, mortgages, inheritance, visitation—all of those components. And I believe it is important to achieve that. I do not [support] marriage itself, . . . as a matter of how I view the world culturally, historically, religiously.[35]

Although supportive of the rights of gays and lesbians and of guaranteeing that marriage benefits are bestowed on homosexual couples, Kerry opposed same-sex marriage on the basis of the cultural, historical, and religious place of marriage in society. He was prepared to allow the states to decide the question.

In the Democratic debates in early 2004, Kerry maintained his support of civil unions and opposition to same-sex marriage. He pledged to fight efforts to link him to the *Goodridge* decision but said he would support a Massachusetts constitutional amendment to ban same-sex marriages.[36] The strongest supporter of gay rights among the Democratic primary contenders supported a ban on gay marriage in his state.

In 2000, Governor Howard Dean had signed the bill legalizing civil unions in Vermont. By early 2004, Dean had emerged as the frontrunner among the Democratic nominees. He supported civil unions but was opposed to same-sex marriage. When asked why, Dean stated: "Because it's easier. . . . And the religious connotation of marriage makes gay marriage a very difficult issue. It is a religious issue. You can't get away from it. You can say, well, some marriage is civil and some is religious, but people in this country think of marriage as a religious institution." [37] The main reason for Dean's opposition to same-sex marriage related to the historical creation and social position of the institution of marriage. Though he strongly supported extending marriage benefits to homosexual couples and opposed the FMA, Dean could not accept the term *marriage*.

Dean's background, perhaps more than that of the other contenders, placed him further left of center than they, and he had to return to the center to show his electability. As the governor who had signed into law civil unions for same-sex couples, Dean attempted to reassure moderate voters that he would respect their opinions regarding the issue. Dean needed to remake his national image in a way that would attract core Democratic constituents as well as moderate and independent voters.

Unlike the Republicans, however, Kerry and Dean did not couch their positions in a defense of the definition of marriage. Much like the American public, they believed in providing homosexual couples the benefits of marriage—the ability to make medical decisions for one another, to inherit property, to make financial decisions—but were against granting the title of marriage. They, like many other Democrats, would be criticized for the inconsistency of their positions and face tough challenges in explaining their support for the group but opposition to the institution. This approach is at heart a political approach, an attempt to make the debate about hearing and respecting all sides of the issue.

Democratic congressional candidates likewise were strong defenders of the rights of homosexuals but lukewarm, at best, to the idea of same-sex marriage. A few Democrats, mainly those in liberal states, advanced the idea of focusing on providing civil unions and the marriage benefits they offered. Stopping short of supporting same-sex marriage, these candidates argued that the need to nurture and support same-sex couples was an important responsibility for government but the relationships of those couples did not warrant the same recognition as marriage. For either religious or political reasons, homosexuals could have everything but the title of marriage. The challenge for Democrats nonetheless was to explain, to an electorate told by Republicans of the threat to marriage, how this solution reaffirmed traditional marriage. The Democrats could not successfully accomplish that task.

In the unusual Illinois Senate race that pitted Democrat Barack Obama against a recent arrival in Illinois, Alan Keyes, the usually articulate Obama explained how his religious beliefs and his belief that homosexuality was a result of nature allowed him to support civil unions. He struggled, however, to explain why his support for civil unions did not extend to same-sex marriage. When the moderator asked whether, given his belief that homosexuality was innate, Obama thought that it was violation of civil and human rights to deny the right to marry to same-sex couples, he replied, "No. I think there are a whole host of things that are civil rights, and then there are other things—such as traditional marriage—that, I think, express a community's concern and regard for a particular institution." [38] When pushed, Obama, like Kerry and Dean, differentiated the individual rights of same-sex couples from the collective rights of the community. Society always took precedence over the equal treatment of same-sex couples.

In the Wisconsin senatorial debates, one of the most liberal Democrats in the Senate, incumbent Russ Feingold, in explaining his opposition to the FMA, highlighted his support for treating gays and lesbians with the same rights as any American, rather than his opposition to same-sex marriage. The amendment wasn't about the possibility of same-sex marriage for Feingold and other Democrats; it was about the treatment of same-sex couples. Equal treatment stopped at the definition of marriage. Tim Michels, Feingold's opponent, nonetheless stressed his view that marriage should only be between a man and a woman and criticized Feingold as not committed to the traditions of this country.[39] Calling the effort to pass the FMA a ploy by Republicans to divide the nation, Feingold refused to engage in the political debate.

Feingold, Obama, and other Democrats still faced the challenge of explaining how they were supportive of full civil rights for lesbian and gay couples but opposed to the expansion of those rights to include marriage. Their efforts were consistent with public opinion, but they were ineffective at countering the Republicans' advantage in framing the issue. They struggled to explain to the American public why the equal treatment did not mean that marriages were "threatened." Homosexual rights advocates were challenged to find a Democrat who thought same-sex marriages did not threaten traditional marriages.

DEMOCRATIC PRONG II: A RENEWED LOVE OF FEDERALISM

The second major argument of the Democratic congressional campaign then became the importance of relying on the states to make the appropriate decisions about the civil right to marry. Democratic candidates thus downplayed the question and focused on the procedural implications of the federal government's involvement. Democrats stated their support for maintaining the current defense of marriage, provided little support for—but no opposition to—civil unions, and argued that the Republican approach was unnecessary in a federal system of government. Marriage had long been the province of the state governments, and to insert the federal government in a state matter was unconstitutional and unnecessary.

Other Democrats adopted the approach used in the 1996 consideration of the Defense of Marriage Act: they expressed their belief that marriage should be between a man and a woman, but they wanted to respect the ability of states to make their own laws. In the Washington senatorial debates, for example, both Democrat Patty Murray and her Republican challenger, Representative George Nethercutt articulated their belief that marriage should be between a man and woman and their support for the Defense of Marriage Act. Murray, however, differed from Nethercutt in that she would not support a constitutional amendment to ban same-sex marriage if DOMA were struck down by the Supreme Court.[40] She believed that the states were fully capable of handling the issue without intervention by the federal government.

Likewise, facing conservative Republican challenger Richard Ziser in Nevada, Senator Harry Reid, the minority whip who became the Senate Minority Leader after Tom Daschle's loss, took the same approach in his moderate state. When asked about his opposition to same-sex marriage and to an amendment to ban such marriages, Reid answered, "So marriage should be between a man and a woman, OK? I agree. But why do we need to have to amend the Constitution when we have the Defense of Marriage Act federally? We have the state Constitution, which has it in it."[41]

Ziser successfully led the state's efforts to amend its constitution to ban same-sex marriage in 2000 and 2002 and questioned Reid's commitment to the moral and religious values of the state. The incumbent and influential party leader had little problem defeating Ziser with 61 percent of the vote in the general election. Whereas this position would not harm incumbents like Reid, it posed a number of complications in other congressional races in which Republicans argued that DOMA was not enough to protect the institution of marriage. In trying to present an alternative to the Republican defense of marriage, the Democrats carried little weight by resting their case on the constitutional limitations of federalism.

Democrats were at a disadvantage in framing the same-sex marriage issue for the 2004 elections. The political conditions of the time were working against them. A minority party with little control of decision-making bodies has few resources to get its message out or to shape the contours of the political campaign. The diversity of opinions and beliefs within the party prevented a single message from being created or distributed to the public. Finally, the party was on the defensive because the Republicans framed the debate to their advantage. At best, the collective message of the Democratic Party was that they basically supported the rights of same-sex individuals and couples but would allow the states and the public to determine the fulfillment of those rights.

ASSESSMENT OF AMERICAN POLITICS

Despite an auspicious beginning, 2004 did not end the way most advocates of same-sex marriage and homosexual rights had hoped. In early

2004 the gay rights movement had made significant advances towards acceptance; by the end of the year the movement seemed like a lost cause. While social conservatives advanced a uniform defense of the institution of marriage in the Republican Party, homosexual rights advocates struggled to find a committed and passionate Democratic message. In the electoral battle over same-sex marriage, the presidential and congressional races demonstrated the ability of a united party to frame the issue as well as the limits of support for gays and lesbians.

Republicans emerged from Election 2004 still controlling the White House, the Senate, and the House of Representatives. They had taken an issue about which the public held mixed views but that was of considerable significance to their base and made it into a galvanizing message that mobilized social conservatives and moderates and had placed the Democratic Party on the defensive. The post-election analysis nonetheless readily credited Karl Rove's strategy of connecting the president's opposition to same-sex marriage with his reelection. By playing early to the concerns of social conservatives, the president excited his base and their turnout was high. Although early polls suggested that moral values defined the election, more thorough analyses indicated that the election was more about terrorism and the economy. In those early reports of the strength of morality, a number of issues had been conflated under the category "moral values." A thorough reassessment showed that morality played a far less significant role in the election than had been supposed.[42]

The electoral aftermath of Election 2004, however, was far less than expected in terms of the success of the marriage issue for Republicans. In January and February 2005, both chambers reintroduced measures to ban same-sex marriage.[43] With weightier political issues such as Social Security, terrorism, the growing possibility of a Supreme Court vacancy, and rising gas prices before it, the Administration placed less emphasis on banning the practice. The passage of thirteen state bans on same-sex marriage and the failure in Congress in 2004 also slowed the Federal Marriage Amendment. Nevertheless, the treatment of the FMA in the 109th Congress suggested that the issue was merely a wedge issue in 2004, intended to galvanize supporters and split the Democratic Party.

With regard to the issue of same-sex marriage, however, Election 2004 was extremely informative. The events and results provided considerable insight into the work that needs to be done on both side of the aisle. The Republican Party clearly outmaneuvered the Democrats on the issue of same-sex marriage. Republicans found an election issue that would mobilize their base without upsetting the opposition. Traditionally, campaigns run into the problem of mobilizing supporters *and* opponents. The Republicans were able to use same-sex marriage to rally the base, motivate the centrists and the undecided, and cause little reaction from the opposition.

The key to this success was their ability to frame the issue—to make the public and private discussions concerning same-sex marriage about how to maintain more than four hundred years of tradition in marriage. In framing the issue, the Republican Party had the advantages of a united party with control of both chambers of Congress, a focused incumbent president in a presidential election year, and a dedicated conservative base that was prepared to cause as little trouble as possible. The Democrats faced the challenge of not alienating mainstream supporters while simultaneously keeping their base of gay and lesbian voters satisfied. Finding a message that would unite the base and the moderates in the face of Republican framing was a difficult task for a party that did not have a definitive position concerning same-sex marriage.

ENDNOTES

1. James N. Druckman, "On the Limits of Framing Effects: Who Can Frame?" *Journal of Politics* 63 (2001): 1041–66; Kathleen E. Hull, "The Political Limits of the Rights Frame: The Case of Same Sex Marriage in Hawaii," *Social Perspectives* 44 (2001): 207–32; William H. Riker, *The Art of Political Manipulation* (New Haven: Yale University Press, 1990).

2. Alan I. Abramowitz and Kyle L. Saunders, "Ideological Realignment in the US Electorate," *Journal of Politics* 60 (1998): 634–52; Melissa P. Collie, "Electoral Patterns and Voting Alignments in the US House, 1886–1986," *Legislative Studies Quarterly* 14 (1989): 107–28; Keith Poole and Howard Rosenthal, "The Polarization of American Politics," *Journal of Politics* 46 (1984): 1061–79.

3. Jeffrey M. Stonecash, Mark D. Brewer, and Mack D. Mariani, *Diverging Parties: Social Change, Realignment, and Party Polarization* (Boulder: Westview, 2002); Paul R. Abramson, John H. Aldrich, and David W. Rohde, *Change and Continuity in the 2004 Elections* (Washington, DC: CQ Press, 2005); William H. Flanigan and Nancy H. Zingale, *Political Behavior of the American Electorate* (Washington, DC: CQ Press, 2005).

4. John C. Green, James L. Guth, and Kevin Hill, "Faith and Election: The Christian Right in Congressional Campaigns, 1978–1988," *Journal of Politics* 55 (1993): 80–91; John C. Green, Scott Keeter, Robert C. Toth, and Andrew Kohut, *The Diminishing Divide: Religion's Changing Role in American Politics* (Washington, DC: Brookings Institution Press, 2000).

5. Kevin P. Phillips, *Post-Conservative America* (New York: Vintage, 1982); Corwin Schmidt, *Contemporary Evangelical Political Involvement: An Analysis and Assessment* (Baltimore: University Press of America, 1989).

6. Quoted in Phil Brennan, "Christian Right Talks of Bolting GOP in 2004," NewsMax.com (May 6, 2003).

7. The Pew Research Center for the People and the Press, *Less Opposition to Gay Marriage, Adoption, and Military Service* (Washington, DC: Pew Research Center, 2006).

8. Darren K. Carlson, *Public OK with Gays, Women in Military* (Princeton, NJ: Gallup Organization, 2003).

9. Walter Isaacson, "Should Gays Have Marriage Rights?" *Time*, November 20, 1989.

10. "Job Rights for Homosexuals Backed in Poll," *New York Times*, September 7, 1992.

11. Alan S. Yang, "The Polls—Trends: Attitudes Toward Homosexuality," *Public Opinion Quarterly* 61 (1997): 477–507; Pew Research Center for the People and the Press *Reading the Polls on Gay Marriage and the Constitution* (Washington, DC: Pew Research Center, 2004).

12. Frank Newport, "Constitutional Amendment Defining Marriage Lacks 'Supermajority' Support: Almost Two-thirds Oppose Same-Sex Marriage, but only 51% Favor Constitutional Amendment." Washington, DC: Gallup Organization. http://www.galluppoll.com/content/?ci=10792.

13. Dahleen Glanton, "In South, Issue of Gay Marriage Exposes Hate and Fear," *Chicago Tribune*, April 8, 2004; George Neumayr, "Marriage on the Rocks (The GOP Needs Counseling)," *American Spectator*, February 21, 2004.

14. *Hillary Goodridge v. Department of Public Health*, 798 N.E.2d 941 (Mass. 2003).

15. Office of the Press Secretary, "Marriage Protection Week, 2003." Press release (October 3, 2003). http://www.whitehouse.gov/news/releases/2003/10/20031003-12.html (accessed March 12, 2005).

16. Office of the Press Secretary, "President Bush Calls for Constitutional Amendment Protecting Marriage." Transcript (February 24, 2003). http://www.whitehouse.gov/news/releases/2004/02/20040224–2.html (accessed March 12, 2005).

17. Office of the Press Secretary, "State of the Union 2004." Transcript (January 20, 2004.) http://www.whitehouse.gov/news/releases/2004/01/20040120–7.html (accessed March 12, 2005).

18. Commission on Presidential Debates, "The Third Bush-Kerry Presidential Debate." Transcript (October 13, 2004). http://www.debates.org/pages/trans2004d.html (accessed March 12, 2005).

19. Republican National Committee, *2004 Republican National Platform: A Safer World and a More Helpful America* (Washington, DC: Republican National Committee, 2004).

20. David D. Kirkpatrick, "Gay Activists in the G.O.P. Withhold Endorsement," *New York Times*, September 8, 2004.

21. Todd Akin for Congress, "Activist Judges." http://www.commercialcloset.org/cgi-bin/iowa/portrayals.html?record=2048 (accessed June 13, 2005).

22. Meg Kinnard, "Diverse Topics on Air in N.C. House Races," *National Journal*, June 30, 2004.

23. Theo Helm, "Foxx, Robinson Both Lean Right," *Winston-Salem Journal*, August 15, 2004.

24. Danielle Deaver and Jim Sparks, "Foxx Beats Robinson in 5th District Runoff," *Winston-Salem Journal*, August 18, 2004.

25. Judith Kohler, "Don't Expect Big Shift in Coors' Positions for General Election, Analysts Say," Associated Press, August 14, 2004.

26. Tom Parsons, "Holt, Lincoln Trade Views in Televised Exchange," Associated Press, October 28, 2004.

27. Seth Blomeley and Laura Kellams, "Observers Surprised at Holt's Showing: Gay Marriage Issue Seen as Aiding Him," *Arkansas Democrat-Gazette*, November 4, 2004.

28. Bruce Schreiner, "Kentucky Democrat Responds to Personal Attacks," Associated Press, October 29, 2004.

29. Senator Ben Nighthorse Campbell resigned at the end of the 108th Congress, and the other four Republican senators were from liberal Northeastern states—Maine, New Hampshire, and Rhode Island.

30. Jim Kolbe, "Statement on a Constitutional Amendment to Ban Gay Marriage," February 24, 2004.

31. Mary Bono, "Clarification on the Congresswoman's Attendance at the Republican National Convention," press release, August 26, 2004.

32. Senators Bob Graham and John Edwards did not attend the forum.

33. Darryl Fears, "3 Support Same-Sex Marriage: Democrats Appear at Rights Forum," *Washington Post*, July 16, 2003.

34. Democratic National Convention Committee, *Strong at Home, Respected in the World: The 2004 Democratic National Platform for America* (Washington, DC: Democratic National Committee, 2004).

35. Human Rights Campaign, "2003 HRC Presidential Forum." Transcript (July 15, 2003) http://www.vote-smart.org/debate_transcripts/trans_25.pdf#search='democratic%20forum%20human%20rights%20campaign (accessed March 12, 2005).

36. Patrick Healy and Frank Phillips, "Kerry Backs State Ban on Gay Marriage: Says Amendment Must Provide for Civil Unions," *Boston Globe*, February 26, 2004.

37. Marc Sandalow, "Dean Supports Gay Unions but Wavers on Saying 'I Do': Presidential Hopeful Stresses Equal Rights over Choice of Words," *San Francisco Chronicle*, December 2, 2003.

38. Keyes for Congress Committee, "Third Debate: Debate Sponsored by WTTW and the City Club of Chicago," 2004. http://www.renewamerica.us/archives/media/debates/04_10_26debate3.htm (accessed June 25, 2005); Nicole Ziegler Dizon, "Illinois Senate Candidates Trade Insults," Associated Press, October 27, 2004.

39. J. R. Ross, "Feingold, Michels Differ over Gay Marriage, Iraq in Debate," *Miami Herald*, October 16, 2004.

40. Jim Brunner, "Murray, Nethercutt Meet in Debate; First Face-Off," *Seattle Times*, October 16, 2004.

41. Dave Berns, "Candidates See Religion's Role in Diverse Light," *Las Vegas Review-Journal*, October 28, 2004.

42. Ted Crow, "Election 2004: How Did One Exit Poll Answer Become the Story of How Bush Won? Good Question," *Washington Post*, December 5, 2004.

43. Faith Bremner, "Republicans Try Again to Ban Gay Marriage," Gannett News Service, January 24, 2005.

THE PRESIDENCY, CONGRESS, AND SAME-SEX MARRIAGE

Craig A. Rimmerman

I have consistently stated that I'll support law to protect marriage between a man and a woman. . . . I strongly believe marriage should be defined as between a man and a woman. I am troubled by activist judges who are defining marriage.

PRESIDENT GEORGE W. BUSH

When I go home from today's work, and I choose, because of my nature, to associate with another man, how is that a problem for you? How does that hurt you?

CONGRESSMAN BARNEY FRANK

Equality is a good start, but it is not sufficient. Equality for queers inevitably means equal rights on straight terms, since they are the ones who determine the existing legal framework. We conform—albeit equally—with their screwed-up system. That is not liberation. It is capitulation.

PETER TATCHELL, BRITISH GAY RIGHTS LEADER

The campaign for same-sex marriage has depended on the courts for much of the success that it has achieved. As the issue has evolved in the 1990s and the early twenty-first century, the legal strategy has proved to be the most effective means for achieving progress on an issue that politicians have exploited as a wedge issue in presidential and congressional campaigns.[1] The political opportunities identified by social movement theorists[2] as crucial factors in determining whether a social movement can achieve its policy demands have largely been concentrated in the judicial system. As this chapter makes clear, Presidents Clinton and Bush, as well as the vast majority of members of Congress, have demonstrated outright hostility to supporting same-sex marriage. This chapter explores the broad political and institutional contexts for evaluating presidential and congressional responses to the issue. In doing so, it discusses the interaction between the president and Congress regarding same-sex marriage over time. Why did Bill Clinton sign the Defense of Marriage Act in the fall of 1996, and why did Congress propose such legislation at that time? In addition, recent debates about same-sex marriage are placed within the broader context of George W. Bush's decision to promote a national constitutional amendment that would effectively bar states from marrying same-sex couples. Why did Bush do so? And how has Congress responded? Finally, it is important to assess why same-sex marriage has emerged as a key wedge issue in American politics and what this means for the lesbian and gay movements as they engage political leaders. It is argued that in the short term, advocates of the practice will likely continue to be thwarted by political elites who perceive that their opposition will help them achieve their political goals, given the potency of same-sex marriage as a potential wedge issue.

THE 1996 DEFENSE OF MARRIAGE ACT

Only in the early 1990s did the debate about same-sex marriage explode on the national scene, despite the fact that lesbians and gay men have been challenging their exclusion from the rights of marriage since the early 1970s. The broad legal rights strategy adopted by the lesbian and gay movements received judicial legitimacy with the Supreme Court of Hawaii's decision in *Baehr v. Lewin*. The relevant background is as follows: In 1991, three couples who were all residents of Hawaii challenged the state's marriage law by filing a declaratory judgment stating that the law was unconstitutional because it "denied same-sex couples the same marriage rights as different-sex couples." They based their claims on the privacy and equal protection clauses of the Hawaii constitution. The Hawaii Supreme Court's 1993 decision rejected the privacy argument but responded more positively to the equal protection argument. It found nothing in the state constitution that prevented lesbian and gay marriage, and it argued that denying same-sex couples access to the benefits and rights associated with marriage is a form of sex discrimination (Rimmerman 2002, 74).

The Supreme Court of Hawaii remanded the case to the state trial court, affording Hawaii the opportunity to present evidence at trial to justify the marriage statute. This new trial was held during the summer of 1996, and because it found that "the state had failed to prove a compelling interest in denying same-sex couples the right to marry," the trial court ruled the state's marriage law unconstitutional. The decision itself "was stayed pending appeal." The case returned to the Hawaii Supreme Court, which on December 9, 1999, issued a ruling of fewer than five hundred words stating, in essence, that the state of Hawaii can bar lesbian and gay couples from obtaining marriage licenses. It also ruled that a 1998 initiative passed by voters legitimized a previous statute that restricted licenses to one man and one woman. The court also, however, opened the door to the possibility that same-sex couples could still be eligible for "the same benefits of marriage—even without the license" (Rimmerman 2002, 74–75).

Shortly after the 1993 *Baehr* decision, there was a well-organized conservative backlash, which served as an augury of the shape of things to come over the next twelve years. For example, the Hawaii legislature passed legislation forbidding same-sex marriage, thus codifying the heterosexual character of marriage. Later, after the trial judge's 1996 decision, the Hawaii state legislature also proposed a constitutional amendment that "would permit the legislature to restrict marriage to opposite-sex couples." This amendment, which appeared on the ballot during the November 1998 elections, was accepted by Hawaii voters, thus dealing same-sex marriage advocates a serious blow (Rimmerman 2002).

As a part of this broader backlash, conservative groups created strategies designed to be implemented prior to the judicial resolution of the *Baehr* case. David Chambers accurately points out that "they provided conservative legislators in every state with draft legislation that would direct their state's courts and other agencies to refuse to recognize a marriage between two persons of the same sex conducted in another state" (Chambers 2000, 294). Why did promoting this legislation prove to be such an effective strategy? It was because the legislation itself served as an important wedge issue by rallying conservatives and dividing liberal legislators from their lesbian and gay constituents. The conservative Right has used this strategy with great success in recent years with respect to same-sex marriage. Chambers offers a compelling explanation for its effectiveness in 1996. His analysis is relevant for understanding how the same-sex marriage issue has played out today: "Many Democratic state legislators across the country either themselves believed that marriage should be limited to one man and one woman, or at least believed that they could not vote against the far right's bill because of the views of most of their heterosexual constituents. So, just as the far right had hoped, many otherwise liberal legislators voted for the bills and infuriated gay and lesbian voters. Gay groups, local and national, were forced to devote huge amounts of effort in nearly every state to persuade legislators to reject the bills" (ibid.).

The conservative backlash also manifested itself in national-level politics during the 1996 campaign season. Same-sex marriage became a major issue in the 1996 presidential campaign when conservative activists and politicians organized a rally condemning the practice three days prior to the Iowa caucuses. Three of the announced Republican presidential candidates attended, addressed the rally, and "signed a pledge to 'defend' heterosexual marriage against the threat allegedly posed by three lesbian and gay couples in Hawaii who had sued the state for the right to marry" (Cahill 2004, 81). This pledge, the Marriage Protection Resolution, had been introduced by a coalition of eight conservative religious groups (Rimmerman 2002, 75). The *Los Angeles Times* observed in April 1996 that "homosexual marriage has abruptly emerged as an emotional flashpoint in the debate about America's cultural mores" (Cahill 2004, 81). It was no real surprise, then, that Republican presidential nominee Bob Dole introduced the federal Defense of Marriage Act (DOMA) in the Senate, though it was surprising to some that President Clinton ultimately signed it into law on September 21, 1996. The Senate had voted 85–14 in September 1996 in favor of the act, which the House had passed by a vote of 342–67 that summer. Congressional hearings about the legislation had turned ugly as Congress members and witnesses warned that if men were allowed to marry other men, "they would soon be permitted to marry children and other animals" (Chambers 2000, 295). Others worried that same-sex marriage would lead to the collapse of Western civilization. Proposed by Republicans with the enthusiastic support of their Christian Right supporters, the legislation was timed perfectly to coincide with the 1996 election season. The law was designed to accomplish two goals:

"(1) prevent states from being forced by the Full Faith and Credit Clause to recognize same-sex marriages validly celebrated in other states, and (2) define marriages for federal purposes as the union of one man and one woman" (Strasser 1997, 127).

What prompted Clinton to sign the Defense of Marriage Act into law? He was clearly worried that the same-sex marriage issue could achieve heightened saliency as a potential wedge issue during the 1996 general election. Having endured the unpleasantness of the debate about gays in the military during the first six months of his presidency, he wanted to avoid a similar controversy about marriage. With this in mind, he signed it into law after midnight, eschewing the Rose Garden ceremony that often accompanies White House bill signings. Understandably, Clinton received strong criticism from some members of the lesbian and gay movements when he did so. Whereas he had reversed his position regarding the military ban, he at least was consistent with regard to lesbian and gay marriage: he had announced his opposition in the 1992 campaign. But those who were most critical of the president argued that DOMA was both unnecessary and highly discriminatory and that Clinton could have vetoed it while still opposing the principle of lesbian and gay marriage. Others understood, however, that Clinton was forced to sign the law in order to avoid attacks by the Christian Right during the 1996 presidential campaign. Indeed, the Dole campaign had run a radio ad that criticized Clinton for supporting an end to the military ban. The Clinton forces responded by releasing their own ad celebrating the President's signing of DOMA. This ad was run on Christian radio stations across the country, despite the fact that the president criticized the authors of the act for attempting to inject such a difficult issue into presidential politics during an election year.

Lesbian and gay rights groups protested the radio ad loudly. In response, the Clinton campaign pulled the ad after two days (Rimmerman 2002, 76). Ever the politician, Clinton recognized the potency of same-sex marriage as a potential wedge issue during the 1996 campaign. In stopping the ad, he helped remind other candidates of how they might balance their desire for electoral victory with the interests of their lesbian and gay supporters.

Could the lesbian and gay movements have done more to force the Clinton administration to support same-sex marriage? Note that it was not a crucial issue for many movement members. Those who think it should be a key goal—individuals such as Jonathan Rauch, Andrew Sullivan, and Bruce Bawer [3]—generally represent the movement's more

moderate to conservative element. But as we know from the military debate that occurred in 1992–93, the movements cannot control when specific issues will come to the fore. And in many ways, the issue of same-sex
marriage could not have come up at a worse time. The Republicans now
controlled both houses of Congress, it was a presidential election year,
and the movements simply did not have the time, skills, or resources to
mount an effective organizing and educational campaign for an issue
that appeared to be unpopular with the American public—certainly not
a campaign equal to challenging the Christian Right's vast organizational resources. Indeed, the Republicans were searching for a wedge
issue when they introduced the Defense of Marriage Act on May 8, 1996.
Rich Tafel, executive director of the Log Cabin Republicans, supported
several of these points when he said, "Marriage is so visceral, such a
negative in the polls. My experience in debating this issue is that if I have
an hour or two hours, I can win, but if I have five minutes, I can't. This is
all being done in five minutes" (quoted in Gallagher 1996, 21). As a campaign issue, opposition to same-sex marriage served several purposes. It
was an opportunity for some politicians to reach out to both the center
and the Right, given the larger public's apparent lack of support for the
issue. And it forced Clinton to tackle a difficult issue at a time when he
did not want to relive the military fiasco of several years before. Clinton
had no choice, then, but to alienate some members of his voting base.

How might Clinton have handled the situation differently? He could
have forbidden his campaign team to broadcast a radio ad supporting
DOMA on Christian radio. That the campaign ran such an ad suggests how badly Clinton and his campaign advisors wanted to straddle
all sides of the issue. He might also have vetoed DOMA while expressing his own opposition to same-sex marriage, arguing that such legislation was being used as a political weapon, without the kind of lengthy
public education and discussion that the issue deserved. We should not
be surprised that Clinton did not follow the latter strategy, given his
previous record with regard to the military ban. For him to take a bold
and creative position, one rooted in educational leadership, would have
been out of keeping with his political character.

But fortunately for advocates of same-sex marriage, the issue moved
out of the national arena and back to the states with the historic December 1999 decision by Vermont's Chief Justice Jeffrey Amestoy that
Vermont's legislature must grant lesbian and gay couples the "common
benefits and protections" that heterosexual couples receive. Not surprisingly, a conservative backlash soon emerged against the decision.

Vermont legislators who supported the civil union legislation were targeted for defeat by Christian Right organizers, and some lost their re-election bids in 2000. Conservative forces throughout the United States immediately moved to preempt attempts to recognize same-sex marriages in their own states. The publicity surrounding the *Baehr* case appears to have done much more for opponents of lesbian and gay marriage than for its proponents. Further, the marriage issue vaulted to the forefront of the movements' agenda without a full and frank discussion of what this rights-based strategy would mean for the movements' organizing and education efforts and for the direction of both short-term and long-term political and cultural change. Same-sex marriage would not manifest itself in the national political scene again until the June 26, 2003 U.S. Supreme Court decision in *Lawrence v. Texas*.

BEYOND LAWRENCE

Andrew Sullivan has argued persuasively that "the single most serious barrier to recognizing the right to marry was a 1986 Supreme Court decision, Bowers v. Hardwick, which upheld state laws criminalizing consensual sodomy" (Sullivan 2004, 106). This is why same-sex marriage proponents (and opponents) viewed *Lawrence v. Texas,* which overturned *Bowers,* as a landmark decision in advancing the interests of the lesbian and gay movements. With the *Lawrence* decision the Court struck down the sodomy laws of thirteen states, laws that ban "private, consensual sexual intimacy" (Cahill 2004, 2), and it "extended the right to privacy—which includes the right to make decisions about one's intimate life—to lesbians and gay men" (Chauncey 2004, 1). In essence, the Court admitted that it had made a grave mistake when it ruled in *Bowers* that states could regulate sodomy. Writing for the 6–3 majority, Justice Anthony Kennedy celebrated "the 'liberty' of gay people to form relationships, 'whether or not [they are] entitled to formal recognition in the law,' and condemned the Bowers decision for 'demeaning the lives of homosexual persons'" (ibid.). But Kennedy also cautioned that the decision does not apply to marriage per se by noting that the legal case opposing the Texas sodomy law "does not involve whether the government must give formal recognition to any relationship homosexual persons seek to enter" (Cahill 2004, 3). And Justice Sandra Day O'Connor argued in her concurrence that the "traditional institution of marriage' was not an issue" (ibid.).

But Justice Antonin Scalia (joined by Chief Justice William Rehnquist) warned of the dangers to the institution of marriage that might result from the *Lawrence* decision: "Today's opinion dismantles the structure of constitutional law that has permitted a distinction to be made between heterosexual and homosexual unions, insofar as formal recognition in marriage is concerned" (Cahill 2004, 3). Scalia's concerns were seconded by conservative politicians and activists in ways that contributed to a shift in coverage by the mainstream news media, some of which suggested that the Court's decision would ultimately lead to the legalization of same-sex marriage. Lesbian and gay movement activists also reacted in ways that provided support for Scalia's claim. For example, Lambda Legal Defense Fund attorney Ruth Harlow, who served as the lead attorney in *Lawrence,* argued, "The ruling makes it much harder for society to continue banning gay marriages" (ibid.). And Patricia Logue, co-counsel in *Lawrence* and also a Lambda attorney, claimed: "I think it's inevitable now. In what time frame, we don't know" (ibid.). The judicial scholar David Garrow perhaps put it best when he said: "There's no getting around the fact that this changes the political and legal landscape forever" (Bull 2003, 36).

The *Lawrence* decision elicited responses from national politicians, as well. At a press conference in late July 2003, President Bush endorsed a federal definition of marriage that defined marriage as being between a man and a woman. He also faced increasing pressure to endorse a amendment to the U.S. Constitution enshrining that definition. Some Republican Party leaders, including Senate Majority Leader Bill Frist (R-TN), went public with their concerns almost immediately. Frist endorsed sodomy laws on the June 29, 2003 episode of ABC's *This Week:* "'I have this fear' that the ruling could create an environment in which 'criminal activity within the home would in some way be condoned . . . whether it's prostitution or illegal commercial drug activity'" (Bull 2003, 38). Frist then endorsed a constitutional amendment that would ban same-sex marriage by stating: "I very much feel that marriage is a sacrament, and that sacrament should extend and can extend to that legal entity of a union between—what is traditionally in our Western values has been defined—as between a man and a woman" (Crea 2003, 1). And he had the continued and enthusiastic support of Senator Rick Santorum (R-PA), who claimed that "the greatest near-term consequence of the Lawrence v. Texas anti-sodomy ruling could be the legalization of homosexual marriage" (Cahill 2004, 3). Of course, Santorum's support was no surprise given his April 2003 warning that if the Supreme Court legitimated the right to gay sex "within your home, then you have the right to bigamy, you have the right to polygamy, you have the right to incest, you have the right to adultery. You have the right to anything" (Hertzberg 2003, 33).

The constitutional amendment that Frist endorsed had been introduced in the House of Representatives by Marilyn Musgrave (R-CO) and five other sponsors on May 23, 2003. Drafted by the Alliance for Marriage, the amendment defines marriage as the union of a man and a woman. Musgrave and her co-sponsors later introduced a slightly reworded version on March 22, 2004, one that would not "bar same-sex civil unions allowed by state law" (Hulse 2004). The goal of the revised amendment was to "broaden support for the initiative and blunt the appeal of alternatives that could leave the definition of marriage up to individual states." Some supporters of the gay marriage ban also had worried that the original amendment went too far and would frighten more moderate voters by nullifying the nation's domestic partner laws and Vermont's civil unions law as well as ban same-sex marriage. The revised amendment therefore states: "Marriage in the United States shall consist only of the union of a man and a woman. Neither this Constitution, nor the constitution of any state, shall be construed to require that marriage or the legal incidents thereof be conferred upon any union other than the union of a man and woman" (Hulse 2004). Musgrave justified the introduction of her original amendment (Senator Wayne Allard, a Colorado Republican, introduced a companion measure in the Senate) by asking: "If we are going to be redefining marriage, who should decide: unelected judges, or the people and their elected representatives?" (Perine and Dlouhy, 2004, 84). It was no surprise that Musgrave, serving her first term in Congress at the time, would lead the charge against same-sex marriage, given that she had organized a successful drive to abolish it as a Colorado state representative prior to her arrival in the House of Representatives. In this way, she linked her state-level experience with her new career on the national stage.

In order for Musgrave's constitutional amendment to be codified into law, it would need a two-thirds supermajority in the House and the Senate. If Musgrave and her supporters in both chambers could garner that much support for it, it would then go to the states, where thirty-eight of the fifty state legislatures (three-fourths of the states) would have to vote to ratify before it could become law. Assuming that all of these challenging constitutional hurdles were overcome, Musgrave's amendment would replace the 1996 Defense of Marriage Act and protect the ban on same-sex marriages from all legal challenges (Perine and Dlouhy 2004, 85).

How did President Bush react to the possibility of such an amendment? In late June 2003 Bush's spokesperson, Ari Fleischer, claimed that the president had never discussed the idea of a constitutional amendment with Frist. Instead, Fleischer said that "the president is proud to support the Defense of Marriage Act. We have a law on the books right now that was signed by President Clinton, that passed with massive, overwhelming bipartisan majorities in 1996. And the president supports that legislation and that's where he stands right now" (Crea 2003, 14).

But the president's position was an evolving one because he and his advisors perceived political opportunities in making same-sex marriage an electoral issue. Bush served notice that he recognized the power of same-sex marriage as a wedge issue when he proclaimed October 12–18, 2003, "Marriage Protection Week." In doing so, Bush signaled his support "for the proposed Federal Marriage Amendment, which would amend the U.S. Constitution to ban same-sex marriage and government recognition of civil unions or domestic partnerships" ("Declaration of Intolerance" 2003, 15). In introducing his proclamation, Bush underscored the importance of traditional marriage for children: "Research has shown that, on average, children raised in households headed by married parents fare better than children who grow up in other family structures. Through education and counseling programs, faith-based, community, and government organizations promote healthy marriages and a better quality of life for children. By supporting responsible child-rearing and strong families, my Administration is seeking to ensure that every child can grow up in a safe and loving home" (Office of the Press Secretary 2003). His statement also highlights the importance of his faith-based approach to social policy and its connections to traditional family structures.

The response to Bush's proclamation from the Log Cabin Republicans was swift and severe. Executive Director Patrick Guerriero recognized the political rationale for Bush's approach to same-sex marriage almost a full year before the 2004 elections: "Early polls indicate that opposition to same-sex marriage could become a wedge issue." Guerriero also recognized that Bush's approach would lead to a "civil war in the Republican party. We are very disappointed to see Bush catering to the extraordinary hypocrisy of the antimarriage groups, which call themselves pro-family and then go around encouraging discrimination against gay and lesbian families" ("Declaration of Intolerance" 2003, 15). He later argued that "using the Constitution as a campaign tool and using gay families as a political wedge sets a new low for shameful campaigning" (Guerriero 2004). And Mark Mead, the political director of the organization, warned that "a federal marriage amendment has the potential to ignite a culture war. As conservative Republicans, we know what can happen when you ignite a cultural war" (Perine and Dlouhy 2004, 84).

The Austin Twelve, the group of hand-picked gay Republicans who had met with George W. Bush in Texas during the 2000 presidential campaign, also reacted with consternation to the president's handling of the marriage issue. Once viewed as the base of Bush's support among gays, the group became increasingly critical of Bush's support of the federal marriage amendment. Rebecca Maestri, the only lesbian in the original group and president of the Northern Virginia Log Cabin Republicans chapter, said that "the Bush campaign people were principally concerned with getting elected [in 2000]. I do feel we were Bushwhacked." David Catania, a District of Columbia councilmember and an outspoken critic of the president's position regarding same-sex marriage, announced his support for John Kerry in the 2004 election. John Hutch, another member of the Austin Twelve and president of a direct marketing firm, claimed that "there's nothing that Bush can possibly do right now to regain the support of gays and lesbians. He would have to publicly go on television, repudiate his position on the amendment and acknowledge that he was wrong to get involved in the process. And he would probably have to go further than that. I just don't see it happening" (Crea 2004). The responses of the Log Cabin Republicans and some Austin Twelve members are reminders of how presidents often disappoint their most fervent supporters. To be sure, Bill Clinton's lesbian and gay supporters reacted similarly to his betrayal with regard to the military and same-sex marriage after he had campaigned fervently for their votes in 1992 and 1996.

With the Massachusetts Supreme Judicial Court ruling of November 17, 2003, the same-sex marriage issue was catapulted further onto the national stage. Politicians in both parties were forced to respond to the court's ruling that "the ban on marriage licenses to gay couples violated the Commonwealth's guarantee of equal protection of the laws" (Sullivan 2004, xvii). The court ruled in 2004 that "no separate-but-equal institution of 'civil unions' would suffice to meet constitutional requirements" (ibid.). Richard Land, president of the Southern Baptist Ethics and Religious Commission, offered an opening salvo in the debate that followed the court's initial decision, and his view represents the Christian Right's perspective well: "The Federal Marriage Amendment is the only way to adequately deal with this judicial assault on the sanctity of marriage being defined as God intended it, the union of one man and one woman" (Foust 2003).

It was only a matter of time before Bush announced his support for the Musgrave amendment. He did so on February 24, 2004, after highlighting the issue in his State of the Union address. Bush declared that "the union of a man and woman is the most enduring human institution" (Sokolove 2004, 1). Why did Bush announce his endorsement at this time? It is clear that he was not eager to take such a step, but the possibility of using marriage as a winning wedge issue during his re-election campaign proved to be too attractive. Once the Massachusetts Supreme Judicial Court legalized same-sex marriage in that state and San Francisco mayor Gavin Newsome began the process of granting marriage licenses to lesbian and gay couples, then Bush and his advisors perceived that his endorsement was a part of a winning electoral strategy. Of course, it should come as no surprise, given his administration's overall record on lesbian and gay rights during Bush's first term.

Nor did it come as a surprise when Bush endorsed a constitutional ban on same-sex marriage on the eve of a Senate vote on the amendment in early June 2006, well into his second term in office. The bill's Senate sponsor, Colorado Republican Wayne Allard, introduced the measure with the support of the White House and the Christian Right. They perceived that this measure could help rally the conservative base in the November 2006 midterm elections, when Democrats stood to make large gains in light of the setbacks associated with the Iraqi war and rising energy prices. It is especially noteworthy that Bush highlighted his support for the amendment with a news conference in the White House Rose Garden on Monday, June 5, the day before the vote. In the end, the Republicans suffered a stinging defeat in the Senate on the vote held to decide whether to have an up-down vote on the amendment itself (the 49–48 vote fell well short of the 60 votes needed).

Bush's attempt to distance himself from the Log Cabin Republicans and the Republican Unity Coalition revealed how far he would go to avoid antagonizing his Christian Right supporters, whose votes he had desperately needed to win the 2000 election and whose votes he perceived he would need if he were to win in 2004 and keep congressional Republicans in power in 2006. The president was also undoubtedly aware that the Christian Right had caused his father considerable difficulty during his one-term presidency when they perceived him as compromising too much on conservative principles. George W. Bush clearly did not want to repeat the political mistakes made by his father. Slightly more than 70 percent of self-identified lesbian and gay voters (more than 2.8 million Americans) cast their ballots for Al Gore in the

2000 election, while Bush received the votes of more than 11 million religious conservatives (Rimmerman 2002, 163). These figures indicate that Bush owed his conservative base his loyalty, given their strong support for him in such a close election and their role in his victory over John Kerry in 2004. The late political scientist Robert Bailey captured well the challenges confronting Bush following his 2000 election "victory": "Gay rights is a no-win situation for Bush. If he aligns with the antigay right wing, the media will accuse him of bigotry. If he doesn't, he'll get attacked by conservatives" (Rimmerman 2002, 163). Bush and some congressional Republicans also recognized that support for a constitutional amendment could turn off potential swing voters who might view the Republican Party as too intolerant. In addition, Republican strategists were well aware that President Bush secured 25 percent of the lesbian and gay vote in the 2000 election, support that both he and Republican Congress members needed in future elections. During a December 2003 interview on ABC television, Bush was asked whether he supported a constitutional amendment that would abolish same-sex marriage. His response reveals his attempt to balance competing interests: "If necessary, I will support a constitutional amendment which would honor marriage between a man and a woman, codify that. . . . the position of this administration is that, you know, whatever legal arrangements people want to make, they're allowed to make, so long as it's embraced by the state" (Perine and Dlouhy 2004, 85). But despite these various political concerns, soon after the *Lawrence* decision was handed down, Bush and his advisors recognized the utility of using same-sex marriage as a divisive political issue.

The Massachusetts Supreme Judicial Court decision provided more support for conservatives who believed that the Republican Party should use marriage as a wedge issue. Indeed, a little more than a month before the November 2004 elections, social conservatives in Congress recognized the potential of using the same-sex marriage issue to mobilize their political base. House leaders brought the revised Musgrave amendment to the floor on September 30, 2004, bypassing the Judiciary Committee and its chairman, F. James Sensenbrenner (R-WI). Sensenbrenner opposes same-sex marriage but has also voiced serious concerns about amending the United States Constitution, thus revealing an important split among social conservatives. In justifying the procedural maneuver, House Majority Leader Tom DeLay (R-TX) claimed that "this debate will spill over into the elections, I think, and rightly so." And Marilyn Musgrave used the latest procedural debate as an opportunity to bash the court system, which, she claimed, has stymied the will of the people: "The trajectory of the courts' decisions is unmistakable" (Perine 2004, 2322). Both DeLay and Musgrave helped President Bush's cause by highlighting the saliency of the same-sex marriage issue in a volatile election year and making the case against the practice with a stridency that the president could not emulate. He was hampered by Cheney's announcement in August 2004 that he did not support the president's determination to amend the U.S. Constitution, presumably out of consideration for his lesbian daughter Mary.

Bush's attempts to appease the Christian Right help explain his discomfort with addressing lesbian and gay civil rights issues during his first term. Since assuming the presidency, Bush had done little to support issues that were of broad interest to the lesbian and gay movements. If anything, he has been openly hostile, as reflected in some of his appointments, such as that of former senator John Ashcroft (R-MO) as attorney general during his first term. As a member of the United States Senate, Ashcroft consistently voted in support of the Christian Right's positions when lesbian and gay issues came up for consideration. Bush's appointment of former Colorado attorney general Gale Norton also did little to comfort the movements because Norton was a vigorous defender of Colorado's Amendment 2, which would have eliminated all lesbian and gay rights laws in the state. Indeed, by the end of his first term, he had no real policy achievements that lesbians and gays could justifiably celebrate. Therefore, his support for a constitutional amendment was merely an extension of his overall approach to gay rights issues since assuming office.

THE IMPLICATIONS FOR THE
LESBIAN AND GAY MOVEMENTS

The results of the 2004 election, which saw the reelection of George W. Bush, the election of a more conservative Congress, the passage of eleven state ballot initiatives banning same-sex marriage, and Election Day exit polls indicating that 22 percent of voters focused more on "moral values" than on other factors (Keen 2004, 20), did not bode well for those supporting same-sex marriage and lesbian, gay, bisexual, and transgender issues more broadly.[4] In the wake of the election, movement leaders held discussions about future strategy and whether more moderate goals and strategies should be pursued in light of the grim election results.

The Human Rights Campaign, the country's largest lesbian and gay advocacy group, accepted the resignation of Cheryl Jacques, its executive director, appointed to its board the first nongay co-chair, and publicly announced a more moderate political and electoral strategy, one that would focus less on "legalizing same-sex marriages and more on strengthening personal relationships" (Broder 2004, A1).

But the reality is that same-sex marriage will now be a part of the national political debate about lesbian, gay, bisexual and transgendered rights for the foreseeable future. And the movement must fashion a political and educational organizing strategy that recognizes and accepts this reality. It is a reality that plays to the strength of the Christian Right's grassroots organizing efforts, because same-sex marriage is the kind of hot-button social issue that can mobilize voters to support conservative candidates and conservative ballot initiatives, as the 2004 election results demonstrate.

I have argued elsewhere[5] that there are three broad strategic directions that the lesbian and gay movements might pursue. The first strategy advocates an exclusive focus on lesbian and gay rights, one that embraces a "let us into the system" approach to political and social change, and one that focuses on narrowly defined issues such as fighting for same-sex marriage and eliminating the military ban. The second posits that the lesbian and gay movements should work to end discrimination and prejudice in its many forms. The third position, which embraces a radical conception of democratic citizenship, argues for a common progressive movement, for building bridges across movements for economic, feminist, and racial justice, and for lesbian and gay liberation. Underlying this perspective is a commitment to political organizing that recognizes the untapped potential of lesbians and gays and their straight allies in America's communities, a potential that must be mobilized to address political and cultural issues if the Christian Right and the corporate-capitalist Right are to be challenged successfully. These political strategies are not mutually exclusive. Indeed, we need all of them to work in concert, especially at this challenging moment in history.

The short-term reality is that the American political landscape, especially at the national level, will be dominated by conservative ideologues who have little patience for challenges to heteronormativity such as same-sex marriage. It is also important to recognize not only conservative Republicans share this view. We have already seen how Bill Clinton used the issue to his political advantage. And during the 2004 campaign, while John Kerry stated his opposition to a constitutional amendment to ban same-sex marriage, he also endorsed the notion that marriage should be between a man and a woman. If there is to be progress, it is likely to come from state-level judicial rulings, as we have recently seen in Massachusetts and California. And the federal constitutional amendment that social conservatives advocate is unlikely to pass given the challenging constitutional hurdles that it faces. But the long-term battle will likely be fought in the court of public opinion. It is here where many Americans who are more tolerant than the national politicians who will represent them may rebel against the ugly discourse that has dominated the same-sex marriage debate over time. If the lesbian and gay movements are to be successful in the long term, they must build coalitions with an array of interests and develop an extensive grassroots educational network in all fifty states, one that can be mobilized when needed to respond to reactionary Christian Right initiatives and to hold lawmakers accountable at all level of the political system for their public pronouncements and their votes. This is hard but necessary work, and there is no one model for achieving success. But it is the work of any successful social movement, especially one that learns from short-term setbacks to build a lasting strategy for meaningful political, social, and economic change.

ENDNOTES

The author thanks Benjamin M. Sio for his excellent work in collecting and organizing background materials integral to the writing of this chapter.

1. A wedge issue is a highly salient issue, one that rallies a candidate's supporters and divides his or her opponent's potential supporters.
2. See, e.g., Tarrow (1998).
3. See Rauch (2004); Sullivan (1996); Bawer (1994).
4. Matt Foreman, the executive director of the National Gay and Lesbian Task Force, vigorously disputed the argument that same-sex marriage hurt John Kerry's campaign for the presidency. Several days after the election, Foreman said: "To blame gay people for the failure of the Democratic message to motivate people is frankly unfair, and frankly, it's homophobic. Yes, the right wing was energized as never before to turn out for George Bush, but it's energized over a whole range of issues. Karl Rove has catered to their every need, with stem-cell research, the ban on late-term abortion, faith-based initiatives, restrictions on funding for overseas contraception, prayer in the schools. Was gay marriage a factor? Yes, along with a lot of other factors" (Belluck 2004). I believe that Foreman's analysis is right on target, especially since Kerry failed to endorse same-sex marriage in the election campaign. Instead, he argued

that the decision should be left up to individual states, which was a way for him to opt out of taking a stand on a salient and controversial issue.

5. See Rimmerman (2002).

REFERENCES

Bawer, Bruce. 1994. *Place at the table: The gay individual in American society.* New York: Simon & Schuster.

Belluck, Pam. 2004. Maybe same-sex marriage didn't make the difference. *New York Times,* November 7. http://www.nytimes.com/2004/11/weekinreview.

Broder, John M. 2004. Groups debate slower strategy on gay rights. *New York Times,* December 9, A1.

Bull, Chris. 2001. Same players, new game. *Advocate,* February 27.

———. 2003. Justice served. *Advocate,* August 19.

Cahill, Sean. 2004. *Same-sex marriage in the United States: Focus on the facts.* New York: Lexington.

Chambers, David L. 2000. Couples: Marriage, civil union, and domestic partnership. In *Creating change: Sexuality, public policy, and civil rights,* ed. John D'Emilio, William B. Turner, and Urvashi Vaid. New York: St. Martin's.

Chauncey, George. 2004. *Why marriage: The history shaping today's debate over gay equality.* New York: Basic.

Crea, Joe. 2003. Frist supports gay marriage ban. *Washington Blade,* July 4.

———. 2004. "Austin 12" divided on Bush: One feels Bush-whacked." *Washington Blade,* September 17. http://washblade.com.

Declaration of intolerance. 2003. *Advocate,* November 11.

Foust, Michael. 2003. Ruling highlights need for marriage amendment, leaders say. November 18. http://www.sbcbaptistpress.org/bpnews.asap?Id=7117 (accessed November 18, 2003).

Gallagher, John. 1996. Speak now. *Advocate,* June 11.

Guerriero, Patrick. 2004. Gay Republicans not for Bush. *Washington Blade,* October 8. http://washblade.com.

Hertzberg, Hendrik. 2003. Comment: Dog bites man. *New Yorker,* May 5.

Hulse, Carl. 2004. Backers revise amendment on marriage. http://www.nytimes.com/2004/03/23/politics/23AMEN.html.

Keen, Lisa. 2004. Did "moral values" tip the scale? *Bay Windows,* November 11.

Office of the Press Secretary. 2003. Marriage Protection Week, 2003. www.whitehouse.gov/news/releases/2003/10/20031003-12.html (accessed October 14, 2003).

Perine, Keith. 2004. House conservatives seek voters' attention with action on gay marriage amendment. *CQ Weekly,* October 2.

Perine, Keith, and Jennifer A. Dlouhy. 2004. Parties worry about political risk in stands on gay marriage. *CQ Weekly,* January 10.

Rauch, Jonathan. 2004. *Gay marriage: Why it is good for gays, good for straights, and good for America.* New York: Times Books.

Rimmerman, Craig A. 2002. *From identity to politics: The lesbian and gay movements in the United States.* Philadelphia: Temple University Press.

Sokolove, Michael. 2004. Can this marriage be saved? *New York Times Magazine,* April 11. http://www.nytimes.com/2004/04/11magazine.

Strasser, Mark. 1997. *Legally wed: Same-sex marriage and the Constitution.* Ithaca: Cornell University Press.

Sullivan, Andrew. 1996. *Virtually normal: An argument about homosexuality.* New York: Knopf.

———. 2004. *Same-sex marriage pro and con: A reader.* New York: Vintage.

Tarrow, Sidney. 1998. *Power in movement: Social movements and contentious politics,* 2d ed. Cambridge: Cambridge University Press.

'TIL DEATH—OR THE SUPREME COURT—DO US PART

LITIGATING GAY MARRIAGE

Karen O'Connor and Alixandra B. Yanus

Today's opinion dismantles the structure of constitutional law that has permitted a distinction to be made between heterosexual and homosexual unions, insofar as formal recognition in marriage is concerned. If moral disapprobation of homosexual conduct is "no legitimate state interest" for purposes of proscribing that conduct, and if, as the Court coos (casting aside all pretense of neutrality), "[w]hen sexuality finds overt expression in intimate conduct with another person, the conduct can be but one element in a personal bond that is more enduring," what justification could there possibly be for denying the benefits of marriage to homosexual couples exercising "[t]he liberty protected by the Constitution"? Surely not the encouragement of procreation, since the sterile and the elderly are allowed to marry. This case "does not involve" the issue of homosexual marriage only if one entertains the belief that principle and logic have nothing to do with the decisions of this Court.

JUSTICE ANTONIN SCALIA, *LAWRENCE V. TEXAS* (2003)

Justice Scalia's remarks in dissent in *Lawrence v. Texas,* a case dealing with the constitutionality of a Texas anti-sodomy law, catapulted the issue of gay marriage onto the public agenda, much as the Court's decision in *Roe* v. *Wade* (1973) had done for abortion. Just as abortion eventually pushed the Democratic and Republican parties further to the Left and to the Right, respectively, Scalia's opinion was a call to the religious and political Right that some, including George W. Bush's top strategist, Karl Rove, believe it turned the course of the 2004 presidential election (Nagourney 2004). This was quite similar to earlier claims that abortion was an important factor in the election of Bill Clinton in 1992 (Abramowitz 1995).

The issue seemed to electrify some voters in 2004, but it did not miraculously appear on judicial dockets and the public agenda. (In 2004, eleven states had ballot measures proposing bans or limitations on same-sex marriage. Commentators argued that these measures were crucial to mobilizing Republican voters, and indeed, Bush won all of these states. But by 2006, when the issue appeared on the ballots of five additional states, prognosticators began to argue that it had lost some of its public salience and might not deliver the Republican victories that it had in 2004 [Johnson 2006].) Rather, scores of individuals and interest groups have been litigating for fuller constitutional rights for homosexuals for decades. We begin this chapter with a discussion of the events that first pushed legal battles about gay marriage to the fore. Next we examine the role of the courts as agents of social change, detailing how the efforts of African Americans and women to achieve rights through litigation served as models for many of the individuals and groups interested in expanding gay rights. We then discuss the approaches adopted by those in the homosexual community to gain rights, as well as the backlash from conservative groups that has affected recent developments in gay rights litigation. Finally, we examine issues that are likely to continue to flood the courts, including the sweep of the United States Constitution's full faith and credit clause in dealing with the patchwork of state laws and their relation to the Defense of Marriage Act (DOMA) as well as divorce and child custody as they relate to gay unions.

A CHALLENGE IN HAWAII

The issue of gay marriage in the courts first leapt onto the public agenda in December 1990 when three homosexual couples—Ninia Baehr and Genora Dancel, Tammy Rodrigues and Antoinette Pregil, and Joseph Melillo and Patrick Lagon—took the unprecedented step of applying for marriage licenses in the state of Hawaii. The couples knew their applications were in blatant violation of the 1985 Hawaii marriage law, which implicitly banned gay marriage by referring to a "man and woman" and a "husband" and a "wife" in its text. Nevertheless, after years of contemplation, the activist couples decided that the political climate was ripe for change.

As expected, their applications were denied by the state's Department of Health in April 1991. This denial provided the couples with the opportunity to file the first serious challenge to a state prohibition on granting same-sex marriage licenses in nearly twenty years.[1] In filing suit in the First Circuit Court of the state of Hawaii, the couples charged that the Hawaii marriage law was a violation of their rights to privacy, due process, and equal protection of the law, as guaranteed by the Hawaii Constitution (Courson 1994).

In October 1991 the First Circuit Court ruled in favor of the Department of Health. The couples and their lawyer, Daniel R. Foley, a private practitioner in Honolulu who previously served as the director of the American Civil Liberties Union (ACLU) of Hawaii, appealed the case to the state's supreme court later that month.

Following this appeal, the case began to garner significant public attention, as revealed in table 12.1. The case also began to gather attention

TABLE 12.1. Growing media attention to same-sex marriage.

YEAR	MENTIONS
1990	38
1991	77
1992	265
1993	291
1994	461
1995	941
1996	4,985
1997	2,041
1998	2,040
1999	1,921
2000	4,143
2001	1,923
2002	2,324
2003	10,514
2004	39,896

Note: The searches were performed in the PAPERS library of the Lexis-Nexis search engine. In each case, the search terms used were "'gay marriage' or 'same sex marriage.'"

from several interest groups on the Left and the Right including the liberal Lambda Legal Defense and Education Fund (now Lambda Legal), the ACLU Foundation of Hawaii, and the conservative Rutherford Institute, which joined the struggle as amici curiae, or friends of the court, at the state supreme court level. The groups' decision to file amicus briefs at this level was a remarkable one because although amicus briefs in these courts are more common than in the past, they still remain relatively rare (Epstein 1994).[2]

The Hawaii Supreme Court's May 1993 ruling in *Baehr v. Lewin* challenged volumes of existing legal doctrine. By a 3–1 margin, the court ruled that the state lacked a compelling public interest to limit civil marriage to heterosexual couples and thus may have been in violation of the equal protection clause of Hawaii's constitution.[3] At least for a short time, it appeared as though gay marriage was on the fast track to approval in Hawaii and perhaps in the United States as a whole. As we will see, however, no successful social movement is without a social, legal, and political backlash. But first we consider the rich historical tradition of litigation by disadvantaged groups to achieve social change.

COURTS AS AGENTS OF SOCIAL CHANGE

Gay rights activists such as the Hawaii couples were not the first groups to resort to litigation to achieve social change. Perhaps the most notable predecessors are African Americans, who, under the aegis of the NAACP Legal Defense and Education Fund (LDF) used the courts to achieve integration in education, housing, and a number of other areas (Vose 1955, 1959). Women's rights groups also made notable efforts to use the courts to gain rights that were not forthcoming from states or the national legislature. Although the work of these groups was largely carried out in the federal courts and gay marriage advocates have mainly litigated in the states, these historical templates remain illustrative.

LITIGATING FOR AFRICAN AMERICAN RIGHTS

The creation of the NAACP Legal Defense Fund in 1939 allowed African American activists to focus their desegregationist efforts on the courts and pursue a direct test case litigation strategy. In such a plan, an interest group uses legal action sponsorship of individual cases as part of a broader strategy to achieve social change.

In attempting to remedy some of the most onerous forms of discrimination suffered by African Americans, for example, the LDF used a series of legal actions to challenge the constitutionality of restrictive housing covenants, which allowed developers to refuse to sell homes to African Americans. In a series of cases that culminated in *Shelley v. Kraemer* (1948), the LDF and its allies convinced the U.S. Supreme Court that state enforcement of restrictive racial covenants violated the Fourteenth Amendment's guarantee of equal protection (Vose 1959).

Under the leadership of chief counsel Thurgood Marshall (who later served on the Court), the LDF then turned its attention to ending institutionalized segregation in other areas of the law. Chief among these was public education, for which the LDF lawyers designed an incremental strategy to invalidate the doctrine of separate but equal accommodation enunciated by the Supreme Court in *Plessy v. Ferguson* (1896). The LDF began its efforts by challenging racial segregation in law schools and, later, graduate schools. These forums, as well as the plaintiffs in each of the cases, were selected strategically by the LDF to prime the Court as it sought to avoid charges that African Americans wanted integration in order to intermarry with whites, a fear enunciated by many southern lawmakers. In a series of cases culminating in *Brown v. Board of Education* (1954), the Court ruled that the segregationist practices were inappropriate and eventually overturned *Plessy*, at least in the area of education.

LITIGATING FOR WOMEN'S RIGHTS

Women's groups also pursued test case litigation, beginning with the notable cases of *Bradwell v. Illinois* (1873), which pertained to a woman's right to practice law, and *Minor v. Happersett* (1875). Later, the National Consumers' League sponsored *Muller v. Oregon* (1908), which related to a woman's right to vote. In what was to become one of the most famous briefs ever filed before the Supreme Court, Louis Brandeis (who was later appointed to serve on the Court) used a wealth of sociological and medical evidence to argue that an Oregon law prohibiting women from working more than ten hours a day should be upheld by the Court (Vose 1957; O'Connor 1980).

Women's rights groups continued to use the courts to achieve legal change in the 1960s and 1970s. Many of these groups used the incremental strategy of the NAACP's Legal Defense Fund as a template for their renewed efforts to facilitate constitutional change through litigation. One of the most notable groups involved in this struggle was the American Civil Liberties Union Women's Rights Project (WRP), which was led by Ruth Bader Ginsburg (who, like Marshall, later served on the Supreme Court). The WRP worked to secure equality for women in a number of areas, including discrimination in the workplace and laws governing civic life. Notable cases brought by the WRP include the sex discrimination cases of *Reed v. Reed* (1971) and *Frontiero v. Richardson* (1973).[4]

LITIGATING FOR GAY RIGHTS

In much the same way that African Americans and women before them were politically disadvantaged by their own lack of representation in government and prejudicial opinions in American society, early gay rights activists faced an uphill battle in trying to achieve social and legal change. Although early gay rights groups such as the Mattachine Society, which was formed in California in the 1950s, engaged in sporadic legal challenges, it was not until the 1970s that the gay rights movement truly began to design a litigation campaign (Brewer, Kaib, and O'Connor 2000). Fueled by the successes of the Gay Liberation Front, the Gay Activists Alliance, and the National Gay and Lesbian Task Force, which successfully lobbied the American Psychiatric Association to remove homosexuality from its list of mental illnesses, a new interest group—Lambda Legal Defense and Education Fund—rose to the forefront. It was later joined by a number of other local and national groups, detailed below.

LAMBDA LEGAL

Lambda Legal, which was founded in New York City in 1972 as the Lambda Legal Defense and Education Fund, can probably be regarded as the NAACP LDF of the gay rights movement. It has sponsored or filed an amicus curiae brief in nearly every major gay rights case brought in the past thirty years and has been at the forefront of designing litigation strategies in all areas of gay law, including gay marriage (Brewer, Kaib, and O'Connor 2000). As the Hawaii case was winding its way through the legal system, for example, Lambda Legal coordinated a litigation campaign and publicly urged gays and lesbians not to bring lawsuits in other states. It feared that challenges beyond the Hawaiian case could jeopardize its overall ability to maintain legal momentum (Duffy 1995).

Since its involvement in the Hawaiian case, Lambda Legal has taken the lead in encouraging gay rights groups to use their local expertise to weigh whether legal challenges would be appropriate in their home cities and states. Lambda Legal has also been at the forefront of efforts to litigate for the legalization of gay marriage in the state of New York. In 2006 the New York Court of Appeals handed Lambda a loss when it ruled 4–2 that the state's ban on same-sex marriage was constitutional. The court further ruled that changes to the state law would have to be addressed by the legislature.[5]

NATIONAL CENTER FOR LESBIAN RIGHTS

The National Center for Lesbian Rights (NCLR) is a public interest law firm founded as the Lesbian Rights Project in San Francisco in 1977. The NCLR is primarily dedicated to advancing the rights of lesbians by means of a program of litigation and public policy advocacy. In the area of marriage, it was most recently the lead counsel in the California case of *Woo v. Lockyer*, in which twelve same-sex couples sued the state for the right to marry; the center's efforts secured a favorable ruling in the California Superior Court March 2005, when a judge ruled that denying gay couples the right to marry was a violation of equal protection and the fundamental right to marry. In late 2006 the cases were waiting to be decided by the California Court of Appeals, where more than 250 groups filed as amici curiae in favor of same-sex marriage rights.

GAY AND LESBIAN ADVOCATES AND DEFENDERS

Founded as Park Square Defenders in Boston in 1978, the organization that is known today as GLAD focuses the majority of its litigation efforts on cases in New England. Although the group has litigated cases dealing with a variety of topics ranging from anti-sodomy laws to employment discrimination cases and cases involving the rights of persons who are HIV-positive, the group is perhaps best known for its work on the Massachusetts case of *Goodridge v. Department of Public Health* (2003). As discussed below, the state Supreme Judicial Court's decision in this case paved the way for Massachusetts to be the first state to legalize gay marriage.

HUMAN RIGHTS CAMPAIGN

Human Rights Campaign (HRC), which maintains headquarters in Washington, DC, was founded in 1980 and is the largest, most well-financed of the gay and lesbian rights groups (O'Connor, Brewer, and Kaib 2000). In general, HRC has chosen to devote most of its efforts to lobbying Congress. The group, however, frequently lends its public prestige and excellent research to litigation for gay rights—including gay marriage cases—through amicus curiae briefs.

AMERICAN CIVIL LIBERTIES UNION LESBIAN AND GAY RIGHTS PROJECT

The ACLU has been integral to a wide variety of interest group litigation campaigns, including the continuing struggle for women's rights detailed above. In 1986 the group widened its scope to include the Lesbian and Gay Rights Project, which brings the prestige of the ACLU to gay rights lawsuits in state and federal courts across the country. Although the project litigates in a wide variety of areas, gay marriage is one of its main focuses. The group has recently served as is counsel or co-counsel in right-to-marry cases in Nebraska, Maryland, New York, Oregon, and California.

FREEDOM TO MARRY

Freedom to Marry is the newest gay rights group, having been founded in January 2003 in New York City. The group, however, does not lack legal expertise. Former Lambda Legal chief counsel Evan Wolfson, whom some commentators compare to Thurgood Marshall and Ruth Bader Ginsburg, heads the group's litigation and public advocacy campaigns (Mauro 2004). As the only gay rights group devoted solely to the goal of marriage, the group is actively involved in the formulation and development of the movement's legal and political strategies.

WORKING TOGETHER: COOPERATION AND CONFLICT

For the most part, these and other groups have worked together with tremendous efficacy to achieve change in states' gay rights laws generally and in marriage laws specifically. Although no single group controls the course of the agenda, at least in public, there appears to be a tremendous interplay of ideas between groups (Mauro 2004).

A few general points should be made regarding the gay marriage movement's litigation strategy. First, it is extraordinarily important to stress that unlike African American and women's rights cases, which were largely brought under the federal constitution, groups litigating for gay marriage have focused their efforts in state courts. This occurs for several reasons. First, marriage has historically been an activity regulated by the states. Second, many state constitutions have broader protections for equality and privacy than the U.S. Constitution.[6] Third, many state courts are more liberal in composition than the federal courts; this makes them a more conducive means for creating legal change.

Second, as part of a national strategy, individual groups have ceded to each other the authority to sponsor cases within their individual locales. This strategy is facilitated by the fact that there is a major litigating group headquartered in most cities with large gay populations—Lambda Legal in New York, GLAD in Boston, and NCLR in San Francisco.[7]

When national groups lack a local presence, the ACLU Gay and Lesbian Rights Project and its local affiliates tend to be the most likely to become involved.[8] Such is the case in states such as Maryland, Nebraska, and Oregon, where no other groups have locally affiliated lawyers with expertise in state and local law. The importance of the ACLU's affiliate structure is illustrated in the case of Hawaii, where the lead counsel for the plaintiffs was a former director of the ACLU's Hawaii chapter.

For the most part, this state-based litigation strategy has allowed gay rights activists to make tremendous legal gains in a relatively short period of time. Most notably, although these groups have yet to win marriage rights in a large number of states, their efforts have succeeded in changing the broader political context in which the U.S. Supreme Court makes decisions. In 1978, for example, the Court refused to review a lower court's decision requiring a university to recognize a gay student group working for the repeal of sodomy laws. In his dissent, one justice wrote, "The question [in this case] is more akin to whether those suffering from measles have a constitutional right, in violation of quarantine regulations, to associate together and with others who do not presently have measles, in order to repeal a state law providing that measles sufferers be quarantined" (*Ratchford v. Gay Lib* [1978]).[9] Only twenty-five years later, that same justice, William H. Rehnquist, presided over a Court that has declared sodomy laws to be in violation of the equal protection clause (*Lawrence v. Texas* [2003]) and refused to review a Massachusetts Supreme Judicial Court decision granting gay couples the right to marry (*Largess v. Supreme Judicial Court* [2004]).

Despite this tremendous progress, however, the gay marriage movement has not been without its setbacks. We explore two of these setbacks and their implications for gay marriage in the courts in the following section.

A CONSERVATIVE BACKLASH AND ITS LEGAL CONSEQUENCES: HAWAII REVISITED AND THE DEFENSE OF MARRIAGE ACT

Most successful social movements experience countermovements, and the gay rights movement has been no exception. Perhaps the clearest call to arms for conservative groups was the Hawaii Supreme Court's decision in *Baehr v. Lewin* (1993), which seemed to signal the imminence of gay marriage in America. Following this decision, conservative and religious activists began to organize their forces for a battle in defense of the traditional American family.

The efforts of these groups were aided by a number of factors, although two are particularly important. First, although conservative public interest law firms began to gain steam in the 1980s (see, for example, Epstein 1985), they continued to gain power—and realize the significance of the gay marriage issue—in the 1990s. In addition, conservative litigation efforts were drastically aided by the creation in 1990 of the American Center for Law and Justice, the litigating arm of the Christian Coalition. Second, the year 1994 signaled the first time Republicans controlled both houses of Congress in forty years. This Congress was decidedly more conservative than its predecessors.

Two events demonstrate the power of these factors in controlling the course of gay marriage in the courts. The first of these is the Hawaii Supreme Court's rehearing of *Baehr*. The second is Congress's passage of the Defense of Marriage Act.

HAWAII REVISITED

After the Hawaii Supreme Court issued its initial ruling in *Baehr v. Lewin*, a series of events was put into motion. First, the case was remanded to the lower courts for reconsideration pursuant to the court's ruling that refusing to grant marriage licenses to same-sex couples did not serve a compelling state interest and was thus a violation of the petitioner's right to equal protection of the laws. Second, a backlash occurred in the Hawaii legislature, and in 1994, legislators passed a bill defining marriage in Hawaii as the union of a man and a woman. This bill also called for the establishment of a Commission on Sexual Orientation and the Law, which was to investigate and issue a report describing the legal and economic benefits of marriage and stating whether public policy reasons existed to extend these benefits to same-sex couples.

Although the trial court was scheduled to reconsider *Baehr* in September 1995, the petitioners, who were now being represented by both Daniel R. Foley and lawyers from the Lambda Legal Defense and Education Fund, requested that proceedings be postponed until the commission issued its report; this motion was granted, and the trial was postponed until July 1996. This appeared to be a major victory for pro-marriage forces because in December 1995 the commission issued its report, which found that "the conferring of a marriage certificate can bestow benefits in other jurisdictions . . . there are substantial public policy reasons to extend those benefits in total to same sex couples" (State of Hawaii 1995).

The next several months were filled with legal maneuvering as the trial was postponed again until September 1996. Then, in December 1996, circuit court judge Kevin S. C. Chang ruled that there was no compelling reason for the state to ban gay marriage. Judge Chang stayed his own decision, however, pending an appeal to the state supreme court.

The plaintiff's victory, thus, was not complete. And, to make matters more difficult for pro-marriage forces, in the time that it took for the state supreme court to hear the case, which was now called *Baehr v. Miike*, the Hawaii legislature approved an amendment to the state's constitution stating that "the legislature shall have the power to reserve marriage to same-sex couples." This measure then was put on the November ballot for the voters' approval, as required for constitutional amendments.

This measure became the launching point for a grassroots battle over gay marriage in Hawaii. Pro-marriage activists were led by groups such as Human Rights Campaign, which is noted for its expertise in grassroots advocacy, and an ad hoc group called Protect Our Constitution. Anti-marriage activists chose to organize into a group called Save Traditional Marriage '98.On Election Day, voters followed the lead of conservative groups, passing the ballot measure by a margin of more than two to one. This was perhaps the first sign of the conservative lobby's staying power in the state of Hawaii, as well as its capacity to mobilize opponents of same-sex marriage.

By the time the Hawaii Supreme Court issued its ruling in the case on December 9, 1999, more than fifty interest groups and interested parties had participated as amicus curiae. What was most astounding about this participation was the growth in the number of conservative groups that participated in support of the state of Hawaii. Whereas only one of the groups that participated as amici in the 1993 case participated in support of the state, more than half of the groups participating in *Baehr v. Miike* supported Hawaii. These groups included the American Center for Law and Justice, the Independent Women's Forum, and countless churches and religious groups.

The growth in the number and influence of conservative groups seems to have had a significant role in the Hawaii Supreme Court's decision. In this case, the court stated that the recently ratified constitutional amendment removed same-sex marriage from the safeguards it formerly was accorded under the state constitution's equal protection clause.

THE DEFENSE OF MARRIAGE ACT

At the same time the Hawaii case was weaving its way through the appeals process, the United States Congress decided to take action. Although marriage is an activity traditionally regulated by the states, the Republican-controlled Congress, with the support of a number of conservative and religious groups, introduced the Defense of Marriage Act. The act, which was billed as an act in defense of the "traditional" American family, defined marriage as "a legal union between one man and one woman as husband and wife." In addition, the law specifically stated that no state would "be required to give effect to any public act, record, or judicial proceeding in any other state . . . respecting a relationship between persons of the same sex as a marriage under the laws of such other state" (U.S. Congress 1996).

The bill was quickly approved by overwhelming margins in both houses of Congress and signed into law by President Bill Clinton (Lewis and Edelson 2000). The very day after Congress approved the act, gay rights activists vowed to take to the federal courts to challenge the constitutionality of this act (Mauro and Howlett 1996). As we discuss below, litigation concerning DOMA remains a serious concern, both today and in the future.

RECENT SUCCESSES

Despite conservative gains such as those detailed above, as well as the election and reelection of a conservative Republican president who has been less than friendly to the idea of legalizing gay marriage, pro-marriage groups have vigorously continued their fight in the courts and in society. In 2003 their efforts were rewarded. First, in June, the Supreme Court handed down its decision in *Lawrence v. Texas*, which, as detailed above, seemed to make gay marriage a logical next step for many gay rights activists. And, on November 18, pro-marriage activists won a major victory when the Massachusetts Supreme Judicial Court declared that "barring an individual from the protections, benefits, and obligations of civil marriage solely because that person would marry a person of the same sex violates the [individual liberty and equality safeguards of the] Massachusetts Constitution."

The court's decision not only paved the way for gay marriage to be legalized in the state of Massachusetts [10] but sparked a movement for gay marriage nationwide. In cities from New Paltz, New York, to Sandoval, New Mexico, to San Francisco, mayors and county clerks performed marriages and issued marriage licenses to gay couples, if only on a temporary basis. In addition, after the success of the Massachusetts case, couples in a number of other states, including Washington, Maryland, and New Jersey, were prompted to challenge or appeal previous rulings on the marriage laws in those states. These direct challenges to state marriage laws constitute only one type of legal challenge we can expect to see as gay marriage continues to be a hot-button issue on the American policy agenda. In the following section we detail only some of the future legal challenges posed by gay marriage.

FUTURE LEGAL ISSUES

As noted above, the regulation of marriage and family law traditionally has been left to the states. That is not to say, however, that at times the U.S. Congress or the U.S. Supreme Court has not stepped in to regulate in these areas. The Court, for example, found unconstitutional Utah's acceptance of polygamy and Virginia's miscegenation statute. Despite interventions such as these, issues of family law have always been considered somewhat sticky by the federal courts.

In addition to these jurisdictional concerns, same-sex marriage raises a number of other constitutional and legal questions that ultimately are likely to be answered by state high courts or the U.S. Supreme Court. These cases fall into several areas, including questions about the scope of the full faith and credit clause of the federal Constitution and questions about family law, including divorce and child custody cases.

THE FULL FAITH AND CREDIT CLAUSE OF THE U.S. CONSTITUTION AND SAME-SEX MARRIAGES

The federal Defense of Marriage Act was Congress's "way of anticipatorily retrofitting the U.S. Code to withstand an 'orchestrated legal assault' by homosexuals seeking access to the array of benefits, rights and privileges its provisions make available to heterosexuals" (*Harvard Law Review* 2004, 2684). Although no state allowed same-sex marriages at the time that DOMA was passed in 1996, the situation in Hawaii had put several state legislatures as well as many members of Congress into near hysteria because of its portents.

To many commentators, however, this federal provision poses a constitutional dilemma because it seems to be in direct contradiction with the full faith and credit clause of the U.S. Constitution. The major purpose of that clause has always been to guarantee that contracts, court rulings, and nonfederal laws made in one state would be binding in others. Without this provision, the portability of court orders and enforcement of state-to-state extradition of criminals and of spousal and child support orders would be nearly impossible. As part of the Constitution, the clause necessarily takes precedence over all other state and federal laws.

There is, however, one potential loophole: courts long have upheld a "public policy" exception to the clause, which allows states not to enforce acts of other states that defy their public policy norms (Paige 1997). Judge Benjamin Cardozo articulated the reasoning behind this exception in *Loucks v. Standard Oil Co.* (1918): "The courts are not free to refuse to enforce a foreign right at the pleasure of the judges, to suit the individual notion of expediency or fairness. They do not close their doors unless help would violate some fundamental principle of justice, some prevalent conception of good morals, some deep-rooted tradition of the common weal" (120 N.E. 198 at 202).

Thus, for example, although a state must abide by another state's crime control provisions, at times governors have refused to extradite criminals to states where the death penalty is a possibility. The question remains, however, whether same-sex marriages fall under this "public policy exception" or whether a federal law that allows states to ignore same-sex marriages performed in another state violates the U.S. Constitution's full faith and credit clause.

Attempts to forecast what the courts might do with such a case are widespread. Many commentators have noted that the enactment by numerous states of post-DOMA statutes or constitutional amendments barring same-sex marriage could be taken as a clear indication to the Court that the public policy norm in some areas is to oppose gay marriage. Support for the practice in the United States is still not strong, and a series of state ballot measures banning same-sex marriages—eleven in 2004 and seven in 2006—were adopted by wide margins. Thus, this public policy exception could be the death knell for federal judicial recognition of same-sex marriages or civil unions in states where they are prohibited.[11]

On the other hand, if state and federal courts follow their recent trend of examining prevailing international norms, the public policy exception may not stand. Spain and Canada, as well as several other countries worldwide, have recently taken major steps in legalizing gay marriages.

FAMILY LAW: CHILD CUSTODY, DIVORCE, AND BEYOND

Although gay rights litigators have made gains in employment discrimination and anti-sodomy cases, change has come much more slowly in family law cases, such as divorce and child custody cases (Sherman 1992). Even in the state where gay marriage is legal, questions of family law continue to pose problems for the courts. Massachusetts, for example, has a mechanism for couples to divorce legally, but the child custody cases that have followed those divorces have not been decided in favor of rights and obligations for same-sex couples that parallel those of their heterosexual counterparts. In late 2004, for example, the Massachusetts Supreme Judicial Court, the same court that issued the decision clearing the way for gay marriage in the state, heard the case of *T. F. v. B. L.*

The plaintiff and the defendant were two gay individuals who, although not married, had conceived a child together. The child was born after the relationship had ended, and the partner who had carried the child sued the other partner for child support. In its decision, the Supreme Judicial Court ruled that the mother's former partner could not be required to pay child support, although she had played an active role in encouraging the artificial insemination process.

This is just one example of a case in which a court has been asked to determine what defines a parent when biology cannot be a factor. This area of law is a particularly thorny one that legal experts expect to become increasingly significant as the number of gay parents continues to grow; in 2000, for example, nearly six hundred thousand same-sex partners shared children (David 2005).

When questions of gay family law begin to cross state lines, it even becomes trickier. One only needs to examine a situation that occurred in Vermont and Virginia in 2004 to see the complexity of these issues. We use the case of *Miller-Jenkins v. Miller-Jenkins* to illustrate the legal confusion as well as the personal heartbreak and financial costs that same-sex married couples may expect.

Lisa and Janet Miller-Jenkins moved from Virginia to Vermont in 2002 to raise their daughter Isabelle, who had been conceived through artificial insemination and born to Lisa in 2001. According to Janet, both women had believed that Vermont, which had legally recognized same-sex civil unions but not marriages in 2000, was a more hospitable place to raise their daughter. When the relationship ended amicably in 2003, a Vermont family court judge awarded Lisa temporary custody of the child and gave Janet liberal visitation rights. Lisa then fled to Virginia, which has some of the strongest anti-gay legislation in the United States. Proclaiming herself no longer gay, she filed suit in a Virginia court seeking sole custody of Isabelle.

Janet contested this motion, arguing that the Vermont court already had jurisdiction in the matter and over any resulting custody disputes ("Lesbian War" 2005). As this case continued, the Virginia county court judge ruled that since the mother now lived in Virginia, the Virginia courts properly had jurisdiction over the case.[12]

On July 1, 2004, Virginia's Marriage Affirmation Act, which bans legal recognition of all forms of same-sex relationships, took effect (Chibbaro 2004). Pursuant to this law, in August, the Virginia judge ruled that Lisa was the sole parent of Isabelle. But in November 2004, the original Vermont family court judge issued a contrary decision recognizing Janet as a co-parent of Isabelle (Lesbian "War" 2005).

Although Janet's lawyer was elated, his exuberance was tempered with concern as to how the complex issues of child custody will play out. He noted that there was "no guarantee that the order will be enforced because of the novel questions it presents" (Finer 2004, A3). As of late 2006, Janet, represented by Gay and Lesbian Advocates and Defenders, had petitioned the Vermont Supreme Court to uphold the lower court rulings and reinstate her rights to see Isabelle, whom she had not seen since June 2004. The case also was on appeal to the Virginia Court of Appeals. It was being watched closely by commentators, many of whom believe that it will be an intrastate family law case such as this one that will bring questions of gay marriage before the Supreme Court (ibid.).

CONCLUSION

For more than one hundred years, disadvantaged groups have turned to the courts to achieve legal change when legislative and administrative avenues have failed. Almost since the beginning, these efforts have been guided by the strategizing and resources of organized interests. The work of groups that litigated for equal rights for African Americans and women illustrate this trend and provide a valuable template for gay rights groups such as Lambda Legal, GLAD, and NCLR that are working to gain the right to marry for same-sex couples.

The earliest recent attempts to litigate for gay marriage rights began in Hawaii in 1993. As the case of *Baehr v. Lewin* wound its way through the judicial system, conservative groups began to organize. By means of legislative actions such as the federal Defense of Marriage Act and judicial involvement by way of amicus curiae briefs, these right-wing organizations began to win victories in the courts. Only after the U.S. Supreme Court's decision in *Lawrence v. Texas* (2003) was new life breathed into gay rights groups' efforts.

Judicial victories at the state level, most notably in the Massachusetts Supreme Judicial Court, have given activists new hope for the success of a litigation campaign. A number of obstacles, including DOMA and questions of family law, however, continue to complicate their efforts.

If previous social movements provide any indication, gay rights groups will eventually move from state courts to federal courts. Then the U.S. Supreme Court will become the arbitrator of questions of same-sex marriage and gay rights. The recent addition of Justices John G. Roberts and Samuel A. Alito, both of whom were appointed by a Republican president, George W. Bush, in 2005, raise new and unique questions about how the Court may react to these claims. If Alito and Roberts are indeed as conservative in their decisions as many commentators predict, their appointment may prove to be a barrier to gay rights groups' success in federal courts. But if these justices are not what commentators expect, they could have the opportunity to be leaders in a constitutional revolution.

ENDNOTES

1. Before the Hawaii case was filed, courts in seven states had rejected the idea of same-sex marriage. Two of those cases, *Baker v. Nelson* (1972) and *Hicks v. Miranda* (1975), reached the Supreme Court. In both cases, the Court refused to review the lower courts' decisions, thereby allowing these decisions, which concluded that states had the ability to define marriage as a union between a man and a woman, to stand (Sherman 1992). Several states, including New Jersey (1982), Pennsylvania (1984), and New York (1990), heard challenges to questions including divorce and property claims in same-sex relationships, but these cases did not involve the act of filing for marriage licenses. The courts' decisions in these cases were consistent with earlier decisions and, like *Baker* and *Hicks*, never received a full hearing by the Supreme Court.

A challenge to the District of Columbia's prohibition on same-sex marriage was decided in the Superior Court of the District of Columbia 1992, at the same time the Hawaii case was in the judicial system. In the D.C. case, two gay men sued the District for the right to marry. On appeal, the District of Columbia Court of Appeals ruled in 1995 that two gay men who were denied a marriage license were not deprived of their right to equal protection of the law. For a full chronology of same-sex marriage attempts, please search "same sex marriage" on www.nolo.com.

2. Part of the reason the case drew so much attention was that it came at a time when the gay rights movement in general was gaining increased recognition and having increased success in courts across the United States (Sherman 1992). In two 1992 cases, for example, gay rights activists won important victories when the Commonwealth of Kentucky's Supreme Court overturned the state's anti-sodomy law and a Florida jury issued a positive finding in a gay job discrimination case (ibid.).

3. By deciding this case with reference to the equal protection clause, the court took the remarkable step of elevating discrimination based on sexual preference to a suspect classification. Suspect classifications, including race or those involving fundamental freedoms, are entitled to the highest level of scrutiny applied by the courts. To date, the U.S. Supreme Court has failed to take similar action.

4. Ginsburg believes firmly in the utility of the equal protection clause and has repeatedly gone on record stating that even the Court's landmark abortion decision in *Roe v. Wade* (1973) should have been framed as a question of male-female discrimination under the equal protection clause and not as a question of a woman's fundamental right to privacy. As Ginsburg and others (especially law professor Richard Karst [1977]) have charged, the conflict in *Roe* and about abortion in general "is not simply one between a fetus' interests and a woman's interests, narrowly conceived, nor is the overriding issue state versus private control of a woman's body" (Ginsburg 1985, 383). Instead, the real concern with abortion is a woman's ability to stand equal to a man in society and have control over her body and her choices.

   Deciding *Roe* on equal protection grounds, Ginsburg has commented, would not have completely eliminated the firestorm of moral and religious concerns that led to the antiabortion backlash. She contends, however, that a ruling made under the equal protection clause would have been more firmly grounded in both legal doctrine and reality. Thus, such a ruling would have been a stronger precedent for later abortion cases (Ginsburg 1985).

5. The case was *Hernandez v. Robles*, 7 N.Y.3d 338 (2006).

6. When gay marriage cases do eventually reach the Supreme Court, litigators will have to make the important decision of whether to file under the equal protection clause or the right to privacy. We do not focus on that decision in order to maintain the clarity of our discussion about state court litigation.

7. Notably missing from this list is Atlanta, Georgia. Although Lambda Legal has a regional office in this city, as well as in Los Angeles, Dallas, and Chicago, southern state and federal courts are far too conservative to justify

an active litigation strategy, especially given the time, money, and other resources that these efforts require.

8. This affiliate strategy also achieved great success in women's rights cases.

9. Note that in 1986, in *Bowers v. Hardwick,* the Supreme Court actually decided a case in which five justices agreed that Georgia's sodomy law was constitutional under the U.S. Constitution.

10. The first gay marriages were performed in Massachusetts on May 17, 2004. Perhaps coincidentally, this date was also the fiftieth anniversary of the day the Supreme Court handed down its decision in *Brown v. Board of Education* (Mauro 2004).

11. The public policy exception is not the only judicial doctrine that is relevant in full faith and credit litigation. The "most significant relationship test," for example, allows the Court to consider a range of factors in determining which courts have jurisdiction over any contract, such as a marriage (Paige 1997). These factors include the state in which the contract was made and the state of residence of the parties making the contract, two characteristics that could have especially potent implications in determining the legal validity of a marriage licensed in one state for citizens of another state.

12. Normally, the federal Uniform Child Custody Jurisdiction Act would determine which state had jurisdiction in the case. But federal courts have yet to determine a standard procedure in cases involving same-sex couples.

REFERENCES

Abramowitz, Alan I. 1995. It's abortion, stupid: Policy voting in the 1992 presidential election. *Journal of Politics* 57:176–86.

Brewer, Sarah, David Kaib, and Karen O'Connor. 2000. Sex and the Supreme Court: Gays, lesbians, and justice. In *The politics of gay rights,* ed. Craig A. Rimmerman, Kenneth D. Wald, and Clyde Wilcox, 377–408. Chicago: University of Chicago Press.

Chibarro, Lou, Jr. 2004. "Landmark" decision in lesbian custody case: Vermont judge rules both partners in civil union are parents. *Washington Blade,* November 26.

Courson, Marty K. 1994. *Baehr v. Lewin:* Hawaii takes a tentative step to legalize same-sex marriage. *Golden Gate University Law Review* 24:41.

David, Sara. 2005. Turning parental rights into parental obligations: Holding same-sex non-biological parents responsible for child support. *New England Law Review* 39:921.

Duffy, Shannon P. 1995. Same sex marriages on the horizon? Lawyers say Hawaii case is test for rest of U.S. *Legal Intelligencer,* May 9, 1.

Epstein, Lee. 1985. *Conservatives in court.* Knoxville: University of Tennessee Press.

———. 1994. Exploring the participation of organized interests in state court litigation. *Political Research Quarterly* 47:335–51.

Finer, Jonathan. 2004. Court says both in gay union are parents. *Washington Post,* November 22, A3.

Ginsburg, Ruth Bader. 1985. Some thoughts on autonomy and equality in relation to *Roe v. Wade*. *North Carolina Law Review* 63:375.

Harvard Law Review. 2004. Note: Litigating the Defense of Marriage Act: The next battleground for same-sex marriage. *Harvard Law Review* 117:2684.

Johnson, Kirk. 2006. Gay marriage losing punch as a ballot issue. *New York Times*, October 14.

Karst, Richard. 1977. Foreword: Equal protection under the Fourteenth Amendment. *Harvard Law Review* 91:1.

Lesbian "War of the Roses" rages on in two states: Vermont judge rules both partners in civil unions are parents. 2005. www.365gay.com/newscon05/060905 parentFeud.htm (accessed June 29, 2005).

Lewis, Gregory B., and Jonathan L. Edelson. 2000. DOMA and ENDA: Congress votes on gay rights. In *The politics of gay rights*, ed. Craig A. Rimmerman, Kenneth D. Wald, and Clyde Wilcox, 193–216. Chicago: University of Chicago Press.

Mauro, Tony. 2004. Trailblazer: Wolfson's fight for the freedom to marry: Same sex marriage advocate sees historical parallels in struggle. *Legal Times*, June 7, 1.

Mauro, Tony, and Debbie Howlett. 1996. Into the courts, away from Congress. *USA Today*, September 11, 4A.

Nagourney, Adam. 2004. "Moral values" carried Bush, Rove says. *New York Times*, November 10, A3.

O'Connor, Karen. 1980. *Women's organizations' use of the courts*. Lexington, MA: Lexington Books.

Paige, Rebecca S. 1997. Wagging the dog: If the state of Hawaii accepts same sex marriage, will other states have to?" *American University Law Review* 47:165.

Sherman, Rorie. 1992. Gay law no longer closeted. *National Law Journal* (October 26): 1.

State of Hawaii Commission on Sexual Orientation and the Law. 1995. *Report of the commission on sexual orientation and the law*. December 8. Honolulu: State of Hawaii Commission on Sexual Orientation and the Law.

U.S. Congress. House of Representatives. 1996. *The Defense of Marriage Act*. 104th Cong., 2d sess., H.R. 3396.

Vose, Clement E. 1955. NAACP strategy in the restrictive covenant cases. *Case Western Reserve Law Review* 6:101.

———. 1957. The National Consumer's League and the Brandeis brief. *Midwest Journal of Political Science* 1:267–90.

———. 1959. *Caucasians only*. Berkeley: University of California Press.

CASES CITED

Baehr v. Lewin, 74 Haw. 530 (1993)

Baehr v. Miike, 1999 Haw. LEXIS 391 (1999)

Baker v. Nelson, 409 U.S. 310 (1972)

Bowers v. Hardwick, 478 U.S. 168 (1986)

Bradwell v. Illinois, 83 U.S. 130 (1873)

Brown v. Board of Education, 347 U.S. 483 (1954)

Dean v. District of Columbia, 653 A.2d. 307 (D.C. 1995)
Frontiero v. Richardson, 411 U.S. 677 (1973)
Goodridge v. Department of Public Health, 440 Mass. 309 (2003)
Griswold v. Connecticut, 381 U.S. 479 (1965)
Hicks v. Miranda, 422 U.S. 22 (1975)
Largess v. Supreme Judicial Court, 125 S.Ct. 618, cert. denied (2004)
Lawrence v. Texas, 539 U.S. 558 (2003)
Loucks v. Standard Oil Co., 120 N.E. 198 (N.Y. 1918)
Miller-Jenkins v. Miller-Jenkins, Va. Cir. Ct. 1051 (2004)
Miller-Jenkins v. Miller-Jenkins, Vt. Fam. Ct. 1051 (2004)
Minor v. Happersett, 88 U.S. 162 (1975)
Muller v. Oregon, 208 U.S. 412 (1908)
Plessy v. Ferguson, 163 U.S. 537 (1896)
Ratchford v. Gay Lib, 435 U.S. 981, cert. denied (1978)
Reed v. Reed, 404 U.S. 71 (1971)
Shelley v. Kraemer, 334 U.S. 1 (1948)
T. F. v. B. L., 813 N.E.2d 1244 (Mass. 2004)
Woo v. Lockyer, 128 Cal. App. 4th 1030 (2005)

THE POLITICS OF SAME-SEX
MARRIAGE VERSUS THE POLITICS
OF GAY CIVIL RIGHTS

A COMPARISON OF PUBLIC OPINION
AND STATE VOTING PATTERNS

Katie Lofton and Donald P. Haider-Markel

The 2004 election season brought the issue of same-sex marriage to the forefront of the national political agenda. Between August and November, thirteen states voted on referenda that amended their state constitutions to ban the recognition of same-sex marriage and, in some cases, civil unions between same-sex couples. This flurry of activity followed the November 2003 decision by the Massachusetts Supreme Judicial Court to strike down a ban on same-sex marriages in that state and the issuance of marriage licenses to same-sex couples in states such as California, Oregon, New Mexico, and New York in early 2004.

Although these events emphasize the recent high salience of same-sex marriage, the issue first gained prominence in 1971 when a Minnesota court became the first in the country to hear a case concerning this issue. Several state courts and legislatures addressed the issue throughout the 1970s and 1980s (Haider-Markel 2001), but same-sex marriage first received significant national attention in 1993. In May Hawaii's Supreme Court ruled that denying marriage licenses to same-sex partners was discriminatory under the state's equal rights amendment (Goldberg-Hiller 2002). Over the course of the next ten years, forty-eight of the fifty states and the federal government introduced laws that limited legal recognition of marriage to opposite-sex couples. In thirty-seven states some version of these laws was adopted, and in 1996 the federal government passed the Defense of Marriage Act (DOMA), which denied federal benefits to couples in same-sex marriages.

Several states' citizens utilized the direct democracy process to codify same-sex marriage bans in statutory or constitutional law. Because such bans pass overwhelmingly in direct democracy contests at the state level, two questions present themselves. First, what factors contribute to voter support for these bans? Second, are patterns of voter support for these bans the same as those that contribute to the success or failure of pro-gay or antigay ballot proposals more generally? Indeed, one can ask whether the popular push to exclude same-sex couples from being allowed to marry is just another battle in the gay civil rights debate or whether gay marriage somehow elicits a fundamentally different response from citizens and policymakers.

In this chapter we employ the morality politics framework to examine these questions in three ways. First, we compare the determinants of individual opinion about gay civil rights to the determinants of individual opinion toward a constitutional ban on same-sex marriage. Second, using exit polls from the 2004 elections, we compare the characteristics of voters who supported state constitutional bans on same-sex marriage to the characteristics of voters who opposed these measures. Finally, we investigate cases where same-sex marriage bans were placed before the voters in state direct democracy contests. In particular, we seek to explain patterns of voter support for these measures and the ways support and opposition to these measures compare to previous gay-related measures in direct democracy contests such as California's 1978 attempt to ban homosexual teachers. Using county-level data from state direct democracy elections held between 1978 and 2004, we develop and test a model of voter support for a pro-gay position in each of these elections. We conclude with a discussion of how patterns of voter opposition to same-sex marriage bans fits within the broader pattern of gay civil rights politics.

STATE POLICYMAKING, SAME-SEX
MARRIAGE, AND MORALITY POLITICS

An uncomfortable tension between judicial and legislative action characterizes the history of state policies regarding same-sex marriage. Although a few cases brought in the 1970s did receive national attention, it was not until the 1993 *Baehr v. Lewin* (later *Baehr v. Miike*) ruling by the Supreme Court of Hawaii that states began to worry that they might be forced to recognize same-sex marriages from other states. In the Hawaii case the state supreme court ruled that the state constitution did not allow Hawaii to ban marriages between same-sex couples because such a policy was unconstitutional gender discrimination. The ruling led most states to adopt statutory bans on same-sex marriage by 2000, caused Hawaii to amend its constitution by constitutional convention to allow the legislature to ban same-sex marriage in 1998, and led the federal government to pass legislation denying same-sex couples the federal governmental benefits afforded to traditional opposite-sex married couples in 1996 (Haider-Markel 2001; Kersch 1997).

What led to such a rapid and consistent state and national government policy response? Two explanations arise. First, same-sex marriage appears to evoke a strong religious-based morality. For example, the Mormon Church, a leader in the push for protection of traditional marriage, argues, "This issue has nothing to do with civil rights. For men to marry men, or women to marry women is a moral wrong" (Goldberg-Hiller 2002, 6). Second, although gay rights advocates have fought to ensure that inclusion of sexual orientation in anti-discrimination laws is viewed as a civil right, the stakes involved in recognition of same-sex marriage make this extension of the civil rights comparison more difficult. The practice not only deals with a set of legal obligations and rights, but it also includes a social and religious component that is not as prevalent in other gay rights issues. Indeed, marriage is a creation of religious traditions and, in social terms, marriage has served as the central organizational structure in society in which children are raised. Meanwhile, most arguments in support of gay civil rights are not typically based in morality, nor are they developed from a perspective that is focused on the needs of gay parents, though certainly these arguments could be made. Thus, it seems clear to us from the outset that same-sex marriage may evoke a stronger version of morality politics that is discussed, but not always evident, in previous research on gay rights (see Barclay and Fisher 2003; Button et al. 1997; Haider-Markel and Meier 1996, 2003; Wald et al. 1996).

The morality politics framework, like the more general policy typology theory developed by Lowi (1972), suggests that the policy type drives the pattern of politics involved. In the case of morality politics, the issue is highly salient to the media and political elites, one side tends to define the issue in terms of a religion-based morality, the issue tends to be symbolic and presented as not technically complex, and citizens, motivated by technical simplicity and high salience, are more likely to participate in the political process (Haider-Markel 2001; Haider-Markel and Meier 1996, 2003; Meier 1994; Mooney 1999). In addition, morality politics tends to be characterized by intense and uncompromising positions, making the issues under consideration seem intractable unless a large majority supports one position or another (Mooney 1999). Thus, in morality politics we should expect that policymaking is strongly influenced by the following:

· Issue salience: morality policies are highly salient
· Partisanship: political parties stake out positions regarding the issue
· Public opinion: given high salience and party positions, policy will reflect public preferences
· Religious beliefs: religious doctrine, adherents, and perhaps groups will play a role in policymaking

In addition, given the lack of technical complexity and high salience, bureaucratic agents and interest groups should normally play less of a role in morality policymaking (Haider-Markel and Meier 1996; Meier 1994; Mooney 1999; Mooney and Lee 1995).

The politics of same-sex marriage, however, may have some special characteristics. This issue has clearly been a highly salient one over the past ten years (Barclay and Fisher 2003). Furthermore, as the issue of same-sex marriage bans has been increasingly decided in direct democracy contests instead of in legislatures (Melzer 2005), interest groups can indeed play a stronger role on the campaign trail than legislative office lobbying (Roh and Haider-Markel 2003). And, indeed, this seems to be the case. For example, as an April 2005 vote on the issue approached in Kansas, gay activists formed a statewide group against the referendum—the first time such a group had formed in Kansas—and religious conservatives pumped at least $182,000 (compared to $80,000 spent by opponents) into a campaign that was nearly guaranteed victory (O'Toole Buselt and Painter 2005).

The characteristics of gay-related policy as a type of morality policy suggest that voting patterns related to same-sex marriage should be influenced by

1. citizen and group forces, including religious values and interest groups, that can influence both issue salience and preferences (Mooney and Lee 1995; Haider-Markel 1999b),
2. political forces, such as partisanship, since elected officials stake out positions (Haider-Markel and Meier 1996, 2003), and
3. environmental forces, such as demographic characteristics that reflect public preferences regarding gay rights and the traditional family (Haider-Markel and Meier 2003).

Previous investigations of the adoption of gay-related policies appear to fit this pattern. In fact, a number of researchers have determined that governments are more likely to adopt antidiscrimination policies when there is higher urbanization, higher Democratic partisanship, higher gay interest group resources, more racial diversity, and weaker religious beliefs (Button et al. 1996; Haeberle 1996; Haider-Markel and Meier 1996; Kane 2003; Wald et al. 1996). In the context of direct democracy contests, these factors weigh heavily on predicting voting patterns (Haider-Markel and Meier 1996), as do potential interest group resources and issue salience (Haider-Markel 1999; Haider-Markel and Meier 2003).

All indications are that same-sex marriage policymaking should reflect morality politics to an even greater extent than gay civil rights policymaking. In fact, Barclay and Fisher (2003) argue that same-sex marriage legislation evokes a more "visceral" reaction than antidiscrimination legislation, and this type of emotional response is what one expects in morality politics (Mooney 1999, 2000). In addition, the speed of policymaking concerning this issue and its high level of salience following the 1993 Hawaii Supreme Court decision (Kersch 1997) and the 2003 Supreme Judicial Court of Massachusetts decision are indicative of morality politics (Mooney 2000; Mooney and Lee 2000). Thus, if in fact the debate about same-sex marriage is "of a different political nature" than previous battles over gay civil rights, as suggested by Barclay and Fisher (2003), we should expect that morality politics variables will be more consistent and stronger predictors of voting patterns in same-sex marriage measures than they are on gay civil rights measures.

STATE-LEVEL GAY MARRIAGE INITIATIVES
AND REFERENDA PRIOR TO 2004

State-level direct democracy proposals to ban same-sex marriage provide interesting test cases for two reasons. The first is that evidence suggests that state legislative passage of bans on same-sex marriage may have more to do with the individual characteristics of the state that any sort of regional diffusion (Haider-Markel 2001a; Barclay and Fisher 2003). The second is that evidence suggests that direct democracy is more conducive to "tyranny of the majority" legislation (Gamble 1997; Haider-Markel and Meier 2003). In a systematic examination of civil rights legislation across the states, Gamble (1997) finds that initiative outcomes are less likely to protect the civil rights of minority groups than are less direct forms of democracy.

Prior to 2004, six statewide initiative votes on banning same-sex marriage had been held in five states: Alaska (1998), California (2000), Hawaii (1998), Nevada (2000, 2002), and Nebraska (2000). (See table 13.1.)[1] In each case the measures were introduced as part of a national response to the Hawaii same-sex marriage ruling. Each of these measures, except California's, was a proposal to amend the state constitution. In California, Proposition 22 was simply a citizen initiative to change statutory law. The measure was popularly known as the Knight Initiative for the Republican state senator who spearheaded the effort. Proposition 22 stated that "only marriage between a man and a woman is valid."

In Nebraska a similar petition effort, directed by the Nebraska Family Council and the Non-Partisan Family Coalition (Bauer 2000) with the support of the United Methodist Church (Ostling 2000), was able to pass a constitutional amendment stating that same-sex marriages were neither valid nor recognized. This was of particular interest given that it followed unsuccessful attempts to pass legislation banning same-sex marriage in the previous year's legislative session (O'Brien 2000). In Nevada the Protection of Marriage initiative required two votes, one in 2000 and one in 2002, to successfully pass a state constitutional amendment that banned same-sex marriage. Unlike the majority of states, none of these three states had statutory laws that specifically banned the legal recognition of same-sex marriage prior to voting on the direct democracy proposals.

In all four elections the measures passed by large margins. This is in contrast to gay civil rights initiatives in general, which have tended to

TABLE 13.1.   Direct democracy measures taken to ban same-sex marriage.

STATE	DATE	DESCRIPTION	FOR	AGAINST
Alaska	1998	Constitutional amendment	68	32
Hawaii	1998	Constitutional amendment	69	31
California	2000	Statutory law	61.4	38.6
Nebraska	11/2000	Constitutional amendment; also covers other relationships	70	30
Nevada	2000	Constitutional amendment	69	31
Nevada	11/2002	Constitutional amendment	67	33
Missouri	8/2004	Constitutional amendment	70.7	29.3
Louisiana	9/2004	Constitutional amendment; also covers other relationships	78	22
Arkansas	11/2004	Constitutional amendment; also covers other relationships	75	25
Georgia	11/2004	Constitutional amendment; also covers other relationships	76	24
Kentucky	11/2004	Constitutional amendment; also covers other relationships	75	25
Michigan	11/2004	Constitutional amendment; also covers other relationships	59	41
Mississippi	11/2004	Constitutional amendment	86	14
Montana	11/2004	Constitutional amendment	66	33
North Dakota	11/2004	Constitutional amendment; also covers other relationships	73	27
Ohio	11/2004	Constitutional amendment; also covers other relationships	62	38
Oklahoma	11/2004	Constitutional amendment; also covers other relationships	76	24
Oregon	11/2004	Constitutional amendment	57	43
Utah	11/2004	Constitutional amendment; also covers other relationships	66	34
Kansas	4/2005	Constitutional amendment; also covers other relationships	70	30

Note: Data are from the respective secretaries of state.

closely divide the electorate, although the gay community tends to lose these battles (Gamble 1997; Haider-Markel and Meier 2003). Variance between counties was significantly different between the states, however with Californian's support for the gay marriage initiative ranging from 31 percent to 81 percent and Nevada 2000 ranging only from 64 percent to 84 percent.

To better understand the politics involved in these direct democracy contests and the applicability of the morality politics framework, it seems fruitful to examine a couple of these cases in more detail. Below we briefly discuss the cases of California and Nebraska.

CALIFORNIA

California presents an especially interesting case given its distinction as one of the more progressive states in the Union and the presence of a highly mobilized gay community. Indeed, the influence of gay political groups in the state is evidenced by the fact that California is one of the few states with a domestic partner registry. It also extends domestic partner benefits to state employees. The state has adopted strong laws regarding discrimination on the basis of sexual orientation in employment, public accommodations, and education, and it bans hate crimes.

Conservative Republicans made multiple failed attempts to pass legislation banning the recognition of same-sex marriages in California.[2] Although voting margins were often close, the failure to pass a ban was due to significant opposition from Democrats and gay lobbying groups and to the successful attachment of amendments that were unpalatable to Republicans.

The first attempt began in late 1995 when Assembly member Pete Knight (R-Palmdale) introduced Assembly Bill (AB) 1982. Before key committee votes, local affiliates of Concerned Women of America flooded the capital distributing copies of *The Ultimate Target of the Gay Agenda: Same Sex Marriage* and information packets presenting the forced recognition of same-sex marriages as imminent. Republican legislators and their staff also attended an information session on legislation to ban same-sex marriage led by the national leader of the Traditional Values Coalition, the Reverend Lou Sheldon. Buoyed by what appeared to be significant public support—a poll of Californian adults revealed that 60 percent were opposed to same-sex marriage (Stall 1996)—conservative Republicans thought the ban would pass through the legislature relatively easily.

The measure did pass the Assembly on a vote of 41 to 31. Only Democrats opposed the bill, though three Republicans abstained from voting. It was strongly supported by Governor Pete Wilson and Attorney General Dan Lungren. The bill was all but killed when a "poison pill" amendment was attached to AB 1982 on July 9 in the Senate Judiciary Committee that would have provided lesbian and gay couples with domestic partner status, including registration and benefits. The committee approved the amendment by a vote of 5 to 3, with all Democrats voting in support (Gunnison 1996; Keen 1996). With the amendment attached, Democratic leaders and gay groups were convinced that Republican legislators would not support the bill (Keen 1996). On the Senate floor Republicans tried to strip out the amendment but failed on a 21 to 20 vote, with a tiebreaker vote cast by the Senate president. With the amendment attached the bill was sent to the inactive file (Keen 1996).

Another 1996 same-sex marriage bill in California was AB 3227. Knight introduced the bill in February when it appeared that his original bill, AB 1982, would not survive in the Senate. Although AB 3227 was similar to AB 1982, it included legislative findings on the issue and attempted more forcefully to establish California policy concerning same-sex marriage in a way that AB 1982 did not. The bill was strongly opposed by Assembly Democrats. Several Republicans wrote a public letter to Knight asking him to withdraw the bill. The bill moved forward slowly, passing the Assembly Judiciary Committee on May 8, just before the May 10 joint legislative deadline for committee action on Assembly bills. Although the bill was scheduled for a floor vote on May 15, Knight apparently did not believe he had the votes to pass AB 3227 and had the bill placed in the inactive file.

In 1997 California Republicans again introduced two measures to ban same-sex marriage: AB 800 and SB 911. Both measures failed committee votes, with SB 911 going down in defeat after the Senate Judiciary Committee attached another "poison pill" amendment that would have entitled same-sex domestic partners to certain benefits.

Once it was clear that the legislature would not pass a ban, conservative Republicans turned to the direct democracy process. The statutory ban on same-sex marriage appeared on the ballot as Proposition 22 in 2000. The measure was divisive in preelection polls, with as few as 57 percent supporting the initiative in October 1999 (Ostrom 1999a). In addition to the seven hundred thousand voters that signed the petition to get the initiative on the ballot, the campaign was able to raise millions of dollars, bolstered by a hefty donation from the Catholic Church (ibid.). The Mormon Church directly supported the initiative, encouraging its members to provide financial and other support (Epstein 1999). The Mormon Church conducted similar campaigns in support of comparable measures in Alaska and Hawaii (Elias 1999). By November the Southern Baptist Convention also officially voiced its support for the initiative (Coleman 1999).[3] Advocates for the Knight Initiative launched a publicity campaign that attempted to appeal to traditional religious views of marriage. Proponents ended up spending more than $7.6 million on the campaign. Meanwhile, opposition groups attempted to portray the Knight Initiative as discrimination and a threat to civil rights (Smith 2000). Although opponents spent more than $4.7 million to defeat the measure, in the end voters overwhelmingly supported the measure by a 61 to 39 percent margin.

NEBRASKA

Nebraska ranks low on a scale of states with gay-friendly policies, but it has also not been a state to adopt significant antigay policies. An anecdotal examination of the initiative to amend the Nebraska state constitution provides evidence of the importance of interest groups and the power of direct democracy. Bills to ban same-sex marriage were proposed every year between 1996 and 2000 in the Nebraska state legislature. In 1998 and 1999, legislative maneuvering by Senator Ernie Chambers of Omaha, a vocal opponent of such legislation, has prevented this legislation from coming to a vote. Chambers, a key member of the Judiciary Committee, managed to keep the legislation stalled in committee. In 1997 the legislature fell one vote short of stopping a Chambers filibuster against one version of the defense of marriage bill (Hammel 2000a). Spurred by the legislature's failure to pass a defense of marriage act, the Nebraska Family Coalition, spearheaded by former state senator Jim McFarland, began a petition drive in support of a constitutional amendment.

McFarland justified the use of the initiative process by stating that only procedural obstacles had prevented this legislation from passing in the legislature. In fact, nearly 67 percent of Nebraska legislators supported the measure in principle (Hammel 2000a). During the petition drive, McFarland defended the amendment, stating that it was "more of an affirmation and clear declaration of public policy" than a "ban on same-sex marriage" (ibid.). The coalition's petition drive, which gathered more than 155,000 signatures, well above the approximately 105,000 necessary, required only about $100,000 in funding (Hammel 2000b, Reed 2000a). Prompted by Vermont's recognition of civil unions, the amendment also sought to prevent recognition of same-sex marriage under "another name" (Reed 2000a).

Following the success of the petition drive that ensured that Initiative 416 would be on the ballot in November, both sides targeted voters. Guyla Mills, a chairwoman of the Nebraska Family Coalition, gave evidence of the strong Christian forces involved, stating publicly: "I personally give credit to Jesus Christ. We give Him the glory. It is something that couldn't have been done without His guidance" (Reed 2000b). A spokeswoman for the "Vote No on DOMA" campaign, M. J. McBride, referred to the legislation as "proactive bigotry in legislation" (ibid.). Preelection polls indicated that although 59 percent of voters overall appeared to support Initiative 416, this increased to 69 percent when those polled lived in a rural setting. Lynn White, a sociologist at the University of Nebraska at Lincoln, suggested that this difference was in part due to exposure in urban areas to homosexual couples: "If you have gay or lesbian neighbors and you see them taking care of children, it changes your view" (Kotok 2000). Those supporting the initiative suggested, however, that the sight of same-sex couples is discomforting to most Nebraskans (ibid.). Groups favoring the amendment were able to raise almost $740,000, but opposition groups were able to raise only about $158,000. Almost $500,000 of the money spent in support of the amendment was raised from out-of-state sources (Reed 2000b). In the end voters passed the amendment with overwhelming support (70 to 30 percent). This support was relatively uniform across the counties.

Anecdotal examination of the drive to pass Initiative 416 in Nebraska suggests that urban areas were less supportive of the measure than were rural areas. The case also demonstrates the importance of organized interest groups, but it is not clear that they shaped the outcome.

MEASURES ON THE BALLOT IN 2004 AND BEYOND

During the 2004 election cycle, thirteen states faced referenda that would ban same-sex marriage (see table 13.1). In total, proponents of these measures spent almost $3.2 million in the campaigns, and opponents spent almost $3.4 million. In all of these states the measures were introduced as a reaction to the November 2003 decision by the Massachusetts Supreme Judicial Court to legalize the practice in that state. In addition, some policymakers may have been responding to the repeal of all state sodomy laws by the U.S. Supreme Court in its *Lawrence v. Texas* decision (June 2003) and to a series of Canadian court rulings on same-sex marriage in 2003 (Knickerbocker 2005). Some of these measures, such as those in Michigan and Ohio, banned virtually any recognition of same-sex relationships. Missouri voted on its measure during an August primary and adopted the change by a vote of 71 percent to 29 percent. Louisiana considered its measure in September, and the remaining states all held their elections to coincide with the general election in November. In addition, Kansas and Texas adopted constitutional amendments similar to those in Michigan and Ohio in 2005 with 70 percent and 76 percent, respectively, voting for the measures. Given the number of measures under consideration in state legislatures in 2006, another twelve states might adopt constitutional amendments banning the recognition of same-sex marriage by 2008.

A FIRST LOOK: NATIONAL OPINION AND STATE VOTING BEHAVIOR WITH REGARD TO SAME-SEX MARRIAGE

We begin our examination of patterns of opposition to constitutional bans on same-sex marriage and the possible different patterns of opposition on this issue in comparison to support for gay civil rights more generally by examining the factors that shape individual-level opinion about these issues. This analysis also tests the propositions of the morality politics framework and provides guidance for our analysis of voting behavior relating to same-sex marriage bans.

We analyzed two questions the Gallup Organization asked of adults nationwide in May 2004. First, Gallup asked respondents: "Should homosexuals have equal rights in terms of job opportunities?" Respondents answering "should not" were coded zero and respondents answering "should" were coded one. Second, Gallup asked: "Do you favor or oppose a constitutional amendment defining marriage as between a man and a woman?" Those favoring an amendment were coded zero and those opposing an amendment were coded one.

On the basis of previous studies of attitudes about gay-related policy, we included a number of control variables (Bowman et al. 2004; Brewer 2002, 2003a, 2003b; Pew Research Center 2003; Sherrill and Yang 2000). These included gender, marital status, parenthood, race, religiosity, income, education, political ideology, and partisanship. We expected that women, whites, the less religious, the wealthy, the highly educated, liberals, Democrats, those with no young children, and the unmarried would be more likely to support equal job opportunities for gays and lesbians and more likely to oppose a constitutional amendment banning same-sex marriage (Brewer 2002, 2003a, 2003b; Haider-Markel and Joslyn 2005; Sherrill and Yang 2000). Following Haider-Markel and Joslyn (2005) we also included an attribution variable based on the question: "In your view, is homosexuality something a person is born with, or is homosexuality due to factors such as upbringing and environment?" Respondents were allowed to refuse these choices and indicate "both" or "neither." We only used respondents who indicated "born with" (42 percent) or "upbringing/environment" (45 percent). These responses were coded zero and one, respectively.

TABLE 13.2. Opposition to a constitutional ban on same-sex marriage and support for equal job rights.

INDEPENDENT VARIABLES	OPPOSITION TO CONSTITUTIONAL BAN	MARGINAL EFFECTS	SUPPORT FOR EQUAL JOB OPPORTUNITIES	MARGINAL EFFECTS
White	.114		.844*	.032
	(.275)		(.404)	
Female	.276		.737*	.020
	(.184)		(.320)	
Age	−.011		−.029**	−.001
	(.006)		(.010)	
Liberal ideology	.547**	.133	.202	
	(.122)		(.197)	
Democratic partisanship	.193**	.047	.091	
	(.059)		(.095)	
Income	.095		.043	
	(.079)		(.132)	
Education	.199*	.048	.304	
	(.096)		(.161)	
Less religious	.252*	.062	.642*	.017
	(.128)		(.302)	
Not married	.343		.095	
	(.201)		(.342)	
No young children	.077		.360	
	(.209)		(.381)	
Believe homosexuality is caused by upbringing or environment	−.797**	−.192	−2.911**	−.103
	(.185)		(.615)	
Constant	−3.256**		2.318	
	(.771)		(1.421)	
(Pseudo) R²	.29		.25	
Log likelihood	787.311		159.376	
χ²	167.625**		104.99**	
Percent correctly predicted	71.60		91.01	
Number of cases	698		701	

Source: The data are from a Gallup national survey of one thousand adults, May 2–4, 2004.

Note: Coefficients are logistic regression coefficients in column 2 and OLS regression coefficients in column 4. Standard errors are in parentheses. Marginal effects is defined as the average change in predicted probability for significant variables moving its value −.5 to +.5 standard deviations from its mean. The dependent variables are based on the following survey questions: (1) "Do you favor (0) or oppose (1) a constitutional amendment defining marriage as between a man and a woman?" and (2) "Should homosexuals have equal rights in terms of job opportunities?" (should not = 0, should = 1).

$^*p < .05$
$^{**}p < .01$

The results of our logistic regression equations are displayed in table 13.2. Both models predict opinions fairly well and generally support our expectations. But as we anticipated, there are also differences across the models. Statistically significant variables predicting opposition to a constitutional amendment include ideology, partisanship, education, religiosity, and beliefs about the causes of homosexuality. Meanwhile, statistically significant variables predicting support for equal job opportunities include race, gender, age, religiosity, and beliefs about the causes of homosexuality. In sum, political orientations such as partisanship and ideology are better predictors of attitudes toward a constitutional ban than they are in predicting support for job protections. This pattern is what the morality politics model would predict: attitudes are more partisan and ideological. Furthermore, religiosity clearly plays a role in each model, but the estimates of the marginal effects of each variable also indicate that religiosity has a greater influence in the same-sex marriage model, relative to the other variables, than in the job opportunities model. Again, this is what the morality politics model would predict: religion-based morality plays a more important role in shaping preferences.

A SECOND LOOK: EXIT POLLS AND THE SAME-SEX MARRIAGE REFERENDA IN THE 2004 ELECTIONS

Next we looked for a pattern of morality politics by turning to exit polls conducted during the November 2004 election, in which eleven states considered constitutional amendments to ban same-sex marriage. Ideally, we would have individual-level exit poll data from all direct democracy contests involving same-sex marriage. Not all of these data are publicly available, however. Thus, below we examine aggregate statistics of voting patterns for eleven contests and individual-level data from exit polls in Ohio.

We compared the state-by-state data shown in table 13.3 by examining differences in voter opposition to the referenda by gender, race, age, religion, religiosity, born-again status, education, urban or rural residence, and voting support for Republican and Democratic presidential candidates.

Comparison of differences in voting based on voter characteristics illustrates a few interesting points. First, there were apparent differences across states. For example, the difference in the percentages of men and women opposing the referendum in Oregon was greater than it was in

TABLE 13.3. Percentage of voters against same-sex marriage amendments, 2004.

VOTER CHARACTERISTIC	ARKANSAS	GEORGIA	KENTUCKY	MICHIGAN	MISSISSIPPI	MONTANA	NORTH DAKOTA	OHIO	OKLAHOMA	OREGON	UTAH
Gender											
Male	24	21	20	37	17	31	23	37	24	41	33
Female	27	26	29	44	13	39	29	39	26	52	35
Race/ethnicity											
White	23	24	24	40	11	34	26	37	24	47	34
Black	34	20	30	41	23	—	—	39	26	—	—
Age, years											
18–29	35	28	32	49	17	43	40	49	30	56	27
60 or older	26	16	22	35	9	28	20	32	20	37	23
Higher education											
No college degree	—	—	—	38	—	—	—	33	—	40	—
College graduate	—	—	—	46	—	—	—	44	—	58	—
Political affiliation											
Democrat	35	36	36	55	25	51	36	56	33	72	75
Republican	11	12	11	22	5	14	13	19	13	14	15
Religion											
Protestant	20	20	22	34	11	25	23	31	21	34	25
None	59	44	39	65	—	73	—	65	43	67	81
Born again	17	11	15	20	6	13	10	14	14	18	—
Not born again	45	31	33	48	23	44	32	45	33	60	—
Church attendance											
Weekly	—	12	16	26	—	—	—	24	—	—	—
Never	—	54	47	65	—	—	—	61	—	—	—
Community Size											
Urban	37	22	29	42	—	49	35	46	29	—	32
Rural	23	18	20	36	13	30	22	33	21	—	36
Voted for Bush	12	12	11	—	—	14	15	19	15	15	16
Voted for Kerry	42	40	47	—	—	64	47	59	43	77	80

Source: Compiled by the authors from November 2004 exit poll data on CNN American Votes 2004 Web site: http://www.cnn.com/ELECTION/2004/pages/results/ballot.measures/.

Note: A dash denotes instances in which the question was not asked.

TABLE 13.4. Opposition to Ohio's constitutional ban on same-sex marriage, November 2004.

INDEPENDENT VARIABLES	OPPOSITION	MARGINAL EFFECTS
Race (white)	.615***	.137
	(.193)	.053
Sex (female)	.221*	
	(.131)	
Age	−.016	
	(.034)	
Conservative ideology	−1.056***	−.252
	(.114)	
Republican partisanship	−.617***	−.147
	(.089)	
Income	.082*	.020
	(.045)	
Education	.348***	.083
	(.066)	
Less religious	.274***	.065
	(.058)	
Not born again	.789***	.188
	(.165)	
Marital status (single)	.363**	.087
	(.150)	
Location (rural)	.009	
	(.063)	
Constant	−2.011***	
	(.631)	
(Pseudo) R^2	.26	
Log likelihood	−723.379	
χ^2	504.69***	
Percent correctly predicted	74.90	
Number of cases	1,430	

Source: Exit poll data from the 2004 general election, as collected in *National Election Pool General Election Exit Polls, 2004.*

Note: Coefficients are logistic regression coefficients in column 1 and marginal effects in column 2. Standard errors are in parentheses. Marginal effects show the average change in predicted probability for significant variables moving its value −.5 to +.5 standard deviations from its mean. The dependent variable is based on the following exit poll question: "How did you vote on Issue 1, defining marriage only as a union between man and a woman?" (yes = 0, no = 1).

*$p < .1$
**$p < .05$
***$p < .01$

Arkansas. Likewise, Democrats in Michigan were more likely to oppose the referendum than were those in Mississippi. Second, despite these types of variations, there were some consistent patterns in opposition to the measures. Overall, females, blacks, youth, the college-educated, Democrats, non-Protestants, those not born again, infrequent church attenders, urbanites, and Kerry voters were somewhat more likely to oppose the measures.

Table 13.4 presents the results of a logistic regression model analyzing opposition to the November 2004 ballot measure amending the Ohio constitution to ban same-sex marriage. The pattern is consistent with the data presented above. In general, Democrats, liberals, women, educated people, and the less religious voted against the measure. The roles of age and urbanization are less clear. Finally, the marginal effects estimates suggest that religious (born-again), ideological, and partisan variables have the greatest relative influence in the model, consistent with our arguments.

The combination of findings based on exit poll data is consistent with previous research on support of gay civil rights (Egan and Sherrill 2005; Wald et al. 1996; Sherrill and Yang 2000) and with the morality politics framework (Haider-Markel and Meier 1996). Furthermore, the largest differences are on religious and partisan dimensions, which is consistent with the pattern we observed in table 13.2, and which fits solidly with our expectation that morality politics would be more apparent in patterns of support of and opposition to same-sex marriage.

A THIRD LOOK: COUNTY-LEVEL VOTING PATTERNS IN DIRECT DEMOCRACY PROPOSALS

For our final confirmatory analysis we examined county-level voting patterns in state direct democracy contests where policy proposals sought to ban same-sex marriage. We compared patterns of voting on these measures to patterns of voting on other gay civil rights issues. Again, we expected that in both types of contests the morality politics model would provide a reasonable set of variables for explaining gay rights support, but key variables from the morality politics framework, such as religion and partisanship, should be relatively more important in models explaining opposition to same-sex marriage bans. We explain key variables and their measurement below.

DATA AND METHODS

For the first part of this analysis we combined the four statewide initiative and referenda votes on same-sex marriage taken prior to 2004 in one model and estimated a separate model of all the similar referenda held in 2004. We then merge both data sets for a combined analysis. The dependent variable was the percentage of the county vote in support of the gay community's position.[4] In our examination of same-sex marriage the unit of analysis was the state level, but for this analysis we shifted to the county level. By so doing, we were able to test the independent variables to see how they shaped the election's outcome.

Unfortunately, if data are aggregated at the county level, individual-level inferences are not possible. Tolbert and Hero (2001) argue, however, that aggregating data at the county level provides some unique advantages. The first is that the data cover the entire population in question, whereas individual-level survey data would necessarily only cover a small percentage of the population. Aggregate data also allow for direct analysis. They argue that this may be particularly important when examining civil rights initiatives given that opinions tend to fluctuate a great deal before and after elections.

INDEPENDENT VARIABLES

A number of variables were suggested by the morality politics model and our analysis above, including partisanship, religious affiliation, gender, minority status, urban residence, issue salience, age, and interest group resources. Although no direct indicator was available to measure the interest group resources of proponents and opponents at the county level, surrogates were available. We measured the potential resources of gay interest groups using census data about the number of self-reported same-sex unmarried partner households in 2000 as a percentage of the total population of households.[5] This measure has been used in the past and is perhaps the most reliable county-level measure of the potential resources of gay interest groups (Haider-Markel and Meier 2003; Hertzog 1996). We expected same-sex households to be positively associated with opposition to the measures.

In measuring the potential resources of groups supporting these measures, the issue becomes mixed with the religious morality elements of the morality politics model. In fact, measures of conservative religious denominations may capture both the potential interest group resources of opponents and the strength of religion-based morality preferences in each county (Haider-Markel and Meier 2003). Indeed, Protestant fundamentalists have played a key role in the introduction and passage of bans on same-sex marriage, whether through the legislature or at the ballot box (Barclay and Fisher 2003; Haider-Markel 2001). Thus, we included the total number of Protestant fundamentalists as a percentage of county population.[6] We expected that a Protestant fundamentalist presence would be negatively associated with opposition to the measures.

In morality politics, partisanship tends to play an important role. In particular, the Republican Party's focus on traditional family values is strongly associated with less support for gay civil rights and same-sex marriage (Lindaman and Haider-Markel 2002). We measured partisanship as the percentage of registered voters who are Democrats. Not all states track the partisanship of voters, however. For states that do not we measured partisanship based on the percentage of county voters supporting the Democratic candidate in the most recent presidential election. The expectation was that Democratic partisanship would be associated with opposition to the ballot measures.

Issue salience is a key component of the morality politics model and should play a significant role in same-sex marriage ballot contests. As policy, same-sex marriage bans were already salient in the states examined in our study because the issue had been placed before the voters. Salience may serve as an intervening variable in shaping the role of interest groups in the policymaking process and may make values a more important component of the debate (Haider-Markel and Meier 1996, 2003). With respect to a highly salient issue, interest groups are less likely to be able to effectively utilize their political and technical knowledge because citizen involvement is high. In these cases, citizens tend to be mobilized to support core values (Haider-Markel and Meier 2003). We captured issue salience by including a measure of the percentage of registered voters who voted on the ballot proposal in each county.

The literature about gay civil rights and the literature about same-sex marriage indicate that a number of additional demographic characteristics may affect the outcome of elections. Social diversity, education, age, and urbanism may further contribute to support for innovative social policy (Wald et al. 1996; Tolbert and Hero 2001). Haider-Markel and Meier (1996, 339) argue, however, that urbanism and education capture a dimension of morality politics by serving as a surrogate for opinion. This is because people living in urban areas and the more highly educated are more likely to be exposed to more diverse lifestyles. Exposure should be associated with greater tolerance (Sherrill and Yang 2000; Yang 2001). Our analysis of public opinion and exit polls above helps confirm this pattern. Education was measured by the percentage of adults with a college degree. Racial diversity was measured by the percentage of the population who report being nonwhite. Age was measured as the percentage of the population that is under the age of forty-five. Urbanism was simply measured as the percentage of county population living in an urban area. In addition, because Yang (2001) finds that women are more supportive of gay and lesbian issues, we included a variable for the number of men per one hundred women.

RESULTS AND ANALYSIS

Before examining the results of our weighted least squares regression models of county-level voting on same-sex marriage measures, recall that we have argued that the politics of same-sex marriage is likely to exhibit stronger morality politics patterns than the politics of gay civil rights more generally.[7] To conduct this comparison in terms of patterns of voting on ballot measures, we also modeled county-level voting on the nine statewide initiatives on gay civil rights, including those in California (1978), Oregon (1988, 1992, and 1994), Colorado (1992), Idaho (1994), Maine (1995 and 1998), and Washington (1997).[8] These measures varied in language and content, but the core issue in each was gay civil rights. Based on the findings in Haider-Markel and Meier (2003) and Lupia's (1994) findings concerning how voters make information shortcuts, we assumed that each of these gay rights measures was similar in the minds of voters. It is interesting that these initiatives, unlike the same-sex marriage bans, which were overwhelmingly supported, often divided the electorate, and that Washington nearly enacted a gay civil rights law. As with the same-sex marriage models, our dependent variable for the gay rights ballot contests was simply the percentage of each county's vote for the measure. All of the independent variables were the same and are compared across the models.

The results of our analysis are displayed in table 13.5. For purposes of analysis, all of the gay civil rights contests were pooled in one data set (column 1), all of the pre-2004 same-sex marriage bans were pooled (column 2), and all of the 2004 same-sex marriage bans were pooled and analyzed in a separate data set (column 3).

In each case the models predicted voting quite well, with nearly all of the variables showing a statistically significant relationship with the dependent variable in the expected directions. Partisanship, Protestant fundamentalism, and being a gay household clearly played a significant role in each of the models. Counties with more Democrats had higher levels of support for the gay rights measures and more opposition to the same-sex marriage measures. Counties with more Protestant fundamentalists were more strongly opposed to the gay rights measures and

TABLE 13.5. Determinants of pro-gay voting patterns by county in state direct democracy contests, 1978–2004.

INDEPENDENT VARIABLES	GAY CIVIL RIGHTS VOTES (1)		PRE-2004 SAME-SEX MARRIAGE BAN VOTES (2)		2004 SAME-SEX MARRIAGE BAN VOTES (3)	
Partisan identification as Democrat	.230***		.055***		.474***	
	(.056)	.230	(.013)	.054	(.019)	.474
Protestant fundamentalism	−.604***		−.332***		−.074***	
	(.194)	−.604	(.040)	−.332	(.013)	−.074
Voter turnout	.064		.277***		.162***	
	(.040)	.064	(.059)	.277	(.013)	.162
Gay household	7.128***		12.495***		8.055***	
	(1.374)	7.128	(1.342)	12.495	(1.243)	8.055
Age >45 years	.944***		.665***		−.126**	
	(.119)	.944	(.173)	.665	(.049)	−.126
College education	.307***		1.087***		.146***	
	(.077)	.306	(.086)	1.087	(.028)	.146
Population diversity	.073*		−.090**		−.199**	
	(.041)	.073	(.043)	−.090	(.015)	−.199
Male-to-female ratio	−.561***		−.006		.206***	
	(.122)	−.561	(.044)	.006	(.037)	.206
Urban residence	.046***		.153***		.175***	
	(.014)	.046	(.020)	.153	(.009)	.174
Constant	47.516**		−25.619***		23.703***	
	(11.257)		(5.789)		(3.711)	
F score	67.66***		68.67***		451.10***	
R^2	.65		.78		.80	
Adjusted R^2	.64		.77		.80	
Number of cases	344		185		1038	

Sources: Haider-Markel and Meier 2003; Lupia 1994.

Note: The dependent variable is the percentage of the county vote favoring a position that was advocated by the gay community. Coefficients are weighted least squares regression coefficients. The weight variable is the number of registered voters in each county. Standard errors are in parentheses. Marginal effects are reported to the right of the standard errors.

*p < .1
**p < .05
***p < .01

more supportive of the same-sex marriage bans. And counties with more same-sex partner households were more strongly opposed to the same-sex marriage bans and more supportive of the gay rights measures. Likewise, more urbanized counties and counties with a more highly educated population were more supportive of gay rights and less supportive of the same-sex marriage bans. Diversity, percentage of the population under forty-five, and the male-to-female ratio did not perform quite as expected. Diversity was positively associated with support for the gay rights measures but negatively associated with opposition to the same-sex marriage bans. This is an indication that the politics of same-sex marriage is different from the politics of gay rights more generally. Indeed, our analysis in tables 13.2 and 13.3 suggested that minorities might be more strongly opposed to same-sex marriage than are whites. Likewise, in counties with a larger youth population, there was more support for gay rights measures and more opposition to same-sex marriage bans prior to 2004. In the 2004 ballot contests, however, there was a weak negative association between youth in a county and opposition to same-sex marriage bans. Perhaps this is a fluke of the data or a pattern in the particular states that addressed the issue in 2004, but it does provide more evidence that the politics of same-sex marriage might be different. Finally, a higher male-to-female ratio is associated with less support for gay rights measures but greater opposition to the same-sex marriage measures in 2004. Again, this finding is consistent with the analysis of public opinion about gay rights that we conducted for table 13.2, but regarding same-sex marriage, research suggests that there should be little difference between the preferences of men and women. Our findings indicate that a higher female population is associated with greater opposition to the same-sex marriage bans. In sum, once again the pattern suggests that the politics of same-sex marriage is different than that of gay civil rights.

Finally, we also suspected that the relative importance of variables in the models would differ. In particular, we argued that partisanship, issue salience, and religious forces should play a greater role in ballot contests involving same-sex marriage than they do in the contests involving gay civil rights more generally. To compare the relative effect, we estimated the marginal effects for each of the independent variables in each model. The marginal effects coefficients (reported to the right of the variable standard errors in table 13.5) for each model suggest that the gay household variable is the most important variable in each model. Although we included this variable as a measure of potential gay interest group resources, we also suspect that it captures underlying values in the population. Where there is a greater diversity of lifestyles and families there should be greater tolerance for nontraditional lifestyles (Haider-Markel and Meier 2003). As such, this variable seems to capture underlying support for core values in regard to equality. Given that such values are an important component of morality politics, perhaps it is not surprising that this variable has greater relative influence in the two models of same-sex marriage voting than in the gay civil rights model.

Our measure of issue salience, voter turnout, performed as expected. Its relative influence was greatest in the same-sex marriage models, which is consistent with morality politics. Yet partisanship and religious fundamentalism did not perform as cleanly as expected. Partisanship played the greatest relative role in the model of 2004 ballot measures and the weakest relative role in the model of same-sex marriage measures prior to 2004. We suspect that this was partly a function of the nature of the states that voted on the issue before 2004, but we cannot be certain. Likewise, although morality was declared to be the key component of the 2004 elections, our measure of religious conservatism was weakest relative to other variables in the 2004 model. In part this seems to be a function of collinearity between religious conservatives and gay house-holds. As the relative influence of gay households increases, the relative influence of religious conservatives decreases. Thus, it seems that there may be a balancing act between core values. As county characteristics suggest greater support for traditional religious values, the relative influence of equality or acceptance for alternative lifestyles might decline, and vice versa. At minimum, this final set of results does indeed suggest that the politics of same-sex marriage is different from the politics of gay rights, but the differences appear to be more complex than we expected. Nevertheless, our results as detailed in each section of this chapter point to a pattern of politics consistent with the morality politics framework.

CONCLUSION

Our exploration of state-level efforts to ban same-sex marriage via direct democracy focused on the proposition that the politics of same-sex marriage exhibits a stronger pattern of morality politics than does the politics of gay civil rights generally. We believed this would be the case because the issue of same-sex marriage appears to invoke a more intense conflict between first principles—in this case, notions of the traditional family as outlined in religious traditions versus equality for all individuals—which is the heart of the morality politics framework.

We tested our proposition in three ways. First, we compared the determinants of individual opinion about gay civil rights to the determinants of individual opinion about a constitutional ban on same-sex marriage using national polls. Second, using exit polls from the 2004 elections, we compared the characteristics of voters who supported state constitutional bans on same-sex marriage to the characteristics of voters who opposed these measures. Finally, we investigated cases in which same-sex marriage bans were placed before the voters in state-level direct democracy contests. In particular, using the morality politics framework, we sought to explain patterns of voter support for these measures and how attitudes toward these measures compared to attitudes toward previous gay-related measures in direct democracy contests such as California's 1978 attempt to ban homosexual teachers.

Our findings are fairly conclusive, and they highlight three important points. First, based on our analysis of individual-level opinion in national polls and voter opposition to same-sex marriage bans in exit polls, individuals are generally supportive of constitutional bans on same-sex marriage though these bans may deny equality to homosexual couples. Based on the trends in support for these measures, it seems likely that voters will support them in virtually any state where they appear on the ballot.

Second, in our examinations of individual-level opinion, exit poll data from referenda banning same-sex marriage, and county-level patterns of voting against these measures, we find that the politics of same-sex marriage is different from the politics of gay rights more generally. In particular, we find that factors suggested by the morality politics framework, such as adherence to first principles, partisanship, and issue salience, play a more prominent role in same-sex marriage politics. Some of our evidence regarding state constitutional bans on same-sex marriage is mixed, however, and this might indicate that changes to statutory law involve a different pattern of politics as opposed to changes in constitutional law.

Third, our results have implications for the broader debate concerning homosexual relationships and families. If the politics of same-sex marriage is in fact different from the politics of gay rights, will we find this same pattern in issues such as civil unions, domestic partnerships, and laws and regulations regarding foster care and adoption by homosexual couples? Such questions are beyond the scope of our study, but we believe our framework would be useful to scholars hoping to understand these other issues as well.

Finally, given the first principles at stake in the debate about same-sex marriage and the lack of desire to compromise by those on either side, the issue may pose problems for smooth functioning of our democracy. Indeed, our democratic institutions are designed for compromise and may become deadlocked on issues for which compromise seems unlikely.

Similar to issues such as abortion, Americans might find themselves in a heated long-term debate in which neither side can claim full victory.

ENDNOTES

1. The 1998 Alaska referendum and the Hawaii referendum are not included in most of our analysis because of data limitations. Hawaii has only four counties, making county-level analysis futile, and Alaskan jurisdictions do not coincide with census data.
2. Unless otherwise noted, information about California is based on correspondence with Jennifer L. Richard, a legislative assistant in the state Assembly, and Laurie McBride of LIFE Lobby.
3. These represent general trends of support. Some California bishops and one Roman Catholic priest did openly oppose the measure (Werner 2000).
4. All voting- and election-related data are from the respective secretaries of state.
5. The 2000 census data are used for all of the case studies because the Bureau of the Census reports that owing to measurement differences, the measures of same-sex unmarried partners from 1990 to 2000 are not directly comparable; however, they are highly correlated. Haider-Markel (1997b) established the validity of this measure for the 1990 reported same-sex unmarried partner households by demonstrating that it correlates highly with membership in gay interest groups.
6. Data are from Glenmary Research Center (2004). Following Haider-Markel and Meier (2003), denominations regarded as Protestant fundamentalist were Churches of God, the Church of Jesus Christ of Latter-Day Saints, Churches of Christ, the Church of the Nazarene, the Mennonite Church, the Conservative Baptist Association, the Missouri Synod of Lutherans, the Church of Pentecostal Holiness, the Salvation Army, the Seventh-Day Adventist Church, the Southern Baptist Convention, and the Wisconsin Synod of Lutherans.
7. Our models were weighted with a variable for the number of registered voters in each county. By weighting the models we were estimating how each of the independent variables is associated with the outcome of each election, not simply the vote in opposition in each county.
8. We did not include Oregon's 2000 ban on gay clubs in schools and Maine's 2000 referendum to pass a gay civil rights law.

REFERENCES

Bailey, Michael, Lee Sigelman, and Clyde Wilcox. 2003. Presidential persuasion on social issues: A two-way street? *Political Research Quarterly* 56 (1): 49–58.

Barclay, Scott, and Shauna Fisher. 2003. The states and differing impetus for divergent paths on same-sex marriage, 1990–2001. *Policy Studies Journal* 31 (3): 331–52.

Bauer, Scott. 2000. Petition will be circulated to effectively ban same-sex marriages in Nebraska. Associated Press, May 23.

Brewer, Paul R. 2002. Framing, value words, and citizens' explanations of their issue opinions. *Political Communication* 19 (3): 303–16.

———. 2003a. The shifting foundations of public opinion about gay rights. *Journal of Politics* 65 (4): 1208–20.

———. 2003b. Values, political knowledge, and public opinion about gay rights. *Public Opinion Quarterly* 67 (2): 173–201.

Button, J. W., B. A. Rienzo, and K. D. Wald. 1997. *Private lives, public conflicts: Battles over gay rights in American communities.* Washington, DC: CQ Press.

Coleman, Jennifer. 1999. California's Southern Baptists back anti–gay marriage initiative, Associated Press, November 17.

Egan, Patrick J., and Kenneth Sherrill. 2005. Neither an in-law nor an outlaw be: Trends in Americans' attitudes toward gay people. *Public Opinion Pros* (February). http://www.publicopinionpros.com/.

Elias, Thomas D. 1999. Mormons join political fray: Church urges members to vote for California ballot issue that could ban gay marriages. *Atlanta Journal-Constitution,* July 29.

Epstein, Edward. 1999. Supervisor hits Mormons for politicking. *San Francisco Chronicle,* July 7.

Gamble, Barbara S. 1997. Putting civil rights to a popular vote. *American Journal of Political Science* 41 (1): 245–69.

Glenmary Research Center. 2004. *Churches and church membership in the United States, 1960–2000* (data CD). Atlanta: Glenmary Research Center.

Golebiowska, Ewa A. 1996. The pictures in our heads and individual-targeted tolerance. *Journal of Politics* 58 (4): 1010–34.

Gunnison, Robert B. 1996. Setback for foes of gay unions: Senate panel dilutes bill against same-sex marriages. *San Francisco Chronicle,* July 10, A16.

Haeberle, Steven H. 1996. Gay men and lesbians at City Hall. *Social Science Quarterly* 77 (1): 190–97.

Haider-Markel, Donald P. 1999. AIDS and gay civil rights: Politics and policy at the ballot box. *American Review of Politics* 20 (Winter): 349–75.

———. 2001a. Policy diffusion as a geographical expansion of the scope of political conflict: Same-sex marriage bans in the 1990s. *State Politics and Policy Quarterly* 1 (1): 5–26.

———. 2001b. Shopping for favorable venues in the states: Institutional influences on legislative outcomes of same-sex marriage bills. *American Review of Politics* 22 (Spring): 27–54.

Haider-Markel, Donald P., and Mark Joslyn. 2005. Attributions and the regulation of marriage: Considering the parallels between race and homosexuality. *PS: Political Science and Politics* 38 (2): 233–40.

Haider-Markel, Donald P., and Kenneth J. Meier. 1996. The politics of gay and lesbian rights: Expanding the scope of the conflict. *Journal of Politics* 58 (2): 332–49.

———. 2003. Legislative victory, electoral uncertainty: Explaining outcomes in the battles over lesbian and gay civil rights. *Review of Policy Research* 20 (4): 671–90.

Hammel, Paul A. 2000a. Same-sex marriages targeted: A conservative group may seek to place a ban on recognition of the unions in Nebraska's constitution. *Omaha World Herald*, April 13.

———. 2000b. Group closer to petition on same-sex union ban. *Omaha World Herald*, April 18.

Herek, Gregory M. 2002. Gender gaps in public opinion about lesbians and gay men. *Public Opinion Quarterly* 66 (1): 40–66.

Hertzog, Mark. 1996. *The lavender vote: Lesbians, gay men, and bisexuals in American electoral politics.* New York: New York University Press.

Kane, Melinda D. 2003. Social movement policy success: Decriminalizing state sodomy laws, 1969–1998. *Mobilization: An International Journal* 8 (3): 313–34.

Keen, Lisa. 1996. Marriage vote to fall on Hawaii trial's eve; California's anti-gay measure stalls. *Washington Blade*, August 30, 1.

Kersch, Ken L. 1997. Full faith and credit for same-sex marriages? *Political Science Quarterly* 112 (1): 117–36.

Knickerbocker, Brad. 2005. Ripples spread as states vote on same-sex marriage. *Christian Science Monitor,* April 7.

Kotok, David. State not ready for gay marriages in poll and words; Nebraskans support ban of same-sex unions; *World Herald* Poll." *Omaha World Herald,* September 17.

Lindaman, Kara, and Donald P. Haider-Markel. 2002. Issue evolution, political parties, and the culture wars. *Political Research Quarterly* 55 (1): 91–110.

Lowi, Theodore J. 1972. Four systems of policy, politics, and choice. *Public Administration Review* 32 (4): 298–310.

Meier, Kenneth J. 1994. *The politics of sin: Drugs, alcohol, and public policy.* Armonk, NY: Sharpe.

Melzer, Eartha. 2005. Kansans to vote on marriage amendment: Polls show closer vote than many expected. *Washington Blade*, April 1.

Mooney, Christopher Z. 1999. The politics of morality policy: Symposium editor's introduction. *Policy Studies Journal* 27 (4): 675–80.

———. 2000. The decline of federalism and the rise of morality-policy conflict in the United States. *Publius* (Winter–Spring): 171–88.

Mooney, Christopher Z., and Mei-Hsien Lee. 1995. Legislating morality in the American states: The case of pre-*Roe* abortion regulation reform. *American Journal of Political Science* 39 (3): 599–627.

———. 2000. The influence of values on consensus and the contentious morality policy: U.S. death penalty reform, 1956–1982. *Journal of Politics* 62 (1): 223–39.

National Election Pool, Edison Media Research, and Mitosky International. 2004. *National election pool general election exit polls, 2004* [computer file]. ICPSR version. Somerville, NJ: Edison Media Research/New York: Mitofsky International [producers], 2004. Ann Arbor, MI: Inter-university Consortium for Political and Social Research [distributor].

O'Brien, Maggie. 1999. Bill before Judiciary Committee would invalidate same-sex marriages. Associated Press, February 26.

Ostling. Richard N. 2000. Methodists seem headed toward keeping stand against homosexual activity. Associated Press, May 9.

Ostrom, Mary Anne. 1999. Battle over an initiative to ban same-sex marriage in California turning bitter. *San Jose Mercury News*, October 15.

O'Toole Buselt, Lori, and Steve Painter. 2005. Getting out the vote on marriage amendment: Whirlwind campaign. *Wichita Eagle*, March 30.

Reed, Leslie. 2000a. Marriage petitions submitted; Gay-union foes gather over 155,000 signatures for Nebraska's proposed constitutional amendment. *Omaha World Herald*, July 7.

———. 2000b. Supporters raise $739,715; Foes of amendment to ban same-sex unions collect $157,992." *Omaha World Herald*, October 31.

Roh, Jongho, and Donald P. Haider-Markel. 2003. All politics is not local: National forces in state abortion initiatives. *Social Science Quarterly* 84 (1): 15–31.

Romney, Lee. 2004. In S.F., a test case for gays; Mayor orders study on legality of same-sex marriages, calling ban unconstitutional. *Los Angeles Times*, February 11.

Sherrill, Kenneth, and Alan Yang. 2000. From outlaws to in-laws: Anti-gay attitudes thaw. *Public Perspective* 11 (1): 20–31.

Stall, Bill. 1996. The *Times* poll: Voters back prop. 209, but margin declining; Opinion: Californians also favor giving judges discretion on three-strikes law and oppose gay marriages. *Los Angeles Times*, July 21, A1.

Tolbert, Caroline, and Rodney E. Hero. 2001. Dealing with diversity: Racial ethnic conflict and social policy change. *Political Research Quarterly* 54 (3): 571–604.

Wald, Kenneth D., James W. Button, and Barbara A. Renzo. 1996. The politics of gay rights in American communities: Explaining antidiscrimination ordinances and policies. *American Journal of Political Science* 40 (4): 1152–78.

Werem, Regina, and Bill Winders. 2001. Who's "in" and who's "out": State fragmentation and the struggle over gay rights, 1974–1999. *Social Problems* 48 (3): 386–410.

Werner, Erica. 2000. Churchgoers, spiritual leaders weighing in on anti-gay marriage initiative. *Associated Press*, March 6.

Yang, Alan S. 2001. *The 2000 National Election Study and gay and lesbian rights: Support for equality grows*. Washington, DC: Policy Institute of the National Gay and Lesbian Task Force Foundation.

THE UNITED STATES IN COMPARATIVE CONTEXT

David Rayside

Thinking through the politics of marriage in the United States and comparing developments there with other countries commonly leads down two distinct paths. One line of analysis points to the "exceptionalism" of the American case, displaying an array of opposing forces unlike those anywhere else, in an institutional context providing unusual openings and impediments. The other approach emphasizes the wide variety within the United States and in the countries with which it is frequently compared and suggests that even with its unusual features, the American case is not exceptional.[1] Elements of both analytical paths apply to a consideration of lesbian and gay marriage. Over the course of the 1990s and the early years of the twenty-first century, public policy and law in several countries moved toward a recognition of same-sex relationships. These developments were most pronounced in Canada and northern Europe but were also substantial in New Zealand, South Africa, Israel, and parts of Australia and within a few American jurisdictions. The result is widespread if uneven recognition of lesbian and gay relationships, with full equality granted nowhere.

Explaining differences in outcome requires a descriptive overview acknowledging the complexity and limitations in changes outside the United States and the importance of pioneering developments on a number of issue fronts within American jurisdictions. This will show very rapid change taking place in Canada and Europe especially while developments in the United States spread slowly and with great struggle, never "taking off."

The first step, though, is to acknowledge that shifts in policy and law are located within broader changes in relationship "regimes." In other words, the social, religious, and political regulation of heterosexual relationships within any country is in constant flux, and in the countries on our comparative horizon these regimes have changed substantially over the past half-century. In some contexts, the particular ways in which these regimes have changed has eased the way toward recognition of lesbian and gay relationships.

FAMILY REGIMES

In public regard and institutional policy, the privileging of some family forms over others maintains a hierarchy of relationships. In the great majority of settings, the top rung in rights, obligations, and social respect is occupied by married heterosexual couples with children, followed by cohabiting or de facto heterosexual couples, monogamous same-sex couples, and then those that deviate more obviously from the marital norm.[2] State policy and law are cornerstones of relationship regimes, and in most jurisdictions, there are scores if not hundreds of statutory provisions that set boundaries around legitimate conjugality, regulating property rights, healthcare decision making, inheritance presumptions, parenting, obligations on separation, immigration, social insurance, taxation, the regulation of conflict of interest, and the legal regulation of sexual activity itself.

Family regimes are echoed in and supported through other institutions. Churches bless some unions and not others and see themselves as having a particularly prominent role in marriage. Newspapers routinely report marriages, births, and deaths in ways that celebrate some family forms more than others. The media in general will portray some relationships as routine and "public" and others as curious or "private."

Employers with family benefit programs recognize some of their employees' relationships and children but not others. Companies advertising products and services related to weddings and children will pitch to some audiences and not others.

Such regimes have undergone significant change in almost all industrialized countries over the course of the past century, and more rapidly in the past forty years. Among the most important changes have been in the norms and law regulating heterosexual marriage. Here we have seen major shifts toward formal equality between women and men, even if much de facto inequality remains. We have also seen an important reconfiguration of marriage toward the model of a contract. Restrictions on who can get married (based on religious affiliation, ethnicity, and race, for example) have been reduced or eliminated in law or in practice. Divorce has been made much easier to secure and the post-separation period governed by implied rights and obligations.

At the same time, in the last half-century, governments, courts, and private institutions have been gradually according some recognition to heterosexual de facto couples. But here we see more differences across countries. Canada has been among the countries at the forefront of recognizing what in that country are called "common law" couples, beginning soon after World War II and accelerating from the 1970s onward. By the mid-1990s, there were only a few areas left with significant differential treatment of married and de facto heterosexual couples by governments and employers.[3] Similar developments occurred in parts of northern Europe and Australia.

There were some states in the United States where particular steps were taken to recognize de facto couples, illustrated by a famous property division case involving actor Lee Marvin and his former partner (decided in 1976). From that time until now, court cases in California, Washington State, and other states have pushed boundaries in the same way, though nowhere to the extent we find in almost all Canadian jurisdictions. Many private employers, too, restrict family benefits to married couples, now a legal impossibility north of the border.

What this has meant is that in some countries, Canada being the best example, activists seeking recognition for lesbian and gay relationships have been able to secure most of the substantive rights and obligations traditionally associated with marriage by claiming equivalence to de facto heterosexual couples. Marriage has come to prominence in recent years, but more for symbolic than substantive reasons. Not so in the United States, where marriage emerged into prominence at a comparatively early state (the early 1990s), with loadings that were both substantive and symbolic.

COMPARATIVE OVERVIEW OF SAME-SEX RELATIONSHIP RECOGNITION

Canadian developments have a particular relevance for understanding the U.S. case, for there are important similarities between the two countries' legal systems, social policy systems, and political cultures.[4] On the other hand, shifts in public opinion and legal-political regulation of marriage highlight what might well be growing contrasts between the two countries' response to morality issues. Developments in a number of northern European countries bear some similarities to those in Canada, but the movement toward full marriage equality has been more conflictual and partial than is commonly believed. The treatment of parenting rights is a particularly dramatic example of the hesitation that has been evident in a range of European countries.

The first significant steps toward recognizing lesbian and gay relationships occurred at the end of the 1980s, with specific statutory recognition being granted in the Netherlands, Sweden and, most significant, in Denmark. (See table 14.1 for the historical spread of recognition of

TABLE 14.1. Historical spread of recognition of same-sex relationships, 1989–2001.

DATE	LOCALE	ACTION
1979	Netherlands	Inheritance and tenancy rights extended to same-sex partners
1984	Berkeley, CA	First U.S. local recognition of partners of government employees
1986	Denmark	Inheritance and taxation rights extended to partners
1987	Sweden	Limited recognition of couples in family law
1989	Denmark	Civil unions legislation, parenting rights excluded
	New York, NY	Court ruling extending inheritance rights to couples
1990–93	Canada	Major court rulings recognizing relationships for employment benefits
1991	Minnesota	Court ruling on guardianship rights for partners
1992	British Columbia	First legislation redefining *spouse* in health decisions
	Massachusetts	First state to extend benefits to partners of some state employees
	District of Columbia	Domestic partner registry created
	New York, NY	Second-parent adoption victory in court (1993–95: victories in five other states)
1993	Hawaii	Favorable court ruling on marriage
	Norway	Civil unions legislation, parenting rights excluded

TABLE 14.1. *(continued).*

DATE	LOCALE	ACTION
1994	Sweden	Civil unions legislation, parenting rights excluded
	Greenland	Civil unions legislation, parenting rights excluded
	Israel	Court ruling on employment benefits
	Spain	Housing rights extended to de facto couples
1994–96	Australia	Specific statutes recognizing same-sex relationships in the Australian Capital Territory
1995	Canada	Parenting legislation in British Columbia; positive court ruling in Ontario
1995–2001	New Zealand	Various specialized statutes recognizing partners
1996	Iceland	Civil unions legislation, parenting rights excluded
	Hungary	Rights in several areas extended to de facto couples, but not in parenting
1997	Hawaii	Civil unions legislation; major exceptions, including parenting
	Netherlands	Civil unions legislation
1998	Belgium	Limited legislation concerning cohabitation
	Oregon	Court ruling on employee benefits
	Spain	Civil unions legislation in Catalonia, parenting rights excluded
1999	Canada	Comprehensive recognition of de facto relationships by Supreme Court ruling, except for marriage
	France	Civil unions legislation, parenting rights and many others excluded
	Vermont	Court ruling on marriage
	California	Domestic partnership legislation, partial recognition
	Australia	Property law amendments include same-sex couples in Queensland and New South Wales
2000	Vermont	Civil unions legislation, excluding all federal law
	Spain	Civil unions legislation in Navarra, including adoption
	Netherlands	Marriage rights legislation, except foreign adoption
2001	Germany	Civil unions legislation, parenting rights excluded
	New Zealand	Rights extended in several areas to de facto couples
	Portugal	Civil unions legislation
	Australia	Some rights extended to domestic partners in Victoria

Sources: Robert Wintemute and Mads Adenaes, eds., *Legal Recognition of Same-Sex Relationships* (Oxford: Hart, 2001); Kathleen Lahey and Kevin Alderson, *Same-Sex Marriage: The Personal and the Political* (Toronto: Insomniac Press, 2004); Yuval Merin, *Equality for Same-Sex Couples* (Chicago: University of Chicago Press, 2002).
Note: Not all significant court rulings are included.

same-sex relationships.) At the same time, we see the first of what would become a steady stream of American rulings extending rights and obligations in particular policy areas, the first major case extending inheritance rights to a surviving gay partner in New York City.

The early 1990s saw a few such court rulings in other American states, most prominently in Hawaii, where the first significant victory with regard to marriage itself was secured.[5] In Canada, however, more sweeping shifts in relationship recognition patterns were being secured, if not as prominently. Several rulings by courts and labor tribunals, many pursued aggressively by labor unions, were making clear that same-sex couples had to be included in employment benefits programs, and perhaps also in many other policy areas.[6]

In the mid-1990s there was a wave of legislation across the Scandinavian countries, creating civil union regimes that widely recognized same-sex couples, though all of them pointedly excluded parenting rights. At the same time (1995), in the Canadian province of British Columbia, the legislature approved changes in adoption that extended almost all adoption rights to gay and lesbian couples. That year also saw an Ontario court ruling that interpreted Canada's Charter of Rights as prohibiting discrimination with respect to such parenting rights.

The year 1997 saw the enactment of the first American regime recognizing lesbian and gay relationships (in partly), with the state of Hawaii enacting a "consolation prize" at a time when marriage was being firmly denied. It was in that year, too, that the Netherlands became the first country to develop a comprehensive civil union regime that did not categorically exclude adoption rights.

A 1999 ruling by the Supreme Court of Canada (*M. v H.*) effectively eliminated any possibility of legally discriminating between same-sex and opposite-sex de facto couples, this in a context in which the differential treatment of married and de facto couples had been minimized (including the area of parenting). As in all previous court rulings and provincial laws (especially in British Columbia), this did not require registration, so that most rights and obligations associated traditionally with marriage would be assumed automatically. The provinces of Quebec and Nova Scotia were soon to create civil union registries, but with this ruling there would be little difference in the extent of recognition anywhere across the country. The federal government and all the provinces and territories were soon having to enact or draft legislation to formalize what the Supreme Court had ordered. This left only the marriage issue unresolved.

From this period onward, we see a wave of steps taken by courts and governments outside North America to recognize lesbian and gay relationships—in Israel, South Africa, New Zealand, and parts of Australia, Argentina, and Brazil—and especially in Europe. A rapidly growing list of countries within the European Union or desperate to enter it from the East enacted civil union regimes, most with major exclusions, parenting prominent among them. Even in Denmark, a 1999 law allowing a partner to adopt the child of a same-sex partner excluded children adopted from a foreign country and "stranger" adoptions from anywhere.[7]

By 2006 the most expansive of the national regimes requiring some form of registration were those in Spain, the Netherlands, Belgium, Sweden, Britain, and Germany. (Only since 2005 have these countries loosened or eliminated restrictions on adoption.) Most other western European countries and a few in eastern and central Europe also had registration systems for same-sex couples, albeit with restrictions (most commonly related to parenting). In late 2006, five of the United States had extended significant recognition to gay and lesbian couples within state and local jurisdictions—all through registration systems. A few countries in Europe and elsewhere extended substantial recognition to same-sex couples without the need for registration: New Zealand (via legislation), Israel, South Africa, Hungary (via court rulings on particular issues), and, of course, Canada.

In 2000 the Netherlands became the first jurisdiction to allow marriage. Even here and at this late date, however, there was nervousness about parenting. Adoption of foreign children was prohibited because of fear that countries that were the source of many such adoptions would take offense. This was second-class marriage, for no previous limitations had been placed on marriage as a result of concerns about how foreign governments would respond to the particulars of the couple. (Only in 2006 was that restriction removed.) When Belgium became the second country to allow gays and lesbians to wed, the right to adopt children was completely excluded until 2006.

Spain legislated the extension of full marriage to same-sex couples in 2005, the first regime outside Canada to do so without glaring discrimination. The European Union was increasingly obliging with at least some form of recognition of gay and lesbian couples in central and eastern Europe. The Union itself was slow to extend such recognition in its own institutions, but several governments saw the recognition of sexual diversity as a mechanism for establishing a progressive human rights record. The Union's move toward strengthening the cross-national mobility of employees might also soon force member states to recognize same-sex unions registered in other countries, even if domestic law extended little such recognition to nationals. The controversies about such steps were becoming more muted in most of Europe, and shifts in public opinion were dramatic (see table 14.2).

Canada saw the first full-fledged lesbian and gay marriages anywhere. In mid-2003, an Ontario appeal court, with the province's chief justice on the bench, ruled unanimously that the Charter of Rights and Freedoms prevented defining marriage in exclusively heterosexual terms and

TABLE 14.2. Public opinion about homosexuality and religion, 1990–2000.

| | HOMOSEXUALITY "NEVER JUSTIFIED" | | RELIGION "VERY IMPORTANT IN MY LIFE" | |
REGION	1990 (%)	2000 (%)	1990 (%)	2000 (%)
North America				
United States	57	32	53	57
Canada	40	27	31	30
Europe				
Belgium	46	27	15	18
Britain	42	25	16	13
Denmark	44	21	9	8
France	42	23	14	11
Germany	50	19	16	9
Hungary	85	88	23	20
Italy	49	30	34	33
Netherlands	20	7	19	17
Spain	46	17	21	19
Sweden	45	9	10	11
Elsewhere				
Australia	*	31	*	23
Brazil	73	56	57	65
South Africa	78	48	66	70

Source: Ronald Inglehart, Miguel Basáñez, Jaime Díez-Medrano, Loek Halman, and Ruud
Luijkx, eds., *Human Beliefs and Values: A Cross-Cultural Sourcebook Based on the 1999–2002
World Values Surveys* (Buenos Aires: Siglo XXI Editores, 2004), tables F118, A006.
*Not asked.

that the elimination of restrictions on gay and lesbian marriage should take effect immediately. That judgment was soon followed by rulings in other cases that extended marriage rights to most of Canada's provinces and territories, and it was obvious that the judicial consensus would soon extend across the country. The federal government was having difficulty securing parliamentary approval of a revised definition for the statute books, but the constitution was being interpreted in ways that made any attempt to turn back the clock more difficult. The Ontario court ruling took effect shortly before its Massachusetts counterpart did so, though the Ontario ruling affected all levels of government and not only the state and local jurisdictions covered by the Massachusetts ruling.

The marriage issue certainly provoked controversy in Canada, and religious conservatives took advantage of a divided and ambivalent public. The Conservative Party, which merged the socially conservative Canadian Alliance and the mid-right Progressive Conservatives, took a strong position opposing the federal Liberal government's 2005 attempt to legislate a changed definition of marriage, but the government's bill passed at mid-year and then survived a Conservative government's attempt to reopen debate in 2006.

What we find overall is that the United States was home to comparatively early pressure to extend family regimes in recognition of sexual diversity. And within its borders we can find jurisdictions that were pioneers in such recognition. Americans were among the first to take up marriage itself, and they secured the first major victory on that issue anywhere in the world—even if it never took effect. Activist successes in securing recognition of same-sex relationships short of marriage were first registered in Canada at about the same time as they were in the United States, but starting in the early 1990s Canadian success took off. Eventually, marriage was opened up. The same thing happened in several European countries and a few countries elsewhere, though in almost all cases only at the end of the 1990s and the early 2000s.

As much as in any country, American shifts in the recognition of gay relationships have varied greatly across regions and localities.[8] Some jurisdictions have reformed policy within their legal terrain as much as any parts of Canada or Europe. Others are as unmoved as the most conservative regions of the industrialized world. The variation within the American system, then, is as great as the variation between countries in the rest of North America and Europe.

EXPLAINING THE AMERICAN "PIONEER" PATTERN

In the decades following World War II, the United States was witness to political activism concerning issues of sexual orientation, and later gender identity, on a scale with few parallels in other countries. The Netherlands was home to a visible movement throughout that time, but by the 1970s American activism was more widespread and visible than its counterparts in any other country and concerned a wider set of issues.

This reflected in part the material conditions allowing for the emergence of identities based on sexual difference. As John D'Emilio and others have argued, the ability to act on homosexual urges increases with capitalism, particularly with the kind of urbanization and dislocation that comes with advanced industrial and postindustrial capitalism.[9] Large cities produce the kind of anonymity that creates spaces for homosexuals' activity, institutions catering to their needs, and networks among them. American cities were hardly unique in providing such foundations for the development of a visible activist movement. What does seem to set the American case a little apart, though, is the extent of geographic mobility that has accompanied its economic growth and the disconnection from extended family that can so often result by accident or purpose.[10]

This provides opportunities not only for sexual diversity to become more visible but also for political identities based on sexual difference to form. Here, too, the American case stands out, for the relative weakness of class as an identifier creates openings for identity formation on other grounds. Canada also has seen a long history of denying the relevance of class, but the pattern is more deeply set in the United States.

The growth of activist movements based on identities such as this had, of course, a model in the civil rights movement. Here was a movement that had worked outside and inside the existing political framework and had marshaled the energies of both reformers and radicals. The women's movement followed this pattern. The social and economic changes in the role of women were advancing in a number of industrialized countries, but American feminists were able to build a more sustained political movement than their counterparts elsewhere, and certainly one with better resources.

An activist movement seeking to extend family regimes to include sexual minorities was able to build on earlier gains secured by the women's movement. The geographic dislocations so characteristic of American family life and the gender challenges presented by the most reformist of feminist groups shifted marriage from some of its most traditional moorings comparative early.

The American GLBT movement was also able to take advantage of the unusual fragmentation of the political system in which they operated. The U.S. system of federalism allows more points of activist entry than do more centralized political regimes. The U.S. system is not generally as decentralized as Canadian federalism, but it is so with regard to questions related to sexual diversity and relationship recognition in particular. The capacity to criminalize sexual activity is in the jurisdiction of American states, as is the capacity to define marriage. (Both areas are within federal control in Canada.) Local governments in the United States often have greater jurisdictional reach than their counterparts north of the border and in other countries. In this way, American decentralization has given sexual minority activists an opening to effect major change in unusually progressive states and localities, and at an early stage.

Building on a long civil rights tradition, American activists seeking the expansion of lesbian and gay relational rights also were able to make use of the courts. This is now a common occurrence in other countries, used with stunning effect in Canada during the 1990s and more recently in such countries as Israel and South Africa, but it began in earnest earlier among American activists. Many pioneering gains, then, were secured because courts in the United States had developed more extensive capacity to challenge government acts than had their counterparts in other countries. In some U.S. jurisdictions, activists seeking change through the courts were able to rely on human rights law that included sexual orientation. Across the country, litigants were also able to rely on large and well-funded activist groups prepared to support litigation—groups such as the American Civil Liberties Union and the Lambda Legal Defense Fund. Such groups have few parallels in other political systems and none with anything like their resources.[11]

The extent of progressive mobilization concerning sexual diversity issues is in part a result of the power of conservative organizing. The religious Right poses a constant threat to the gains that have been made, and the institutional fragmentation of the American system allows for their intervention at many points and at any time. This requires a degree of vigilance that calls for considerable institutionalization, and it depends on garnering resources from supportive communities that no GLBT movement in any other country could hope to attract. The threats posed by religious and secular conservatives on other policy fronts also help secure support from groups and constituencies that might not otherwise expend time and resources for gay-related causes.

But with all these advantages and openings, the American activist movement as a whole has never achieved the point of takeoff that its counterparts in Canada, northern Europe, and a few other settings have achieved, even when movements elsewhere have usually operated with a fraction of the resources available in the United States. Why?

EXPLAINING THE ABSENCE
OF AMERICAN TAKEOFF

The strength of religious conservatism is the single most important barrier to the recognition of same-sex relationships in the United States, and the most powerful explanation for the lack of takeoff there.[12] In comparison to Canadians, and especially to citizens in most European countries, Americans are highly religious and more likely to be religiously conservative.[13] The United States is also home to an unusual array of well-funded organizations on the religious Right that are prepared to place opposition to gay rights at the center of their agendas and to mount concerted opposition to any political or legal recognition of sexual diversity.

Among North American and European countries, most indicators of religiosity place the United States at one end of a spectrum. Table 14.2 displays responses to a World Values Survey question about how important religion is in a person's life, and it shows a remarkable 57 percent of Americans saying "very important"—higher than any other country in those regions. Gallup polling shows even sharper contrasts, with a 2003 survey showing that 60 percent of Americans declared religion to be very important in everyday life, compared to 28 percent of Canadians and 17 percent of Britons.[14] Another World Values question finds that 60 percent of Americans attend religious services at least once a month, compared to 36 percent of Canadians and an average far below that in western Europe.

Strong religious belief is widely associated with opposition to the recognition of gay and lesbian relationships. Many supporters of same-sex marriage and other forms of recognition for gay and lesbian couples can be found among religious believers, but they are in a minority. Support is much stronger among nonpractitioners, including Roman Catholics.[15] Among regions where support for same-sex marriage has increased most dramatically and disapproval of homosexuality has declined most rapidly are the predominantly Catholic areas where religious practice has fallen off sharply (for example, Spain, France, and Quebec).

What is also prominent on the American landscape is the hold of conservative forms of religiosity. When asked by Gallup if the Bible is to be taken literally, 34 percent of Americans said yes in 2005, compared to 17 percent of Canadians and even fewer Europeans.[16] A variety of indicators might be used in assessing levels of religious conservatism, but they generally agree that such levels are two to three times higher in the United States than in Canada. In the least "religious" regions of the United States (for example, the Pacific Northwest), levels of religiosity and of conservatism are higher than anywhere in Canada, apart from quite specific regions within such provinces as Alberta and British Columbia.

What further distinguishes the American case is the extent to which religious conservatism has spawned political organizations that preoccupy themselves with mobilizing antigay constituencies. There are many such organizations, some specializing in litigation, some in direct mail campaigns, some in lobbying. The largest is Focus on the Family, with more than one thousand staff members and with radio broadcasts reaching huge audiences across and beyond the United States. What strengthens the political capacity of the religious Right is its core foundation in explicitly conservative Protestant churches. Their church-attending adherents are a highly receptive constituency, meeting together at least weekly before a conservative pastor or minister. The costs entailed in marshalling networks of such religious leaders to antigay causes are not necessarily great, though the resources available to conservative political groups allow more grassroots mobilizing than is possible for any other activist movement.

In Europe and elsewhere in North America, these explicitly conservative Protestant denominations are not as strong. The largest Protestant denominations in northern Europe and Canada are either more doctrinally centrist (as is true of most Lutheran churches), progressive (as is distinctly true of the United Church of Canada), or internally divided (for example, the members of the Anglican Communion). Religious conservatism is an important current among Roman Catholics, but the church hierarchy's political mobilization concerning sexual diversity issues is not as effective as the mobilizing of conservative Protestant denominations since their constituencies are less likely to attend church and less likely to follow the hierarchy's dictates.

Religious conservatives in the United States have in the past three decades gained great leverage over the Republican Party in most parts of the country. Their success is reflected in party platforms at all levels, in the willingness of campaigners to play antigay cards in elections, and in the preparedness of legislators to press for statutes to encode their antigay views, often with levels of party discipline that are very high by American standards.

Several western European countries have Christian Democratic parties generally sympathetic to positions taken by the Roman Catholic Church, but their pursuit of antigay agendas cannot compare with the ferocity of such pursuit among American Republicans. They are also faced with the harsh reality of declining church attendance and increasing popular wariness of following the political dictates of the hierarchy on matters related to gender and sexuality. Popular referenda held in Italy during the 1980s, for example, led to massive defeats for the positions taken by Christian Democrats and the Roman Catholic Church on questions of divorce and abortion. Polling conducted in Spain in 2004 showed that two-thirds of the population supported the government's marriage legislation, despite ferocious opposition from the Vatican and the Spanish hierarchy.

In Canada, religious conservatives form an important core constituency for the new Conservative Party, and they did secure three-quarters of delegate support for a resolution opposing same-sex marriage in their 2005 founding convention. The party's leadership, though, has been scrambling to tone down the moral conservatism of the party, knowing that it must do so to secure larger popular support outside the western provinces. In Canada as in Europe, there are more right-wing politicians than in the United States who recognize the inconsistency between opposing government intervention in the economy and supporting government regulation of morality. In that sense, neoliberalism and neoconservatism are seen to be in some tension with one another. At the provincial and federal levels in Canada, most parties on the Right have been much more preoccupied by lower taxes and deregulation—the neoliberal side of the right-wing agenda. They have campaigned and voted against major advances in the recognition of same-sex relationships, and especially marriage, but they have not sought to roll back advances already made.

The identity of the party in power has an obvious impact on governmental willingness to extend policy recognition to same-sex couples. Equity has been very difficult to secure in the United States where Republicans have controlled the executive or either legislative house at the state or the federal level, and in some cases even when they are a minority throughout but a strong one. Most instances in Canada where governments have acted without court pressure have had Liberal or New Democratic Party governments. Significant steps toward gay and lesbian relationship recognition in Britain, New Zealand, the Netherlands, and most of Nordic Europe have come when governments have been center-left.

The forces of resistance to recognizing sexual diversity in the United States benefit from a political system deliberately designed to be cumbersome. At the federal and state levels, power is more fragmented than in parliamentary systems, where power is generally concentrated in cabinets and prime ministers' offices. The power of American legislatures is greater, and power within them less concentrated, than in almost all parliamentary systems. The relative unity of Republican opposition to any steps designed to recognize sexual diversity makes change in policy very difficult to effect, especially when a minority of Democrats are uneasy about the risks of electoral identification with pro-gay causes.

Resistance also benefits from the near-constant threat of referenda on issues related to sexual diversity. The mobilizing capacity of the religious Right has allowed it to secure enough signatures to place many issues on state ballots and to secure victories on many of them. With regard to marriage in particular, they are able to win over very large majorities to their side. There are more than a few Democrats who fear the impact of having such measures on the ballot at the same time as they are up for election. In almost all other countries referenda are unusual and are difficult or impossible to secure by means of popular initiative. This does not prevent politicians from being nervous about taking on pro-gay positions, but it lowers the anxiety and reduces the likelihood that an election will focus on sexual diversity issues.[17]

Another factor that has slowed the recognition of gay and lesbian relationships has been the high cost of health care benefits in the United States and the rhetorical wedge this provides to opponents. Sexual minorities are widely (though inaccurately) perceived to be materially advantaged, so the prospect of their acquiring expensive benefits, especially those that can be portrayed as a drain on the public treasury, can be used by conservatives in marshalling resistance. In most of Europe and Canada, state support for health care of individuals is substantial enough that the material costs of extending recognition to same-sex couples is modest. In Canada, too, most of the substantive rights and obligations traditionally associated with marriage were extended to all de facto couples before the issue of same-sex marriage came to the fore, so the question of costs, however modest, was already settled.

Bolstering the resistance to recognizing sexual diversity in the United States, and in regard to marriage especially, is the fear of social disintegration that seems so widespread there. In any country experiencing rapid economic change, fears about social cohesion and family solidarity increases. There, however, those fears are especially acute. The geographic and social mobility and the free market ethos that have opened up spaces for the expression of sexual difference also create anxiety about the retention of "family values"—anxiety with few parallels in European and other North American societies. Nowhere else does there seem to be so much support for radical individualism and at the same time anxiety about the inevitable atomization that results from it. Gallup polling conducted in 2004 showed that only 35 percent of Americans were satisfied with the moral and ethical climate, in stark contrast to the 59 percent of Canadians who expressed satisfaction. As the Canadian pollster Michael Adams has put it, Americans "seem inclined to latch on to traditional institutional practices, beliefs, and norms as anchors in a national environment that is more intensely competitive, chaotic, and even violent." [18]

That anxiety may well be reinforced by the "muscularity" of American nationalism, a characteristic associated with the country's imperial standing in world politics.[19] Concerns about the strength of American moral fiber have parallels with late nineteenth-century Britain, at the height of that country's imperial expansion, and it can be no coincidence that conservatives in the United States so often cite the "decadence" of the late Roman Empire as prominent in their explanations of its decline. The superpower status of the United States also secures the social and political prominence of the military and reinforces opposition to any moves that would weaken its masculine strength. Homosexuality, of course, becomes linked to weakness both within and beyond the military. It is not that other countries' military systems are categorically and equitably open to sexual minorities and women—it is that their hierarchies are less fixated on that issue and that the military plays a less prominent role in those countries' affairs.

In some parts of the United States, courts have played an important role in securing recognition for same-sex relationships. The absence of American takeoff is also, however, a product of the absence of leadership in the area of sexual diversity rights by the U.S. Supreme Court. This comes partly from the appointment of conservative justices by Republican presidents. It also comes from the wide latitude given for conservative interpretation by the generality of the equality rights provisions in the American Constitution.

In a few other countries (for example, South Africa and Israel) courts have taken important leads on the right of sexual minorities, nowhere more comprehensively than in Canada.[20] Marriage rights and relationship rights more generally were extended in Canada because of court challenges, with rulings based on a Charter of Rights and Freedoms that contained more elaborate and robust rights language than exists in the U.S. Constitution. Judicial appointments also had not been as politicized as in the United States, and equality rights in any event had been less subject to either partisan or judicial polarization. Cries of judicial "activism" have been leveled at courts when they ruled favorably on cases involving sexuality, but such charges have not been pursued as unrelentingly as in the United States. There have been calls for reform of the process of judicial appointment, but there are few Canadian admirers of the American system and the politicization that has flowed from it.

FACTORS EXPLAINING CANADIAN
AND EUROPEAN TAKEOFF

The accelerating rate of change in Canada and elsewhere is explained in part by a number of factors identified already. Compared to the United States, Canada has a relatively weak religious Right. The political Right in Canada is also not as influenced by religious conservatism as its counterpart is in the United States, and the Right in northern Europe especially is less so. The political systems at the provincial and the federal levels in Canada and in almost all European countries are less fragmented than their American counterparts, and although this has often allowed governments to resist legislative action to recognize same-sex relationships, it has allowed them to proceed when induced or forced to by the courts. In Canada, the Charter has been a vehicle by which lesbian and gay activists have been able to secure change, and this has in turn helped increase public acceptance of their rights.

The extent to which de facto heterosexual relationships were recognized in Canadian law and public policy contributed to the recognition of de facto gay and lesbian couples and to their public acceptance. These changes reduced the substantive distinction between marriage and cohabitation and may well have reduced the symbolic rigidity surrounding marriage.[21] They certainly allowed many gains in substantive recognition of same-sex relationships without the need to raise the more highly charged issue of marriage. Sweden is the European case that most closely parallels the Canadian in the policy recognition of de facto heterosexual relationships, and it was unquestionable a help in securing political approval for the recognition of civil unions for gay and lesbian couples.[22]

In northern Europe and to some extent in Canada, the expansiveness and coverage of the welfare state eased the extension of recognition to same-sex couples, since the additional costs associated with including them in state social insurance benefits were likely to be negligible. Particularly where social insurance is most generous, in northern Europe, the substantive importance of marriage for securing social policy protections is also reduced.

There are additional factors that have eased change and contributed to the acceleration of its pace. Canada has a relatively strong labor movement, though it has been politically weakened with the growing clout of neoliberalism since the mid-1970s. It is a much stronger economic and political force than its American counterparts, and it has been among the leading labor movements internationally in taking up issues related to sexual diversity.[23] Unions have been prominent in pursuing the recognition of same-sex relationships in the workplace and in political arenas and have supported many cases brought before courts and labor tribunals. In Europe, strong labor movements have been associated with progress toward gender equality, in turn associated with moves toward the recognition of same-sex couples, though most European unions have been relatively slow to take up sexual diversity specifically.[24]

Another factor is the extent to which acceptance of diversity has been incorporated into the Canadian self-image. In Canada's political class, and to some extent the population at large, the country is often seen in a positive light as a social "mosaic" and contrasted to the American "melting pot."[25] The mosaic imagery is meant to suggest that there is less assimilationist pressure on ethnic and cultural minorities than in the United States, and for that matter, in most European countries. Apart from its aboriginal populations, Canada is an immigrant country, but unlike such immigrant societies as the United States and Australia, there was never a strong sense of Canadianness to which newcomers were expected to adapt.

There is some mythology embedded in this imagery. Canada had a long history of discriminatory immigration policy and practice, and there have been waves of anti-immigrant sentiment, much of it with strong racial undercurrents. The most lasting of the cultural differences in Canada, that between the speakers of English and of French, has often enough in the past not been accompanied by particularly strong bonds of mutual understanding.

But for most of Canada's recent history, no single group defined either by region or by culture has been able to impose its will on the rest of the country on the basis of a demographic majority. This is starkly evident in Canada's major cities, particularly in Toronto and Vancouver, which are among the most ethnically and racially diverse in the world. This is clearly not welcomed by all, but it is by some, and it is acquiesced in by many more. Prejudice and discrimination remain widespread, but the experience of many who migrate there from Europe, Africa, Asia, or even parts of the United States is that there is more acceptance of difference. Pew Research polling conducted in 2002 found Canada to be the only country among forty-four surveyed in which a majority agreed with a statement that immigrants have a good influence on the country, and it was a strong majority of 77 percent.[26] In the United States, 49 percent agreed.

How transferable such patterns are to other forms of difference is unclear, but an argument can be made that they have helped sustain a certain toleration of difference both at the official level and, in a limited and perhaps largely pragmatic way, in the general population. They may also have helped create a degree of legitimacy for group rights, even in an environment that has not had as long a history of rights claims as the United States. The absence of an imperial past, and the relatively low-key forms of nationalism that exist in Canada as a whole, allow more room than exists in many other countries for acknowledgment of group differences. Quebec's nationalism has at times been an exception, and strong currents within it are not easily accepting of ethnic differences within, but that, too, is changing.

The prior recognition of other forms of difference has played a role in a few parts of Europe. The need to acknowledge minority religious and political interests emerged relatively early in the Dutch case and may well have secured a pattern of accommodation that was then applied to sexual minorities.[27] But the record of the Netherlands and of most continental European countries is not outstanding with regard to the social and political recognition of ethnic and racial difference, and explicitly xenophobic political mobilizing has been a recurrent feature of electoral politics across the continent.

It is not the case that advances have been secured in Canada and other countries because the activist pressure for them has been larger in scale, better-funded, or more skillfully deployed than in the American case. The Canadian GLBT movement has been a critical source of pressure on governments and an essential stimulus to favorable court rulings. It has not, however, had nearly the resources of its American counterparts. What has helped, of course, is that it has not faced anything like the kind of opposition that can be mobilized by the American religious Right. Organizing by this movement in Canada has increased dramatically in recent years, most prominently with the growth of a branch of the huge U.S. group Focus on the Family. The base constituency, however, remains less than half the size of its American version. And GLBT advocates have not faced the same number of extremely conservative media personalities that Americans confront. The same is true for European movements, which, on the continent in particular, have benefited from a long history of visible anticlericalism.

CONCLUSION

A number of factors have slowed American recognition of same-sex relationships: the power of religious conservatism, its capture of the

Republican Party, the popular fear of social disintegration, the weakness of the welfare state, the resistance to recognizing rights and obligations for de facto couples, the low level of unionization, the particular form of nationalism, and the complexity of the political system. What is also characteristic of the American case is a large and resourceful activist movement constantly pressing for recognition of sexual diversity. Whatever its limitations, it has strong allies in civil liberties groups, the women's movement, progressive religious circles, significant elements of the labor movement, and major currents in the African American civil rights movement. This has led to major steps toward the recognition of gay and lesbian relationships in many urban areas and in a few states. It has also produced a rapid spread of recognition of domestic partners in employee benefit programs, particularly in the educational sector and in large corporations.

What is distinctive about the American pattern is that early pioneering has never been followed by any takeoff period. Every step, in almost every region, comes from hard struggle against well-organized opponents who will regularly try to prevent any recognition of sexual diversity and undo gains secured earlier on. No region of the country is spared this struggle, and no gain can ever be fully secured. Where movement toward equity has been won in other countries, it is rarely at risk of reversal. In Canada, northern Europe, and a few other countries such as New Zealand, Israel, and South Africa, we also see a pattern of takeoff once a certain legal and policy foundation is established.

It is easy, though, to overstate the rapidity of change across Europe or in other industrialized liberal democracies. Gains are highly uneven across Europe, and there is far from a legal or political consensus on the importance of widely recognizing same-sex relationships, let alone marriage. The most influential of the European Union's institutions have moved toward a recognition of same-sex relationships with excruciating slowness. Across Europe there is still a great deal more skittishness about extending parenting rights to lesbian and gay couples than is commonly recognized, and this is no small matter. The fears about parenting have roots in the most insidious of stereotypes about the risks that homosexuality poses to children. The symbolic and substantive significance of excluding, limiting, or delaying parental rights in civil union and marital regimes cannot be overstated.

The Canadian case displays the same takeoff pattern that we find in parts of Europe, and few political voices hint at rolling back the recognition of gay and lesbian relationships apart from the marriage question.

This issue remains divisive, and there is no guarantee that a Conservative majority government in Ottawa would not try to impose legislative impediments to the recognition of same-sex marriages, even if it knew that such impediments were unconstitutional. The majority of Canadians, however, would prefer to turn the page and move on.

The United States is an unusual case, in part because of the extraordinary range of legal and political outcomes across states and localities. It is also unusual in several characteristics that impede the march to equity. But it is not as exceptional as is widely believed. A great majority of Americans now believe in extending recognition to lesbian and gay couples, if only a minority favor marriage. Most large corporations extend their family benefits coverage to the same-sex partners of employees. A steadily growing number of U.S. states and municipalities extend some form of recognition to such partners of their own employees. Openly lesbian and gay characters make regular appearances on American television dramas, even if their portrayals have limitations. In everyday life, sexual diversity is as visible in American society as in any. And across a wide range of regions and localities in the United States, countless lesbians, gays, bisexuals, and the transgendered are asserting the right to be visible.

There is no American policy takeoff, and that is unusual, but there is unrelenting pressure for greater equity, applied against great odds. That, too, is unusual.

ENDNOTES

1. John Kingdon artfully treads a middle path in *America the Unusual* (New York: Worth, 1999).
2. On the parameters of traditional constructions of family, see Mary Bernstein and Renate Reiman, eds., *Queer Families, Queer Politics* (New York: Columbia University Press, 2001); Valerie Lehr, *Queer Family Values* (Philadelphia: Temple University Press, 1999).
3. A few provinces moved more slowly in this direction, within their jurisdictional sphere, and Quebec continues to be exceptional in its differentiation between married and de facto couples who have not registered for a civil union, largely within its Civil Code.
4. Among the useful surveys of comparative developments are Robert Wintemute and Mads Adenaes, eds., *Legal Recognition of Same-Sex Partnerships: A Study of National, European and International Law* (Oxford: Hart, 2001); Kathleen Lahey and Kevin Alderson, *Same-Sex Marriage: The Personal and the Political* (Toronto: Insomniac, 2004); Martin Dupuis, *Same-Sex Marriage, Legal Mobilization, and the Politics of Rights* (New York: Peter Lang, 2002),

chap. 6; Yuval Merin, *Equality for Same-Sex Couples: The Legal Recognition of Gay Partnerships in Europe and the United States* (Chicago: University of Chicago Press, 2002); Kees Waaldijk and Matteo Bonini-Barraldi, eds., *Sexual Orientation Discrimination in the European Union* (The Hague: T.M.C. Asser, 2005); and Lee Badgett, "Variations on an Equitable Theme: Explaining International Same-Sex Partner Recognition Laws," 2004.

5. There are several good reviews of American developments, including William N. Eskridge Jr., *Gay Law* (Cambridge: Harvard University Press, 1999); Jason Pierceson, *Courts, Liberalism, and Rights* (Philadelphia: Temple University Press, 2005); Daniel Pinello, *Gay Rights and American Law* (New York: Cambridge University Press, 2003); and Daniel Pinello, *America's Struggle for Same-Sex Marriage* (New York: Cambridge University Press, 2006).

6. Rulings by the Supreme Court of Canada in the early 1990s formally turned down the claims of gay litigants, but they did so in language that made clear the court's inclination to read the equality provisions of the Charter of Rights (section 15) in ways that included sexual orientation. A number of lower courts and labor tribunals then took up this interpretation. For more on this, see Cynthia Peterson, "Fighting It Out in Canadian Courts," in *Laboring for Rights: Unions and Sexual Diversity across Nations*, ed. Gerald Hunt, 37–57 (Philadelphia: Temple University Press, 1999).

7. See Merin, *Equality for Same-Sex Couples*, chap. 3; Dupuis, *Same-Sex Marriage*, 129.

8. This point is made in most analyses of political advances and setbacks in the United States. See, e.g., James Button, Barbara Rienzo, and Kenneth Wald, "The Politics of Gay Rights at the Local and State Level," 269–89, and Donald Haider-Markel, "Lesbian and Gay Politics in the States," 290–346, both in *The Politics of Gay Rights*, ed. Kenneth Wald, Craig Rimmerman, and Clyde Wilcox (Chicago: University of Chicago Press, 2000).

9. John D'Emilio, *Making Trouble* (New York: Routledge, 1992), chap. 1.

10. One particularly important outgrowth of this pattern is the extent to which young American adults attend postsecondary institutions that are at a considerable geographic remove from their homes.

11. Jason Pierceson points to the importance of tracking state-level judgments in assessing legal change concerning sexual diversity issues in *Courts, Liberalism, and Rights*. David Richards also points to significant court decisions at all levels in *The Case for Gay Rights* (Lawrence: University Press of Kansas, 2005).

12. Among the informed analyses of American distinctiveness or of comparative developments that have come to similar views are Barry Adam, "The Defense of Marriage Act and American Exceptionalism: The 'Gay Marriage' Panic in the United States," *Journal of the History of Sexuality* 12 (April 2003): 259–76; and Badgett, "Variations on an Equitable Theme."

13. Several analysts of gains and setbacks with regard to sexual orientation issues in the United States, of course, talk of this as a crucial factor explaining variations across localities and states. See, e.g., Kenneth Wald, James Button, and Barbara Rienzo, "The Politics of Gay Rights in American Communities:

Explaining Antidiscrimination Ordinances and Policies," *American Journal of Political Science* 40 (November 1996): 1152–78; Donald Haider-Markel and Kenneth Maier, "The Politics of Gay and Lesbian Rights: Expanding the Scope of the Conflict," *Journal of Politics* 58 (May 1996): 332–49; and Barry Adam, "Defense of Marriage Act." Scott Barclay and Shauna Fisher ("The States and the Differing Impetus for Divergent Paths on Same-Sex Marriage, 1990–2001," *Policy Studies Journal* 31, no. 3 [2003]: 331–52) downplay the role of religious conservatism but do so in part as a result of a deeply flawed indicator.

14. Julie Raj, "Worlds Apart: Canada, Britain, and the United States," www.gallup.com.

15. Surveys conducted in Canada and the United States regularly show that Roman Catholics on the whole are no more conservative than are others with respect to issues related to sexual diversity.

16. Josephine Magwa, "U.S. vs. Canada: Different Reads on the Good Book," www.gallup.com.

17. It is unclear from the evidence whether the wave of anti–gay marriage referenda that were passed in the 2004 election strengthened the Republicans' hand, but the general point remains that many Democrats fear such referenda. See Ken Sherrill, "Same-Sex Marriage, Civil Unions, and the 2004 Presidential Election," report for the National Gay and Lesbian Task Force, 10 December 2004. http://thetaskforce.org/downloads/MarriageCUSherrill2004.pdf.

18. Michael Adams, *Fire and Ice: The United States, Canada and the Myth of Converging Values* (Toronto: Penguin Canada, 2003), 52.

19. Barry Adam makes this point in "Defense of Marriage Act," as do I in *On the Fringe* (Ithaca: Cornell University Press, 1998), chap. 7. See also Mary Fainsod Katzenstein, "The Spectacle of Life and Death," in *Gay Rights, Military Wrongs: Political Perspectives on Lesbians and Gays in the Military*, ed. Craig Rimmerman, 229–48 (New York: Garland, 1996).

20. There is an exaggerated belief expressed in some American constitutional discussions that the conservatism of the U.S. courts with regard to sexuality issues is exceptional or unusual in the industrialized West; see, e.g., Pierceson, *Courts, Liberalism and Rights*, and Richards, *Case for Gay Rights*. They and others overstate the shift in jurisprudence in Europe and elsewhere, including the European Union–level courts.

21. This point is made by Robert Wintemute and Kees Waaldijk, "Strasbourg to the Rescue," 713–32, and Kees Waaldijk, "Towards the Recognition of Same-Sex Partners in European Union Law," 635–53, in *Legal Recognition of Same-Sex Partnerships: A Study of National, European and International Law*, ed. Robert Wintemute and Mads Andenaes (Oxford: Hart, 2001).

22. See Merin, *Equality for Same-Sex Couples*, chap. 2.

23. I have pursued this question in detail in "Equity and Solidarity in Comparative Perspective," in *Equity, Solidarity and Canadian Labour*, ed. Gerald Hunt and David Rayside (Toronto: University of Toronto Press, forthcoming). See also Gerald Hunt, ed., *Laboring for Rights: Unions and Sexual Diversity across Nations* (Philadelphia: Temple University Press, 1999). Barry Adam, in

"Defense of Marriage Act," agrees that the relative weakness of American labor has been a factor in slowing progress in the United States.

24. Yuval Merin makes this case in *Equality for Same-Sex Couples,* 46–47.

25. Seymour Martin Lipset, for example, in *Continental Divide* (New York: Routledge, 1990), is a longstanding proponent of the view that significant value differences distinguish Americans from Canadians. Michael Adams (*Fire and Ice*) argues that there is now a values divergence, whether or not it issues from historically embedded patterns. Neil Nevitte is among the prominent dissenters; see Nevitte, *Decline of Deference* (Peterborough, Ont: Broadview, 1996).

26. This is reported in Adams, *Fire and Ice,* 66–67.

27. This factor is easily overstated in the Dutch, Danish, and Scandinavian cases. There are no strong indicators of an unusually high level of acceptance of racially distinct minorities in these societies.

CONTRIBUTORS

PAUL R. BREWER is an associate professor of journalism and mass communication at the University of Wisconsin at Milwaukee. His research on public opinion about gay rights has appeared in the *Journal of Politics, Political Communication,* and *Public Opinion Quarterly.* He is currently working on a book manuscript titled *Public Opinion and the Politics of Gay Rights.*

SEAN CAHILL is the director for the Policy Institute of the National Gay and Lesbian Task Force, a think tank that conducts research, policy analysis, and strategy development to advance the equality and understanding of lesbian, gay, bisexual, and transgender people. Cahill is the author of *Same-Sex Marriage in the United States: Focus on the Facts* (2004) and "The symbolic centrality of gay marriage in the 2004 presidential election" in *The Future of Gay Rights in America* (2005), along with many other book chapters, academic journal articles, and studies. Forthcoming books include *Family Policy: Issues Affecting Lesbian, Gay, Bisexual, and Transgendered People* and *Education Policy: Issues Affecting Lesbian, Gay, Bisexual, and Transgendered Youth.*

DAVID C. CAMPBELL is an assistant professor of political science at the University of Notre Dame. His research has centered on Americans' civic engagement, including the ways their engagement is shaped by religion. He is the author of *Why We Vote: How Schools and Communities Shape Our Civic Life,* co-author of *Democracy at Risk: How Political Choices Have Undermined Citizenship, and What We Can Do About It,* and editor of *A Matter of Faith? Religion in the 2004 Presidential Election.*

JOHN D'EMILIO is professor of gender and women's studies and history at the University of Illinois at Chicago. He is the author or editor of half a dozen books, including *Sexual Politics, Sexual Communities, Lost Profit: The Life and Times of Bayard Rustin* and, with Estelle Freedman, *Intimate Matters: A History of Sexuality in America.* D'Emilio was also the founding director of the Policy Institute of the National Gay and Lesbian Task Force.

GRAHAM B. GLOVER is a doctoral student in political science at the University of Florida. A graduate of Concordia Seminary in St. Louis, Missouri, he is also the pastor of Good Shepherd Lutheran Church in Chiefland, Florida. His dissertation (expected 2008) is titled *Confronting Relativism: The Political Theology of Pope Benedict XVI.*

C. ANN GORDON is associate professor of political science at Ohio University. She received her PhD from the University of Southern California in 1999. She is co-editor of *Anticipating Madam President,* co-author of *When Stereotypes Collide: Race, Gender, and Videostyle in Congressional Campaigns,* and author of *Playing Politics: An Active Learning Approach to American National Government.* She has been honored by a Goldsmith Research Award from the Joan Shorenstein Center on the Press, Politics and Public Policy at Harvard University and the Carrie Chapman Catt Prize for Research on Women and Politics (co-recipient), awarded by the Catt Center at Iowa State University.

DONALD P. HAIDER-MARKEL is associate professor of political science and director of the Survey Research Center at the University of Kansas. His research and teaching are focused on public policy, public opinion, and political participation. He has authored and co-authored a book, book chapters, and more than thirty refereed articles in a range of issue areas including the environment, civil rights, gun policy, and terrorism.

CELINDA LAKE is one of the Democratic Party's leading political strategists, serving as tactician and senior advisor to the national party committees and to dozens of Democratic incumbents and challengers at all levels of the electoral process. Her work also took her to advise fledgling democratic parties in several postwar Eastern European countries, including Bosnia, and South Africa. Lake and her firm are known for cutting-edge research on issues including the economy, health care, the environment, and education and have worked for a number of institutions including the Democratic National Committee, the Democratic Governor's Association, the White House Project, America Coming Together, the AFL-CIO, the SEIU, the CWA, the IAFF, the Sierra Club, Planned Parenthood, the Human Rights Campaign, Emily's List, and the Kaiser Foundation.

KATIE LOFTON has her MA in political science from the University of Kansas. Her research interests include public policy and statistics.

DEWAYNE L. LUCAS is an assistant professor of political science at Hobart and William Smith Colleges. His research focuses on the influence of partisan and electoral factors on the voting behavior of members of the House of Representatives.

KAREN O'CONNOR is a professor of political science and director of the Women and Politics Institute at American University in Washington, DC. She has written, co-authored, or edited several books, including *American Government: Continuity and Change* (8th ed., 2004), *Women, Politics, and American Society* (4th ed., 2004), *Women in Congress: Running, Winning, and Ruling* (2002), and *No Neutral Ground: Abortion Politics in an Age of Absolutes* (1996) as well as many scholarly articles and book chapters. She is the past chair of the Law and Courts section of the American Political Science Association and the past president of the Women's Caucus for Political Science and the Southern Political Science Association.

ELIZABETH POPP is a graduate student in the Department of Political Science at the University of Illinois at Urbana-Champaign. Her research interests include the study of elite political rhetoric, public opinion, and mass-elite linkages.

DAVID RAYSIDE is professor of political science and director of the Mark S. Bonham Centre for Sexual Diversity Studies at the University of Toronto. He has an academic interest in sexual diversity issues, having written on such topics as antidiscrimination legislation in Ontario, public opinion and gay rights, AIDS politics in Canada, and GLBT engagement with mainstream political milieux in Canada, Britain, and the United States. His *Queer Inclusions, Continental Divisions* (forthcoming) is a comparative analysis of Canadian and American developments in the political recognition of same-sex relationships, the extension of parenting rights to same-sex couples, and the response to sexual diversity in public schooling. These research pursuits have been matched by an activist engagement with issues related to gender and sexual orientation.

ELLEN D. B. RIGGLE is associate professor of political science and associate director of the Gender and Women's Studies Program at the University of Kentucky. She received her PhD in political science from the University of Illinois at Champaign-Urbana in 1990. Her current research interests include the effects of minority stress, legal status, and policy on same-sex couples and GLBT individuals. Her research has been published in journals such as *Psychology, Public Policy and Law, Professional Psychology: Research and Practice,* and *Sexuality Research and Public Policy.*

CRAIG A. RIMMERMAN is professor of public policy studies and political science and currently holds the Joseph P. DiGangi Endowed Chair in the Social Sciences at Hobart and William Smith Colleges, where he has taught since 1986. A former American Political Science Association Congressional Fellow, Rimmerman teaches courses in public policy, social movements, and democratic theory. He is the author, editor, or co-editor of a number of books, including *The Politics of Gay Rights* (co-edited with Kenneth Wald and Clyde Wilcox, 2000), *From Identity to Politics: The Lesbian and Gay Movements in the United States* (2002), and *The New Citizenship: Unconventional Politics, Activism, and Service* (3d ed., 2005). Rimmerman is currently working on a book that examines the contemporary lesbian and gay movements' political organizing strategy in light of three key policy areas: HIV/AIDS, military integration, and same-sex marriage.

CARIN ROBINSON is a PhD candidate in American government at Georgetown University. She has contributed to a number of books on the subject of religious beliefs and political behavior. She is co-author of *Onward Christian Soldiers? The Religious Right in American Politics*, 3d ed.

MARK CARL ROM is an associate professor of government and public policy at Georgetown University in Washington, DC. He has written *Fatal Extraction: The Story of the Florida Dentist Accused of Infecting His Patients with HIV and Poisoning Public Health* (1997), *Public Spirit in the Thrift Tragedy* (1996), and *Welfare Magnets: A New Case for a National Welfare Standard* (1990, with Paul E. Peterson), among many other scholarly publications. Rom received his BA magna cum laude from the University of Arkansas and his MA and PhD in political science at the University of Wisconsin at Madison in 1992. He believes that one hundred years from now Americans will not even wonder why same-sex marriage was a major political controversy.

SHARON S. ROSTOSKY is associate professor of counseling psychology at the University of Kentucky. She received her PhD in counseling psychology from the University of Tennessee in 1998 and is a licensed counseling psychologist. She has published numerous articles on adolescent sexuality and sexual minority youth and on minority stress and relational issues for same-sex couples. Her work has appeared in the *Journal of Counseling Psychology*, the *Journal of Adolescence*, the *Journal of Sex Research*, and *Professional Psychology: Research and Practice*.

RONALD G. SHAIKO is a senior fellow and the associate director of the Nelson A. Rockefeller Center for Public Policy and the Social Sciences at Dartmouth College. Prior to teaching at Dartmouth, he was awarded the Fulbright Distinguished Chair in American Politics at Warsaw University in Poland in 2000–2001. For the decade of the 1990s he taught at American University. During that time he served as an APSA Congressional Fellow in 1993–94 and as a Democracy Fellow at the United States Agency for International Development from 1997 to 1999.

SHAUNA SHAMES is a PhD candidate in American government at Harvard University. Her main areas of interest are women, gender, feminism, and politics, and she has published articles and book chapters on women as candidates, feminism in the United States, public opinion concerning same-sex marriage, abortion, and gender consciousness. She has also served as assistant to the president of the National Organization for Women, research director for the White House Project (a national women's leadership nonprofit), and coordinator of the Haven Coalition, a group dedicated to ensuring abortion access for low-income women.

BARRY L. TADLOCK is an assistant professor in the Department of Political Science at Ohio University. He teaches courses in American national government, legislative processes, and the American presidency. His research involves identity politics. Along with Ellen D. B. Riggle he co-edited *Gays and Lesbians in the Democratic Process: Public Policy, Public Opinion, and Political Representation* (1999). He and C. Ann Gordon have investigated media portrayals of lesbian and gay candidates, candidate choice in elections involving gay men and lesbians, and interest group and media framing of the same-sex marriage issue. His other research interest concerns the impact of welfare reform in Appalachian Ohio.

KENNETH D. WALD is distinguished professor of political science at the University of Florida and the co-author of *Religion and Politics in the United States* (5th ed., 2006) and *The Politics of Cultural Differences* (2002). Together with the editors of this volume, he co-edited *The Politics of Gay Rights* (2006).

CLYDE WILCOX is professor of government at Georgetown University. He has written and edited more than twenty books on religion and politics, gender politics, campaign finance, and science fiction and politics. He is co-editor of *The Politics of Gay Rights* and *Women in Elected Office: Past, Present, and Future* (2d ed.). He recently published the third edition of *Onward Christian Soldiers? The Christian Right in American Politics*.

ALIXANDRA B. YANUS is a graduate student at the University of North Carolina at Chapel Hill. She holds a bachelor's degree from American University, where she received the University Award for Outstanding Scholarship at the Undergraduate Level. Her research interests are in American politics and the courts. She is currently working on several research projects that examine external influences on judicial decision making in the U.S. Supreme Court and state supreme courts.

INDEX

riage, 261–68; and sexual orientation nondiscrimination laws, 160

Denmark: adoption rights in, 346; inheritance and taxation rights in, 344; public opinion about homosexuality and religion, 348

Department of Education, opposition to, 164

Deukmejian, George, 23

devaluation, of same-sex couples, 66, 68, 77

Diamond, S., 166

disease, homosexuality as, 46, 47

Disney, 12–13

District of Columbia: ban on same-sex marriage, 308n1; domestic partner registry, 344

divorce, 9, 10, 117, 305, 343; no-fault, 159, 163, 179

Dobson, James, 138

Dole, Bob, 276, 277

domestic partner registry, 320, 344; Belgium, 347; Britain, 347; Germany, 347; Netherlands, 347; Spain, 347; Sweden, 347

domestic partnerships, 51, 52; and NCGO, 194

Domestic Partners Rights and Responsibilities Act, 20–21, 26

Donovan, T., 177

DontAmend.com, 199, 206

Douglas, James, 20

due process, and ban on same-sex marriage, 293

Dukakis, Michael, 182n21

Eagle Forum, 164, 199, 206

Edgar, Bob, 99

education, and perception of gays, 100, 209, 238, 324–26, 326–29, 331; state laws impacting, 166–67

educational discrimination, 24, 87, 320; and Christian Right, 159, 161; racially-based, 295

Edwards, John, 33n47, 253

Eisenstadt v. Baird, 56

Elliot, John, 113

emotional response to issues, 317

employment benefits: in Israel, 345. *See also* benefits to domestic partners

employment discrimination, 24, 46, 47, 87, 216, 305; California legislation, 320; Florida case, 308n2; public opinion

regarding, 324–26; and religious organizations, 175; sexual orientation nondiscrimination laws, 160

Employment Nondiscrimination Act, 170, 233–34, 235

Episcopal Church, 5, 98–99; and homosexuality, 143; sacred scripture and homosexuality, 112–13, 114; and same-sex marriages, 143

EqualMarriage.org, 206; Web site, 199

equal protection, 41, 88, 299; and antimiscegenation laws, 7; and ban on same-sex marriage, 26, 283, 293, 294; and civil marriage, 80; and gay marriage cases, 308n6; in Hawaiian law, 39–40, 274–75; and issue framing, 203–4, 208; in issue framing, 202; marriage as civil right, 6; in Massachusetts law, 249–50; in public opinion polls, 222; suspect classifications, 308n3; in Vermont law, 20, 27–28; Web site presentations, 199–200

Equal Rights Amendment, 135, 145, 164

Ettelbrick, Paula, 41

European Union, 347, 360

evangelical churches, 4–5, 50, 86, 93, 352–53; and antidiscrimination policies, 330–35; and attitudes toward antidiscrimination laws, 233–34, 238–39; and same-sex marriage, 132, 137, 138–39

Evangelical Lutheran Church of America, 5, 94, 99; sacred scripture and homosexuality, 112

Evans, George, 94

evolution, teaching of, 159, 179

Exodus International, 171

experiences of prejudice, 68–69

Fair Michigan Majority, 86

Falwell, Jerry, 182n21

families of origin, support from, 67–68, 72, 73

family, changing conceptions of, 46, 47–48, 50–51

family laws and GLBT families, 87, 161–63, 282, 342–44, 355

family medical leave, 51

Family Protection Act, 50

family regimes, 342–44

Family Research Council, 16, 157, 182n21, 206, 245; and Arlington Group, 139, 143; and domestic partner benefits, 160; and gay partners of 9/11 victims, 163; Mayday

minority stress (*continued*)
    public health issue, 67; and relationship
    formation and maintenance, 69–74
Minor v. Happersett, 295
Mississippi: adoption rights in, 167; ban on
    same-sex marriage in, 327, 328; educa-
    tional issues in, 181n18; parenting laws
    in, 167; same-sex marriage in, 86
Missouri: ban on same-sex marriage in,
    323; congressional elections in, 256–57;
    domestic partner benefits, 168; same-sex
    marriage in, 152n14, 195
mixed-race marriages, 226–27
Mongiardo, Daniel, 257
Montana: ban on same-sex marriage in, 327;
    same-sex marriage in, 86
morality politics, 335–37, 356; and bans
    on same-sex marriage, 314, 315–17; in
    California, 320–22; county-level voting
    patterns, 329–35; described, 316
Moral Majority, 138, 182n21
Mormon Church, 125n2, 315, 321; and same-
    sex marriage, 139
Moseley-Braun, Carol, 261
Muller v. Oregon, 295
municipal governments, and domestic
    partnership rights, 194
Murray, John Courtney, 125n6
Murray, Patty, 265–66
Murray, V. M., 70
Musgrave, Marilyn, 194, 281, 285–86
M. v. H., 346

National Association for the Advancement
    of Colored People (NAACP), 54–55;
    Legal Defense Fund, 294–95
National Association of Social Workers, 162
National Black Lesbian and Gay Leader-
    ship Forum, 49
National Center for Lesbian Rights, 51, 88,
    297
National Coalition of Gay Organizations
    (NCGO), 193–94
National Council of Churches, 99
National Election Study, 135–37, 160, 217,
    221–22; of homophobia, 223; Pilot
    survey, 222
National Gay and Lesbian Task Force
    (NGLTF), 15, 42, 51–52, 92, 94, 101,
    206, 296; and anti–gay marriage ballot
    campaigns, 157; opinion polls, 228–29;
    Web site, 199

nationalism, 359, 360
National Latino/a Lesbian and Gay Orga-
    nization, 49
National Opinion Research Center, 10
National Organization for Women
    (NOW), 98
National Policy Roundtable, 89
National Religious Leadership Roundtable,
    94, 97
natural law, 8
Nebraska: ACLU in, 299; adoption rights
    in, 167; ban on same-sex marriage,
    33n53, 318, 322–23; Family First, 140;
    foster parenting by gays, 167; parenting
    laws in, 167; same-sex marriage in, 195
Nebraska Family Coalition, 322
Nebraska Family Council, 318
Nethercutt, George, 265–66
Netherlands, 349, 359; civil unions in, 345,
    346; domestic partner registry, 347;
    inheritance and tenancy rights in, 344;
    marriage rights legislation in, 345; pub-
    lic opinion about homosexuality and
    religion, 348
Nevada: ban on same-sex marriage in, 318,
    319; congressional elections in, 266;
    parental notification laws, 166; same-
    sex marriage in, 195
New Democratic Party, 354
New Jersey: ban on same-sex marriage
    in, 303; divorce and property claims,
    307n1
New Mexico, same-sex marriage in, 313
New Paltz, New York, 303
Newsom, Gavin, 24, 85, 249, 284
Newsweek, 216; opinion polls, 225
New York: adoption rights in, 344; ban on
    same-sex marriage in, 60, 297; divorce
    and property claims, 307n1; same-sex
    marriage in, 313
New York City: inheritance rights in, 344,
    345; Stonewall riots in, 193
New Zealand, 341, 346, 360; recognition of
    same-sex partners, 345
Nixon, Richard, 40
NoGayMarriage.com, 199
Non-Partisan Family Coalition, 318
North Carolina, congressional elections
    in, 257
North Dakota: adoption rights in, 167;
    same-sex marriage in, 86, 327
Norton, Gale, 286